Cracked spine — EW 3/24/18

DATE DUE

SEP 1 7 2003			
3-18-04 14:234 3710			
JUL 1 3 2004			
JAN 3 1 2005			
3/11 8 IL 38342885			
JAN 0 5 2012			

Demco, Inc. 38-293

COUNSELING FAMILIES

An Introduction to Marriage and Family Therapy

THIRD EDITION

David L. Fenell and Barry K. Weinhold
University of Colorado – Colorado Springs

LOVE PUBLISHING COMPANY®
Denver • London • Sydney

Library of Congress Control Number: 2002112204

Copyright © 2003, 1997, 1989 by Love Publishing Company
P.O. Box 22353
Denver, CO 80222

Printed in the U.S.A.
ISBN 0-89108-300-6

Contents

12. Treating Families With Special Needs   311

13. Research in Marriage and Family Therapy   339

Preface

In actual practice, much of marital and family therapy is delivered, and will continue to be delivered, by counselors who are trained primarily in individual and group therapies. We believe that all therapists should be prepared as fully as possible to provide effective treatment to couples and families. Research suggests that, although many counseling practitioners would like to become more proficient in family therapy, few received any formal family therapy training in their graduate studies (Gladding, Burggraf, & Fenell, 1987).

According to a survey ("Training of Clinical Psychologists," 1981), clinical psychologists in private practice work with marital and family problems approximately 40% of the time, yet fewer than 5% of the psychologists surveyed had any formal coursework in marriage and family therapy in their graduate programs. Conversely, many therapists trained specifically in marriage and family reported that their programs focused almost exclusively on systems-based couple and family treatment with little individual and group therapy training in their curriculum. In either case, we believe that a more thorough training process that includes planned coursework in individual counseling, group counseling, and marital and family counseling would improve the practice of psychotherapy.

In *Counseling Families* we attempt to accomplish this task. We provide the reader with information about how the basic core skills that are necessary, but not sufficient, to perform individual and group therapy may be used to counsel couples and families. The core skills presented in this text are frequently translated into practice differently in individual, group, and family therapy situations. Nonetheless, these skills are essential to the successful practice of psychotherapy, whether with individuals, groups, or families. In addition to these core therapy skills, we describe more advanced individual and group counseling interventions that may be employed by the counselor with more complicated problems presented by individuals, groups, and families.

In their preface to Volume 1 of the *Handbook of Family Therapy*, authors Alan Gurman and David Kniskern (1981b) justified their decision not to discuss certain approaches to family therapy, including cognitive, rational emotive, behavioral, person-centered, Adlerian, gestalt, and transactional analysis therapies. They acknowledged that these approaches have exerted salient influences on the practice of individual and group therapy and that elements of these approaches have been incorporated into the work of some family clinicians. Nonetheless, Gurman and Kniskern concluded, "These therapeutic approaches have not yet exerted a significant impact on the field of family therapy" (p. ix). Although they recognized Virginia Satir's tremendous impact on the family therapy field, they opted to exclude her theory as well because no clearly discernable school or therapeutic method has evolved from her significant contributions.

Volume 2 of the *Handbook of Family Therapy* (1991) addressed the evolution of the theories covered in Volume 1 and introduced several new systems-based theories. Gurman and Kniskern continued to omit individual and group theories (except behavioral theory) that are often employed successfully in therapy with couples and families.

Gurman and Kniskern recognized that for family therapy to emerge as a respected and autonomous addition to the mental health-care delivery system, it was necessary to clearly distinguish family therapy from long-accepted individual and group approaches to treatment. The effort of the early family therapy pioneers was to ensure that family therapy was recognized as a new and radically different paradigm for treating psychological problems and would not be seen as merely another theory of treatment subsumed by the professions of psychology or psychiatry. At the current and more mature stage of development of the psychotherapy profession, however, we believe that much is to be gained by bridging the fields of individual and group therapy with marital and family therapy.

Training in marriage and family therapy has frequently been characterized by requirements or strong recommendations that trainees undergo personal counseling. We believe that such recommendations are appropriate during training programs and later when needed. We believe that the therapeutic abilities of trainees will be enhanced by the opportunity to examine their own family histories as well as their personal values, assumptions, and beliefs. This opportunity is an increasingly important facet of the expanded training paradigm for therapists. This activity provides the counselor in training with the ability to experience what it is like to be a client. More important, however, is the opportunity for the counselor to examine blind spots, unfinished business, and other issues that might interfere with the ability to be an effective practitioner.

Thus, with this book we hope to bridge the gaps between individual, group, and family therapies. We believe there is too much fragmentation among the helping professions today in battles for turf. Counselors from virtually all types of professional training programs work with marital and family problems. We want each counselor to be as well rounded and capable as possible. We hope this book will encourage counselors and other helping professionals with individual and group training to fully recognize that they already possess the skills necessary to work with many problems presented by couples and families. In addition, we want to encourage therapists to build on their already considerable skills in individual and group counseling by gaining specific knowledge of marital and family therapy theories based on general systems theory and the recent development of narrative and other nonsystemic family treatment approaches.

Too often we hear of counselors avoiding the use of systems theories that may be applied for the benefit of their clients because they believe these theories are unnecessarily clinical and do not sufficiently emphasize the importance of the therapeutic relationship between the client and the therapist. In this text we confront that belief directly by emphasizing the importance of the relationship between the client family and the counselor throughout. We acknowledge and report on the significant body of research that suggests that the therapeutic relationship is necessary to facilitate therapeutic change in individuals, groups, and families.

Moreover, we believe that therapists who are not able to integrate the key concepts of family systems theory therapy into their counseling practice may not be able to provide the most effective help to certain couples and families. This is not to say that family theory is the answer to all problems, but it does offer an alternative paradigm that can be effective with many clients and can be particularly helpful in situations in which more traditional methods of intervention have been tried and have not been effective. Thus, we hope this book will encourage counselors to explore family theories and techniques and perhaps integrate them into their repertoire and use them along with the other effective helping skills they have already developed.

Terms Used in This Book

In this text marriage and family therapy is referred to simply as *family therapy,* because most family therapists view the marital dyad as one important subsystem of the larger family system. Thus, family therapy implies treatment of the marital couple as well as the entire family. The terms *counselor, therapist* and *psychotherapist* are used interchangeably throughout this text. In addition, the terms *marriage and family counselor* and *marriage and family therapist* are used interchangeably. In our judgment, there is little, if any, difference between a trained professional counselor and trained psychotherapist. Both have the task of helping individuals, couples and families alleviate human suffering and are accorded equal status in this book.

Overview of the Book

This third edition of *Counseling Families: An Introduction to Marriage and Family Therapy* has been reorganized in a way that we hope will assist counselors in developing basic knowledge and skills in marriage and family therapy. Moreover, this new edition has been revised and expanded to provide the reader with an understanding of the important emerging theories designed to help couples and families.

In Part I of this text we update our presentation of the development of the family therapy movement. We reemphasize the need for counselors skilled in providing therapy to couples and families through our discussion of the application of specific family therapy theories and techniques to specific presenting problems. The third edition also includes several new problem areas that may be treated with family therapy such as families with Alzheimer's disease, families with HIV, rural families, military families, families with gifted children, and families with chronic medical problems. Further, we systematically introduce the profession of family therapy through the presentation of key terms that will enable the reader to conceptualize family problems and develop effective interventions to help families alleviate their problems. We expand our presentation of the healthy marriage and healthy family and, in addition, describe 12 core counseling skills taught in most counselor training programs and demonstrate how these well known skills may be used in working with couples and families.

In Part II we present individual, systems-based and narrative theories of psychotherapy and describe how these approaches may be used in working with couples and families. Because of their strong emphasis on the phenomenological nature of humans, the transpersonal models of treatment are included in Chapters 9 and 10, covering the humanistic, existential, and transpersonal theories.

The theories presented in Part II of this text are organized into three major classifications:

1. Theories based on psychodynamic concepts
2. Theories based on cognitive/behavioral concepts
3. Theories based on humanistic, existential, and transpersonal concepts.

Many counselor-training programs classify theories into these three categories to assist students in organizing their thinking about the various theories and in identifying appropriate theory-based intervention strategies to use in their work with couples and families. In addition, we have expanded the coverage of theories in this edition by including internal family system theory (Schwartz, 1995).

The organizational categories used here are also helpful in that they serve as a bridge linking individual and group counseling theories with the most closely related systems theories. This feature, unique to *Counseling Families,* provides a logical developmental step from the study of less complex individual theories to the study of more complex systems theories. In our training of hundreds of counseling students over the years, we have discovered that their initial familiarity with the individual theories most closely related to family theories creates a developmental bridge leading the students to a more rapid and in-depth understanding and application of systems theories. Presenting systems theories by first linking them developmentally to closely related individual theories greatly facilitates students' mastery of the more complex systems theories presented in this text.

We hope the organization of this text will enable the reader to discover that many key principles of individually oriented psychodynamic theories also may be relevant to family systems approaches based on psychodynamic theory. Similarly, cognitive/behavioral and humanistic, existential, and transpersonal theories used in individual treatment will have elements in common with corresponding systems-based theories. These classifications will provide familiar ground for the reader in the developmental process of learning to employ systems theories in the treatment of problems presented by couples and families.

The individual theories presented that are based on psychodynamic concepts include the classic psychoanalytic theory of Freud; Adlerian theory, and Berne's transactional analysis. The systems theories presented that are based on psychodynamic concepts include Bowen's family systems theory, Framo's intergenerational systems theory, and Schwartz's internal family systems theory. The individual theories based on cognitive/behavioral concepts include Ellis' rational emotive behavioral therapy and the behavioral and social learning theories of Jacobsen, Falloon, Patterson, and others.

The systems theories presented based on cognitive/behavioral concepts include Minuchin's structural family therapy, the functional family therapy developed by Barton, Alexander, and Parsons, the brief strategic therapy of the Mental Research Institute group. The individual theories with a humanistic, existential, and/or transpersonal base presented in this edition include Rogers' person-centered therapy, Perl's gestalt therapy, and Moreno's psychodrama and transpersonal therapy as described by Wilber and Mindell. The systems theories presented that are based on humanistic, existential, and/or transpersonal concepts include Satir's communication theory, Whitaker's symbolic–experiential systems theory, narrative therapy as employed by White and Epston, and the Weinholds' developmental systems theory.

In Part III of the text, we have made other significant changes in this third edition. Two new chapters have been added: Chapter 11 introduces the use of conflict-resolution strategies with couples and families. Chapter 12 continues to address the treatment of families with special needs and has been updated with more current information. Chapter 13 contains new expanded and updated coverage on research in marriage and family therapy. Chapter 14 continues to cover professional issues and ethics in marriage and family counseling.

We have included as appendices the ethical standards of both the American Association for Marriage and Family Therapy and the International Association for Marriage and Family Counseling. Finally, we have added a glossary of key family therapy terms.

Purpose of the Book

The purpose of this third edition of *Counseling Families* is to provide mental health professionals who are trained and experienced in individual counseling theories and techniques with the knowledge and skills to begin working with couples and families using systems concepts under supervision. We have presented a model that describes how to employ the basic counseling skills taught in most counselor training programs to facilitate change in couples and families. At the beginning of each chapter is a brief summary statement, to lead the reader into the chapter, a list of key concepts covered in the chapter, and questions for discussion that direct the reader to key concepts of each chapter. This material will be useful to the student who is preparing to read the chapter for the first time, and later when reviewing the material for periodic examinations. This edition has a new companion Web site to help students understand the content and synthesize the material and allow students to discover new information and explore fresh ideas.

Acknowledgments

The authors would like to thank the many individuals who have made this text a reality. We would especially like to thank our publisher, Stan Love, and our editors, Carolyn Acheson and Erica Lawrence, who made sense of our writing and helped clarify our ideas. We also would like to thank the counseling and family therapy professionals who reviewed the text and made important suggestions for improving it. Finally we would like to thank all the professors who have adopted the text for use in their classes and the students who have used the text. The suggestions from professors and students have been invaluable in revising the text and making it more user-friendly and current.

About the Authors

The third edition of *Counseling Families* has been revised and edited after the tragic events of September 11, 2001. The terrorist attack on the United States changed us all, and the authors of this text and our families are no exception. Barry Weinhold was appointed professor emeritus upon his recent retirement from the University of Colorado at Colorado Springs. He continues to be active in developing and delivering leading edge resources for shifting consciousness through the Colorado Institute for Conflict Resolution and Creative Leadership, a non-profit institute that he co-directs with his wife, Janae. He is currently involved in conflict resolution trainings, executive coaching and leadership training, directing the Kindness Campaign, (a bullying prevention program for schools and families) and writing books. The Weinholds have authored or co-authored twenty-three books and are currently working on several new books. More information about their current programs and projects can be found on their website at www.weinholds.org

David Fenell was recalled to active duty as a lieutenant colonel in the United States Army. He has been working in the selection and assessment of Special Forces soldiers who have been the most active participants in the war on terrorism. Dr. Fenell completed his revisions for this edition of the text from his quarters at Fort Bragg, North Carolina. When released from active duty, he will return to the University of Colorado at Colorado Springs and resume his teaching and research in marital and family therapy. The Fenell family is heavily committed to the war on terrorism. First Lieutenant Nathan Fenell is a platoon commander with the 3rd Battalion, 5th Marines, is deployed in Okinawa. Navy ensign Maija Fenell is deployed with the Sixth Fleet on the USS LaSalle in the Mediterranean Sea. Ruth Ann, loving wife and mother, is completing her graduate degree in counseling and working in the counseling office of Cheyenne Mountain High School, Colorado Springs while providing moral support to her husband and two children. Ruth Ann, and all the countless others who have sent family members into this war on terrorism have demonstrated their own kind of courage. They, too, are called upon to serve—and they serve well.

PART ONE

Introducing and Understanding Marriage and Family Therapy

▮ CHAPTERS

Counseling Families: An Introduction

In this chapter, we will show why counselors and other mental health professionals should be trained to work with family-related problems. We will discuss several specific family-related problems and suggest how counselors may help resolve these problems more effectively if the family or portions of the family are included in treatment.

Family-related problems
Two-career families
Marital dysfunction
Single-parent families
Drug and alcohol abuse
School-related problems
Families with a gifted child
Families with children with disabilities
Child-management problems
Adolescent depression and suicide
Problems with adult children leaving home
Care of elderly parents
Elderly family members with Alzheimer's disease
Rural families
Families with chronic medical problems
Families with an HIV-positive member

QUESTIONS FOR DISCUSSION

1. Why is it important for counselors and other mental health professionals to have the knowledge and skills necessary to work with couples and families?

2. What are some specific counseling problems that may best be treated with family therapy? How might family therapy help?

3. The terms **counselor** and **psychotherapist** are used interchangeably throughout this book. Do you agree with this usage? Why or why not?

4. Which specific family-related problem discussed in this chapter would you consider most difficult to treat? Why? Which would be the easiest? Why?

5. How might family members support the addictive behavior of an alcoholic or drug-abusing member even though they report that they want the member to change?

Marriage and family therapy has become an increasingly important mental health treatment approach. The social, economic, and political demands placed on families today far exceed those of previous generations and can create considerable stress for family members. Helping professionals have recognized that counseling an individual without considering, and frequently without including, other family members makes lasting change less likely. Because societal pressures have increased family stress and because more families are seeking help through therapy, counselors and therapists need to be prepared to treat psychological problems that occur in the context of the family.

Specific areas of concern today include the pressures of families in which both parents work, the unique stresses experienced by single-parent families, problems with school-related issues, ranging from problems with gifted students to those with developmental disabilities. Other issues include burgeoning alcohol and drug abuse, higher suicide rates in the teenage population, and increased life expectancy resulting in worries about caring for elderly parents including those with Alzheimer's disease. Moreover, family therapy can be helpful in working with families who have a member who is HIV-positive, and families with members who have other chronic medical problems.

These are a few of the emerging issues that well trained counselors must be aware of and be able to handle effectively. Counselors must understand how the issues mentioned above, as well as other family problems, affect every member of the family unit. This awareness enables therapists to impact the family by implementing change strategies with the focus of the intervention on *any* family member. This is a key family therapy concept that states: *Change in one family member affects the entire family.* Much more will be said about this important concept throughout this text.

Influence of the Family

A practicing counseling professional is presented with numerous client problems that other members of the client's family may cause, encourage, or support. More and more therapists are recognizing the difficulty of successfully treating clients with psychological problems that have their roots in the family. Clients treated without involving the family are often helped as a result of treatment. But when the changed clients return to the family without the support of therapy, they tend to revert to former patterns of dysfunctional behavior because, while the client has changed, the rest of the family has not. This introduces a second important concept in family therapy: *The family system is powerful.*

If the behaviors of the rest of the family members remain constant, the client is likely to revert to former dysfunctional behaviors that the family system supports and reinforces. Therefore, the well-trained counselor has to understand how to effectively treat psychological problems that the family reinforces and supports. This treatment often involves participation of all the family members in therapy. Several of the most commonly encountered family problems are described in this chapter.

Two-Career Families

Economic pressures on the family have contributed to an increase in the number of women in the workforce and the number of two-career families in the United States. Developing an effective two-career lifestyle raises many new issues and questions for the couple. Frequent issues that dual-career couples raise in therapy are (Fenell, 1982):

1. How will the necessary household duties be divided with both spouses working?
2. How will young children be cared for?
3. How will finances be managed?

When these issues for the two-career family are not resolved, marital counseling may be indicated. If only one spouse were to come for treatment, the therapeutic alternatives would be limited because the counselor would deal with the perceptions and feelings of only one partner. With both spouses present in treatment, however, new rules can be negotiated that identify and respond to the needs and concerns of both partners. If both partners' needs are considered, there is a better chance that mutual agreements can be made and that lasting change will take place.

Marital Dysfunction

One of the most common reasons for seeking psychotherapy is for assistance in resolving marital problems. Frequently, couples have complex and serious disagreements and do not have the communication and problem-solving skills necessary to resolve them (Sperry & Carlson, 1991). When treating one spouse alone, the therapist is limited to only that spouse's perceptions of the problem. Moreover, when a spouse is treated individually for marital problems, deterioration in the marital relationship is more likely (Gurman & Kniskern, 1978a) than if both partners are treated together. Thus, the counselor should possess the skills necessary to engage both spouses in the counseling process (Whitaker & Keith, 1981; Wilcoxon & Fenell, 1983, 1986) and should be capable of treating the couple conjointly as well as individually.

A spouse treated for marital problems in individual sessions is likely to achieve personal therapeutic growth. The spouse not in treatment also may see improvement in the partner as emotional issues that previously were brought to the partner at home, and perhaps dealt with ineffectively, are now being handled in therapy. Demands on the spouse at home decrease. Thus, everyone involved may believe the client is improving as long as therapy continues. But, when therapy ends with no real change in the couple's interaction pattern, the differences between the spouses actually may increase and make resolution of the marital difficulties less likely. The anger and disappointment the couple may experience at the return of their problems may complicate the marital situation and perhaps lead to divorce.

If the presenting concern is a marital problem and the goal is to resolve this problem, the counselor should attempt to involve both spouses in treatment. Conjoint marital therapy is the treatment of choice for marital problems because it offers the therapist a more realistic picture of the marital problems. Also, the partners work together to resolve their problems and do not grow farther apart as could be the case if only one of the partners were in treatment (Gurman & Kniskern, 1978a).

◼ *Single-Parent Families*

Because of the high divorce rate in the United States, the number of single-parent families has continued to increase. There are nearly 6 million single-mother households in the United States (Goodrich, Rampage, & Ellman, 1989), and fathers currently head nearly 2 million single-parent families, a dramatic increase (Davis & Born, 1999). Thus, counselors must be prepared to respond to the problems that both male and female single parents experience.

The parent with custody of the children faces a myriad of problems that must be resolved to effectively support and nurture the family. Single parents frequently feel the pressures of time while trying to meet the needs of the children, their own personal needs, and work responsibilities. This stress can spill over on the children and create difficulties. Although some children of single parents do fine, one study suggests that children of single-parent families may have more problems than children from two-parent families in adjusting, handling challenges at school, and forming stable relationships with others (Wallerstein, 1992).

When single parents experience increased stress levels, they may begin to lose a sense of control of their children, families, and perhaps of themselves. Often children sense the lack of control experienced by the parent and respond by becoming symptomatic, frequently developing health problems, or beginning to act out at school and home. Counseling with the single parent, the children, and available support persons is frequently an effective way to help moderate the tension and stress in this difficult situation.

Another serious issue the single parent may face involves issues of custody, child support, and parenting time. These issues are rarely resolved successfully without the participation of all concerned parties in the counseling process.

◼ *Families With Drug and Alcohol Problems*

When a member of a family has a problem with drug and alcohol use, all other members of the family are affected by the abuser and influence the abuser for better or for worse. In addition to assisting the abusing client, counselors must help other family members deal with their feelings about the abusing client and about their ineffective attempts to change the abuser's behaviors. Furthermore, some family members may inadvertently engage in specific behavior patterns that support the continuation of the drug or alcohol abuse.

Children may become overly responsible and handle duties that a parent would normally perform. These children often are referred to as *parentified,* as they are required to act parentally to allow the family to function. The actions of parentified children allow the parents to continue their substance abuse and often erode the child's self-esteem. Moreover, this family pattern deprives the child of normal developmental experiences that may impact the child in significant relationships later in life.

The spouse or children of the alcoholic person often behave in a way that has been described as *co-dependent.* This term describes a spouse who has such a tremendous neurotic need to maintain the marriage relationship that he or she is unwilling to seriously challenge the drug-dependent partner's dysfunctional behavior. Thus, the co-dependent person helps perpetuate the presenting problem of drug dependency or addiction. Murphy (1984) consolidated other roles that family members take in an alcoholic family.

Similar roles may be identified in the families of drug abusers and even in families with other symptoms (Stevens & Smith, 2001). The *enabler*—often called co-dependent—allows the drinking behavior to continue by serving as a rescuer for the abusing family member. The *scapegoat* is the child who gets into trouble to distract the family members from the pain caused by the alcohol abuser. The *hero* is the family member who continues to function well and also may serve to demonstrate that the family is a good family despite the substance abuse. The family often marginalizes the *lost child,* and the pain this person feels is rarely acknowledged. Finally, the *clown* is the family member who distracts family members from the substance abuse problems through humor and cute antics.

George (1990) summarized several "rules" that are characteristic of most families with a substance-abusing member.

1. Resist any change, and remain the same. This is accomplished by not talking about the problems in the family.
2. Don't trust family members and oneself.
3. Ignore and deny feelings.

4. Maintain that the problems are caused by some factor other than the substance abuse.

Maintaining these rules becomes the goal of all family members unless they receive help. Much research demonstrates that all family members play a role in maintaining the problem and treatment should include family sessions that identify family roles and rules in the maintenance of the problem. Thus, counseling with the family as well as with its individual members is a clear necessity in drug and alcohol abuse situations (Edwards & Steinglass, 1995; George, 1990; Stevens & Smith, 2001).

School-Related Problems

Parents and teachers often suggest that children who are having difficulty in school receive counseling. When the difficulties are related to problems at home or conflicts between the school and home, counseling the child alone is rarely effective. Parents, siblings, teachers, school counselors, and administrators should be involved to gain an accurate assessment of the problem. Participation of the family as well as significant school personnel is necessary to establish effective cooperation between the school and the family and to identify ways that both systems—the school and the family—might be able to support the changes the student makes. The counselor must have excellent skills to facilitate the cooperation of these two important systems and thereby enhance the effectiveness of students who are having school-related problems (Lambie & Daniels-Mohring, 1993).

School Phobia

The NEA estimates that 160,000 students miss school every day because of phobias (Fried & Fried, 1996). Nichols and Schwartz (2001) describe a problem involving school phobia. Children who experience school phobia frequently live in families that have weak overprotective parental structures and an inability to control their children. When it is time for these children to go to school, they rebel, either by refusing to go to school or by creating significant turmoil for the parents and school staff.

School-related problems such as these are rarely handled effectively by working with the child alone. Family therapy usually is required, and integrating school personnel in treatment is extremely important. Minuchin and Fishman (1981) have described structural family therapy techniques that are helpful with these problems. Their ideas will be presented later in this book.

We believe that systems-based family therapy training is essential for school counselors. All school counselor trainees in our program at the University of Colorado at Colorado Springs must complete a course in introductory family therapy theory and techniques and a skills training laboratory course that emphasizes the application of systems theory interventions. These courses are graduation requirements for all our school counselor trainees. Graduates of our program have reported that the family therapy module of instruction has contributed to their effectiveness as school counselors in resolving family-based problems, as well as in consultation with teachers and administrators concerning systems-based issues within their schools.

Gifted Students

School counselors also are involved in the appropriate education of gifted students. Often the parents of gifted students are overinvolved with their student and the educational system, which may lead to the student's underachievement and acting out. Conversely, some parents are not aware of their child's abilities and do not provide support for their development. The school counselor is most effective in helping the gifted family by meeting with the student, parents, and teachers to best determine how to maximize the educational experience for the student while attempting to develop an appropriate level of involvement by the parents. Without the participation of all elements of the family and educational system in this process, a successful outcome is unlikely.

Students With Disabilities

Students with disabilities and their families present similar challenges for the school counselor. Convening a meeting of all elements of the family, educational, and, when necessary, medical systems leads to the most productive planning for educating these students. Parents, siblings, and school personnel all want the best for their students with disabilities.

But the best attempts to be helpful to the students are often the reason that they do not develop. When family, friends, and school personnel do "too much" for the student, it robs the student of the initiative to try new behaviors. Thus, the student does not develop and may even regress. Family meetings involving the school counselor, student, parents, and involved school personnel can be the key to helping students with disabilities reach their full potential (Fenell, Martin, & Mithaug, 1986).

▇ Child-Management Problems

Family counseling is often helpful when parents have difficulty managing their children's behavior (Minuchin & Fishman, 1981). Frequently, the behavior of the acting-out child promotes disagreement between the parents on how to manage and discipline the child. When the disagreement is not resolved quickly, increased stress and instability in the marriage and the family may result and the child may become the family scapegoat (Barker, 1992). This stress, in turn, precipitates the child's additional acting-out. Rather than work on issues of conflict concerning disagreement in child-management styles, the parents repress that conflict and intensify their focus on the child. The child often becomes worse because he or she senses the tension in the marriage and the increased focus on his or her behaviors, and responds by further acting-out. Also, the parents' overinvolvement with the child and his or her problem behavior often reinforces the maintenance of the acting-out behavior.

Family therapy is the most effective way to accurately identify how the role played by each family member helps to maintain or increase the problem. Family therapy can help change the dysfunctional interactional patterns between the acting-out child and the other family members and thereby help all family members identify other issues that are present in the family. When this is accomplished, the family typically develops a more functional and pleasant family life.

▇ Adolescent Depression and Suicide

The number of adolescents suffering from depression and, in severe cases, contemplating suicide have increased alarmingly. More and more pressure is being placed on adolescents to engage in behaviors they are not physically or psychologically prepared to handle. Parents may hold excessively high expectations for their teenagers and demand excellence in all aspects of activity, or perhaps the adolescents believe their parents hold these expectations when their parents actually do not. In either case, when adolescents do not live up to the real or perceived parental expectations, they may develop depression. When the depression is severe, the adolescent might consider suicide.

Family therapy is an excellent treatment modality for problems of adolescent depression in reaction to perceived parental, school, and social pressures because it sensitizes all family members to causes of the depression and, in cases of suicidal potential, educates family members about warning signs and ways to deal with the problem. Through family therapy, all members of the family discover what each can do to support the improvement of the depressed member and what behaviors are not particularly helpful and should be decreased or eliminated.

The therapist will want to encourage all family members to be present and ensure that each is able to discuss the impact the depressed member is having on him or her and on the family as a unit. Each member is given the opportunity to think of ways to support the depressed member, and the opportunity to check out the idea with the client to see if it is, indeed, helpful. As each family member makes small but significant changes in behavior, the depressed adolescent often improves.

If the depressed member does not improve, or worsens, consultation with a psychiatrist who has family systems training may be suggested. The psychiatric consultant might prescribe medication or, in the most serious cases, hospitalization for the depressed member. All ethical standards require that the counselor respond to imminent suicidal behavior in ways that ensure the client's welfare (AAMFT, 2001; IAMFC, 2001). When harm to the client is likely, this imperative takes precedence over the ethical requirement to maintain confidentiality (Jurich, 2001). Additional information on responding to a suicidal client through family interventions is presented in Chapter 12.

Adult Children Leaving Home

A relatively recent phenomenon in our society arises in facilitating the departure of adult children from the parents' home. On the one hand, parents want their adult children to become autonomous but, on the other hand, some parents do not believe that their children will be able to succeed on their own. These parents sometimes send subtle messages to their children suggesting that they will not be successful. Noted family therapist Murray Bowen (1978) suggested that the negative messages transmitted by parent to child result from anxiety the parent has about himself or herself. Rather than deal with that anxiety, the parent often transmits it to the child. These children grow into adults who doubt their own ability to succeed without parental support and may eventually project the same anxiety onto their own children, perpetuating the problem. Exploring the dynamics involved in this situation in family counseling may help the adult son or daughter leave the home and also provide assistance to the parents as they learn effective behaviors that support the departure.

A related situation is the "boomerang" adult child. In this situation, the adult child has successfully differentiated and "left the nest." But, for some reason—usually divorce or a financial setback—the adult child returns to the parents' home. This often gives rise to problems concerning authority and responsibility in the home. When these problems are not resolved adequately, family treatment can be beneficial.

In another common contemporary situation, the grandparents assume parental responsibilities for their grandchildren. Many older individuals who have already raised one family are assuming the care of their grandchildren because of the irresponsibility or unfortunate setbacks of their own children. This situation can lead to unexpressed feelings by the child, the parents, and the grandparents. Family therapy can help identify a plan for responding to the situation and help family members communicate more effectively about their plans and expectations concerning this parenting arrangement and its impact on the child, parents, and grandparents.

■ *Care of Elderly Parents*

As life expectancy lengthens, many couples are finding themselves responsible for the care and support of their aging parents. As one spouse finds his or her interactions with the elderly parents consuming more and more time, the partner may feel unimportant or ignored in the marriage relationship. One spouse may feel that he or she is playing "second fiddle" to the other spouse's parents while the spouse with the parents in need of assistance feels pulled and guilty no matter what course of action he or she chooses. These situations can place extreme stress on the marriage and the individual marriage partners (Montalvo & Thompson, 1988). This stress is exacerbated when the demands from aging parents coincide with problems the couple may be having with their grown children leaving home.

Assisting the spouses in working through the issues related to the support of elderly parents may help to resolve tensions in the marriage created by this frequently unexpected demand. Including the elderly parents in some of the sessions can be useful, to gain their perceptions of the situation and their ideas concerning what they need from their adult children. Often, to avoid hurt feelings, elderly parents do not tell their adult children that some of the help they provide is not needed. New awareness often emerges as a result of family therapy to everyone's delight.

One of the most devastating problems confronting families with elderly members is Alzheimer's disease. This form of incurable dementia has predictable effects on family members. Initially they hope that the disease will not progress. When that hope is dashed, many family members react by withdrawing, which is not helpful to the primary caregiver. Although concern for the patient is important, even more important is the concern for the primary caregiver of the Alzheimer's patient. The caregiver is frequently an elderly spouse who is adamant about not placing the spouse in institutional care. But the requirements of caring for an Alzheimer's patient can be more than the spouse is physically able to manage. Thus, other family members and friends must be constantly on the alert for signs that the caregiver may not be taking adequate care of himself or herself. Often a family consultation including friends and other members of the caregiver's support system is needed to help family members decide how each can best contribute to the care of both the Alzheimer's patient and the primary caregiver.

▇ *Family Therapy in Rural Communities*

Rural families present unique challenges for the counselor. Most family therapy training programs prepare therapists to work with clients in urban locations. However, clients in rural areas differ from those in urban areas in significant ways (Fenell, Hovestadt, & Cochran, 1985;

Hovestadt, Fenell, & Canfield, 2002). Three specific areas that therapists must be aware of when working with families in rural communities are: (a) the traditional sex roles that are often part of the rural community; (b) the lack of confidentiality in rural settings, and (c) the traditional religious values of much of rural America.

Therapists trained in urban settings and conditioned to more egalitarian sex roles may have difficulty accepting and joining with clients who maintain a different perspective. Therapists must not impose their values while helping the family resolve its issues. This can be a daunting challenge when the therapist's values are quite different from the family's values.

Family therapists in rural settings often meet their clients in the community and must be comfortable in this environment. Moreover, other community members know the family is in treatment and are aware of the family's issues. These community members may try to engage the therapist in discussions about the family. The family therapist must tactfully handle these situations by acknowledging the caring of the community members while at the same time not breaking confidentiality. At times, with the family's permission, including extended family and relevant community members in treatment might be helpful in developing a community system to support the changes resulting from therapy.

Another area to which the therapist must be able to respond relates to the traditional religious values held by many families in rural settings. While a therapist may see many possible options to resolving a situation, the family may have more limited choices because of its strong religious convictions and the behaviors these beliefs will permit them to employ. To be successful in the rural community, the family therapist must be comfortable with these realities. Counselors who are not comfortable in the situations described will have a difficult time gaining acceptance in rural communities, and without acceptance it becomes difficult to help rural families deal with their problems (Fenell, Hovestadt, & Cochran, 1985; Hovestadt, Fenell, & Canfield, 2002).

Families With Chronic Health Problems

When an individual develops a serious medical problem, its impact reverberates throughout the family. The demands of the illness frequently require family members to reorganize their activities in response to the illness. A growing body of evidence suggests that family dynamics can affect many illnesses for better or worse (Campbell, 1986, as cited in Nichols & Schwartz, 2001). Disruption to the family caused by the onset of the illness can lead to emotional problems for the sick individual and other members of the family (Nichols & Schwartz, 2001).

Medical family therapists work in conjunction with the family and the health care system to help families experiencing serious medical problems maintain as normal a lifestyle as possible. If the illness is impending, the therapist can help the family prepare for it. If it is already present, the therapist can help family members identify negative impacts of the disease and make changes that are appropriate.

Illness interacts with the family dynamics, structure, life-cycle stage, and belief about the course of the illness (Nichols & Schwartz, 2001). By increasing the family's awareness of these characteristics, the therapist assists the family in utilizing its resources to best respond to the realities of the disease. Goldenberg and Goldenberg (2000) identified two additional areas in which family therapy may complement medical treatment. The first is in the area of noncompliance with medical advice. Individuals who are noncompliant often are helped through family interventions as other members are enlisted to support the patient's following medical orders.

The second area relates to overutilization of medical services, which may occur when individuals are overstressed by family problems and develop physical symptoms in response. They hope that the doctor will "fix" them, when in reality the family problems are the source of the symptoms. These patients often overutilize medical services and underutilize family therapy. The physician often prescribes family therapy for these patients to break the overutilization cycle.

▪ *The Need for Family Therapy Skills*

In this chapter we have presented numerous family-related problems that demonstrate that counseling with families offers potential for problem resolution that is not possible when working with individual clients. Although therapy with individuals has a definite place in mental health service delivery, family treatment ought to be the treatment of choice in many situations. Therefore, the challenge is for counselors and psychotherapists to develop the knowledge base and skills necessary to respond to the myriad of problems that occur in marriage and the family.

■ Conclusion

Most counselors and psychotherapists receive training in basic helping skills, including empathy, respect, warmth, genuineness, concreteness, self-disclosure, and immediacy. Most helping professionals are trained to use these skills with individual clients or in groups. Although many counselor training programs offer a few academic courses in marriage and family therapy, few offer practicum or internship experiences of significant duration to allow the counselor to develop effective skills with couples and families (Gladding, Burggraf, & Fenell, 1987).

Most counselor training programs have little room in their curricula for marriage and family therapy coursework and training because of the significant requirements for courses supporting individual and group psychotherapy. Only 24 of the 153 Council on Accreditation for Counseling and Related Educational Programs (CACREP) have received accreditation in marriage and family counseling/therapy (CACREP Connection, 2001). Thus, many graduate students interested in family therapy must receive formal training in marriage and family therapy beyond the master's level through continuing professional education (Fenell & Hovestadt, 1986).

A further obstacle for students desiring to develop marriage and family therapy skills is the perception that marriage and family therapy, practiced from a systems perspective, is radically different from what is taught in a master's program that focuses on individual and group therapies. Because of the mystique and different terminology surrounding marriage and family therapy, counseling professionals often believe they are not adequately prepared to work with couples and families. This book demonstrates ways in which counseling students can begin to apply many of the basic skills learned in individual and group work to work with couples and families. Further, we will show how these skills form bridges linking individually oriented counseling theories to systems theories, which will increase the reader's confidence and abilities to help couples and families.

The question is not whether counselors will work with couples and families. Because of the tremendous demand for family therapy services, practicing professional counselors certainly will encounter clients experiencing family-related problems. The important question is: Will counselors be adequately prepared to help clients who seek help with marriage and family related problems? This book is designed to provide counselors with information they need to begin to provide supervised therapy to couples, families, and others experiencing relationship difficulties. Each chapter will bring the reader closer to the goal of being able to begin to work with couples and families under the supervision of a competent marriage and family counselor.

The Family as a System

This chapter presents basic and essential information concerning family therapy. To be effective in working with couples and families, the counselor has to understand the concepts that define the uniqueness of family therapy and be able to conceptualize family problems systemically. This means that the counselor has to recognize the family as a functioning organism connected by relationships, history, and shared experiences. Further, the effective family counselor must be able to conceptualize the family system as the client and the focus of treatment. In addition, the counselor must develop the skills necessary to connect with each family member and develop interventions that impact the entire family system.

In this chapter we provide a brief history of the family therapy movement and introduce several of the therapists who founded the movement. Then we provide specific information about family system functioning. Key areas covered are the elements of family functioning, including family health, family dysfunction, and family assessment.

Double-bind hypothesis
Identified patient
Schizophrenic family
Family as a living system
Subsystems
Paradigm shift
Circular causality
Family homeostasis
Subsystem boundaries
Adaptability and cohesion
Disengaged families
Enmeshed families
Family life cycle
The circumplex model

QUESTIONS FOR DISCUSSION

1. How can family systems theory be helpful to the counselor in professional practice?

2. What are the major differences between systems theory and individual theory?

3. Which terms and concepts introduced in this chapter describe your own family? How are they appropriate for your family?

4. How can the circumplex model be used in understanding and assessing family functioning?

5. What are key characteristics of effective communication? Why is communication essential to effective relationships?

6. How is the concept of family life cycle development helpful in family therapy?

7. What elements of the history of the family therapy profession seem most important to your understanding of helping families?

This chapter introduces key family therapy terms and concepts. A thorough understanding of these terms and concepts will facilitate understanding of the family therapy theories presented later in the book. Most of the theories of individual psychotherapy are based on the assumption that psychological problems reside within the individual; if the therapist can help resolve issues that are internally disturbing to the individual, therapeutic cure has occurred. This notion that the *locus of pathology* resides within the individual is deeply rooted in contemporary American society, in which individual achievement is highly valued and rewarded. When a person is successful, he or she is viewed as having "made it" as an individual; the individual possesses the characteristics that made the success possible.

Personal failure and psychological problems are viewed as deficits that also reside and are maintained within an individual. If a person is unable to succeed or has psychological problems, the overwhelming preponderance of social opinion suggests that the person has some character defect or flaw. Given the importance of individuality in this society, it is not difficult to understand why psychological problems are viewed primarily as being within the individual and why treatment of psychological problems focuses on the individual. In this text we propose an alternative systems view to this traditional understanding of psychological problem formation.

Evolution of Marriage and Family Therapy

Until the late 1940s and early 1950s, psychological theories were rooted primarily in the idea that problems reside within the individual. About this time, maverick psychiatrists and psychologists began exploring the notion that psychological problems could be caused by dysfunctional interactions between persons rather than by some individual character flaw or personality defect. To better understand what conditions led these pioneers in family therapy to develop new theories of problem formation based on dysfunctional interaction patterns, we will briefly outline the history of the family therapy movement.

Family Therapy: Setting the Stage

Sigmund Freud is the acknowledged father of psychotherapy. All therapies have their origins with psychoanalytic theory. Freud was perhaps the first to recognize the importance of the family in the development of sound mental health. He believed that successful passage through a series of developmental stages between birth and late adolescence was necessary for development of a sound personality.

According to Freud difficulties could arise at any of the stages to create psychological problems in the individual. He believed that resolution of the Oedipal and Electra stages of development are especially critical to sound development, because it is here that healthy relationships with parents and persons of the opposite sex are established. In the widely quoted case of Little Hans, Freud (1909) actually trained a father to help treat his son to resolve the son's phobia of horses. This case is one of the earliest examples in the psychology literature of family intervention.

Alfred Adler was one of Freud's colleagues and followers. He broke from Freud, however, by emphasizing the importance of the individual's *perception* of early life events rather than the actual events themselves as critical in the development of mental health problems. Adler believed that individuals make early decisions about themselves based on these perceptions, and that awareness of these choices allow individuals to make new and more effective life decisions.

Moreover, Adler emphasized the importance of family interactions in the formation of personality and developed a theory based on the effects of *birth order* on behavior. He also established the first child guidance facility. Adler emphasized the *social nature* of humans and believed that all have a basic drive to be socially productive. Further, he viewed all *behavior as purposeful*—an idea that many family therapists have adopted. Adler's belief that individuals' perceptions of events are more important than the events themselves is an idea adopted most recently by narrative family therapists, as well as social constructivists (Corey, 2001; Gladding, 2002).

In the 1930s, marriage counseling emerged as a new field. Psychoanalysts had been treating individuals with problems in their marriage but rarely had treated the couple together. The psychoanalysts focused on the neuroses of each individual. Early marriage counselors, in contrast, directed their treatment to what was wrong in the marriage rather than what was wrong with each individual. Pioneers in marriage counseling were Paul Popenoe, Abraham and Hannah Stone, and Emily Mudd (Broderick & Schraeder, 1991).

The next significant event in the development of marriage and family therapy was the establishment of the American Association of Marriage Counselors in 1945. This organization has evolved into the American Association for Marriage and Family Therapy (AAMFT), the primary professional organization for marriage and family therapists.

Family Therapy: An Emerging Profession

The next breakthrough in the development of the field of marriage and family therapy resulted from the work of therapists in the early 1950s who studied schizophrenia. These researchers began to recognize that patients' symptoms improved when they were hospitalized but deteriorated when they were brought in contact with significant family members.

This finding encouraged researchers at the Mental Research Institute in Palo Alto, California, to study the communication patterns between schizophrenic patients and members of their families. From this research emerged the *double-bind hypothesis* of dysfunctional communication (Bateson, Jackson, Haley, & Weakland, 1956). According to this hypothesis, parents send confusing and contradictory messages to the schizophrenic patient. No matter how the patient responds to the message, the patient's answer or response is inevitably incorrect or inappropriate. Thus, the patient is in a "no win" situation because no rational response is acceptable. For example, a mother might say to her child, "You never tell me you love me." Then the child responds and tells the mother she is loved. The double-binding mother responds, "You only tell me that because I made you—you don't love me at all." Thus, the child is in an untenable situation and in a captive environment, one that offers no escape.

It was believed that schizophrenic patients retreat into psychoses to avoid dealing with the repeated and inescapable double-bind messages and the untenable position in which these messages place them. The mother of the schizophrenic patient was often detected as the person communicating the double-bind messages. However, fathers also have contributed to this communication pattern by withdrawing and not confronting the mother on her behavior toward the child. The reason mothers were most frequently detected in double-bind relationships with the schizophrenic offspring was that the mothers had more intense and frequent contact with the patient than the fathers did. Thus, the mothers' opportunities for engaging in dysfunctional interactions with the schizophrenic child were much greater than the fathers'. The key finding was that one parent would create the double-bind and the other would collaborate by withdrawing and not confronting the spouse's behaviors.

The double-bind research conducted by Gregory Bateson, Don Jackson, Jay Haley, and John Weakland (1956) had a tremendous impact on the mental health field. Therapists began to realize that the dysfunctional communication patterns in schizophrenic families also exist in less intense forms in other families. The member of the family who exhibited symptoms was recognized in the family therapy literature as the *identified patient* of a dysfunctional family. As a result of this research, implications of the double-bind communication theory extended beyond schizophrenic families. The researchers believed that dysfunctional communication patterns are at the root of many family problems and that therapy could focus on improving communication between members rather than identifying and treating a pathology within a dysfunctional family member.

When the problems in communication between family members were corrected, the symptoms of identified patients were frequently found to diminish or disappear. Writing about the numerous significant contributions of the Mental Research Institute to family therapy, Bodin (1981) stated that the double-bind theory "stands as perhaps the most definitive landmark in the revolutionary shift from an individual to systems focus in concepts of psychopathogenesis" (p. 281). Another pioneer in the family therapy field, Virginia Satir (1983, 1988), worked with Bateson and his family communications research group at the Mental Research Institute in Palo Alto. After several years of research with Bateson, Satir left the group and developed her own unique style of family therapy, combining humanistic and systemic characteristics.

Two of the earliest publications on family therapy were *The Psycho-dynamics of Family Life* by Nathan Ackerman (1958) and John Bell's (1961) monograph, *Family Group Therapy*. These books began to pop-ularize family therapy and systems theory, and discussions of systems theory began to emerge in colleges and universities.

Another early contributor to the family therapy movement is Lyman Wynne, whose early research focused on dysfunctional communication within families with schizophrenic members. Wynne coined the term *pseudomutuality* to describe families that appear to be open, caring, and clear in their relationships and communication patterns when this is really not the case. *Pseudomutual families* develop elaborate patterns of relating that often are superficial and disguise underlying relation-ship problems.

Offspring from pseudomutual families often grow up doubting themselves and their perceptions of reality (Wynne, Ryckoff, Day, & Hirsch, 1958). Wynne's later work includes an extensive overview of family therapy research (Wynne, 1988) and expands the definition and functions of family therapists to "family consultants" and "systems consultants." Consultants would focus more on assessing system dynamics and strengths attending to the agenda of the client (Wynne, McDaniel, & Weber, 1987).

Another psychiatrist and first-generation family therapist, Murray Bowen (1960, 1961, 1976, 1978), also conducted research with schizo-phrenic families in the 1950s. Under Bowen's care, the mothers and fathers of patients lived in the hospital with the patient to facilitate fam-ily treatment. Carl Whitaker (1976; Whitaker & Keith, 1981), also a psychiatrist, began bringing spouses, and eventually children, into ther-apy as early as 1944. Both Bowen and Whitaker developed family ther-apy theories that will be reviewed in later chapters.

Salvador Minuchin, too, has had tremendous impact on the family therapy field. He developed structural family therapy theory. Those entering the family therapy profession often adopt this model because it is simple, straightforward, and quite powerful in producing family change. Emerging from the structural model was strategic family ther-apy. Several variations of strategic therapy took hold under the leader-ship of well known leaders in the profession including Jay Haley, the Palo Alto group, the Milan group, and others. These therapies intro-duced techniques that, while powerful, often were not as respectful of the client families as some therapists believed was appropriate. This issue was not addressed until the feminist critique of the family therapy movement began.

Family Therapy: Recent Changes

The *feminist critique* of family therapy, coupled with the postmodern and constructivist family therapy movements, began to challenge the approaches of many of the most established family therapy theories. The feminists believe that the major theories of family therapy served to keep women in stereotypical roles. The feminists advocated a therapy that advanced women's issues and women's privilege.

The *constructivists* and *postmodernists* who began deconstructing family therapy and looking at its component elements believed that many of the family therapy theories in vogue were not respectful of the client's realities and attempted to impose a solution rather than engage the families in finding their own solutions. Moreover, some of the frequently used family therapy techniques such as *paradox*, often known as *reverse psychology,* were viewed as manipulative and not genuine.

Because of these critiques, family therapy began to evolve into a kinder and gentler approach. *Narrative therapy* and *social constructivist* approaches emerged along with *internal family systems theory* (Nichols & Schwartz, 2001) and *emotionally focused couple's therapy* (Greenburg & Johnson, 1988). Relationship-based approaches such as Rogers' (1961) *person-centered therapy* began to influence family therapy.

Counselors are trained extensively in the use of relationship skills that are viewed as critical in work with individuals, couples, and families today. Through the effective use of these relationship skills, coupled with effective use of family systems theory, counselors can maximize their assistance to the families they treat.

▇ Developing a Family Systems Perspective

To understand family systems and to practice counseling from a systemic approach, therapists must understand that *systems exist at many levels*. One of the easiest ways to understand the concept of living systems is to examine the human being. The human is a living system composed of *subsystems*, which in turn are composed of other subsystems.

Subsystems

The biological human is composed of a nervous system, a digestive system, a circulatory system, a skeletal system, a respiratory system, and a reproductive system. Each of these systems is a subsystem of the total human system. Furthermore, each of these subsystems is composed of other subsystems. The circulatory system, for example, consists of the veins, arteries, and the heart. Each of these subsystems is composed of other subsystems. The heart, for example, is composed of cells, and the cells are composed of cellular subsystems. For the body to be healthy, all subsystems must function effectively and cooperatively. If the heart were not functioning properly, the other subsystems (and the human being) would be radically affected.

Just as humans are living systems composed of subsystems, each individual lives in a subsystem of a larger living system, as shown in Figure 2.1. This point is essential in learning to provide therapy for

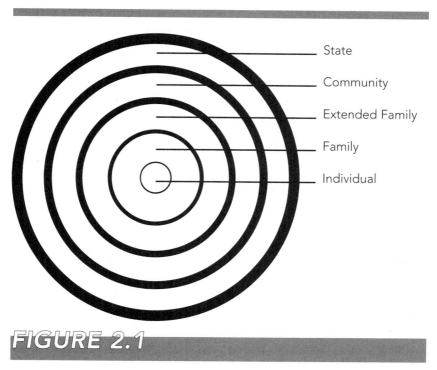

State
Community
Extended Family
Family
Individual

FIGURE 2.1

Levels of System

families: *The individual human is a subsystem of a larger living system called the family.* The family is part of a living system called the extended family, which is part of a larger system called the community. The community is part of a larger system, perhaps known as the state, which is also part of a larger system, and so on.

Because of these interrelationships between systems and their subsystems, if a problem arises in one of the subsystems of a biological organization or a social organization, that problem frequently affects other subsystems of the organization. This concept is most important when a therapist treats a family in which the problem seems to reside in only one of the members. Systems therapists recognize that, although an individual exhibits the presenting problem, it may be maintained by behaviors of other family members. Furthermore, the systems therapist recognizes that the problem behavior affects the behavior of other members of the family system.

The family theorists and researchers introduced previously were initially schooled in models of psychotherapy that emphasized treatment of the individual. These models focused on problems of an *intrapsychic* nature—problems that resided within the mind of an individual. Each of these theorists sought to understand the nature of problem formation in a more inclusive theoretical orientation. Rather than viewing the client's problem as being intrapsychic in nature, they came to view the psychological problem as a symptom of *dysfunctional patterns* (Minuchin, 1974) in the identified patient's family system. Thus, they presented a new way of conceptualizing problem formation. With this new conceptualization of problem formation came new models and strategies for problem resolution.

The movement from an individual perspective to a systems perspective of problem formation and resolution is called a *paradigm shift* (Haley, 1971), a term frequently used in the family therapy literature. To most effectively employ systems-based counseling interventions, therapists must make this paradigm shift and learn to understand how an individual's symptoms are one aspect of a family's interactive sequences of behavior and may serve to stabilize and maintain the current family system.

A classic example of this concept is the case of a child whose symptoms divert the concern of the parents from their marital problems and thoughts about divorce to the problems of the child. By manifesting psychological symptoms, the child has preserved, at least temporarily, the unity of the family through the symptomatic behavior. The parents rarely dwell on their marital problems when they are needed to help their child. The result of the child's symptomatic behavior is the preservation of the larger system, the family. Thus, the symptoms of the child signify a larger problem with the family system.

Linear and Circular Causality

Therapists who make the paradigm shift can differentiate between *linear causality* and *circular causality* in the formation of family problems. Linear causality refers to the concept of cause and effect. One person's action causes another person's predictable reaction. An example of linear causality is:

cause   *effect*

husband drinks ——————> wife nags

In this linear model, the husband's drinking causes his wife to nag. This explanation is perfectly acceptable, but it may not be a complete explanation. If we were to ask the husband to explain his drinking, he might report:

cause   *effect*

wife nags ——————> husband drinks

Again we have an acceptable linear, cause-and-effect explanation for the behavior. The husband drinks because he cannot tolerate his wife's nagging, and the drinking dulls his anger toward her.

Circular causality considers both explanations and incorporates them in a more complete *systemic* conceptualization of the problem. The wife nags to stop her husband from drinking and her husband continues to drink because it helps him tolerate his wife's nagging. This circular understanding of the problem is:

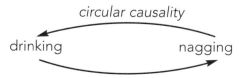

A counselor working with this couple would understand the problem more completely by conceptualizing it through the circular causality

model. According to this view, the behavior of both persons maintains the problem behavior. The couple's problem may not necessarily be either the drinking or the nagging but, rather, their inability to resolve the power struggle concerning who will control the relationship.

Understanding Family Health and Dysfunction

One of the most striking characteristics of family systems therapy is in how the systems therapist defines the presenting problem and conceptualizes the location of the problem. In most counseling theories the focus of treatment is the individual because the problem is believed to reside within the person. Family therapists base their work on the concept of systems theory suggested by Ludwig von Bertalanffy (1968). He proposed that systems are composed of interrelated parts and that the organization of the interrelated parts constitutes a higher-level system.

A family, composed of its individual members and all their relationships, is one such higher-level system. Family systems therapists choose to conceptualize the family as the unit to be treated in therapy rather than identifying one family member of the system for treatment, as is common among individual therapists. Systems therapists recognize that dysfunctional behavior exhibited by the symptomatic individual in the family is merely a manifestation of other problems within the family system.

For many family therapists, the whole family system, rather than a single individual in the family, is recruited for treatment. The symptoms that one family member exhibits are viewed as a part of the dysfunctional interaction patterns of the family rather than a character or personality flaw residing solely within the individual. Another way of stating this is that the *identified patient,* or symptom bearer, may be signaling, with his or her symptoms, a more encompassing problem within the family's organization.

Typically, the identified patient in a family is one of the children. When the child's symptoms become disturbing to parents or teachers, individual therapy for the child is usually recommended. If individual treatment is successful and change is maintained, the problem was truly an individual issue with the child and not a manifestation of a more complex family problem. But, if the treatment is not successful and the frustration of the parents or school officials continues, the parents may seek further therapy. This is the stage where family therapy is often considered as an option.

When a family seeks family therapy, it is not necessarily because the members understand that the problem is systemic in nature. In truth, a family rarely is aware of the interactional nature of the identified patient's symptoms prior to entering family therapy. Instead, the family is there because other forms of treatment have not been successful and the members want help. Often the family comes to understand the systemic nature of the symptoms as representative of a problem with the family through the learning that takes place in the later phases of family therapy.

Family Subsystems

Salvador Minuchin (1974) has described family systems in a helpful and understandable manner. He conceptualized the family system as composed of smaller units called subsystems. Among the subsystems that may exist within the family are the *spousal subsystem,* the *sibling* (children's) *subsystem,* the females' subsystem, the males' subsystem, and individual subsystems. In addition to these, other subsystem configurations may exist, such as mother–son and father–daughter subsystems. Each family system has a set of *rules* that govern the behaviors of the family members, and each member has certain *roles* to play in the family. These rules and roles are key to understanding the functions of the family's subsystems. According to Minuchin, the therapist's responsibility is to identify and work to change the key family subsystems involved in maintaining the presenting problems.

Homeostasis

When all members abide by the family rules and act in ways consistent with their roles, family *homeostasis* (Minuchin, 1974), or balance, is achieved. Homeostasis is the tendency of living systems to desire to be at rest or in balance. Living systems, including families, attempt to achieve and maintain homeostasis. When a family member deviates from the established family rules or roles, homeostasis of the family system is threatened. At this point, the other family members begin to engage in corrective behaviors in an attempt to return the deviating member of the system to accepted ways of acting, thereby restoring the family homeostasis.

A classic example of homeostasis is the human body maintaining its temperature of 98.6° on a hot day through perspiring. The perspiration begins as the body overheats. It evaporates on the body to cool it to the appropriate temperature and maintains homeostasis. A related example is that of a thermostat. The thermostat senses the temperature of the air in a room and, if the temperature is too low, it provides for heat. If the thermostat senses that the temperature is too hot, it shuts down heat production until heat is needed again. Thus, the thermostat regulates a consistent temperature and maintains homeostasis.

Families, too, exhibit homeostatic mechanisms. For example, a family rule might be that teenage children will be home by 9 o'clock on school nights. The parents allow for some fluctuations in the arrival time of the teenager, but when she returns home more than an hour late, the parents become upset. If this becomes a recurring pattern, the parents begin rule-enforcing measures to bring the system back into balance. As long as the daughter maintained her behavior within an acceptable range and did not upset the family homeostasis, she had no problems with her parents. But, when she regularly returned home more than an hour late, breaking a family rule, the parents' tolerance level and family homeostasis were challenged and the parents took measures to regain family system homeostasis.

As long as the daughter follows the family rule, homeostasis is maintained and relationships are good. If she does not follow the rule and is disciplined, additional problems, such as hostility and resentment, may negatively affect relationships between the daughter and her parents and further upset the family's homeostasis. When the parents agree that the problems with their daughter cannot be solved by their current efforts, they might seek individual therapy for the daughter's "acting-out" behavior. If the problem is one of an overly rigid family structure rather than simply a rebellious daughter, individual treatment is not likely to be effective in the long run. Thus, family therapy might be the next attempt at obtaining help for their problem. Family therapy would examine the parents' rules and behaviors along with the daughter's rebelliousness. This approach is likely to produce cooperation in rule setting and lead to more positive and long-lasting results than individual treatment. It might help the family restore homeostasis with a set of more functional family rules.

Boundaries

The flow of information from one subsystem to another is controlled and regulated by the *boundaries* between the subsystems. Boundaries are created primarily by the rules the family establishes for regulating information flow between and among members. Families that are very private and do not share many thoughts and feelings have *rigid* boundaries. These families are very nondisclosive and live in homes where closed bedroom doors ensure privacy. Families that share any and all information have *diffuse* boundaries. These families often live in homes where closed bedroom doors are not allowed and family members have detailed information about one another.

For instance, a husband and wife may have a relatively impermeable boundary around their subsystem that generally does not allow the children to participate in their spousal interactions. The husband and wife also serve in the roles of mother and father to their children. When the couple is in the *spousal subsystem*, participation of the children is discouraged by family rules. When the couple is in the *parental subsystem*, the subsystem boundaries are permeable and inclusion and appropriate participation by the children are encouraged. The family as a whole system may have a permeable boundary that readily includes members outside the family, or it may have a rigid boundary that makes inclusion of "outsiders" difficult. The character of the boundaries of the family determines the flow of information within the family and the inclusion or exclusion of participants in the family system and subsystems.

As part of the assessment process, family therapists try to identify the type of boundaries that exist between family subsystems and between the family and the outside world. If the boundary functions are not facilitating healthy family interactions, by either restricting the flow of clear communication or by impeding its flow, the therapist will intervene to assist the family in changing the boundaries and the rules that define those boundaries and the interactions among family members.

Adaptability and Cohesion

Two characteristics of families that may be used for diagnostic purposes are *adaptability* and *cohesion*. Olson, Sprenkle, and Russell (1983) developed a *circumplex model* to assess families on these dimensions. Shown in Figure 2.2, this model has been widely used in assessing family health and dysfunction.

Referring to the figure, the constructs of adaptability and cohesion each have four levels. Thus, a possibility of 16 types of families may be identified through the use of this model. *Adaptability* refers to the family's ability to modify its rules, roles, and structure in response to the pressures and conflicts of family life. *Chaotic* families have little

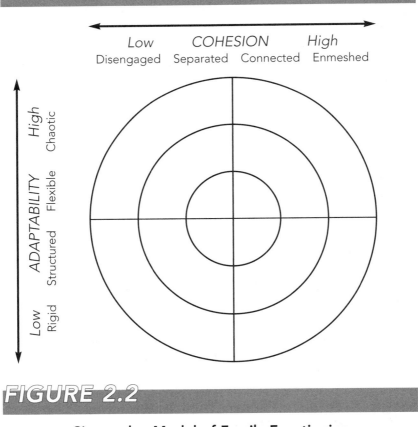

FIGURE 2.2

Circumplex Model of Family Functioning

Source: "Circumplex Model of Marital and Family Systems: VI: Theoretical Update" by D. H. Olson, D. H. Sprenkle, and C. Russell, in *Family Process*, *22*(1), 1983, p. 71. Used by permission.

structure for dealing with the problems of family life; rules are unclear and frequently not enforced. *Flexible* families are receptive to change and have the ability to resolve problems through appropriate changes in rules and roles. *Structured* families are less able than flexible families to modify rules and roles; however, these families are able to adapt and change when necessary. *Rigid* families are reluctant to change rules and roles and tend to maintain the status quo at all costs.

Cohesion refers to the extent of togetherness in the family and the amount of individual autonomy granted to family members. *Disengaged* families have low cohesion. Members are afforded maximum autonomy and may not identify significantly with their family. *Separated* families value individual autonomy, but they have a sense of family unity and identity.

Connected families value closeness and may prefer it; however, connected families also recognize and support development of autonomy in their members. *Enmeshed* families value family closeness above all. In enmeshed families, to sacrifice togetherness for independence is considered a major violation of family rules. The 16 types of families possible in the circumplex model are identified by the level of adaptability (high, mid-range, or low) and the level of cohesion (high, mid-range, or low) present in the family. Assessment of the family using the circumplex model as a basis for discussion with the family can be helpful in understanding the family and in expediting the family-change process.

Families in the midrange of the circumplex model have moderate scores on the adaptability and cohesion scales. Families with moderate scores are believed to exhibit characteristics of family health. Families at the extremes of the two dimensions are more likely to exhibit characteristics of family dysfunction. Olson and his colleagues caution, however, that all families with extreme scores are not necessarily dysfunctional and that some mid-range families are dysfunctional. In general, however, the mid-range families tend toward healthier functioning.

A summary of the characteristics of healthy and dysfunctional families is provided in Table 2.1. Counselors who plan to work with families have to understand family functioning and be able to classify families based on the characteristics they exhibit. The information provided in Table 2.1 should help the family counselor understand and classify family functioning.

TABLE 2.1

Characteristics of Healthy and Dysfunctional Families

Family Health	Family Dysfunction
Subsystem boundaries are clear and may be altered as family requires.	Subsystem boundaries are rigid or diffuse and are not subject to change.
Family rules are clear and fairly enforced. Rules may change as family conditions change.	Rules are unchanging and rigidly enforced, or family has no rules or methods of organizing behavior.
Family members have a clear understanding of their roles and may seek changes in their role as conditions change.	Roles are rigid and may not be modified, or roles are not clearly defined and members are unsure what is required to meet expectations.
Individual autonomy is encouraged, and a sense of family unity is maintained.	Individual autonomy is sacrificed for family togetherness, or autonomy is required because of lack of family unity.
Communication is clear and direct without being coercive.	Communication is vague and indirect or coercive and authoritarian.

Family Communication

The research by Bateson et al. (1956) hypothesized that the double-bind communication style described earlier in this chapter contributes to the development of schizophrenic symptoms in family members. Similar dysfunctional communication patterns were shown to be a feature of other family systems with less severe symptoms in one of their members, such as acting-out or depressive reactions. Thus, one important objective for many family therapists is to help their clients recognize and modify dysfunctional patterns of communication. This change in communication patterns often leads to the resolution of symptoms. Clear, concise and open communication skills are hallmarks of effective family functioning.

Communication is vital to healthy family functioning because members have to be able to express their thoughts, feelings, and desires to others (Satir, 1983). When family members are unable to do so, psychological problems may develop in one or more family members. Alexander and Parsons (1982) maintain that an effective negotiation style is an important general goal for all families because negotiation is the key to resolving the myriad differences that arise in families. These authors believe that effective family communication involves the following characteristics:

Brevity

Communication must be short and to the point. This avoids confusing the listener with too much information.

Source Responsibility

Wants and needs are expressed most effectively in "I statements." These allow the sender of the message to take responsibility for the wants, thoughts, or feelings expressed. By maintaining source responsibility, the sender avoids making accusations to the listener and keeps the communication flow on a positive level.

Directness

When it is necessary to identify behaviors in others that have been problematic, the communicator should identify the person and the behavior directly. Directness avoids the problem of not clearly identifying what is needed for change to occur. An indirect statement would be, "No one in this family ever helps me in the kitchen." A more effective statement would be, "I need more help from you in the kitchen."

Presentation of Alternatives

Effective communicators are not overly demanding; they present alternatives to solving a problem. In addition, they are open to alternative solutions suggested by the listener. For example, a husband may say to a wife, "I can't get all the rooms painted by the time your parents come. Would you like me to start on the first floor or upstairs?"

Congruence

Effective communicators present messages that are consistent or congruent at all levels. The verbal message is consistent with the nonverbal message, and the message is appropriate for the context of the conversation. If a husband needs more affection from his wife, he should ask for this in a pleasant manner with congruent body language rather than asking for this with a critical tone and demanding scowl on his face.

Concreteness and Behavioral Specificity

Effective communicators specify clearly what behavior is needed from the listener. Rather than saying, "You complain too much," the effective communicator would say, "I become angry when I hear you complain about my not helping in the kitchen." This level of specificity permits the communicators to know exactly what they need to work on.

Feedback

Effective communicators seek clarification from each other in a way that does not interrupt the purpose of the interaction or change the topic of discussion. For example, when a wife tells her husband that his "long work hours are creating distance in the relationship," she could seek feedback by asking him what he understood her to say. Possibly, the husband heard criticism from his wife when she wanted him to hear that she was lonely. This feedback technique is an important way for couples to be sure their communication is clear.

Dysfunctional communication is frequently part of the problem of families entering treatment. Family therapists can help families identify and modify their dysfunctional communication patterns by educating clients about the components of effective communication and by allowing clients to *practice these skills during counseling sessions* where feedback can be provided by both family members and the therapist. This "in session" practice and feedback involving all family members and supervised by the therapist is one of the features that sets family therapy apart from individual treatment.

Family Life Cycle

Professional counselors and other psychotherapy practitioners must be able to design therapeutic interventions appropriate for the developmental stage of the individual receiving treatment. Therapists who treat marital and family difficulties may find the concepts of family life cycle development useful in their work with couples and families. Just as individuals move through predictable stages in their development, families pass through predictable stages of development.

Carter and McGoldrick (1980) have suggested that families move through stages of development in the process of marriage, childrearing, and preparing for life as a couple with grown children. Typically, three generations of the family are involved in the life cycle process. Carter and McGoldrick suggested that specific developmental tasks must be accomplished at each of the developmental stages of the family, as described below.

1. *The unattached young adult.* During this stage, parents and children come to accept the separation that has developed between the generations. The offspring begin to develop intimate peer relationships and establish a career pattern.
2. *Marriage: The joining of two families.* During this stage, the offspring commit fully to establishing a new family system through marriage. Critical events are the realignment of relationships with extended family and peers to meet the requirements of marriage.
3. *The family with young children.* During this stage, the couple must change the family system to make room for the child or children. The parents must increase their role responsibilities to include parenting, and they must adjust their relationships with each other and with the older generation, which assumes new roles and responsibilities as grandparents.
4. *The family with adolescents.* During this often stormy stage, parents must allow more autonomy for adolescents. Adolescents begin to move out of the family system and begin to seriously seek autonomy. Parents deal with mid-life career and relationship issues and begin preparing to assume responsibilities of caring for the older generation.
5. *Launching children and preparing for married life without children and parents.* During this stage, the parents help the children leave the family to establish their own lives. In addition, the spouses begin to renegotiate their relationship as a two-person system. During this stage, the couple may adopt the new roles of in-laws and grandparents. Finally, they must deal with the disability and death of their own parents during this stage.

6. *The family in later life*. During this stage, the couple deals with passing the torch to the next generation. Specifically, the two of them must maintain their own interests in the face of declining health, support a more central role for their children (middle generation) in the family, create a place for themselves in the family system without trying to control the middle and youngest generations. Ultimately each partner must prepare for and perhaps deal with loss of the spouse and prepare for one's own death.

As counselors consider this family life cycle, specific issues emerge at each of the stages. Knowledge of these stages prepares counselors to identify effective interventions to help their clients deal with these significant issues in acceptable ways. This knowledge enables counselors to reassure family members that events that seem stressful to the family may be normal aspects of family development and can be handled as such rather than as psychological dysfunction.

For example, parents frequently become overly critical of their teenagers when the son or daughter begins the normal process of establishing independence from the parents. Parents often diagnose their adolescent as having emotional or psychological problems during this stage when the teenager is actually engaging in the normal life cycle process of differentiating from the family of origin. Although differentiation is often painful for the parents and children alike, it is not necessarily a sign that the adolescent has psychological problems. When the counselor assures the parents and the adolescent that what is happening in the family is quite normal in family development, the stress and anxiety that had been present are often significantly reduced and healthy family functioning is enhanced.

The therapist should be careful when *normalizing* family developmental issues. If normalization is not done effectively, family members may believe that their problems are being discounted. The family therapist, while normalizing certain predictable developmental issues, also may reassure the family that there are more effective ways to deal with the issues. Family therapy may be extremely useful in learning to implement these more effective solutions.

The model of family development described in this chapter is based on the rules and roles of the traditional family with three generations and two parents. Although many of the developmental tasks described are appropriate for nontraditional family systems, such as remarried families and single-parent families, other minority and alternative family types, such as single-parent families, frequently have additional tasks to accomplish. Specific issues of nontraditional families will be treated in Part Three of this book.

Summary

This chapter has provided a brief history of the family therapy movement and important concepts required to understand the family as a living system and appropriate focus of treatment in family therapy. The reader has been introduced to several key leaders in the development of the family therapy movement including Bateson, Haley, Weakland, Jackson, Satir, Whitaker, Bowen, Wynne, and Minuchin. The ideas developed by these family therapy pioneers continue to define much of the work in family systems therapy today.

The family has been described as being composed of several subsystems, and intervention strategies have been identified. The circumplex, communications, and family life cycle models were presented to help the reader understand and assess normal and abnormal family functioning.

SUGGESTED READINGS

Broderick, C. B., & Schraeder, S. S. (1991). The history of professional marriage and family therapy. In A. S. Gurman & D. P. Kniskern, Eds., *Handbook of family therapy* (Vol. 2). New York: Brunner/Mazel.

Carter, E. A., & McGoldrick, M., Eds. (1980). *The family life cycle: A framework for family therapy.* New York: Gardner Press.

Minuchin, S. (1974). *Families and family therapy.* Cambridge, MA: Harvard University Press.

From Individual Counseling to Marriage and Family Therapy: Building Theoretical Bridges

This chapter provides the reader with information about the similarities and differences between individual and systems theories. Too often the differences between individual and systems theories have been emphasized without sufficient consideration of their similarities. Effective therapists use both individual and systems theories appropriately in clinical practice. To understand when and how to use individual and systems theories, the therapist must be aware of the similarities and differences between the theories and the strengths of each approach. This chapter also presents a five-step procedure that may be used to treat family problems by therapists with experience in individual counseling. Finally, we will describe the classification scheme used to organize the individual and systems theories presented in Part Two of the book.

KEY CONCEPTS

Locus of pathology
System as client
Joining
Systems therapist as expert
Expanding the definition of the problem
Paradigm shift
Brief family therapy

QUESTIONS FOR DISCUSSION

1. What are the major similarities between individual and systems theory approaches to counseling?

2. What are the major differences between individual and systems theory approaches to counseling?

3. What can the counselor do to expand the definition of the presenting problem in family therapy? Why is this important?

4. Why is it important to join with each family member in family counseling?

5. What basic counseling techniques may be used in the joining process?

6. Why do family systems counselors consider it important to treat the whole family as the client?

7. How can family systems theory be helpful to the counselor in professional practice?

*I*n the past, much emphasis has been placed on the differences between counseling for individuals and marriage and family therapy. As Gurman and Kniskern (1981b, p. xii) stated, transactional analysis, client-centered, rational-emotive, Adlerian, cognitive, and Gestalt therapies have been the primary influences in individual and group therapy. Although Gurman and Kniskern acknowledged that some family therapists have adopted aspects of these theories in their work with couples and families, they suggested that the theories have not yet exerted a significant influence on the family therapy field.

In part, these theories about therapy for the individual have not been very influential in family therapy because of a perceived dichotomy between the practice of individual and group therapy and family therapy. This dichotomy in essence is based on the idea that individual and group theories conceptualize problems as existing within individuals and that, for the most part, these problems are maintained by the actions of the individual or by past experiences. Family therapy, based on systems concepts, assumes that psychological problems in an individual are conspicuous elements of a more encompassing problem that involves the individual as well as those in that person's environment or interpersonal system. Most often, the *interpersonal system* is composed of the members of the identified patient's family.

We believe that this dichotomy between individual/group theories and systems-based theories may not be helpful for therapists with traditional individual and group therapy training, for it fails to recognize that the skills these therapists currently possess can be used effectively to help couples and families. Effective therapists should be able to conceptualize problem formation in clients from both individually oriented models and systems-based models. It is our experience that many counselors believe they are in some way being disloyal to their theoretical position if they do not adhere to the concepts in exactly the same way as the founder of the theory. This observation applies to counselors who adhere to either individual or systems-based theories. We have found that the most effective therapists are those who have identified a theoretical approach that is consistent with their own value system, and who are open to modifying their approach in response to client need, new information, and research results.

The purpose of this chapter is to clarify how counselors who have experience working from individually based theories can build bridges linking their current way of conceptualizing problem formation to a model of helping that is systems-based. To begin this process, it is important for the reader to understand the similarities and differences between individual and family systems therapies.

Similarities Between the Theories

For counselors to comfortably cross the bridge from individual to systems-based treatment, they need to reaffirm their awareness that the ultimate goal of all counseling theories, including individual and systems theories, is to help alleviate human suffering. Once the counselor recognizes that the goal of therapy is the same for all approaches, the question becomes: What is the best way to incorporate theory and technique to alleviate this human suffering? We believe that counselors who do not incorporate systems-based family therapy in their skill repertoire may not be as well-equipped to help their clients as a therapist who is able to conceptualize and treat from both individual and systems-based theoretical orientations as the client's needs dictate.

A second similarity between individual and systems-based theories is that each respects the dignity of the client. The client seeks the services of the therapist. The therapist, in turn, attempts to help the client resolve the difficulties that are negatively affecting the client's life. To be successful in helping the client, the therapist must clearly communicate that he or she respects the attempts, however ineffective, the client has made to resolve the current problems. Moreover, the therapist communicates, through respect, that the client possesses the resources necessary to make significant life changes.

If counselors accept that both individual and systems theory treatments seek to alleviate human suffering and respect the dignity of their clients, it will become easier to adopt a systems perspective in treatment. Counselors who operate from the perspective of counseling the individual need not give up their current knowledge and skills in alleviating human suffering and will not be asked to surrender their belief in the dignity of the client, as these characteristics are shared by both individual and systems theorists.

Differences Between the Theories

There are four specific differences between theories for treating individuals and systems theories used in family therapy. These differences highlight specific factors in the conceptualization of problem formation that should be examined and incorporated in a systems perspective. The four major differences are presented next.

Locus of Pathology

Traditionally, therapists for individuals have conceptualized the locus of pathology (or the location of the problem) as being within the psyche of the individual client. According to this model, problems occur because the client has not resolved certain issues in his or her current or past experiences. The therapist helps the client examine and resolve these internal psychological issues and conflicts.

The systems therapist does not discount this model. However, the systems therapist considers an alternative hypothesis of problem formation and locus of pathology. Although the client's problem may lie within the individual's psyche, systems theorists assume that the client's problems occur as a result of dysfunctional interaction patterns between significant persons within the client's social context. This social context is frequently the client's family. Thus, for the systems theorist, the locus of pathology is within the client's social system or family. From a systems perspective, the problems experienced by one family member are believed to be conspicuous elements of a dysfunctional family. Thus, for the systems theorist, the locus of pathology is found in the client's entire social system or family.

Focus of Treatment Interventions

From an individual theorist's perspective, the focus of treatment is generally on the individual client. The therapist concentrates on helping the client explore his or her past and present world and discover what could be changed to make his or her life more satisfying. In counseling the individual, the therapist gathers information based primarily on the client's perceptions of what has occurred and is occurring in his or her life. If the client is having problems dealing with a member of his or her family system, the therapist may help the client discover ways to change his or her behavior to respond more effectively to the stable conditions in the family.

The family therapist's focus of treatment is on the family system of the client. The person with the problem in the family is referred to as the *identified patient*, or *IP*. Frequently, the family therapist will treat the identified patient's entire family and will assist the family members in changing the ways they relate to each other and to the identified patient. If the therapy is successful, all family members change their patterns of interaction and the symptoms of the identified patient decrease in intensity and duration and may eventually disappear. In family therapy the therapist must deal with the perceptions of *all* the family members in addition to responding to the actual interactions and behaviors of the members of the family system.

The therapist for an individual client usually has access only to the client's reports of the other family members' behaviors, but the family therapist can actually observe the behaviors of the identified patient and other members of the family system during the sessions. This is a major strength of family therapy. Based on observations of family interaction patterns, the systems therapist helps each member of the family adjust his or her behavior to a more satisfying state for all concerned. In family work, everyone has the opportunity to change—not just the identified client. Systems therapists believe that lasting change is more likely when all members of the system are participating in that change.

Unit of Treatment

The individually oriented therapist generally treats only the individual client in therapy. Based on the theoretical assumption that the locus of pathology is within the individual, treating the individual alone makes sound theoretical sense and may be the treatment of choice.

Family therapists often seek to treat the entire family in therapy, or at least to counsel the members of the family most involved in the presenting problem. This approach, they believe, not only increases the options and alternatives for change but also resolves the presenting problems and helps the entire family more quickly and effectively than individual therapy. Because systems therapists conceptualize the *locus of pathology* as occurring within the family system, treating as many members of the system as possible is considered to be the treatment of choice.

Duration of Treatment

In general, therapists for individuals attempt to help clients resolve internal conflicts that may have roots imbedded deeply in the past. Thus, treatment continues until the client has not only fully worked through problems that occurred in the past but is also functioning effectively in the present. This type of treatment may be quite lengthy, often lasting a year or more depending on the specific presenting problem and the theoretical orientation of the therapist. Such lengthy treatment also has the disadvantage of creating the possibility of client dependence on the counselor.

Family systems theorists typically attempt to provide brief treatment for the resolution of family-related problems. The systems theorist wants to help families alter their current patterns of dysfunctional behavior and then terminate the therapy in as brief a time frame as possible. Family members learn to depend on each other, rather than on the therapist, in the resolution of their difficulties. Families are encouraged to return to therapy only if further difficulties occur at a later date. Although wide variations in length of treatment can occur, family therapy tends to be briefer than most forms of treatment for individuals, often lasting six months or less. The systems therapist is not trying to help family members resolve longstanding internal conflicts. Rather, the systems therapist expects to help the family resolve only its immediate crisis through alteration of the current pattern of dysfunctional interaction among the members.

Individual Counseling Theories in Family Treatment

We have often heard counselors trained in individual and group theories report that they do not think they are adequately trained to work with families because they lack expertise in systems theory. We believe that counselors with training and experience in individual and group therapy can begin to work effectively under supervision with couples and families, using core counseling skills they have already developed (Fenell & Hovestadt, 1986). Moreover, the theories focusing on counseling individuals presented in most counselor training programs can be employed in working with couples and families, as we will demonstrate in subsequent chapters of this book. Core counseling skills may be used to accomplish a series of five steps that are important in both individual and family systems therapy. These five steps are described next.

Establish Effective Relationships With Family Members

To help an individual or a family change through psychotherapy and to develop a productive counseling relationship, the first step for the therapist is to establish an effective relationship with each individual involved in the treatment. In our judgment, the skills counselors develop in their training programs for counseling individuals (such as empathy, respect, and genuineness) that enable the therapist to establish a therapeutic relationship with clients are the same skills the family therapist needs to develop a working relationship with a family system in family therapy. In family therapy, establishing an effective working relationship with the family members is known as *joining* (Minuchin, 1974). Joining with each family member is an important prerequisite to further work in therapy.

Establish Self as Expert

Establishing the self as an expert who can help the family change is a step that some counselors may find inconsistent with effective therapy. Many counselors trained in therapies for individuals have been taught a person-centered theoretical orientation (Rogers, 1961). This orientation is based on the assumption that the client is the expert concerning the problem and that the client will resolve his or her own problems if the therapist can provide an effective relationship with the client. We contend, however, that even nondirective therapists establish themselves as experts in helping their clients, although they accomplish this through empathy, warmth, and genuineness rather than through more readily observable therapeutic behaviors.

Establishing yourself as an expert in helping the family change may be accomplished directly or indirectly. If a direct approach is chosen, the counselor may give specific suggestions to family members to help the family change dysfunctional patterns. The therapist may share with the family his or her perceptions of what is taking place in the family and what may need to be changed. Direct leadership may also be asserted by referring to experts in the field or citing research relevant to the presenting problem. For example, a therapist may assist a couple in marital therapy using direct leadership by citing a research study on characteristics of long-term marriages (Fenell, 1993a).

If expert leadership is established indirectly, the counselor becomes a significant *source of self-esteem* for the members of the family through demonstrating genuine caring, respect, and understanding of each family member. Basic relationship skills taught in most counseling programs, such as empathy, respect, warmth, and genuineness, are particularly effective in establishing expert leadership indirectly and may be effectively employed by counselors who are beginning their work with families.

Expand the Definition of the Problem

To work most effectively with a family, the counselor must frequently define the presenting problem as one that exists and is maintained within the family system rather than one that resides entirely within the psyche of the identified patient. The definition of the problem is often expanded in this way and this redefinition enhances the effectiveness of many systems-based interventions (Haley, 1983). If the family continues to believe the problem is solely the responsibility of the identified patient, the members are less likely to make changes that could positively affect the outcome of treatment.

The counselor can help the family expand the definition of the problem by applying skills used in therapy for individuals. For example, the counselor is already trained to identify problem behaviors exhibited by the client and to communicate to the client how the behaviors maintain the undesired symptoms. In the same manner, the counselor may observe and identify behaviors or communication styles in other family members that directly or indirectly affect the identified problem.

By using effective relationship skills learned in most counselor training programs, the counselor may help other family members discover how their behavior is part of the problem and identify what they may do to institute change.

A classic example of expanding the definition of the problem occurs when a family comes to therapy seeking help with an acting-out child. The therapist may quickly discover that the parents hold quite different opinions about how to best deal with the child's behavior. The family therapist will use this information and attempt to expand the definition of the problem to include the parents. The therapist will help the parents recognize that they send contradictory and confusing messages to the child and that the parents' behavior places the child in a bind that may have precipitated the acting-out behavior. As mentioned previously, excellent observational skills are necessary to detect important family patterns.

The therapist must accurately describe the actual behaviors of the family members in the expanded definition of the problem. By using actual family behavioral data in the expanded definition, the therapist increases the likelihood that the family will accept the expanded definition. Furthermore, if the therapist has joined with the family members and established expert leadership through the use of excellent communication skills, the chances of the family accepting the new definition of the problem is further increased.

Expanding the definition of the problem is important in family treatment. If the family's definition of the problem is maintained, the family will remain the expert on the problem. If the family is the expert, it will continue to employ different variations of the ineffective solutions it has previously attempted. If a new or expanded definition of the problem is presented and accepted by the family, the *therapist becomes the expert* on the problem and its resolution, and the process of change will often be expedited. When the therapist becomes the expert on the problem, the family will often defer to the therapist and more enthusiastically try new behaviors and solutions to their problem.

Engage All Members in Solving the Problem

After the counselor has successfully expanded the definition of the problem to include other family members, it is necessary to engage the family members in solving the problem. This step can often be accomplished during a session by asking two family members to discuss how the newly defined problem can be resolved. Often, when encouraged to participate, the less verbal family members will have excellent new insights into how the family can behave in more effective ways, and the therapist should be certain all members are included in the process of problem resolution.

Remember that the family is likely to discover new and more effective ways to deal with the problem once it is redefined. Family members are not dealing with the same insoluble problem that brought them to therapy. Rather, they are dealing with a new and expanded version of the problem, which may lend itself to new and creative solutions involving all members of the family system.

Make a Paradigm Shift

The last and possibly most difficult step in the process of working effectively with family systems is making the *paradigm shift* to systems thinking. Counselors are well trained to accept new ideas and to implement them when they are in the best interest of their clients. Systems therapy offers avenues for therapeutic change that cannot be easily achieved from other theoretical orientations. Thus, the well-trained counselor will want to be able to use systems therapy when it is in the best interests of the client family.

Each of the four steps listed above can be accomplished by the well-trained counselor. However, these steps will be nothing more than a set of techniques to be routinely followed if they are not supported by consistent systems-based theoretical assumptions and actions. Therefore, counselors who work with family systems need to make the paradigm shift from conceptualizing the problem as existing within the individual to conceptualizing the problem as a conspicuous aspect of a dysfunctional family system.

Too often counselors adopt a way of helping and adhere to the tenets of the theory as if it were a religion. Counseling theories are not religions; they are models developed to help clients make life changes. If one model for helping does not work, effective therapists will want to try other models. Systems theory offers a powerful alternative helping paradigm that counselors can employ with clients. However, this model cannot be effectively implemented if the counselor cannot or will not conceptualize the family as a living system and as the focus of treatment.

Classification of Theories

The theories in this book have been organized into three categories to aid the reader in understanding the material presented. The categories are psychodynamic, cognitive/behavioral, and humanistic, existential and transpersonal theories. The classification scheme builds on the work of Levant (1984), who developed a multilevel classification system for family therapy theories. The present classification system is unique in that it describes how theories developed to treat individual problems can be used in working with couples and families. Further, several major family therapy theories are presented that may be incorporated by counselors and psychotherapists after appropriate training and supervision.

Each of the theories will be presented in the same organizational format for the purposes of comparison and to develop the bridge between individual and systems theories. First, we will present the *background* for each theory and clarify why and how each theory was developed. Second, we will present the *philosophical tenets* of each theory and discuss the *assumptions* underlying each theory. It is of critical importance that counselors understand the assumptions underlying their method of providing therapeutic assistance to clients. Third, the *major techniques* associated with each theory will be described, including the major interventions used to bring about therapeutic change. In addition to describing these three areas for each individual and systems theory, case examples demonstrating the actual use of each theory are included. Finally, the *strengths* and *limitations* of each theory will be presented.

Summary

As you study each of the theories in this book, it is important to note that certain theories will make more sense to you and be more acceptable and relevant than others. This is as it should be. Each theory is based on certain assumptions and philosophical tenets. Counselors are most comfortable with theories that are based on philosophical tenets similar to their own beliefs about the development of psychological problems and the alleviation of these problems. We suggest that you initially become familiar with the theories that seem most relevant and most promising for the client and client family and use those theories in clinical practice. Then, after becoming grounded in one or more theories, carefully consider and implement theories that are less comfortable, when in the best interests of your client or family. When you are thoroughly grounded and very comfortable with a familiar theory, you will have the ability to move from that theory to study other theories carefully. A return to the familiar is always possible if the study of the new theories becomes too uncomfortable. We believe that having a strong theoretical home base permits the student to engage in a more thorough exploration of other theories.

This book describes the major individual and systems theories that can be employed in family counseling. Several of these theories may serve as a comfortable home base as the counselor studies other systems models developed for treating families.

SUGGESTED READINGS

Horne, A., & Ohlsen, M., eds. (1982). *Family Counseling and Therapy*. Itasca, IL: Peacock.

Levant, R. (1984). *Family Therapy: A Comprehensive Overview*. Englewood Cliffs, NJ: Prentice Hall.

Minuchin, S., & Fishman, C. (1981). *Family Therapy Techniques*. Cambridge, MA: Harvard University Press.

Using Core Counseling Skills in Marriage and Family Therapy

In this chapter, twelve core counseling skills taught in most counselor education programs are described. Each of the twelve skills is identified, and recommendations are made concerning how the skills may be applied in individual, group, and family therapy.

KEY CONCEPTS

Rapport building
Joining
Information gathering
Minimal encouragers
Genogram
Structuring
Information giving
Reflecting content
Reflecting feelings
Summarizing
Self-disclosure
Confrontation
Interpretation
Reframing
Behavior change
Closure

QUESTIONS FOR DISCUSSION

1. Why is rapport building important in individual, group, and family counseling?

2. What steps should the family counselor take when joining with a family?

3. What is a genogram, and how is it useful in family counseling?

4. How is reflection of content different from reflection of feeling, and why are they important in counseling?

5. What is reframing, and why is it important in counseling?

6. What are the components of behavior change skills, and how are these used in individual, group, and family counseling?

7. Which skills described in this chapter do you believe are most important in the helping process?

8. Can you think of a situation where use of the feeling cross would be helpful? Describe the situation.

The five fundamental steps described in the previous chapter suggest a framework for counselors trained in individual therapy to begin working with couples and families. We assume that counselors who begin to work with couples and families are trained in the use of specific core therapeutic skills and have qualified supervision available. In this chapter we will describe twelve core counseling skills that may be used in individual, group, and marriage and family counseling. We will demonstrate how these core skills, which are already in the repertoire of most counselors, may be used as a bridge from individual and group counseling to marriage and family counseling.

Core Skill One: Rapport Building

In counseling the individual, rapport building involves behaving in an attentive manner toward the client both verbally and nonverbally. Examples of good nonverbal attention would be sitting facing the client, maintaining good eye contact, and being relaxed. Verbal attention would include staying with the topic the client brought up and not changing the subject.

In group counseling sessions, rapport building is more difficult because of the number of people involved. The basic premise is the same, however, as with the individual. The goal in group therapy is to let the group members know you are "with them" and that you accept them rather than approve or disapprove of them. It is also useful to pay close attention to the verbs the clients use in their sentences, which will indicate their favorite way of accessing information (visual, auditory, or kinesthetic).

Research has shown that matching a client's way of accessing information is an effective way to build rapport. If a client says, "I am clear (visual) that it wasn't my fault," you might match that by saying, "You don't see why people are blaming you." Eye movements can also provide visual clues. People look up when accessing information visually, side to side when accessing in auditory ways, and down when feeling something kinesthetically. The key to letting them know you are with them is matching their verbal and nonverbal behavior (Dilts & Green, 1982).

In marriage and family therapy, rapport building with clients is called *joining* (Minuchin, 1974). Working with a couple or family requires establishing rapport with each individual in the family. The effective therapist must join with each member of the family system and the significant subsystems of the family.

Joining With Each Family Member

Each person in a family has a story to tell. Each individual needs to tell his or her story and to know that he or she has been heard and understood by the counselor. Thus, excellent listening skills and effective verbal and nonverbal communication skills are essential in order for the counselor to let the individual know that understanding has occurred. If rapport building, or joining, is successful, the counselor will become a significant source of self-esteem for each family member (Minuchin & Fishman, 1981). When the family members look to the counselor to meet some, or most, of their self-esteem needs, the counselor's power in the family and ability to intervene effectively with the family will increase.

Unlike group counseling, in family therapy the story that each family member tells will be related to the story of every other member. The effective counselor will hear and understand each version of the story without favoring any of the versions. This skill takes practice, as the counselor's own values frequently support one family member's position over the others. If the counselor's values do become obvious, the ability to intervene in creative and powerful ways becomes limited as the counselor is "sucked" into the family system and loses therapeutic objectivity.

Joining With the Family

In addition to successfully joining with each individual, the counselor must be able to join with the entire family and the significant subsystems within the family. The counselor must identify important patterns of behavior that the family exhibits and respect these patterns.

Moreover, the counselor must be able to identify family rules early in the treatment and attempt not to violate these rules unintentionally.

Finally, there are significant subsystems in the family, such as the husband-wife, parental, and sibling subsystems. The counselor must identify and join with these subsystems. If the counselor does not join the significant (powerful) subsystems, these powerful units can hinder the therapy process. Just as individuals need to feel valued, so do family systems and subsystems. If the counselor is successful at rapport building, the prognosis for assisting the family is enhanced.

Core Skill Two: Information Gathering

In individual counseling, *open-ended questions* help the counselor gather more information than closed questions. An open-ended question allows the client to respond in several ways; a closed question lends itself to yes-no responses. An example of an open-ended question would be: "Tell me about your relationship with your husband." A closed question would be: "Do you get along with your husband?" *Minimal encouragers* also aid in information gathering. A minimal encourager prompts the client to provide additional information, as, for example, in "Tell me more" or "Give me an example of that."

In group counseling, the same techniques can be employed. The use of open-ended questions and minimal encouragement statements can have a modeling effect when used in a group. Group members may begin to use this technique with each other if it is effectively modeled by the counselor.

In marriage and family therapy, the counselor must obtain information from several persons, as in group counseling. However, the information obtained in family counseling will have a central theme and will be related to issues the family is confronting. In family counseling, the therapist needs an additional skill: *blocking information* provided by a family member who is not being addressed or who is attempting to control the flow of information in the family interview.

For example, the identified patient may be providing information to the counselor about the family situation when the mother interrupts with, "Be sure to tell him about how rude you were to your father yesterday." At this point, the counselor must block the mother's attempt to control the son's responses. The counselor can accomplish this by saying, "Thanks for your concern, Mrs. Smith; however, at this point I'm interested in Tom's thoughts about the situation. If you will be patient with me for a few minutes, I will get to you and find out what you are thinking and feeling about the situation." The family counselor must begin to use blocking techniques early in the therapy to prevent more powerful family members and subsystems from controlling and limiting the flow of information provided by the family.

Another helpful information-gathering tool used primarily in family counseling is the *genogram*. The genogram is a visual depiction of the family tree that frequently covers three generations of the family. Important family information is reported on the genogram, such as names of family members, ages of family members, marital status, divorces, significant life events, and years of deaths. The genogram is a useful aid that frequently helps the counselor elicit important information concerning the family members, the problems in the family, and the emotional reactivity in the family to various members and events. The genogram also may demonstrate how certain problems are transmitted from one generation to the next (McGoldrick & Gerson, 1985). An example of a three-generation genogram is shown in Figure 4.1.

■ *Core Skill Three: Structuring*

In counseling sessions for individuals, structuring the nature, limits, and goals of the session can help the client make better use of the session. It lets the client test out and clarify (1) where he or she is, (2) who the counselor is, (3) how the counselor can or cannot help him or her, and (4) what common goals and expectations each person has for the session. Structuring also clarifies:

1. *Time limits.* Example: "We have agreed to a one-hour appointment today."
2. *Role limits.* Example: "I see my role as helping you explore your problems and concerns and helping you find solutions that are personally satisfying."
3. *Process limits.* Example: "I will help you by pointing out obstacles that I believe are getting in your way and preventing you from solving your problems."
4. *Action limits.* Example: "I will ask you to try out new ideas outside the session and report back to me."

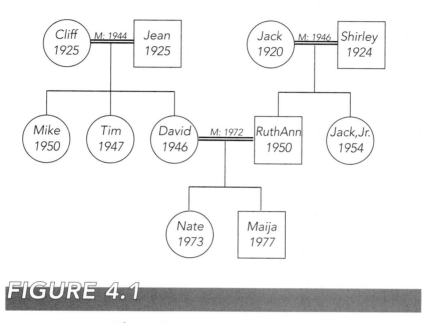

FIGURE 4.1

Three-Generation Genogram

The counselor should involve the client in the structuring process by asking open-ended questions such as, "What motivated you to come see me?" and "How may I be of most help to you?"

In group counseling, the skill is practiced in a similar way. The main difference is that in a group more time has to be devoted to structuring so all members have an equal opportunity to become involved. The time spent structuring the purpose and goals of the group is often time well spent because it helps the group members use the group time more effectively, helps encourage reluctant members to participate, and limits the participation of dominant group members.

In marriage and family therapy, structuring is of critical importance. When a couple or family enters therapy, the clients are frequently locked in a mutually reinforcing pattern of dysfunctional behavior. Despite the pain family members experience, they continue to repeat the same behaviors because those behaviors are reinforced by the complementary behaviors of other family members. A family can quickly overwhelm a therapist with dysfunctional sequences of behavior if the therapist does not take control of the session from the outset. In family therapy, this structuring begins with the initial telephone contact. Often, the person contacting the therapist will have already decided who needs treatment. The family spokesperson is already active (1) in setting up therapy, and (2) in determining who should be present in treatment. The therapist must recognize that the family member's attempts to control treatment, no matter how well intentioned, may have the effect of maintaining the dysfunction. Helping the family engage in new behavior sequences can be accomplished most effectively when the therapist is able to structure the therapy without seeming authoritarian to the family members. For example: The mother may call to set up a therapy appointment and tell the therapist that everyone can attend except her husband, who is too busy with his work. The therapist must respond in a way that acknowledges the mother's concern for her husband's schedule, but that also includes him in the therapy, as his presence is important to the treatment.

▬ *Core Skill Four: Information Giving*

There are times in counseling sessions for the individual when the therapist must give information to the client. At these times, called *teachable moments*, facts or data about experiences the client is having may expand the meaning or learning for the client. The three main purposes of information giving are (1) to identify alternatives, (2) to evaluate alternatives, and (3) to correct erroneous information. In giving information, it is important to be accurate and to reveal information gradually, only when the individual most needs it. In a group counseling session, this skill may be utilized in much the same way as in a session with an individual. There are many opportunities to teach group members concepts that will help them function more effectively in the group and outside the group.

In marriage and family therapy, information giving takes on an increased importance for two reasons: (1) As marriage and family therapy tends to be brief, clients need information to begin making changes relatively quickly in the therapy; and (2) to alter dysfunctional patterns, the family or couple needs to understand what these dysfunctional patterns are. The therapist identifies the dysfunctional patterns and provides the information the family needs to understand the pattern and change it. The information provided by the therapist should meet the following criteria:

1. The information is understood and accepted by the family.
2. The information does not overwhelm the family.
3. The information is accurate.
4. The information is provided at the appropriate time.

Without giving helpful information, the counselor's ability to help the family change their currently dysfunctional patterns of behavior is greatly reduced.

Core Skill Five: Reflecting Content

As a skill for counseling individuals, reflecting content is (1) a way to convey to clients that you understand them, (2) a way to help clients crystallize their thoughts and feelings by having them restated in a more concise manner, and (3) a way for the counselor to check his or her perceptions to make sure they are consistent with what the client is trying to convey. Although the focus is on content, the counselor also recognizes the client's feelings. For example, if a client says, "I don't know about him—one moment he is as nice as can be and the next he is a real jerk," the counselor might say, "He seems like a pretty inconsistent guy who is hard for you to be with. His erratic behavior keeps you pretty confused."

As a group counseling skill, the reflection of content simply changes from a focus on individual content to a focus on group content. Whenever group members seem to ignore, avoid, or deny some important content, the group therapist should intervene and draw out, identify, and reflect the content. There are three specific skills involved: (1) eliciting group content, (2) identifying group content, and (3) reflecting group content. These skills are described next.

1. *Eliciting group content* usually means asking open-ended questions and making statements that draw out the content. For example, the counselor may say: "Sammy, I noticed you avoid looking at other people when you talk to them. What is going on with you? What do other members notice about this?"

2. *Identifying group content* means helping group members identify issues that they have overlooked. For example, the counselor may say: "Most of you seem to have trouble with certain subjects. I noticed that when Bill mentioned having trouble with his mother everyone got quiet, and Jim changed the subject. What have others noticed about this?"

3. *Reflecting group content* means restating or clarifying some issue in your own words. For example, the counselor may say: "It seems to me that several of you are saying that you have problems in dealing with people in authority. Will you give me feedback on my perceptions?"

Reflecting content is an important skill for the marriage and family therapist. For the counselor to provide information to clients about their current patterns of behavior, the counselor must be able to assess current interaction patterns. When the counselor notices a certain repetitive behavior that may require modification, he or she reflects the observation of that behavior to the family. For example, the counselor may say to the family: "I notice that whenever Bill seems to have trouble gathering his thoughts, dad jumps in to help him." At this point, the counselor should check out this observation with those directly involved as well as with other family members.

In addition, this skill is critical in the joining process in the early stages of family therapy. If each member of the family feels that he or she has been heard and understood, the family is more likely to place trust in the therapist, which improves the prognosis for therapy. One of the most effective ways to ensure that family members feel heard and understood is to accurately reflect the content of each family member's communications in therapy.

▩ *Core Skill Six: Reflecting Feelings*

This skill is used in counseling individuals to help clients move toward more complete self-awareness and self-understanding. In reflection of feeling, the counselor expresses the central concern the client is feeling. There are three aspects to this skill: (1) listening for feeling, (2) timing, and (3) reflecting the feeling. In listening for feelings, listen for what is not being said. You may watch nonverbal behaviors, such as a person's breathing, a sigh, a blush, a stammer, or a swallow, as clues to feelings. Verbal clues include the use of feeling words and tone of voice. Good timing requires that the counselor wait for an appropriate moment before reflecting, being careful not to cut off an internal flow or disturb the focus of thought. It is also important not to lag behind the client. Reflecting feelings requires the use of a *feeling word* when the client may not have said one. If a client says, "I wish I could talk to my dad like this," the counselor might say, "You have been a little *afraid* to be open with your dad."

The Importance of Reflecting Feelings

In group counseling, feelings are often overlooked or not dealt with. Most people have been conditioned not to express feelings in public. Therefore, a group counselor must help elicit, label, clarify, and reflect individual and group feelings. A group member might say: "It is hard to bring up things like that." The therapist replies: "You seem scared to talk about your problems in a group. Do any other group members share this feeling?"

According to several marriage and family therapy theories (Fisch, Weakland, & Segal, 1982; Haley, 1971; Minuchin, 1974), reflection of feeling is viewed as important in the joining process, when intense feelings about the family situation are often expressed. The counselor must accurately hear and reflect the feelings. As emotional catharsis is usually not encouraged in family therapy, feelings are not pursued unless their expression is critical to establishing more effective family patterns. However, the therapist must be careful not to discount the client's feelings even though their expression may not be contributing to specific problem resolution. In such a situation, the counselor would want to hear, understand, empathize, and reflect the feeling. When the time is appropriate, the counselor should ask if the client is ready to move to another issue. This technique contrasts with theories about counseling individuals, which teach the therapist to help the client *stay with the feeling* and *work through* it fully before moving to other issues.

The views of many family therapists toward client feelings are different from those of individual or group therapists. Family therapists recognize that family problems may evoke a great deal of affect. However, this affect is dealt with only to the extent necessary to allow the client to move on to aspects of therapy that are viewed as being more helpful in changing dysfunctional interaction patterns of all family members.

The Feeling Cross Technique

Frequently, counselors working with individuals, groups, couples, or families encounter clients who are not skilled at recognizing and reporting their feelings. This often occurs in marriage counseling when the wife complains that her husband does not understand her feelings about their difficulties or express his own feelings about the marital issues. When the counselor asks the husband to report his feelings, the husband automatically shifts into a cognitive, rather than affective, response. The communication sequence might go like this:

Counselor: Your wife is telling us that you do not recognize her feelings about the situation and that you have even less awareness about your own feelings. Can you tell your wife and me how you feel about the marital difficulties you two are currently experiencing?

Husband: I know she says I don't have feelings, but I do. I think she is so down on me that no matter what I do I am wrong.

Counselor: How does it feel to be wrong no matter what you do?

Husband: I've always thought she was frustrated with me.

Counselor: Yes, but tell us how you feel.

Husband: I think I'm not being appreciated.

This sequence of the counselor asking for feelings and the client reporting thoughts could continue for a while. In fact, it often mirrors the communication sequence that the couple uses.

One good way to interrupt a dysfunctional sequence between therapist and husband is by using the *feeling cross* technique developed by Fenell (1990). In this technique, the counselor draws a cross on a chalkboard or piece of paper (see Figure 4.2) and in each quadrant writes a feeling word: *happy, sad, angry,* and *scared.*

Then the session continues as follows:

Counselor: I've just drawn a feeling cross with the four major feelings listed, one in each quadrant. Can you read each feeling for me?

Husband: Sure, that's easy—happy, sad, angry, and scared.

Counselor: Great! Now, when you say that you feel that you are wrong no matter what you do, that your wife is frustrated with you,

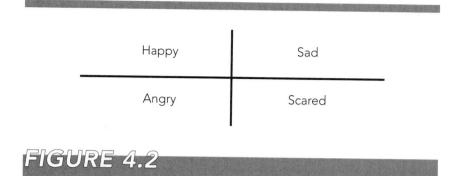

FIGURE 4.2

The Feeling Cross

and that you are not appreciated, you have a feeling or feelings about this. Please touch the word on the feeling cross
that comes closest to how you feel now.

Husband: Well, there is anger for sure, but mainly I feel sad because
the marriage that I want so badly seems to be out of my
reach, and I'm scared I won't be able to make it better.

Counselor: So you feel sad and scared. Can you tell your wife how you
feel like you told me just now?

The husband tells his wife, thereby demonstrating that he does feel and
care about the situation, and the couple begins a new sequence of communication behaviors. The feeling cross can be given to the couple to
display on the refrigerator.

When using this technique, a couple of additional points should be
considered. First, men usually have more difficulty with feelings than
women, but not always. This technique can be applied to anybody.
Second, when the client points only to *angry* and does not include *sad*
or *scared*, the therapist explains to the client that anger is a *surface* feeling and that below the surface is always sadness, fear, or both. The
counselor then asks, "As you feel your anger, tell me what other feelings you experience." The client almost always will recognize one or
both of the more vulnerable feelings of sadness or fear and report this
to the counselor and, more importantly, to the spouse. Once deeper
feelings are introduced into the communication between partners, the
intensity of the anger in the relationship dissipates almost immediately,
allowing the couple to have hope that the marriage might improve.

▮ Core Skill Seven: Summarizing Content and Feelings

At times in individual therapy, the counselor wants to recapitulate, condense, or crystallize the essence of what the client said and felt. Although this skill resembles reflection of content and feeling, it is more comprehensive and covers more of what the client said and felt. Summarization can be used at the beginning of a session to review aspects of the previous session or at the end of a session to review what has happened. This technique can also be used when a client rambles, isn't clear, is at the end of a discussion on a particular topic, or is in conflict.

Summarization can be used in similar ways in group counseling except there is an emphasis on summarizing the collective content and feeling from the group as a whole or of several people. In a group, themes or processes should be summarized from time to time to help group members stay focused.

In marriage and family therapy, summarization pulls together critical aspects of the session for the family. Counselors will want to be certain that their summarizations include the thoughts of as many family members as possible. If the summarization of content and feeling focuses on only one member, the family (and perhaps the therapist) may have lost sight of the problem as a dysfunctional system rather than a dysfunctional individual. As noted previously, the family therapist will generally use summarization of content more frequently than summarization of feeling.

▮ Core Skill Eight: Self-Disclosure

Unless counselors and therapists understand themselves, they will find it difficult to understand others. In counseling individuals, there are times when counselors will want to share personal thoughts, feelings, and experiences that relate to a client's situation. At a basic level, self-disclosure involves listening to the client, reflecting content and feelings, and telling the client what you think or feel about what is being said. Carkhuff (1969a) described this skill as counselor *immediacy.*

In group counseling, self-disclosure can be a very useful way to give group members feedback on how their behavior affects others. For example, a group member may be critical and judgmental about his spouse. The group counselor says: "You seem so angry that I feel afraid of you when you talk that way about your wife. I get angry and want to shut you up. Can you respond to my feelings, John?" Group members may also comment on their perceptions of John's and the counselor's behaviors.

In marriage and family therapy, the use of self-disclosure is sometimes appropriate. When family members are not genuinely reacting to each other, for example, the therapist may share his or her reactions about the behavior with a member who is particularly receptive to the therapist and aware of the family's withholding information. If the counselor is on target with the self-disclosure, frequently one or more members of the family will feel more comfortable sharing the same perceptions and confronting other family members about the situation.

Family therapists must be careful not to use self-disclosure inappropriately. Frequently, counselors think self-disclosure means to share or describe a situation they experienced that was similar to what the client or family is experiencing. Because family problems are widespread and therapists are not immune to family problems of their own, it is possible that the family's behaviors or interactions will remind the therapist of a similar situation in his or her own life. The therapist should rarely discuss the similar situation with the family because it takes the focus off the family and puts it on the therapist. In general, therapists should not share this kind of personal information unless they are certain it will be therapeutic for the family by normalizing the problem or putting the family more at ease.

▨ *Core Skill Nine: Confrontation*

In a counseling session with an individual, a counselor may notice a discrepancy between what the client is saying and how he or she is behaving—for example, if a person is talking about a sad subject and laughs. Such discrepancies almost always have some significance for the person. They may indicate a conflict in feelings or an attempt to avoid or deny facing feelings. By confronting these discrepancies, the counselor may help the client gain insight into the problem or bring the problem out into the open so the client can deal with it. Confrontation is most effective when done from a caring position that shows respect for the client and validates him or her as a worthwhile individual. The counselor's tone of voice, posture, and gestures all contribute to the success of the confrontation.

In a group counseling situation, confrontation takes on even greater importance. Interaction within a group often reveals patterns of behavior more quickly than sessions with individuals. Within a group, members often assume roles identical to the ones they experience outside the group. Through effective confrontation, the counselor can help members understand their behaviors and change problematic behavior patterns.

Confrontation in marriage and family therapy is similar to confrontation in group counseling. However, in group counseling the client comes to recognize a pattern of behavior in the group that is similar to his or her behavior outside the group. The client must then leave the group to try new behaviors in the social setting. Furthermore, the people in the client's social setting will not be participating in the treatment and may not be prepared to reinforce the client's new behaviors. In family therapy, not only are all members experiencing their roles in the therapy but they are each in a position to change their roles with the awareness, support, and reinforcement of other family members outside the therapy session. Thus, the change is more likely to be maintained because all family members are participating in that change.

Confrontation in marriage and family therapy serves the same function as in individual and group therapies. It helps the client, group, or family recognize that what is expressed and the behavior exhibited may be incongruent. Confrontation helps the individual, group, or family clarify what it wants and encourages movement toward that goal.

■ *Core Skill Ten: Interpretation*

Interpretation in a counseling session with an individual means the counselor presents the client with a new frame of reference through which the client can view the problems and better understand the situation. This advanced skill relies on the counselor's mastery of reflection of content and feelings. The accuracy of the interpretation and the client's readiness to receive it determine whether the client can utilize the information. The counselor has to take the essence of what the client has said, summarize it for the client, and add new information for the client to consider. The following example illustrates this. A client with a record of absenteeism states, "I really feel bad about missing so much work." The therapist could respond with an interpretation: "You are worried about your absenteeism. You know how the company views absenteeism, and you are probably afraid you may get fired the next time it happens."

In group counseling, interpretation may include some aspect of the group process or the interaction of several group members. For example, a group member continually rescues other members whenever there is even a mild confrontation. The therapist may offer the following interpretation to the rescuer: "I have noticed that you jump in and try to protect everyone who is challenged by the group. You seem to have a real need to take care of other people. In my experience, people who have a need to protect others usually feel pretty scared and insecure themselves. Is that true for you?" In this situation, the data for the interpretation included the behavior of the client in the group context as well as the counselor's experience with other clients.

In marriage and family therapy, effective interpretation is often crucial to helping the family. When family members come into therapy, they are generally stuck in behavior patterns that seem appropriate to them given the actions of the identified patient. To help the family change, the therapist needs to understand the current behaviors of family members and recognize that these represent their *best attempt* to resolve the problems they are facing. One of the therapist's first interpretations is to acknowledge the family's genuine attempts to resolve the problem and to suggest that current methods are not resolving it. In fact, these efforts to change the identified patient may even make the problem worse.

Family members usually appreciate this interpretation because it shows them that the therapist understands that they have been trying to change and that the therapist is proficient enough to recognize that these attempts have not been effective in solving the problem. Furthermore, this interpretation *engenders hope* in the family that through therapy other ways to solve the problem may be possible.

Another interpretation critical to helping the family resolve its problems occurs when, given the information the therapist obtains from the family, the therapist presents a new understanding or interpretation of the problem. As long as the family's initial definition of the problem is used in the therapy, the family remains the expert on the problem and may disqualify many of the therapist's suggestions for alternative behavior. Typically, a family spokesperson will say, "We have tried that, and it didn't work." This type of response greatly reduces the therapist's ability to intervene effectively.

To avoid this situation, the therapist interprets the problem situation in a new way and offers the family a new understanding of the situation. This type of interpretation is called *redefining the problem* or *reframing*, and it presents the family with a new problem to solve. Because it is a new problem, the family is no longer the expert and turns to the therapist as the expert for help in resolving the problem.

A very simple example of redefining the problem can be shown by a couple beginning marital therapy. The couple is frequently in much turmoil and a great deal of anger may exist. Once the therapist determines that the couple is serious about wanting to improve the relationship, the wife's "pressuring the husband to express his feelings" may be redefined as her "need to hear that she is loved and valued by him." In the same manner, the husband's "withdrawal" may be redefined as "his feeling badly that he is unable to meet his wife's needs." Clearly, this type of interpretation must be done carefully and with appropriate timing. Attempting to redefine the problem when the partners are venting their anger toward each other or are not ready for a redefinition would almost certainly be ineffective.

Core Skill Eleven: Behavior Change

In counseling sessions with individuals, bringing about behavior change is an advanced skill and employs all the preceding skills. There are four stages in the process, each employing different skills.

1. *Identifying and clarifying the problem* involves use of rapport building, information gathering, structuring, reflection of content, and reflection of feeling.
2. *Establishing workable goals* requires the use of information gathering, information giving, summarization, and self-disclosure.
3. *Establishing criteria for effectiveness of the action plan* may require the use of confrontation and interpretation as well as reflection skills so both client and counselor will know when the objectives of therapy have been achieved.
4. *Implementation* involves summary skills, reflection skills, confrontation, interpretation, and closure skills—in short, the skills needed to help the client make desired changes.

In group counseling, these same skills would be useful with the additional advantage that other group members can support the changes individual members are making. Group support of its members is one of the major strengths of group therapy.

In marriage and family therapy, changing the behavior of family members is critical to system change, which is the goal of family therapy. The steps described above are appropriate for family therapy if the counselor considers the expanded uses of the core skills for working with couples and families. As the family therapist identifies and clarifies the problem, she should remember that for systems therapy to be effective, the problem should be defined as an element of the functioning of the family system. Several family members should be identified as important in both the definition and the resolution of the problem.

Establishing workable goals is also important in marriage and family therapy. Determining those goals with the family based on a redefinition of the presenting problem increases the probability of successful interventions.

The marriage and family therapist, like any other therapist, must establish criteria to evaluate the effectiveness of the treatment. In family therapy, the most basic way to evaluate effectiveness is to look for change in the identified patient. Change in the identified patient, however, is not the only way to evaluate the effectiveness of the therapy.

Frequently, through change in other family members, the behaviors of the identified patient no longer have the power and influence over the family that they previously had. The behaviors of the identified patient may be relatively unchanged, but the ability of the other family members to accept or deal with the behaviors may be greatly improved. This development may be viewed by all as therapeutic success. Systems therapy offers the therapist *multiple criteria* for evaluating effectiveness. A major strength of the family systems approach to therapy is that there may be several therapeutic outcomes perceived as effective change by the family members. The therapist should be aware that system changes often occur in ways quite different from what might be expected. Such unplanned changes are every bit as effective as changes produced by well-designed treatment plans.

Behavior change in marriage and family therapy is most likely to occur when the therapist has:

- successfully joined with each family member and the family system,

- established himself or herself as an expert who is highly qualified to help the family solve the problem it confronts,
- expanded the definition of the problem to include the entire family and demonstrated how several family members are maintaining the problem through their own behaviors,
- engaged all significant family members in the solution to the problem, and
- conceptualized treatment and provided interventions from a family systems orientation.

■ *Core Skill Twelve: Closure*

One of the most common problems in counseling individuals is termination and closure. Inexperienced counselors report that termination is a difficult time in the counseling process. Closure skills enable the counselor and the client to accomplish the following:

1. Bring a particular issue or problem to some resolution.
2. Bring a session to an end.
3. Terminate work with a client.

In the first instance, it is sometimes necessary for the therapist to ask, "Have we gone as far as we can on this problem? Is resolution complete?" If there is a specific contract with the client, it is easier to reach a mutual decision about whether resolution is complete in terms of meeting the goals of the contract. Without a contract, the counselor should summarize what has been covered, ask probing questions, and reflect content and feelings to complete the closure. Some counselors are timid and avoid closure, and others may be too aggressive and close a topic prematurely. Summarizing skills are useful in closing a session. It is usually helpful to ask the client to summarize what he or she got out of the session and to reevaluate the structure of therapy in light of the contract you have with the client.

Final termination may require several sessions to complete and usually involves self-disclosure and interpretation of the current status of the client as well as a thorough review and summary of the therapeutic contract. Some therapists write a formal evaluation of the treatment so that if the client returns to therapy or goes to another therapist a comparison can be made with the present level of functioning.

In group counseling sessions, closure of an issue being dealt with by one group member has to be complete before the emphasis can shift to another group member. Closure of a group session provides a transition for all the group members and gives them a chance to either complete unfinished business or contract to complete it outside of the group. In the final termination of a group, it is important to review the life of the group and take care of any unfinished business group members may have with each other. Some time should be spent on closure when an individual terminates from the group. Some group counselors allow graduates of a group to return for visits or remain in the group to support the work of others.

Closure in marriage and family therapy generally follows one of two patterns. In brief forms of family therapy, closure of the therapy occurs as soon as possible after the family has begun more functional behavior patterns. To keep the family in therapy after it has made basic family system changes would imply that the changes are not real or will not last. Family systems theorists believe that changes made by a family will be self-reinforcing and foster even greater change outside of therapy. Clients should be encouraged to end treatment as soon as possible and should be invited to return if and when other problems develop. The therapist needs to be able to identify when system change has occurred and should ensure that the *family feels responsible for that change* and feels capable of maintaining the change. For the family members to maintain their change, they must believe that they, not the therapist, are responsible for the good things that occurred in treatment. If the family believes the therapist is responsible for the change, it is less likely to be maintained.

In a second form of closure that occurs in family therapy after the family has made system changes, the therapist offers the family the opportunity to either terminate or remain in therapy for a time to process and learn how the changes took place as well as how to bring about similar changes when necessary in the future. This *psychoeducational approach* (Johnson, 1987) supports the idea of teaching families what it takes to bring about family system change. After this teaching stage of the therapy, termination occurs.

As you may have observed, the intense, personal relationships that are frequently established in group and individual counseling may not develop in family therapy. Therefore, many of the dependency issues that occur in the termination of individual and group treatment do not normally occur when effective family therapy ends.

◼️ *Summary*

In this chapter we have shown how twelve core counseling skills used in individual and group counseling may be effectively used in work with couples and families. Systems therapy in work with couples and families applies the basic core skills in unique ways. To most effectively help couples and families, counselors should seek additional supervision of their work to receive feedback on their counseling skills in the resolution of marital and family system problems.

In Part Two, we will discuss counseling theories that are already familiar to most counselors for individuals, show how these theories may be employed in work with couples and families, and introduce some important systems theories.

SUGGESTED READINGS

Alexander, J., & Parsons, B. V. (1982). *Functional Family Therapy*. Pacific Grove, CA: Brooks/Cole.

Carkhuff, R. (1969). *Helping and Human Relations: Selection and Training*. New York: Holt, Rinehart, & Winston.

Carkhuff, R., & Anthony, W. A. (1979). *The Skills of Helping: An Introduction to Counseling*. Amherst, MA: Human Resources Development Press.

Ivey, A., & Authier, I. (1978). *Microcounseling: Innovations in Interviewing, Counseling, Psychotherapy and Psychoeducation*, 2nd ed. Springfield, IL: Charles C Thomas.

Ivey, A., & Gluckstern, N. (1984). *Basic Influencing Skills*, 2nd ed. Amherst, MA: Microtraining Associates.

Ivey, A., & Matthews, W. J. (1984). "A Meta-Model for Structuring the Clinical Interview." *Journal of Counseling and Development 65*, 237–243.

PART TWO

Helping Couples and Families: Bridging Individual and Systems Theories

■ **CHAPTERS**

Psychodynamic Theories in Family Treatment

In this chapter, we will show how classical and neoclassical psychoanalytic approaches can be adapted to family therapy. The work of Harry Stack Sullivan is presented as the most family-oriented approach of this type. In addition, Adlerian approaches to family therapy are presented. Rudolf Dreikurs and Raymond Lowe are two Adlerians who have developed applications of this theory for work with families. Finally, a transactional analysis (TA) approach to family therapy is discussed. Building on the work of Eric Berne, Ruth McClendon's approach to TA-oriented family therapy is described.

KEY CONCEPTS

Psychosexual stages
Psychological birth
Object constancy
Symbiotic relationships
Individuation
Inferiority complex
Ego states
Strokes
Narcissistic needs
Intrapsychic conflict
Transference neurosis
Phenomenological orientation
Concept of indeterminism
Natural and logical consequences
Injunctions
Permission

QUESTIONS FOR DISCUSSION

1. What are the unique aspects of psychodynamic family theories?

2. With what kinds of family problems would these approaches work best? Why?

3. With what kinds of family problems would these approaches not work? Why not?

4. Which psychodynamically oriented therapy techniques can be used most effectively in working with families?

5. As a therapist using a psychodynamic approach with a family, how would you determine the developmental issues of each of the family members?

6. How might a psychodynamically oriented family therapist handle the resistance to therapy of a family member?

7. What information would an Adlerian family therapist collect on each family member? What methods would the therapist use to collect this information?

8. How would a TA-oriented family therapist work with a family in which the father is an alcoholic?

The term *psychodynamic* is generally used more broadly than the term *psychoanalytic*. Psychoanalytic theories refer to Freudian principles, such as resistance, repression, narcissism, transference, libido, id, ego, and superego, as well as to Freudian techniques, such as free association and dream interpretation (Freud, 1949). Psychodynamic theorists attempt to understand the dynamic interplay of the conflicting components and experiences of the mind. They may or may not use Freudian principles or techniques. According to our definition, if a psychodynamic theory does use Freudian principles or techniques, it can be called psychoanalytic; if it does not, it is called psychodynamic. Using this definition, Sullivanians, Adlerians, Jungians, and TA theorists are classified as psychodynamic but not psychoanalytic. In this chapter, we will cover traditional psychoanalytic theory as well as two psychodynamic approaches, the Adlerian and TA theories.

Goals of Psychodynamic Approaches

Using psychodynamic family therapy, the therapist develops insight into the family as a social unit and how family members' intrapsychic development is affected by relationships. Using such an approach, the therapist can help each family member become aware of his or her projections and take responsibility for them, which requires each family member to develop an *observing ego* to understand and integrate these awarenesses. The psychodynamic family therapist also aims to help family members set appropriate and functional ego boundaries between themselves and other family members.

One of the goals of such an approach is to strengthen and preserve the family as a social unit without interfering with the functional autonomy of each individual family member. The family and intimate family relationships are seen as excellent vehicles to help promote completion of unresolved parent-child conflicts left over from early childhood. Therapy is used to facilitate this completion process. Therapy attempts to help family members neutralize and integrate aggressive and libidinal urges so that their behavior is motivated more in the service of the ego (enlightened self-interest) and less by impulse and intrapsychic conflict.

The Process of Psychodynamic Approaches

In general, psychodynamic family therapy involves a four-stage process.

1. *The therapy contract.* The contract includes all the administrative details of therapy, such as fees, vacations, appointment times, and so forth. The ability of clients to keep their agreements made in the therapy contract and to successfully negotiate changes as needed is seen as a clear indication of their functional level.

2. *The initial phase of treatment.* In this phase, the couple or family members gain insight into the communication patterns of the family unit. In addition, tools for effective conflict resolution are taught, and therapeutic alliances are established.

3. *The working-through stage.* The therapist actively attempts to help a couple or family members strengthen alliances with each other by helping them to reveal previously unexpressed feelings, share secrets, and develop more trust and empathy. Transference and countertransference are used to help bring out unconscious patterns of communication that are deeper than those brought out in the initial phase of treatment. These patterns often show up as resistances at this stage and should be confronted and worked through for successful therapy to take place.

4. *Termination.* When a termination date is set, conflicts and defenses often emerge. This conflict signals the need for the couple or the family to identify and work through anxiety about the impending loss. The therapist also should help clients

review and identify the therapeutic gains they made during therapy.

The goal of this phase is to help each family member reduce his or her anxiety and ambivalence about separation, to reinforce the therapeutic gains that were made, and to develop usable tools for continued growth. It is important that each person accept and understand the integrity of every other family member and be able to resolve conflicts with a minimum of psychic injury to themselves or others. Some couples or families attempt to prolong therapy rather than deal with their feelings of loss. A tapering off of sessions and periodic follow-up sessions can help a family or couple resolve this issue.

Advantages and Disadvantages of Psychodynamic Approaches

Psychodynamic family therapy provides the therapist with a conceptual framework for understanding conscious and unconscious behavior in the context of marital and family relationships as well as a developmental framework for behavior. Freud's psychosexual stages of development, when combined with Erikson's psychosocial stages of development, provide a comprehensive model for understanding behavior at every age. The model helps to bridge the gap between inner experience and outer, social behavior.

Psychodynamic approaches offer conflicted families and couples an opportunity to achieve cognitive mastery of some causes of human suffering as well as an opportunity to learn effective interpersonal communication skills and correct misperceptions and distortions of experience that other approaches ignore. The therapeutic relationship can be used as a tool for change. Many people enter therapy because of poor relationships. This approach centers on using the therapist-client relationship as a model for teaching new relationship skills.

But psychodynamic approaches also have disadvantages. The techniques are limited in this approach, and techniques from other approaches often have to be employed. The focus on the past may lead the therapist to overlook present causes of dysfunctional family behaviors. The approach tends to overemphasize pathology rather than wellness, and there is a tendency for the therapist who is not clear on his or her own intrapsychic conflicts to create a "power-over" relationship with clients that does not get worked through.

Moreover, the transference relationship between each person and the therapist can dilute the powerful transference relationships between husband and wife or mother and child. Because the focus is often on individual behavior change rather than changes in the family structure, structural problems can be overlooked, which may cause families to maintain dysfunctional aspects despite individual changes.

■ Classical and Neoclassical Psychoanalytic Approaches

Freud (1949) did not do family therapy as we now think of it. His major contributions to family therapy came from his theory on the cause of dysfunctional behavior in families. We will discuss this theory later in this chapter. Freud contributed to an understanding of the important influences of the family matrix on the development of the personality of the individual. His theory identifying the psychosexual stages of development helps us begin to chart the course of early child development and shows the importance of the early parent-child relationship for the subsequent personality development of the individual. In Freud's (1963) classical case histories, such as the case of Dora and the case of the Wolf-Man, we can see Freud's analysis of the role of family dynamics in shaping the personality and the possible psychopathology of the individual.

Colleagues of Freud also studied the influence of the family on child development (Flugel, 1921; Spitz, 1965), but psychoanalysts did not begin treating the whole family until the early 1950s, when child analysts began to treat the mother and child together (Paolino & McCrady, 1978). However, development of analytic forms of family therapy had to wait for the theoretical work of Harry Stack Sullivan (1947, 1953, 1954), Erich Fromm (1941, 1947), and Erik Erikson (1946, 1950, 1959) to provide the psychosocial focus.

Sullivan, the most family-oriented of all the American analysts, saw the growth and development of the child as a response to the social environment of the family. In addition, he was the first to demonstrate that schizophrenia could be treated by psychotherapy. He also was more interested in the clinical application of his work than in the theory itself. A number of early leaders of family therapy were heavily influenced by the work of Sullivan, including Don Jackson, Virginia Satir, and Murray Bowen.

Philosophical Tenets

Freud was influenced by scientific realism and logical positivism, which placed emphasis on the objective knowledge of subjective experience. According to this view, the process of knowing requires an external interpreter to understand the preexisting structure of the personality. There is an essence, or preexisting human nature, that controls and governs behavior. The instinctual drives of the individual are what control human behavior.

Psychoanalytic theory assumes that much of human behavior is determined by past experience. Humans are unconscious of the process and content of their reality. They are enslaved by their past until the unconscious parts of their behavior can be brought into consciousness. In addition, the ultimate basis of morality is conscious reasoning; it is based on scientific principles that have to be understood and integrated into one's life.

Theoretical Constructs: Theory of Cause

The works of Freud, Sullivan, and, more recently, Margaret Mahler (1968; Mahler, Pine, & Bergman, 1975) showed that the human infant begins life in a symbiotic relationship with a significant mothering figure and gradually during the first two or three years of life goes through a set of developmental stages that enables the individual to achieve an independent and relatively autonomous emotional separateness from this mothering figure. The successful completion of this developmental sequence enables the person to establish a coherent sense of self, which allows the individual to develop object constancy or a constant sense of who he or she really is. Mahler calls this development the "psychological birth" of the individual.

Failure to complete this developmental process forces the individual to remain trapped in dependent relationships, never quite able to "go it alone," and to have difficulties in differentiating between himself or herself and others. These individuals remain stuck in infancy until they can learn to achieve some degree of separateness. They adopt a false sense of self that is acceptable to those they feel they are dependent on, and they gradually lose sight of their true selves. As adults, these people often have a hard time developing values or beliefs that are clearly their own. Frequently, they become excessively involved in causes, beliefs, leaders, and ideologies that they hope will provide them with the sense of stability and direction they cannot provide for themselves. If they find very few ways to establish their own identity and their lack of differentiation is severe, they may become psychotic. Neurotic behavior comes from the same source. Such people constantly need praise and cannot tolerate criticism. They look to others to build up their fragile sense of self-esteem, and they take any criticism as rejection or hostile assault.

In families where there are a number of such individuals, there is constant emotional upheaval over the competition for praise and reassurance. Reality is distorted by these overwhelming needs. Projections abound, usually derived from repressed or split-off aspects of the individual who doesn't have enough self-esteem or ego strength to own or integrate the repressed or split-off material.

In couples, the symbiotic process is recapitulated when each partner fills in a missing part for the other to make up one complete person. This process leads to a survival orientation and a dependency relationship based on control. If either partner tries to break out of this dependency and assert his or her own needs in the face of the demands of the other or attempts to establish his or her own self-identity, he or she can expect the partner to pull out all the stops and use every form of manipulation, exploitation, pressure, rejection, and force to maintain the dependency.

In families, one member is sometimes singled out as the family scapegoat or "whipping boy" to help all the others maintain their dependent patterns. Even in a psychoanalytic approach, the interrelationship of all family members is recognized. The mobilization of one family member in the direction of autonomy and individuation will likely be seen as a threat to the security of the other family members. Therefore, some psychoanalytically oriented family therapists will insist on seeing all family members in family therapy. Others may combine individual therapy with each family member with occasional family therapy sessions.

Psychoanalytic approaches emphasize that there is a close relationship between spouse-spouse and parent-child relationships. Individuals come to the marriage relationship with unresolved narcissistic needs, and they seek to have these needs met in the marriage. When they are

CASE EXAMPLE

Psychodynamic Family Therapy

Mr. and Mrs. Smith had been married for three years when they first entered therapy. The reason they gave for seeking therapy was that Mrs. Smith, age 27, was interested in having children, while Mr. Smith, age 36, was not. When they got married, each had assumed that the other shared his or her values and goals about a future family.

In the initial phase of therapy, both shared rather openly their disappointments about the lack of common values on this issue. Mrs. Smith idolized her father and performed to meet his standards, but she felt she always fell short. She behaved toward her husband much the same way and believed she was "bad" for holding an opinion different from his. Mr. Smith, the only boy in his family, was adored and pampered by his mother and sisters. His father was cold, distant, and demanding. He expected compliance from his wife and looked to her to support the correctness of his views.

In the middle stage of therapy, Mrs. Smith began to understand the transference aspects of her relationship with her husband, and she developed more autonomy and self-esteem. She became more involved in her career and more sure of her wishes to have children. The therapist supported her growth. At the same time, Mr. Smith grew more fearful of parenthood. He now could separate his wife from his mother, but he wanted to express his creativity in his career and not in his family. He saw the therapist as being similar to his father and complained of the therapist's "cold, analytical style."

Videotape was used to help resolve the transference neurosis between Mr. Smith and the therapist. Mr. Smith began to see what was happening and gradually worked through his anger and sadness about his father. He saw that his fear of having children was related to a fear that if he became a father, he would be just like his father. He finally consented to his wife's wishes, and the couple went ahead and started a family. They continued in marital therapy during this time, and both were able to resolve their intrapsychic conflicts and become effective parents and loving partners in their relationship.

not met and their efforts are frustrated, the couple often has children and hopes the children will meet these needs. The child then becomes an object to fulfill the unmet needs of the parents; as such, the child cannot meet his or her own needs to develop a separate self. Thus, the cycle starts all over again with the next generation. As the child grows up in that family, this battle of wills is constantly played out until the child leaves home to start his or her own family in an effort to get the needs met that went unfulfilled while he or she was growing up.

Main Therapeutic Interventions: Theory of Change

Psychoanalytic literature gives much more attention to a theory of cause than to a theory of cure. The recovery of the true self and the resolution of childhood intrapsychic conflicts seem to be the important goals of psychoanalytic theory. Freud (1949) defined healthy functioning as the ability to work productively and to love and to be close to other people. This goal, of course, requires neutralization and integration of aggressive impulses and childhood complexes so people can behave toward themselves and others more in service of their ego and less by impulse and intrapsychic conflict.

According to psychoanalytic theory, the cure of neuroses and psychoses comes when the patient brings his or her intrapsychic and unconscious conflicts to conscious awareness and then works through the conflicts in the context of a safe therapeutic relationship. The fundamental belief in psychoanalytic theory is that the full expression of repressed or suppressed emotions and thoughts has more value than any therapeutic act on the part of the therapist. The cure for these conflicts or complexes is for the client to become aware of them and express all the formerly unconscious material in the therapy session as the therapist listens without judgment.

Psychoanalytically oriented family therapists tend to believe that insight must come first and then appropriate behavioral changes will follow. Behavioral techniques may be employed only to achieve immediate symptomatic relief, but these techniques are seen as deterrents to reaching and solving deep intrapsychic conflict. On the contrary, patients are taught that they have nothing to fear from any thought or feeling, no matter how irrational it might seem.

As the patients feel safe and secure in the therapeutic setting, the transference neurosis develops, which then provides the vehicle for patients to work through and resolve the conflicts. Transference is a regressive phenomenon by which unconscious childhood conflicts are brought to the surface. By utilizing the therapeutic alliance and by reexperiencing the conflicts within the transference situation, the patient is able to apply his or her more adult modes of thinking and reality testing to the childhood problem. Because the patients are now adults and have stronger egos, they usually have more options available to them to resolve the conflict than they did as children. The therapist has to be less intimidating or threatening than the patient's parents were for the transference to be worked through and the childhood conflicts resolved.

In the initial stages of therapy, the therapist attempts to (1) determine the ego strengths and weaknesses of each family member, (2) determine their motivation for therapy, (3) define the goals of therapy, and (4) establish a therapeutic alliance.

Once the therapeutic alliance is established with each family member, the therapist can begin to interpret the unconscious material imbedded in the conscious statements of the clients as well as interpret the resistance and maladaptive ego defenses of the clients. Done repeatedly over time, this technique leads the client to acquire new and adaptive defense mechanisms. Through interpretation, the therapist attempts not to extinguish or encourage aggressive expression but to understand the source of the aggression and its effects on others in the family.

Videotape playback can also be used as an adjunct to therapy. Sessions are videotaped and then played back and analyzed by the therapist and the clients. This helps the client develop an observing ego and become more aware of nonverbal messages and unconscious material present in the session. Videotape is also useful when clients are denying or resisting some information or interpretation. It can also be useful in helping therapists monitor their own countertransference tendencies and make sure they do not interfere with the therapy process.

Adlerian Approaches to Family Therapy

Adlerian family therapy has its beginnings in child guidance centers founded by Alfred Adler in Vienna during the first quarter of the twentieth century. This type of therapy focuses on relationship problems between parents and children.

Alfred Adler was a colleague of Freud but broke away from him in 1912. Adler stated that the personality was unified and not broken into id, ego, and superego, as Freud believed. Adler's social views were shaped by the writings of Charles Darwin and David Lamarck. He formulated the theory that humans have an innate social interest that enables them to contribute to the welfare of others without thought of reward (Adler, 1927).

Although Adler visited the United States frequently from 1926 to 1937, it was one of his students, Rudolf Dreikurs, who established Adlerian family therapy in this country. Dreikurs established a family counseling center in Chicago in 1939, and Chicago remained the center of Adlerian work until 1952, when some of his students opened a center at Iowa State University. In 1959, Raymond Lowe established an Adlerian center at the University of Oregon (Lowe, 1982).

Philosophical Tenets

Adlerian psychology was perhaps the first theory to take a phenomenological orientation toward therapy. Adlerians focus on the subjective reality of the client and how their world view or lifestyle determines how they organize their behavior. Adlerians adopt a *concept of indeterminism*, which means they believe that neither heredity nor environment determines one's behavior; rather, the individual's creative power determines what a person will or will not do.

Adlerians tend to focus more on operational reality than on ultimate reality, which they agree can never be known completely. They take the stance that what is good is determined by prevailing social values. The family is seen as a social instrument to teach sound values and help people live effectively in a democratic society. All behavior is seen as purposeful and goal-oriented (teleological versus deterministic view). The focus is more on the present and future than on the past (Corey, 2000).

Theoretical Constructs

Theory of Cause
Adler saw all behavior disturbances as (1) a failure to develop appropriate social interest, (2) a faulty lifestyle, and (3) a mistaken goal of success. He said that clients do not suffer from a disease but from a

failure to solve life problems. Therefore, Adlerian family counseling is more of an educational model than a medical model of therapy.

Disturbances can result from either permissive or authoritarian parenting methods. In either case, children grow up with distorted views of how to get along with others. Permissive methods give the child the impression that they have no social responsibility for their behavior, and authoritarian methods teach them to fear authority and, ultimately, to rebel against it. In either case, a child can develop inferior feelings or an inferiority complex. People often compensate for these feelings of inferiority by attempting to master their environment or strive toward superiority. As such, inferiority feelings are strong motivators for purposeful, goal-oriented actions (Corey, 2000).

Theory of Change

The cure for disturbed behavior in Adler's framework is the use of democratic parenting methods that enable the child to establish effective limits and participate effectively in the decisions that affect him or her in the family, the school, and the larger community. To help shape the behavior along socially acceptable lines, Adlerians use the concepts of natural and logical consequences for behavior. A *natural consequence* is one that occurs naturally as a result of some action, as in sticking a finger into a light switch. Such consequences provide a natural way for humans to learn to modify their own behavior. *Logical consequences* refer to logical, agreed-upon outcomes of behavior. For example, a child who repeatedly interferes with another person by not coming to dinner on time should be told how the behavior affects the parent and that if the behavior continues he or she will not be scolded but will not be served dinner and will have to fix his or her own dinner. Depending on the age of the child, this could be a consequence or a punishment. Consequences should enable the child to assume responsibility for his or her behavior; punishment requires others to assume responsibility. Because the behavior of parents has to change before the behavior of children can change, there is inherently more responsibility placed on the parents, who are presumably more mature and able to change.

Main Therapeutic Interventions

The main goal of Adlerian family counseling is to facilitate improvement of adult-child and parent-child relationships. The therapy sessions are geared toward teaching family members the skills and understanding they need to achieve and maintain effective relationships that enable everyone to grow in ways useful to themselves and to those they relate to, including the family, the neighborhood, the nation, and the world.

To accomplish this goal, the therapist attempts to help parents understand the dynamics that contribute to poor relationships and then to teach them constructive alternatives. The essential techniques therapists use include the following (Lowe, 1982):

1. *The initial interview.* This stage is an important part of Adlerian family therapy. The structured interview form that is usually used includes: (1) structure of the sessions, (2) information on the family constellation, (3) presenting problems, (4) working hypotheses by the therapist, (5) a description of a typical day in the family, (6) a children's interview, and (7) teachers' reports and recommendations. This information is used to diagnose children's goals, to assess the parents' discipline methods, to understand the family atmosphere, and to develop a plan of action.
2. *Role playing.* The therapist attempts to have family members act out how they perceive their situation. This technique helps the therapist teach new responses and new communication skills.
3. *Recognition reflex.* The therapist watches the response of the children to specific events. The responses are usually nonverbal, such as a slight smile or a twinkle in the eye.
4. *Disclosure and interpretation.* Adlerians use interpretation and disclosure of their own observations as a way to teach parents and children new responses.
5. *Action-oriented techniques.* Adlerians may use homework and other similar ways to promote effective practice of skills. Family councils are also recommended so that family members can practice their newly acquired skills.
6. *Information giving and teaching.* Part of the session may be devoted to teaching and giving information necessary for new learning to occur.
7. *Limit setting.* The therapist models and teaches parents how to set effective limits.
8. *Minimizing mistakes.* The therapist emphasizes what can be done rather than what was done that was wrong.

9. *Encouraging family fun.* The therapist encourages family members to plan fun activities together as a way to strengthen their work in therapy.

Limitations of Adlerian Family Therapy

Very little research has been done to date on Adlerian family therapy. It seems to be most useful when the family pathology is not severe. It is limited in that it is very information-oriented and does not place much emphasis on the value of the therapeutic relationship. Moreover, family members can overadapt to the authority of the therapist and learn only enough to please the therapist rather than making lasting changes in the family system.

CASE EXAMPLE

Adlerian Family Therapy

Mr. and Mrs. Jones and their family of four children have been referred to an Adlerian family therapist because of the disturbing behavior of one of the children, Jimmy, who is 10 years old. As they discuss their typical day, the therapist finds out that Jimmy refuses to sit and eat with the family at meals. He also refuses to help out by running errands and will not cooperate with other family members. The therapist interviews the children with the parents out of the room and then brings them in and makes the following interpretation: "Jimmy is playing the role of helpless child and is the underdog in the family. Jimmy is also confused about who's boss in the family and needs to have his dad model how to be a man. Otherwise, he feels defeated and unable to do things for himself. We are going to show you, Mr. Jones, how to be a more effective role model for your son." The therapist then instructs Mr. Jones to play with his son and teaches him how to give Jimmy positive attention rather than negative attention (Lowe, 1982).

Transactional Analysis Approaches to Family Therapy

Building on the theoretical work of Eric Berne (1961), the founder of transactional analysis (TA), many practitioners have applied TA to family therapy. TA is an interactional therapy based on the assumption that current behavior is based on past experiences and that these past experiences cause us to make decisions about who we are, who other people are, and what the world is like. These decisions form our life script, which we can change with increased awareness and skills. Because TA was developed primarily as a group approach, it was relatively easy for practitioners to apply it to marital and family therapy. However, TA still emphasizes the dynamics of the individual, and the basic goal of TA family therapy centers on the therapy contract each person makes with the therapist. TA therapists approach work with family members cognitively, affectively, and behaviorally. Each client requires a blend of these three dimensions to make necessary changes (Corey, 1991).

Philosophical Tenets

TA is one of the most philosophically diverse theories because its practitioners often use techniques based on many other theories, such as Gestalt, behavior therapy, and psychoanalytic therapy. As a psychodynamic theory, TA therapists still hold to the theory of an essential human nature, but there is disagreement over what the essential human nature is. Harris (1967) postulated an essential "not-OK-ness," sort of like original sin, while James and Jongeward (1971) disagreed and saw humanity as basically okay.

There is a strong phenomenological emphasis in TA as well. The meaning people give to their experiences, rather than the experiences themselves, determines how they act. The importance of the subjective reality of the client is stressed, but this reality can be understood through a set of objective laws and principles. Finally, most TA therapists regard it to be necessary for the client to gain insight about his or her behavior for change to be possible.

Theoretical Constructs

Theory of Cause

According to Berne (1961), the interplay of three *ego states,* parent, adult, and child, determines an individual's personality. These ego states parallel in certain ways the structure of the personality in psychoanalytic theory. The child and id, parent and superego, and adult and ego exercise many similar functions. Thus, we have included TA among the psychodynamic theories. The pattern of *strokes* people receive determines how they view themselves and others. Strokes are verbal and nonverbal signs of acceptance and recognition, and they can be either positive or negative, conditional or unconditional.

The most damaging strokes are negative conditional or unconditional strokes, which often come from parents and other adults in the form of injunctions ("Don't be close," "Don't be you") and counterinjunctions ("Be perfect," "Try harder"). These injunctions and counterinjunctions cause people to make decisions about themselves and others such as, "I can't be who I really am" or "I am stupid." Berne (1972) saw people as victims of their injunctions and the decisions based on them.

Mary and Robert Goulding (1979) disagreed with Berne, seeing people as making conscious choices and decisions that are adaptive and changing them when they cease to be adaptive. The Gouldings insisted that many decisions children make are not the result of parental injunctions but of faulty thinking and fantasies on the part of the child. Berne (1961) discussed two types of problems that affect the structure of the personality, exclusion and contamination. *Exclusion* means that a person is stuck in stereotyped or rigid responses; the person responds from only one ego state, such as the parent ego state or the child ego state, and excludes the other two. Contamination means that material from one ego state overlaps with another, causing a double signal. A person may sound like he or she is responding from the adult ego state while using parental gestures, for example.

All of the stroking patterns, games, injunctions, and decisions make up a *life position.* There are four basic life positions that people adopt: (1) I'm OK—You're OK; (2) I'm OK—You're not OK; (3) I'm not OK—You're OK; and (4) I'm not OK—You're not OK. Generally, once a life position is chosen, it remains somewhat fixed until some intervention such as therapy occurs to help people change the stroking patterns, injunctions, and decisions. The life position was seen by

Berne (1972) as representing a basic existential decision that colors all our perceptions of our transactions with the world. The life script tells us how to act out our basic life position and as such determines the patterns of our thinking, feeling, and behaving (Corey, 1991).

Theory of Change

To change a decision, a script, or a basic life position, TA therapists believe that people have to take responsibility for their own behavior and stop blaming their problems on other people. For most people, this is the most important and often the most difficult step in changing. Clients are seen as having the power to change their own lives. To make that shift, some clients have to reexperience aspects of their past; others can take this step in the present without much reference to the past.

Although TA is designed to help clients develop both emotional and cognitive awareness, the focus is clearly on the cognitive aspects. Understanding and insight into the functions of the ego states and the life script are usually seen as necessary for lasting behavior change to take place. Those who combine Gestalt techniques with TA theory place less emphasis on insight and cognitive understanding than on decisive action. More traditional TA approaches, however, rely on cognitive teaching methods to teach the client how to better understand his or her own behavior. In either case, the client is encouraged to develop tools to solve his or her own problems. The autonomy of the client is seen as an important part of the process of change.

Main Therapeutic Interventions

The primary techniques used in a TA approach to family therapy vary with the stages of family therapy. McClendon (1977) proposed three main stages in a TA approach to family therapy: (1) determining the family dynamics, (2) therapy with each family member, and (3) developing a functional family.

Stage One: Determining Family Dynamics

The therapist looks for the patterns of communication among all family members, not just the problem member. The intention is to identify each person's role in the dynamics of the family's problem. The therapist might *interview* or use *open-ended questions* with each member about his or her role in the family. While doing this, the therapist watches how others behave. For example, when the father talks, the mother looks away and the oldest boy starts playing with a pencil. These observations are shared with the family to increase their awareness of family dynamics.

Interpretation of family dynamics may be used as well. The therapist may also use a story or *metaphor* to illustrate a point or give family members *permission* to do or say things they seem reluctant to do or say. The therapist may *confront* family members on discrepancies between their perceptions and their behavior. Therapists may also confront statements that reinforce injunctive or old script messages and give information on healthier responses, such as changing "I can't," "I won't," or "I have to" to "I choose to," "I will try," or "I will do it."

Stage Two: Therapy With Each Individual

The focus of this stage of therapy is on individual psychodynamics and life script analysis. Clients become aware of their preferred ego states when interacting with others. The client may then choose to employ other ego states that are more functional for a given situation. This focus may require the therapist to see family members in individual therapy, work on individual issues within a family therapy framework, utilize group therapy, or work conjointly with the couple and not the family. Gestalt or psychodrama techniques may be employed to help individual family members identify and change their script decisions.

Stage Three: Developing a Functional Family

Reintegration aimed at developing a functional family structure is the focus of this stage. A functional family structure is one in which each person can meet his or her basic needs; the structure is designed to support the maximum development of each family member. Teaching people how to negotiate and get what they want and need is one of the techniques used during this stage. Homework assignments may be given to test the effectiveness of the family structure. In this stage, family members actively ask for what they want while also giving freely to support others.

Limitations of TA Approaches

Little research has been done on this approach comparing it with other approaches. One limitation of TA is that it offers a cognitive approach

CASE EXAMPLE

Transactional Analysis Family Therapy

The White family was referred for therapy by a school counselor who had worked with Sandy. Sandy was doing poorly in school, daydreaming in class, and withdrawing from peers. The family consisted of the father, Jim, age 38; the mother, Susan, age 34; and two children, Sandy and John, ages 9 and 4. The Whites had been married for twelve years.

The initial session consisted of the family members introducing themselves and telling what they thought the problem was and why they had come to family therapy. Jim was on the offensive, saying that he thought the problem was his wife's inability to handle the children. He said he resented that Susan called him at work to complain about the children. Susan complained about the lack of emotional support she got from Jim, who, she said, was always working late. Sandy replied by saying she didn't know what the problem was or why they were in family therapy. John said that Sandy sometimes picked on him and teased him. Part of the session was devoted to a discussion of what the family members wanted to accomplish. Jim and Susan made a contract to spend more time together. They both agreed that the goal for the session was to help Sandy resolve her problems. The therapist worked with Sandy to get her to open up about her problem. She reported that no one liked her at school and that her mother

(continued)

to understanding behavior but offers very few techniques for changing behavior. Thus, it is often combined with other techniques such as Gestalt and psychodrama. Moreover, practitioners can use the structure and vocabulary of TA to avoid genuine contact with clients. Finally, clients are taught jargon that can lead them to believe they are changing when in reality they are just using new words to describe their problems. Use of jargon also can be a defense they can hide behind.

(CASE EXAMPLE continued)

picked on her at home. She began to cry, saying, "No one likes me and I can't do anything right." It became clear that Sandy felt as if she were the victim, Susan was the persecutor, and Jim was the rescuer, although all three of them played all of these roles at different times. The therapist worked with the family, teaching ego states and identifying dysfunctional interaction patterns, making sure to include all family members in the assessment.

In the second phase of therapy, Susan worked on the anger she displayed with the children, especially Sandy, and her fear of expressing her needs and wants directly to Jim. Gradually in the session she began to identify what she wanted. She wanted more contact with Jim and more freedom to develop her own interests outside the home. She was encouraged to join a women's therapy group and ask for more time with Jim. As the result of script analysis, Jim learned that his life script included a pattern of working hard and keeping distant from the family. Jim saw that he was modeling his life after his father and decided to change his earlier script decision and spend more time with his family.

The final phase of therapy centered on couple work with Jim and Susan to restabilize the family, while Susan continued to attend her women's therapy group. Sandy's problems at school subsided, and her teachers reported that she was more attentive and had made one friend.

Summary

This chapter reviewed the psychodynamic theories that have been adapted for use in marriage and family therapy. Representative psychoanalytic, Adlerian, and TA theories were described to show how these theories are being applied in working with families. These theories help to bridge individual therapy and family therapy.

In the next chapter, the major psychodynamically oriented systems theories that have been used in marriage and family therapy will be described. The skills and techniques of these systems theories will be presented, and we will show how they can be used in family therapy.

SUGGESTED READINGS

Erskine, R. G. (1982). "Transactional Analysis and Family Therapy." In A. M. Horne & M. M. Ohlsen, eds., *Family Counseling and Therapy*. Itasca, IL: Peacock.

Lowe, R. N. (1982). "Adlerian/Dreikursian Family Counseling." In A. M. Horne & M. M. Ohlsen, eds., *Family Counseling and Therapy*. Itasca, IL: Peacock.

Nadelson, C. C., & Paolino, T. J. (1978). "Marital Therapy from a Psychoanalytic Perspective." In T. J. Paolino & B. S. McCrady, eds., *Marriage and Marital Therapy*. New York: Brunner/Mazel.

Sager, C. J. (1981). "Couples Therapy and Marriage Contracts." In A. S. Gurman & D. P. Kniskern, eds., *Handbook of Family Therapy*. New York: Brunner/Mazel.

Psychodynamic Systems Theories

In this chapter we introduce the reader to three major family systems theories with psychodynamic roots. The systems theories of Murray Bowen, James Framo, and Richard Schwartz were selected for presentation here because each has taken the family and the therapist into the realm of intrapsychic processes. Both the Bowen and the Framo theories have been used for more than 20 years, have been reported widely in the literature, and are practiced by many family therapists. Moreover, both of these theories emphasize the effect of family-of-origin experiences during childhood on later functioning as an adult, a parent, and a spouse. Schwartz's theory is relatively new and looks at the individual's internal and intrapsychic system. It holds promise for pioneering the use of systems concepts with individual clients. Each of the theories presented in this chapter has a systems base and underlying assumptions that are psychodynamic in nature.

Emotional illness
Family of origin
Differentiation of self
Family projection process
Fusion
Internal Family Systems (IFS)
IFS exile
Multigenerational transmission process
Emotional cutoff
Triangulation
Family-of-origin sessions
Couples group therapy
IFS manager
IFS firefighter

QUESTIONS FOR DISCUSSION

1. What are the major goals of Bowen's family systems therapy?

2. How may the differentiation-of-self scale be used in family therapy?

3. What are four ways by which fused families may dissipate the anxiety related to the fusion?

4. Why did Framo believe that sessions with one's family of origin are so effective?

5. What is Framo's three-phase approach to family therapy?

6. What are the specific goals of the family-of-origin session?

7. What are some of the issues in your own family of origin that have been highlighted in this chapter? Do you think family-of-origin therapy would work on these issues? Why, or why not?

8. Is internal family systems (IFS) theory really systems-based? Defend your answer.

9. What is the goal of IFS? What is the role of the IFS therapist?

10. What are the manager, exile, and firefighter in IFS? How do they function?

The three systems theories selected for discussion in this chapter are rooted in psychodynamic theory. Both Bowen's family systems therapy and Framo's family-of-origin theory have been widely used for many years in marriage and family therapy. Schwartz's internal family systems therapy is relatively new and rapidly gaining a strong following. First we will discuss Bowen's pioneering work in family systems theory, followed by Framo's refinements in family-of-origin theory, and finally introduce Schwartz's internal systems therapy.

■ *Bowen's Family Systems Theory*

Murray Bowen (1913–1990) was the leading proponent and developer of *family systems theory*. His shift to the family systems movement began in the early 1950s when family therapy was in its infancy. A psychiatrist, Bowen was working at Menninger's Clinic with schizophrenic patients and their families. During this time, Bowen developed the concept of *mother–patient symbiosis*, which stated that the mother and the infant could form an intense bond that would not allow the mother to differentiate herself from the self of the child (Bowen, 1960, 1961). This intense emotional bond could make it difficult for the mother to give up the child in later years. Other psychodynamic symptoms, such as maternal deprivation, hostility, rejection, and castration anxiety were seen as secondary features of the intense attachment. Bowen believed that schizophrenia was a result of this *emotional stuck-togetherness* of the mother and child (Kerr, 1981).

Later Bowen modified his initial theory to include the whole family constellation in his understanding of schizophrenia in a patient. He came to recognize that a reorientation of his psychodynamic thinking would be required to work effectively with families. In his work with patients with schizophrenia, he began hospitalizing entire families and

stopped all therapy with individuals to focus on family group [
ment. Bowen later recognized that the characteristics a schizoph
family exhibits are similar to symptoms in many dysfunctional fan
and that the concepts of family systems theory can be employed w
wide range of family problems (Kerr & Bowen, 1988).

Philosophical Tenets and Key Theoretical Constructs

To understand the key concepts of family systems theory fully, i
important to understand that Bowen hypothesized that individu
encounter problems in their families and in other systems when they
are *emotionally impaired*. By emotionally impaired, Bowen meant that
the individual was not able to "distinguish between the subjective feeling process and the intellectual thinking process" (Bowen, 1971).
When this impairment occurs, the individual cannot establish an "I
position" to state his or her beliefs. Rather, emotionally impaired persons work toward togetherness and agreement in their statements and
discourage individuality and differentiation.

This inability to differentiate the feeling and thinking processes is
called *emotional illness* and is much more than a disorder of the mind.
Bowen believed that emotional illness is a disorder of relationships. He
discontinued use of the term *mental illness* in favor of the term *emotional illness* to describe what occurs in family relationships to cause
emotional impairment of one or more members.

Emotional Triangle

Bowen considered a three-person emotional triangle to be the basic mol-
ecule of any emotional system. He believed that a two-person system
was unstable, especially during conflict, and always would pull in a
third person to create stability. These emotional triangles tend to have
two stable sides and one side that is conflictual. For example, two children might be in conflict. Often they attempt to bring in another sibling,
parent, or friend to lend support to one or the other's position. This third
person is not in conflict with either party and may or may not take a side.
The mere presence of the third person adds stability to the conflictual
two-person system. In marital therapy, it is the counselor who becomes
"triangled" into the unstable couple system and lends stability and support through the therapy provided. This creates the emotional triangle
which, according to Bowen, is fundamental to all family systems.

rentiation of Self from Family of Origin

rentiation involves an individual's ability to develop a strong
of self and to choose behaviors that are not based on the influ-
s of others. Bowen (1978) described the level of differentiation as
degree to which one's self fuses or merges into another self in a
e emotional relationship. Bowen developed a *conceptual scale* to
cribe level of differentiation, with zero indicating the least differen-
ion and maximum fusion and 100 representing maximum differen-
tion or autonomy.

The level of differentiation is believed to be established in childhood and is a reflection of how adequately the child is able to establish
a sense of self separate from his or her parent or parents. If a child has
parents who are quite fused and undifferentiated, the child is unlikely
to be able to establish a high level of differentiation of self during childhood. The level of differentiation is thought to be stable throughout life
unless specific actions such as family therapy are taken to change it.
Those who are less differentiated from their family of origin have a
more difficult time separating "reason from emotion" and often are
controlled by their emotional system. Fenell (1993b) described a technique that employs Bowen's *differentiation-of-self scale* in helping
couples renegotiate the rules of their relationship and separate emotions
from reason in their communication process.

Bowen postulated two levels of self. The *solid self,* on the one hand,
is the part of the self that develops slowly and from within. It develops
firmly held convictions that may be changed from within through
rational processes but never through coercion by others. The *pseudoself*, on the other hand, is made up of the beliefs, values, and opinions
held by others. Emotional health is more likely to be found in persons
whose solid self is in control of their behaviors.

Individuals with low levels of differentiation of self live in a world
dominated by emotions. They are not readily able to distinguish facts
from feelings. Their rational processes frequently are clouded by their
emotional experiences. Much of their energy goes into seeking love
and approval or punishing others for not providing that approval. Thus,
they have little energy left for engaging in productive, goal-directed
activities. These people have a greater incidence of emotional and
physical problems.

For persons with low differentiation of self to feel satisfied, they must receive tremendous amounts of validation and recognition from others. Those lower on the differentiation-of-self scale may be reluctant to express their opinions if they would not meet the approval of significant others. They are unable to provide self-approval and are emotionally driven.

Those with higher levels of differentiation of self are aware of the differences between thoughts and feelings. They are able to experience both and are able to acknowledge feelings without allowing their feelings to dominate the rational process. These people are able to state their positions on issues clearly and are open to modification of their positions based on new information and internal choice. The differentiation-of-self scale is shown in Figure 6.1.

Family Projection Process

The family projection process is related to the emotional triangle in that it describes how parental problems can be projected onto a child. Family projection occurs when one parent is more emotionally focused on the child than the other parent is. Because of traditional gender roles, the mother is more often the emotionally enmeshed parent. The husband

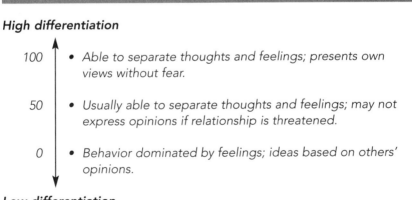

High differentiation

100 — • *Able to separate thoughts and feelings; presents own views without fear.*

50 — • *Usually able to separate thoughts and feelings; may not express opinions if relationship is threatened.*

0 — • *Behavior dominated by feelings; ideas based on others' opinions.*

Low differentiation

FIGURE 6.1

Differentiation-of-Self Scale

senses his wife's anxiety about the child and supports her in her emotional overinvolvement. The child quickly feels the mother's anxiety and may begin to behave in ways that confirm the mother's need to be overinvolved. With her husband's support, the mother focuses her energy on relieving the child's anxiety rather than on dealing with her own.

This activity gradually leads to increased emotional impairment for the child, and significant behavior problems often develop in adolescence. The father continues to support this behavior pattern either by backing the mother or by withdrawing from the situation when he disagrees with her. Eventually, if problems become severe, another party (frequently a counselor) will be "triangled in" to help stabilize the emotional system.

Nuclear Family Emotional System

The concept of the nuclear family emotional system is a logical extension of the family projection process. The family system seeks to attain balance and stability, but, the family's attempt to balance the system may be at the expense of a vulnerable family member. All families maintain some level of *fusion,* the act of losing one's sense of individuality in a relationship. Those who experience fusion to a greater degree are driven by their emotional processes and are less able to employ their intellectual processes. Families with high levels of fusion have a high level of anxiety which often leads to a variety of family problems. Families have four ways of dissipating their anxiety.

1. *Establishing emotional distance.* When persons are emotionally reactive to each other and are unsuccessful at managing that reactivity, they tend to create distance between themselves and the other (Kerr, 1981). This distancing may not be a conscious choice but, instead, a means to avoid the nuclear family emotional process. When distancing occurs, togetherness needs may be met in other relationships and extramarital affairs can occur.

2. *Marital conflict.* Through marital conflict, spouses can meet their needs for emotional closeness and distance. These needs, however, are not met through choice but, rather, through a cycle of intense anger and conflict over an issue that involves withdrawing from the partner and conflict (emotional distance) and making up and forgiving (emotional closeness). Marital conflict in itself does not harm the children unless they are made to feel guilty or responsible for the conflict.

3. *Dysfunction of one spouse.* Another way to remove the anxiety created by the nuclear family emotional system is through the dysfunction of one spouse. In this situation, one partner becomes submissive and the other becomes dominant. In this type of marriage, each spouse believes that he or she is adapting to the other spouse. The partner who adapts the most becomes a "no-self" (Bowen, 1971) and is susceptible to physical illness, emotional illness, or social dysfunction such as alcoholism. These dysfunctions tend to become chronic and may be difficult to reverse.

4. *Projection onto children.* Projection occurs through the family projection process previously discussed. Children become impaired when the fusion or lack of differentiation of the parents is projected onto the child or children. Typically, because of traditional family roles, the most intense fusion may occur between the mother and an identified child. The fusion, however, can be between the father and the child in certain circumstances. When the child is impaired, the parents are able to focus their attentions on the child and ignore their personal anxiety concerning their lack of differentiation from their own families of origin and from each other which, according to Bowen, is the source of the problems.

Multigenerational Transmission Process

Bowen conceptualized the development of emotional illness as a multigenerational process in which undifferentiation or fusion is projected onto one or more of the children over a series of generations, leading to increased emotional illness with each succeeding generation. This concept, more than any other, places Bowen's systems theory among the natural systems of the universe (Friedman, 1991) and puts the focus on the historical development of symptoms over several generations. Bowen believed that people marry partners with similar levels of differentiation of self. When these couples produce children, one (or more) of the children possesses a lower level of differentiation of self than the parents do. (It must be noted that one or more of the children is likely to have a higher level of differentiation than the parents.)

The child with the lower level of differentiation then marries at his or her level of differentiation and produces a child who has a lower differentiation. This child marries at his or her level, and the multigenerational transmission process continues. Over the course of 10 or more generations, this process may produce a severely impaired offspring. The impairment can be schizophrenia or one of many other significant problems such as serious antisocial behavior, severe chemical dependency, or severe psychosomatic physical disability (Kerr, 1981).

The multigenerational transmission process may be slowed by favorable life circumstances that calm the anxieties of one generation. If a generation severs itself from the emotional intensity of another generation, this *emotional cutoff* may slow the multigenerational transmission process. Although emotional cutoff is commonly thought to solve the problem of emotional fusion between the generations, it actually only slows the process. It generally does not stop the dynamics that maintain the multigenerational transmission process. Frequently, couples say that their problems with the older generation were solved by moving away. Bowen would suggest that the problems may have been forestalled temporarily but would have to be dealt with through one of the four mechanisms described in the earlier discussion of the nuclear family emotional system (Anonymous, 1972).

Bowen believed that the birth order of the children can serve as a predictor of adult behavior. Toman's (1961) study of birth order gives 10 profiles of sibling positions. The most common are seen in the oldest and youngest children. Typically, the oldest child assumes an overfunctioning role and believes that he or she has the ability to control family events. The youngest child, who is often taken care of by older siblings, tends to be more reluctant to take initiative and may wait for others to be helpful. These patterns are adaptive and functional for some, but when there is emotional illness characterized by intense fusion and lack of differentiation of self, the birth order patterns are likely to be dysfunctional to the individual in marriage and other close relationships.

Main Therapeutic Interventions

When families request therapy, they are asking the family systems therapist to help resolve problems in the identified patient. As Bowen suggested, the identified patient is not the source of the problem; the problem has arisen because of emotional fusion within the family. This emotional fusion leads to emotional responses and problematic situations that intensify the already charged emotional environment. Thus, the therapist's first task is to deal with the emotionally charged situation in the family and neutralize it as much as possible.

The therapist is the key to neutralizing the emotional system in the family and must be able to remain outside the emotional forces in play. For the therapist to remain outside the emotional field, he or she must be reasonably differentiated. Bowen required therapists training with him at the Georgetown Family Institute to work on issues of differentiation of self from family of origin to prepare them to assist their client families to do the same. The method Bowen used for his own differentiation process is enlightening and is recommended reading for all family therapists (Anonymous, 1972).

The therapist neutralizes the family's emotional system by using reason to respond to each of the emotionally charged issues the family members raise. While this process is taking place, the therapist begins to introduce the family to a systems understanding of the problem. If the emotional atmosphere has been neutralized, the family will be more readily able to rely on their intellect and conceptualize the interplay among the members that is leading to impairment of one of the children. Bowen (1971) attempted to resolve the problems of symptomatic children through work with the family. He defined the family as the two most responsible family members. This family unit of treatment, according to Bowen, is almost always the husband and wife.

Prior to 1960, Bowen included the children in therapy. He believed his results were less than satisfactory because the parents terminated the therapy when the child's symptoms were sufficiently reduced without resolving issues of the parents' differentiation from their families of origin. After 1960, Bowen instructed the parents to enter therapy without the symptomatic child and explained to them in the initial session that problems are a result of the parents' dysfunctional relationship and that changes in the child's symptoms will occur automatically if the parents are able to redefine and modify their relationship. Bowen believed that his approach allowed the parents to focus on their relationships and the issues regarding their own differentiation of selves from their families of origin and how their lack of differentiation may be affecting the child.

Bowen (1978) believed that the therapist has four main functions in assisting the family:

1. Defining and clarifying the relationship between the spouses.
2. Keeping self detriangled from the family emotional system.
3. Teaching the functioning of emotional systems.

    4. Demonstrating differentiation by taking an "I position" during
       the course of therapy. (pp. 247–252)

Bowen suggested that spouses avoid discussing with each other subjects that create anxiety for their partners and for themselves. Thus, Bowen did not have the spouses talk to each other but, instead, to him. Bowen instructed the spouses to talk to him in the most objective and low-key manner possible. This technique prevents the spouses from engaging in emotional reactivity to each other and allows them to hear more accurately what is being said because they are not emotionally connected in the conversation. Early in the therapy process, Bowen asked the spouses to report their rational thoughts and reactions to him. Later in therapy, as the partners were better able to separate the emotions from their thoughts, he sought the couple's subjective opinions and feelings.

When one partner's comment created an emotional overreaction in the other and an interruption occurred in therapy, Bowen suggested that the therapist quickly turn the communication flow away from the couple and back to the therapist–client relationship by increasing questions to one partner and not attending to interruption by the other. In this phase of therapy, the goal is to keep the couple talking about their thoughts, feelings, and reactions *to the therapist* rather than acting out these feelings and reactions with each other.

This first phase of therapy is critical. Because the spouses are talking to and through the therapist, they are able to really hear what the other is saying, perhaps for the first time in the relationship. Speaking to the therapist instead of the partner increases understanding, removes the emotional reactivity from the relationship, and allows the spouses to move on to other issues in the therapy.

If therapy is to proceed effectively, the therapist must remain *detriangled* from the family's emotional system. To successfully maintain detriangulation, the therapist has to be sufficiently differentiated from his or her own family emotional system and able to stay outside of the couple's emotional system. The therapist has to understand the nature of relationships and how two-person relationships always stabilize by involving a third party to form triangles. The therapist should focus on the process of what is happening in the session without becoming emotionally involved in the content.

This ability is critical to helping the family change, because one of the key assumptions of family systems theory is that "the emotional problem between two people will resolve automatically if they remain in contact with a third person who can remain free of the emotional field between them, while relating to each" (Bowen, 1971). One way a therapist can gauge if he or she is outside the emotional force of the relationship is to attempt to demonstrate to each person that some of their most cherished assumptions concerning the relationship have alternative interpretations. When the therapist is unable to respond with alternative conceptualizations for the situation, he or she is probably emotionally caught in the triangle.

Another technique used in family systems therapy is to teach the functioning of emotional systems to the family. This process begins by the therapist's use of "I messages," which communicate the differentiated position of the therapist and model effective behavior for the couple. Through the use of I messages, the therapist can communicate his or her knowledge concerning emotional systems without expecting clients to necessarily accept the concept.

Later the teaching is done through parables, metaphors, and descriptions of similar family situations. Much later in therapy, when the emotional reactivity and anxiety are quite low, the teaching can be didactic. When couples understand the functioning of emotional systems and are able to relate to each other, their children, and their parents in a differentiated way, therapy has been concluded successfully.

Strengths and Limitations of the Family Systems Approach

Like all theories of psychotherapy, Bowen's family systems theory has strengths and limitations. The major strengths of the approach are:

1. It conceptualizes problem formation from a systems perspective. Symptoms are viewed as the result of interactions between and among family members over several generations.
2. It does not diagnose and label an individual as having mental illness. Rather, it conceptualizes emotional illness as a systems-based phenomenon that does not label any single member of the system.

CASE EXAMPLE

Bowen's Family Systems Therapy

Mrs. Brown has contacted a family systems therapist because of problems she and her husband are having with their son, who has been getting into trouble at school and has not been doing his homework. The therapist suggests that the best way to approach the problem is for Mr. and Mrs. Brown to come into therapy to discover how they can best help their son.

Once the Browns come for therapy, the therapeutic procedures we have described are followed. The therapist helps them define and clarify the nature of their own relationship by remaining detriangled from his clients' emotional system. As their anxiety regarding their son begins to lessen, they note that considerable emotional reactivity exists between the two of them.

The therapist helps them move from reactions to each other based on emotions to interactions based on reason. During this portion of the therapy, the counselor describes the functioning of emotional systems to help the spouses gain insight into what happened to them in their families of origin and what has to happen in the future to establish differentiated selves in their current families.

Through this process of therapy, Mr. and Mrs. Brown begin to react less emotionally to their son, and gradually his problems at school begin to decrease. They start to react as differentiated selves within the family and respond to family problems through intellect rather than emotion. Specifically, the couple recognizes the following changes through therapy:

1. *More realistic understanding of the influences of their families of origin on their concerns about their son.*
2. *An ability to recognize anxiety that is related to their previous experiences and an ability to minimize projection of that anxiety onto their son and onto each other.*
3. *An ability to remain in sustained intimate contact based on rational choice rather than neurotic dependency.*
4. *An ability to allow autonomous functioning of their children and each other without fear that this is harmful to the family.*

3. It conceptualizes emotional illness as resulting from a multi-generational transmission process and recognizes the importance of assisting clients in differentiating from their families of origin.
4. It recognizes the importance of neutralizing the emotional process that occurs in families to permit the couple to progress to more advanced stages of therapy.

The limitations of this approach are:

1. Because the focus of treatment is on the marital dyad, the effects of children on the system may not be fully considered.
2. Concepts such as the differentiation-of-self scale are not fully developed and have little empirical validation.
3. The approach may overemphasize past experiences at the expense of current functioning.
4. The approach may not give enough emphasis to the importance of affect in problem resolution.
5. The approach frequently requires a longer time commitment to therapy than some other systems approaches.

Bowen's family systems theory is a good example of a systems theory with psychodynamic roots. The theory relies on understanding past experiences in development of the family emotional system. The importance placed on family-of-origin experiences and differentiation of self places Bowen's family systems theory in the category of psychodynamic family systems theories.

▓ *Framo's Family-of-Origin Theory*

James Framo, trained as a clinical psychologist, developed a family therapy theory based on the importance of dealing with the issues that emerge in a person's developing years in the family of origin. Although Framo's theory is presented in this chapter on systems theories with psychodynamic roots, it would be safe to say that Framo himself may not have classified his theory in this way. Framo seemed to believe that Foley's (1974) classification of his theory as that of an "integrationist" accurately described what he tried to accomplish. Furthermore, Framo "wince[d]" when he found himself categorized as a psychoanalytic family therapist (Framo, 1981). We agree that Framo was not a psychoanalytic family therapist in the classical sense, but he was indeed one of the most widely recognized practicing systems theorists. Nonetheless, we believe that although Framo was clearly a systems thinker, many of his assumptions about therapeutic change had psychodynamic roots; thus, his inclusion in this chapter.

Framo began treating couples and families in 1958. He continually revised and modified his therapeutic approach to meet the needs of families in distress. James Framo died unexpectedly on August 22, 2001. He was 79 years of age.

Philosophical Tenets and Key Theoretical Constructs

Framo's work was based heavily on the concepts of object relations theory as developed by Fairbairn (1954). Framo believed that families can best be treated by depth therapy and that marital and family problems result because individuals have not resolved issues that existed in their families of origin. These unresolved issues become an introjected part of the individual's personality. Thus, the individual may treat persons in close interpersonal relationships, such as spouse and children, in a manner that is based on the experiences from the family of origin rather than on actual behaviors of the family members.

Furthermore, Framo believed that when individuals deal with these issues in therapy with members of their families of origin actually present, issues that are problematic in the current marriage and with children may be resolved. Framo believed that one session with the family of origin may be more powerful in resolving current problems than several individual, marital, or family sessions (Framo, 1981). The specific tenets of Framo's (1982) theory are:

- The primary motivation in persons is to establish a successful relationship with another person.
- The early relationships of children with their parents creates frustrating experiences that the child cannot change. These negative experiences are incorporated in the child's personality as introjects to surface later in life.
- The individual then forms close relationships through marrying and having children. The individual forms these relationships in a way that allows the frustrations experienced in the family of origin in childhood to be re-created with the spouse and children.

- Intrapsychic problems result because of unresolved conflicts in the family of origin.
- People select marriage partners who will precipitate reexperiencing unresolved family-of-origin conflicts.
- Unresolved issues from the family of origin often are projected onto the children. When this occurs, the children may develop symptoms.
- Problems may be best resolved by returning to their source through sessions *with* the family of origin.
- When individuals explore the past to resolve issues with their families of origin, they are better able to perceive and relate to their own spouse and children as they actually are rather than as symbols of unresolved conflict in the family of origin.

Main Therapeutic Interventions

Framo is most widely recognized for his work with his clients and their families of origin (Framo, 1981). This is the approach that will be addressed here. When problems arise in a family through symptoms in one of the children or through marital conflict, the therapist sees the family for a few sessions to deal with the crisis that has brought the family or couple into treatment. Once the crisis is under control, the marital couple may profit from continued work that will explore and perhaps correct the underlying circumstances that created the situation that brought the family to treatment.

Specifically, Framo developed a three-phase treatment program that has provided successful therapy for his patients. The phases of the treatment program are (1) therapy with the couple, (2) couples group therapy, and (3) family-of-origin therapy.

Therapy With the Couple

Each stage of treatment has specific goals and techniques. During the first stage, the therapist works with the couple with the primary goal of establishing a solid working relationship with each spouse, based on mutual trust. This goal is accomplished through the use of the relationship skills of the therapist, who (1) comes to understand the wife as an individual, (2) comes to understand the husband as an individual, and (3) comes to an accurate understanding of the relationship. The therapist spends the first several sessions learning about the couple without deliberate attempts to intervene (Framo, 1982). He or she seeks diagnostic information by asking relevant questions in several areas, including:

- Information about the referral source
- Basic demographic information about each spouse
- A brief statement of the problem from each spouse
- Duration of marriage and age of children
- Previous therapy and results
- Reasons for mate selection
- Prior marriages
- Family's reaction to mate
- Fight styles
- Whether spouses love each other
- Commitment to marriage
- Characteristics of the marriage
- Quality and quantity of sexual relationship
- Motivation of each for therapy.

Once each partner has had the opportunity to discuss these issues, the therapist has a much better sense of the quality of the relationship and the problems that are present. This initial phase of the therapy provides the therapist and the couple ample opportunity to develop a trusting relationship before beginning the intervention stage of couple therapy.

After a trusting relationship with each spouse has been established, the therapist must focus on the remaining therapeutic goals of treatment: (1) husband's goals, (2) wife's goals, and (3) therapist's goals. Framo believed the family therapist must discover a way to conduct therapy that meets the expectations of the husband, the wife, and the therapist. If the husband and wife are not having their goals met, they are likely to drop out of treatment. If the therapist is not able to meet his or her goals, the chances of successful intervention decrease. In all phases of treatment, including couple therapy, couples group therapy, and family-of-origin therapy, the therapist must be aware of the clients' changing goals and expectations and work to meet these goals in the context of the therapist's own treatment goals.

When the therapist's relationship with each spouse is solid, the therapist begins to defuse intense conflicts present in the marriage. This goal is accomplished through basic interventions, such as communication skills training and negotiation training, as well as by emphasizing the positive characteristics of the relationship. After any immediate crisis issues are defused, the therapist begins the process of educating the couple about object relations theory and how issues that have been long unresolved in the family of origin may be responsible for the present difficulties in the marriage and family.

Framo also introduced his desire to have the spouses deal directly with their families of origin in therapy at some later date. Framo recognized that the notion of dealing directly with the family of origin causes great anxiety for many clients. He assured them that they will be adequately prepared to meet their families and most likely will benefit from the encounter.

Couples Group Therapy

To best prepare couples to meet with their families of origin, Framo found that the couples group therapy format is most advantageous. The couples group format is suggested as a step toward the family-of-origin work for numerous reasons.

- It is reassuring to each person in therapy to know that other couples have similar fears and anxieties about dealing with their families of origin in therapy.
- By participating in a couples group, the individuals come to recognize the universality of problems that individuals have with their families of origin. Thus, the couple feels more normal and self-accepting.
- Couples in a successful group come to trust each other and share information that might not emerge in individual couple therapy. Furthermore, group members may be quite receptive to feedback and support from other couples.
- The genuine caring the couples feel for each other is therapeutic.
- Through feedback from group members, the couples usually come to modify their goals in productive ways.
- Through feedback and modeling by other couples, the spouses come to recognize their unrealistic expectations of their mate.
- Through effective leadership by the therapist, the group members are assisted in exploring the genesis of their unrealistic expectations of their spouses. This process returns the focus to the importance of resolving issues with the family of origin.

- Despite each person's fear of dealing with the family of origin in therapy, members of the group are almost always supportive of other members who are having their family-of-origin session. This group support often is instrumental in helping members develop the courage and resolve to invite their parents to family-of-origin sessions.

The couples group is usually composed of three couples. Ideally, these couples are at various stages of their preparation for the family-of-origin sessions—one couple graduating, one couple in the middle of couples group work, and one couple joining the group after individual couple therapy sessions have just been completed. Framo used the couples group format unless for some reason it was not possible to place a couple in the group. He has found that the groups are most successful when the couples are at a similar family development stage as well as being similar in other ways.

In summary, the couples group helps the spouses further understand their own relationships and improve them. It creates a sense of community in which the couples support each other in their attempts to recognize and confront unresolved issues from their families of origin that are affecting their current relationships. Moreover, it provides support for the members inviting their parents to join them in therapy, and a place to debrief after the family-of-origin sessions.

Family-of-Origin Therapy

As individuals become ready to meet with their families of origin, preparations are made to convene a family-of-origin session. Needless to say, the couple does not always become ready for these sessions at the same time, and this is not necessary. When a spouse returns to the couples group after meeting with the family of origin, the encouraging effect on the other spouse and the other group members may be significant.

Prior to having the family-of-origin session, the client is thoroughly prepared. Normally, Framo met the family of origin on a single day with four hours devoted to the session (Framo, 1981). Despite the initial reasons clients give for why the family-of-origin sessions would be impossible, the success rate of engaging the family in therapy is quite high. Framo believed that when the client recognizes the importance of the meeting, the client will communicate that importance to members of the family of origin and they will participate. This belief has been supported by experience in Framo's practice of family-of-origin therapy.

The key goal of the family-of-origin session is for the client to make contact with the family and have a "corrective experience" with the family (Framo, 1981). The family-of-origin session is held without the spouse. Framo believed that having the spouse present in these sessions could easily detract from the purpose of correcting the perceived problems between the generations and between siblings. If the spouse were present, much of the attention could be placed on the spouse and the couple's relationship, and the main goals of the family-of-origin work would be missed.

The specific goals for the family-of-origin session are as follows.

- The client makes contact with the family of origin, parents and siblings, in a way that is based on adult (rather than child) interaction.
- The therapist may discover what attitudes developed in the family of origin are being projected onto the client's spouse and children.
- The client may increase differentiation (Bowen, 1971) from the family of origin, which will lead to enhanced relationships with members of the family of origin as well as with the current family.
- The meeting sets the stage for getting to know the parents as real people and to share important thoughts and feelings with them.
- The meeting provides the client with an opportunity to forgive the parents for their mistakes, real and perceived, and to tell the parents that they are loved. The importance of this goal cannot be overstated.

Framo found that the family-of-origin sessions were usually positive for all participants. Normally, the spousal relationship is enhanced and relationships with parents and siblings are improved. Occasionally, however, some issues emerge that may increase tensions between the family of origin and the client. Thus, the immediate effects of the session may not be positive. Clients are prepared for this possibility and are encouraged to use the group for support if this is the outcome.

Moreover, when individuals complete their family-of-origin work, they may recognize that their marriage is based on projections and unfinished business with the family of origin rather than on love and respect for the spouse. In these cases, the couple may decide not to work on correcting the projections in therapy, and the result may be divorce. Although these negative outcomes are uncommon, clients should be made aware of the possibility that they may occur. Framo views family-of-origin work as the "major surgery" of family therapy and cautions that this therapy is not without its risks (Framo, 1981).

Framo's family-of-origin therapy is an active and directive approach to resolving issues affecting the family that have their roots in the family of origin. He believed that working with an opposite-gender co-therapist was the most effective way to provide treatment. The opposite gender co-therapy team allows the therapists to relate to the same gender and opposite gender clients. It alleviates the clients' fears that alliances by gender may occur. Further, the co-therapy team through effective collaboration is much better able to respond to the myriad of issues that emerge in therapy. One therapist may become extremely involved in the content and affect of the situation presented, while the other may remain more detached and objective. Co-therapy teams make it possible to more effectively meet the needs of the couples. Other important techniques used in this approach are as follows.

- Framo did not meet with one spouse alone. He set an appointment when both can be present. If this was not possible, he referred the couple to a colleague who treated spouses separately.
- The couple is prepared for family-of-origin sessions gradually and without coercion from the therapist. Preparation begins early in the individual couple sessions and continues more vigorously during couples group sessions.
- Spouses are asked specifically about events occurring in their families of origin. If the therapist does not seek this information, couples normally will not view it as relevant to the current problems.
- Couples in the group who are willing to meet their families of origin help prepare couples who are reluctant.
- The group members and co-therapists encourage family-of-origin work, which causes the couple to prepare for this event. Thus, the other problems in the relationship diminish in importance and

CASE EXAMPLE

Framo's Family-of-Origin Therapy

Mr. and Mrs. Taylor were having difficulties with their marriage. She complained that her husband was indecisive and she couldn't rely on him. Mr. Taylor reported that his wife was domineering and unsupportive of any attempts he made to exert leadership. Thus, he had begun to give up on the marriage.

The couple came to therapy for help in making the marriage better. The family-of-origin therapist, working from Framo's model, treated the couple in marital therapy to reduce the tension, anger, and hurt feelings through teaching communication and negotiation skills, establishing trusting relationships with both partners, and understanding each person's experience of the marital difficulties.

During this stage of treatment, the therapist introduced the idea of having family-of-origin sessions so each person might come to understand how some of the present behaviors developed and to seek ways to eliminate the problematic behaviors. The therapist engaged both spouses in discussions about their families of origin and the issues that existed within their families. At this point in treatment, they entered couples group therapy because they were ready to begin more advanced work on their marital problems.

In the group setting, Mr. and Mrs. Taylor came to feel accepted and cared for by the other two couples in the group. These couples were working on relationship issues not unlike those of the Taylors. In the couples group, the Taylors recognized that their marital issues might be the result of problems that began in their families of origin.

Mr. and Mrs. Edwards, another couple in the group, were in the final stage of preparation for their family-of-origin sessions. Both were excited about the possibilities, yet fearful at the same time. The support the Edwards couple received from the therapists and the group was positive and instrumental in helping each of them have successful meetings with their families of origin. The Edwards' report to the group about their experiences encouraged the Taylors to begin serious preparation for dealing with their own families of origin. The focus on preparing for the encounter with their respective families pulled the two closer together as they supported each other's attempts to prepare for the family-of-origin sessions. Thus, their original marital problems became less of a focus in therapy and at home.

(continued)

(CASE EXAMPLE continued)

    Several weeks passed before Mrs. Taylor was ready for her family-of-origin session. When the day finally arrived, she was apprehensive. She went into the session armed with a list of issues to discuss with her parents and brother. Although many of the issues were not discussed because of time limitations, several of the most critical issues were covered, and Mrs. Taylor was provided with a wealth of information about herself and her family. Through the family-of-origin session, Mrs. Taylor discovered that her own father was passive and was content to let her mother deal with any problems that emerged. Mrs. Taylor had not accepted this pattern and was angry with both parents because neither tried to change the situation.

    Mrs. Taylor had been certain that she would not be domineering like her mother because she would marry a stronger man than her father. But she discovered that she had re-created in her present marriage what she thought she would avoid. Thus, she was faced with the need to deal with her anger toward her parents as well as her anger toward herself for creating a similar situation.

    These insights provided Mrs. Taylor with plenty of information, and she was able to forgive her parents and establish more positive relationships with them. Furthermore, she discovered that her brother had similar feelings that he had not expressed before. This revelation opened the door for an improved relationship with her sibling. Finally, and perhaps most significant, she recognized that some of her husband's lack of assertiveness was the result of her need to make him be the way she wanted him to be rather than accepting him as he was. This insight led to immediate marital improvements.

    A few weeks later Mr. Taylor was ready for his family-of-origin session. He discovered that he had never felt adequate in relation to his father. The tasks he was asked to perform were never done quite well enough. Mr. Taylor had grown up feeling that it didn't matter how hard he tried; he would not be adequate. Thus, he married a woman who re-created that feeling.

    Through the insights the Taylors achieved in family-of-origin therapy, they were able to establish a more productive marriage and more meaningful ties with their families of origin. Knowing how their behaviors were driven by unresolved family-of-origin issues helped the Taylors move forward both as individuals, as a couple, and as parents to their own children.

the relationship is strengthened as the spouses work together for their family-of-origin sessions.

- Resistance to the family-of-origin sessions is to be expected. The combination of the therapists' interventions and group support emphasizes the importance of the sessions. The therapist does not pressure the spouses into the sessions but allows them to become ready at their own pace. One partner may become ready for the family-of-origin session well before the other spouse. This is not a problem, however, as the spouse who has had the session can encourage the one who has not.
- The therapists help each person develop an agenda of issues to be discussed with the family of origin. This assures the client that the session will have real purpose.
- Spouses are not included in the initial family-of-origin session. These sessions are between the client and his or her family.
- The spouse may be included in a later family-of-origin session if problems exist in the in-law relationship.
- The therapist and the couples group members encourage others to do family-of-origin work.
- As the family-of-origin session nears, calls from family members to the therapist are to be expected. The therapist encourages family-of-origin members to consider any issues they have with their son or daughter and be prepared to raise them in the session.
- To ensure a productive family-of-origin session, the therapist makes certain that caring among the family members emerges. If the session is too focused on negative content, the session may become an unproductive gripe session with a potentially negative outcome.

Strengths and Limitations of Framo's Approach

Family-of-origin therapy has several strengths.

1. It is the only therapy that actually has the client deal with issues from the family of origin directly with the family in a session.
2. This theory recognizes that problems in the present marriage may be the result of unfinished business in the family of origin.
3. It recognizes the therapeutic power of the couples group and uses that power to help clients develop in their relationships.

4. This approach offers the opportunity for individuals to create more meaningful relationships with their families of origin through direct contact about significant issues.

Framo was aware that this approach was not for everyone and acknowledged the limitations of the therapy (Framo, 1981).

1. Family-of-origin work is not for couples with relatively minor marital difficulties that do not require intensive work.
2. Some couples do not have access to their families because of death or some other circumstance.
3. This approach may highlight the need for therapy with the individual. If therapy for the individual is indicated after family-of-origin work is completed, Framo encouraged referral to a therapist who specializes in such work.
4. This approach relies on the assumption that current problems are a result of past experiences in the family of origin. It may not be effective with clients who are unwilling to accept this assumption.

Internal Family Systems Theory

Richard Schwartz and his colleagues at the Institute for Juvenile Research of Chicago (Nichols & Schwartz, 2001) developed the internal family systems theory because existing models of family therapy were not sufficiently powerful to help their clients with the eating disorders anorexia nervosa and bulimia. This theory "expands systems thinking beyond the boundaries of family into the realm of intrapsychic process" (p. 427). While Schwartz considers this theory to be integrative, his view of personality as a multifaceted construct and his focus on the intrapsychic "internal parts" of the client's personality suggest that this theory fits best within Chapter 6 of this text, "Psychodynamic Systems Theories."

Philosophical Tenets and Key Theoretical Constructs

Schwartz developed the internal family systems (IFS) model out of frustration with limitations of the family therapy approaches they had been using previously to treat clients with eating disorders. Schwartz believed that for his clients to get better, they would have to explore the intrapsychic natures of their personalities. He created a unique way to help his clients examine their psychological dynamics by framing their psyche as a "family of inner voices or parts" (Nichols & Schwartz, 2001, p. 427).

Sub-Personalities or "Parts"

Like many other individual theorists, Schwartz's notion that the psyche is divided into *parts* is not new. Fritz Perls (1969), among others, believed that the healthy personality is a *gestalt,* or whole that may be splintered into unrecognized or dominant elements that drive a person's behavior and affect. Moreover, the various aspects of the whole, when acknowledged, accepted, and integrated, lead to a healthy personality with the ability to choose behaviors rather than have behavior driven and controlled by unacknowledged aspects of the self.

Schwartz's definition of the personality is similar to Perl's. Therefore, a critical challenge early in treatment for the therapist is to introduce this framework of parts to the client and gain the client's acceptance of the framework. Once the client accepts this reframed definition of the psyche, the therapist is able to help the client identify the struggling *parts* of the personality.

For example, a part of the client might want to eat in a healthy way while another part might be afraid of gaining weight and becoming unattractive and want to greatly restrict her diet. By using systems principles such as *joining* and accepting each of the parts of the internal system, Schwartz is able to help the client come to accept herself and begin to sort out the competing drives within the personality. Finally, the therapist supports the client in identifying the healthy and unhealthy parts of the personality. Then the therapist and client work collaboratively to strengthen the healthy parts of the psyche while minimizing the effects of the negative parts.

Internal Client Systems and External Family Systems

Several major assumptions support the internal family systems model.

1. *Internal* systems interact like *external* family systems. Therefore, change in one part of the internal systems must precipitate change in all the other parts of the system as well.

2. The parts can be *joined with* and related to just as if the parts were members of a family.

3. When parts are explored in a family setting, family members come to understand, appreciate, and tolerate each other. Thus, change occurs between and among members of the external family system while the focus of treatment is on the internal system of the client and other family members.

4. *Key parts* exist within the client's psyche, and these parts must be acknowledged and respected to gain access to the other parts of the internal system. Resistance occurs when these key parts are not addressed appropriately in treatment. The model assumes that the individual has a *drive toward health* and that key parts want the internal system to heal. But the key parts are protectors of the internal system and need assurance that the healing can be done safely by a caring and competent counselor. Schwartz calls these key parts *managers,* and they ensure that help can be provided in a safe manner before allowing other parts to participate (Nichols & Schwartz, 2001, p. 428).

5. Internal systems can function to keep painful thoughts and experiences out of awareness. This assumption is similar to Freud's (1949) concepts of the unconscious and defense mechanisms. The *managers* may keep these painful parts out of awareness in an effort to protect the individual. These unconscious parts are called *exiles.*

6. When an *exiled* part is greatly upset, the client will incur great pain or anxiety. The client will behave in ways that are an attempt to quell the pain. Often these behaviors are unhealthy and are viewed as symptoms of psychopathology by self and others. The behaviors might include acting out, binge eating, or the excessive use of drugs or alcohol. Acting out parts are called *firefighters* in this model because firefighters attempt to put out the fire of pain and anxiety through any means possible.

7. Each individual has a *core self* that may be difficult to access and often is unrecognized by the client. This part contains the leadership and compassion that allow the client to deal effectively with the other internal parts and with the other members of the family. The core self must be differentiated from the other parts in a manner similar to the way Murray Bowen (1978) helped family members differentiate from their families of

origin. When the core self is differentiated and discovered, it is able to serve as healer for all aspects of the client's internal and external system problems. A corollary to this assumption is that all people, even those with severe symptoms, possess an inherent wisdom that will direct a healthy transformation of the individual.

Main Therapeutic Interventions

The interventions in IFS therapy involve the following elements.

The Relationship With the Client

Internal family systems theory is more than a series of techniques (Schwartz, 1995), but certain techniques are essential for success when employing this model. First, this approach requires a therapist who genuinely values the client and the client family. Of equal importance is the therapist's ability to demonstrate this caring to the client. If the client does not feel valued through the joining process, trust will not develop and exploration of the "parts" is unlikely. Thus, improvement will be elusive.

Identification of Parts

After trust has been built, the therapist begins the process of identifying the aspects of the client that are dominant and controlling behavior and those that are less well recognized. This can be accomplished in individual sessions or in family sessions. In the family sessions, additional power may be added to the therapy as other members often see strengths in the identified client and in other family members. Often the members have not recognized or acknowledged these strengths. Power is added through family treatment because the client comes to see other family members as "flawed" as well, and feelings of isolation diminish. This phase of therapy, however, can be conducted effectively even if other members of the family are not available.

Listening to the Parts

For therapy to progress, the counselor must be able to respond effectively to each part as it emerges. For the less desirable parts to emerge, an atmosphere of trust must exist and the client must feel heard and understood. Carl Rogers (1961) would call this counselor quality *accurate empathic understanding.* This quality can be demonstrated to the client by listening to the deeper messages and feelings conveyed and by communicating, through accurate reflection to the client, the understanding of these deeper messages and feelings.

Empowering the Healthy Parts

During this phase of therapy the strengths of the individual are identified and built upon. As the therapist and other family members help the client identify healthy parts, trust among the members builds. The healthy parts then can be encouraged to take more control over the client's behaviors. As the healthy parts take control, problematic behaviors decrease.

Disempowering the Unhealthy Parts

Everyone has strengths and weaknesses. Therefore, negative aspects of self will be uncovered and discussed. An important technique for the therapist is to ensure that the client understands how that part was useful to the client in providing protection from pain and anxiety. For instance, a client who recognizes and seeks to eliminate a heavy drinking pattern will feel validated when the counselor acknowledges that the drinking served to minimize the client's pain and that new ways to do this will be recognized through the treatment.

Finding the Core Self

At this point in therapy, the counselor asks the client to have the *managers* and *firefighters* assume less prominent roles in the personality. This will allow the core self to emerge. As it is emerging, the therapist and other family members, if present, acknowledge and value its emergence. As the client and other family members come to recognize this core self, it is expected that in the future this core will take the leadership in self-regulation and in interactions with other family members. When this occurs, behavior patterns shift away from dysfunction and toward health.

Linking to the External Family System

Linking can be employed through individual counseling, but it is more powerful when used in a family context. In the family setting all members explore the parts of themselves and share their self-awareness with all the other family members. Thus, the identified client will come to understand that all family members have healthy and unhealthy aspects to their psyche. This increases trust and understanding among family members and creates a climate in which they can support each other though the various strengths identified in each member that emerge through this process. Finally, the family members learn how the therapist is able to listen, trust, and draw out the positive elements of each person, and they are better able to do this themselves with each other in the future.

CASE EXAMPLE

Ted was expelled from school for rowdy behavior in class and disrespect for his teachers. He also was disrespectful at home to his parents and brothers. His mother contacted an internal family therapist for help with Ted's problem.

The counselor met with Ted alone for the first few sessions. She established a relationship built on caring and trust. Gradually Ted began to talk about the parts of himself that were rebellious and disrespectful to others. At the same time, the counselor helped Ted identify the positive parts, which included being a good friend to his buddies, being a good athlete, and being bright and able to do well academically. The therapist asked Ted if he would be willing to bring in his family and discuss the parts of himself that he had discovered. He agreed to invite the family to join him.

In that session, all family members identified healthy and unhealthy parts of themselves and their core self that moderated and controlled the other "parts." The family members were asked to discuss how they could access the core selves in each other when it was important. A process was developed and practiced in the next family session.

Therapy terminated with Ted and all family members feeling better about one another and knowing each other in a way that most families do not achieve. Finally, Ted was much more self-aware and able to call on his core self to deal with issues that emerged at home and at school.

Strengths and Limitations of the Approach

Internal family systems theory is applicable for use with individuals and families. It unites the concepts of individual therapy and family systems therapy in a clear and usable way. The theory recognizes the importance that respect for the client plays in therapeutic change and emphasizes the relationship between client and counselor. Finally, the theory integrates concepts from a wide range of theories and can be used with a wide range of clients and client families. The approach does a nice job of linking the internal intrapsychic system of the individual with the external family system of the larger group.

The main limitations of the approach are the absolute dependence on the client's accepting the definition of the psyche as composed of competing parts with a core self located somewhere in the psyche and the assumption that internal and external systems function similarly. This primary concept is treated as an immutable fact rather than one of many helpful ways of conceptualizing problem formation and problem resolution. Moreover, the notion that internal parts respond like members of an external family system, while interesting, requires research support. The concepts of manager, exile and firefighter may be overly simplistic with little research available to support them or the efficacy of the IFS approach.

Despite the lack of research, the model relies heavily on individual theory concepts and techniques that have been well established for years. Integration of the individual concepts and techniques with family therapy remains an important contribution to the field.

▉ Summary

Murray Bowen, James Framo, and Richard Schwartz have developed theories of family therapy with psychodynamic roots. Each theory places heavy emphasis on the impact of early intrapsychic, childhood, or family-of-origin experiences on current family functioning. Counselors will want to understand the key theoretical tenets and techniques of each of these approaches to be able to effectively employ them in their work with couples and families.

SUGGESTED READINGS

Bowen, M. (1978). *Family therapy in clinical practice.* New York: Jason Aronson.

Framo, J. L. (1982). *Explorations in marital and family therapy.* New York: Springer.

Hovestadt, A. J., & Fine, M., Eds. (1987). *Family of origin therapy.* Rockville, MD: Aspen.

Schwartz, R. C. (1995). *Internal family systems therapy.* New York: Guilford Press.

Cognitive/Behavioral Theories in Family Treatment

In this chapter, we will describe the application of rational emotive behavior theory (REBT) to family therapy as a representative of the various cognitive theories. In addition, behavioral family therapy, based on social learning theory, developed by Gerald Patterson and others is described as a representative of various behavioral approaches to family therapy.

KEY CONCEPTS

Modeling
Cognitive errors
Irrational beliefs
ABC theory
Contingency contracting
Behavioral assessment
Reinforcement
Cognitive restructuring
Behavioral rehearsal

QUESTIONS FOR DISCUSSION

1. How might the REBT therapist deal with a family member who is making irrational statements to another family member?

2. Do you think the REBT therapist should teach family members a philosophy of life? Can the therapist avoid imposing his or her values?

3. How would the REBT therapist deal with a family member who starts crying and exclaiming that she feels picked on by the other family members?

4. How would a behavioral therapist handle the aggressive behavior of an older brother toward his younger sister during a family therapy session?

5. What criteria might a behavioral therapist use to determine whether the therapy has been successful?

6. How might a behavioral therapist work with a family in which the mother is an alcoholic?

Cognitive and behavioral approaches are often treated separately in the literature, but because they share similar philosophical underpinnings and a common focus on objective behavior, they may be considered together (Baucom & Epstein, 1990; Meichenbaum, 1977). In this chapter, we will present these theories together as the cognitive/ behavioral approach.

Beck (1976) describes *cognitive therapy* as an approach that addresses the formulation of psychological problems in terms of incorrect premises and a proneness to distorted imaginal experiences. These incorrect premises and distorted internal images, also called *cognitive errors*, lead to incorrect emotional and behavioral responses to external events. Cognitive therapists attempt to change the thought patterns, beliefs, and attitudes of their clients, which they believe will lead to lasting behavior change (Ellis, 1991). Behavior therapy, on the other hand, focuses on changing specific behaviors in predetermined ways and deals only with observable events in the environment that can be objectively measured. Behavior therapy, also known as the *social learning approach*, does not require insight or a change of thinking or attitudes to be effective. This approach posits that symptoms are actual problems and that by changing behaviors, thoughts and feelings will also change as a result.

The chief contributors to cognitive therapy are Albert Ellis (1962, 1991, 1993), Aaron Beck (1976, 1991), and Donald Meichenbaum (1977). Important behavioral therapists are John Krumboltz and Carl Thoreson (1969, 1976), Joseph Wolpe (1958, 1969), Gerald Patterson (1971), Ian Falloon (1991), Richard Stuart (1980), Neil Jacobson (1989), and Arnold Lazarus (1971, 1981). Many behavioral therapies are based on the theoretical and research efforts of Albert Bandura (1969, 1977) and his social learning approach.

An example of a cognitive/behavioral approach can be seen in the case of a high school sophomore who is referred to the counselor's office because he is not paying attention in class, not following the teacher's instructions, and making wisecracks that disrupt the classroom. A counselor using a cognitive approach would attempt to understand the student's internal logic and help him identify the self-defeating messages with which he indoctrinates himself. For example, the student may believe it is "essential" that he be the focus of attention at all times. The counselor would help him understand that it is certainly enjoyable to be the center of attention but definitely not essential. As the student challenges this irrational idea with a more rational one, he is able to begin to change his acting-out behavior. The counselor would attempt to help the student change his self-defeating attitudes and beliefs, hoping this would improve his classroom behavior. Role playing and rehearsal techniques may be used to teach the student ways to improve his behavior.

A counselor using a behavioral approach would assume that the problem behaviors were the result of prior learning and reinforcement. The counselor would try to find reinforcement contingencies to use to help the student change the identified undesirable behavior. The counselor might also involve the teacher in the process by encouraging the teacher to reinforce the student's more acceptable behaviors with attention or grading credit and to ignore (or not reinforce) less acceptable behaviors. In this way, the counselor would assist the student in learning new and more effective behaviors.

A critical component of the behavioral approach is the counselor's development of a specific method to assess the student's behavior changes. This assessment is frequently quantified; for example, how many times did the student interrupt class discussion during the day? The behavioral counselor would expect the frequency of the undesirable behavior to decrease over time while more desirable behaviors increase.

This chapter will cover two of the main cognitive/behavioral approaches to family therapy: the rational emotive behavior therapy approach of Albert Ellis and the social learning approach of Gerald Patterson and the Oregon Social Learning Center staff. We begin the discussion with the general goals of the cognitive and behavioral approaches.

◼ *Goals of Cognitive Approaches*

The two general goals of a cognitive approach are to minimize self-blame and to minimize blaming others. Specific outcomes that result from these two goals include the following:

- enlightened self-interest that respects the rights of others;

- self-direction, independence, and responsibility;
- tolerance and understanding of human fallibility;
- acceptance of the uncertainty of life;
- flexibility and openness to change;
- commitment to something outside oneself;
- risk taking and a willingness to try new things; and
- self-acceptance.

Goals of Behavioral Approaches

The general goal of behavior therapy is development of a systematic application of experimentally established principles of learning for the purpose of changing unwanted or dysfunctional behaviors. More specific outcomes relating to the problems of the family members are also sought, including the following:

- learning to ask clearly and directly for what one wants;
- learning to give and receive both positive and negative feedback;
- being able to recognize and challenge self-destructive behaviors and thoughts;
- learning to become assertive without becoming aggressive;
- being able to say no without feeling guilty;
- developing positive methods of self-discipline, such as regular exercise, controlling eating patterns, and eliminating stress;
- learning communication and social skills; and
- learning conflict resolution strategies to cope with a variety of family situations.

The Process of Cognitive/Behavioral Approaches

Therapy is seen as a learning process that might be viewed as follows:

1. *The courtship stage.* In this stage, the therapist assesses the problem and builds rapport. The assessment process might include standardized marital assessment devices, therapist or client ratings of the particular behaviors deemed necessary to be changed, and a clinical interview. Rapport building with each of

the family members is necessary for movement to the next stage to occur.

2. *The engagement stage.* This stage is characterized by a solidification of the therapeutic relationship. The therapist conveys commitment to the couple or family and specifies what the client is expected to contribute to the process. Goals may be determined at this stage and a plan developed to achieve these goals.

3. *The marriage stage.* This stage has two important features: (1) enhancement of communication skills between and among family members, and (2) development of a written therapy agreement to aid in the change process. The goals of the training in communication skills include teaching conflict resolution skills, teaching family members how to reduce and clarify misunderstandings, increasing positive verbal interaction, and increasing the appropriate expression of feelings. Written marital or family agreements generally involve an agreement by each family member to engage in certain specified behaviors desired by others in the family as well as an agreement on what positive or negative consequences should occur if the specified behaviors are or are not present.

4. *The disengagement stage.* In this stage, responsibility is gradually shifted from the therapist to the family members. Members are often encouraged to hold family meetings between therapy sessions and to report on the results of those meetings. In conjunction with these family meetings, family members construct and successfully carry out the agreements they make with each other. This phase provides the therapist with concrete evidence of the family's ability to solve its own problems and gets the family ready for termination.

Advantages and Disadvantages of Cognitive/Behavioral Approaches

One of the main advantages of cognitive/behavioral therapy is that it is based in research. Much research has been done to show that appropriate reinforcement contingencies can alter problem behaviors. Second, the therapist is an active participant in the therapy process and can often model effective behavior for the client. By staying with very specific observable behaviors and by using written contracts, the clients can easily understand the goals and track the progress of their own therapy. Finally, this approach allows for use of many diverse intervention methods.

Cognitive/behavioral therapies have been particularly effective in the treatment of depression and in stress management (Beck, Rush, Shaw, & Emery, 1979). These approaches work well with clients who have good reasoning ability. Both cognitive and behavioral approaches tend to be brief treatment modalities.

But cognitive/behavioral therapy also has disadvantages. Critics have accused it of focusing too much on symptoms and ignoring underlying problems. In addition, the approach may be too directive and, in the hands of an unethical therapist, can be used to manipulate the client. The theory has also been criticized as having a myriad of techniques with no integrating theory to tie them together. Beck (1991) disagrees and articulates the development of cognitive theory over the past 30 years. He believes the research has supported the theoretical constructs of cognitive therapy.

▓ *Rational Emotive Behavior Therapy*

Ellis (1962) first developed rational-emotive therapy (RET) in the 1950s. Because this approach emphasizes the reciprocal interactions among cognition, emotion, and behavior, Ellis later renamed his theory "rational emotive behavior therapy (REBT)" (Corey, 1996; Ellis, 1995). He uses the ABC theory of REBT to work with individual clients as well as couples and families (Ellis, 1991, 1993):

Problem Formation

- **A** is the *activating* event,
- **B** is the irrational *belief* about the activating event, and
- **C** is the *consequences* of the belief about the activating event.

For example, a couple complains that their son is not being as respectful as they would like. The more they insist on respect, the less they receive. The couple are becoming angry and upset, and this affects their own relationship and their relationships with their other children.

In this case the REBT therapist would help the couple identify the ABC of their presenting problem. The activating event (A) is the son's lack of respect. The consequence (C) is that the couple becomes angry and the boy is even less respectful. What this couple is not aware of is their belief (B) about the activating event. In this case, the therapist helps the couple identify their belief that "It's absolutely essential that their son show respect at all times, and if he does not, they are 'bad' parents and he is a 'bad' son." This belief would be considered an *irrational belief* because of its demanding nature and its lack of acceptance of human imperfections. The therapist helps the couple recognize that it is not their son's lack of respect that causes their anger but *their personal beliefs* about their son's behavior. Once the couple can *dispute* their irrational belief with a more rational one, such as: "It is preferable to have our son show respect, but it is not crucial. We can still admire the good in him even if he does become difficult at times. Moreover, we do not take responsibility for his actions." As the couple integrate this new, more rational belief, they stop demanding, and gradually their son's behavior toward his parents may improve.

Ellis said that irrational beliefs are effectively *disputed* (at point *D*) by challenging them logically, empirically, and rationally. This rational process causes clients to reevaluate these beliefs and actually change them to new, more effective beliefs. Ellis developed REBT as an individually oriented therapy but saw implications for its use in marital and family therapy situations. Prior to developing REBT, Ellis practiced classical psychoanalysis. He found that no matter how much insight clients gained or how well they understood how their childhood affected their present behavior they improved only slightly and often developed new symptoms. He began to realize that the clients constantly reindoctrinated themselves with irrational and childish beliefs about how they should be, how others should be, and how the world should be.

Problem Resolution

- **A** is the *activating* event,
- **B** is irrational *belief* about the activating event,
- **C** is the *consequences* of the belief about the activating event,
- **D** is rationally *disputing* the belief about the irrational activating event, and
- **E** is the *effect* of rationally disputing the irrational belief.

Ellis's thoughts differ from psychoanalysis in that he believes humans are basically irrational. He believes that this irrationality is a natural characteristic and not the result of early training. He also views humans as creatures of habit who are lazy and will take simple preferences such as a desire for love, approval, success, and pleasure and redefine them as needs or necessities. While humans are prone to irrational thought, they are capable of rational thinking that leads to a mentally healthy lifestyle. Based on these assumptions, Ellis directly attacks the self-defeating value system of clients and not clients themselves. He supports the individual but strongly attacks faulty ideas, traits, and performance (Ellis, 1974).

Philosophical Tenets

Ellis (1962) believes in an *a priori* human nature. He thinks humans are born with strong biological predispositions to be socially involved with others. According to Ellis, humans are also naturally predisposed to disturbance and have a tendency to act against their own best interests. Their other innate values are: (1) to stay alive, (2) to enjoy themselves, (3) to live in a social group and get along with others, (4) to work productively, and (5) to seek activities that are pleasurable and satisfying.

In line with this philosophical belief, he traced the philosophical roots of his theory back to Epictetus, an early stoic philosopher who wrote that "people are disturbed not by things, but by the view which they take of them." Ellis focuses on objective thoughts, which he believes must be understood to change subjective feelings.

Ellis believes that absolute values corrupt logical and reasonable values, which are more situational. He also seems to trust the external collective values and believes the social nature of man dictates that social values are most important in guiding rational thoughts and behavior.

Theoretical Constructs

Theory of Cause

Ellis stated clearly that it is not a person's behavior that has to be changed but rather a person's irrational beliefs. The cause of these beliefs, according to Ellis, is the human condition. He claimed that our basic nature is irrational, and no event or person is to blame for causing these beliefs to develop. Ellis (1993) reports that because of their nature humans are easily disturbed and that these disturbances are evident when individuals are alone, in families, or in other groups. The disturbances are the result of individuals constructing strong goals, values, and desires that initially are functional and add to their happiness. These goals, values, and desires later are elevated into grandiose demands, shoulds, oughts, and musts. When humans create these absolutes, they also create conditions that lead to their unhappiness and emotional disturbances. He identified several absolutes that lead to emotional difficulties:

- I must perform well and be approved of by the important people in my life. If I don't perform well, it is horrible or awful, and I can't stand it. I am a terrible person if I fail to perform well.
- Other people should always treat me fairly and be considerate of my needs. It is horrible if people don't treat me the way I want to be treated. They are bad individuals and cannot be trusted.
- Life must be the way I want it to be, and if it isn't, I can't stand living in such a world. It is terrible and unacceptable.

Ellis said that if family members subscribe to one or more of these core beliefs, various forms of emotional disturbances and dysfunctional behavior will result. Referring back to the ABCDE model, presented earlier, problems emerge when an (a) *activating* event occurs and the (b) *belief* about the event is irrational and leads to unpleasant (c) *consequences.*

Theory of Change

For clients to change their beliefs, Ellis said that they have to learn three basic insights:

1. The causes of the emotional problems of family members are their irrational beliefs, not any external environmental condition.
2. Family members engage in self-conditioning by repeating these irrational beliefs over and over to themselves. Even if they did originally learn these beliefs from their parents, they are now responsible for the dysfunction they are causing themselves.
3. Family members will change their beliefs by being aware of them *and* by working and practicing to think, feel, and act against these irrational beliefs. That is, according to the

ABCDE model, presented earlier, change occurs when the client (d) *disputes* the irrational belief. The (e) *effect* of disputing the irrational belief with a rational one is to feel better, to act more productively, and to think more clearly.

Self-acceptance is also a major factor in the theory of cure in REBT. Ellis believed that his approach taught his clients to fully accept themselves, other people, and the world, and thus live happier, more enjoyable lives. He identified several kinds of acceptances that are necessary for therapeutic change (Ellis, 1993). These are:

- Accept human fallibility
- Accept the human tendency to demand
- Accept that humans may be uncaring and unloving
- Accept that humans are prone to some degree of disturbance
- Accept that we are responsible for our own disturbance by turning desires and preferences into absolute and grandiose demands
- Accept that humans choose their behaviors and that choices need not be absolute or demanded
- Accept oneself unconditionally
- Accept others unconditionally
- Accept that humans experience unchangeable frustrations
- Accept that humans may choose not to disturb themselves.

Main Therapeutic Interventions

Three main sets of techniques are used in REBT: (1) cognitive techniques, (2) emotive techniques, and (3) behavioral techniques. Each is described briefly.

1. *Cognitive techniques.* Family members are confronted about the beliefs that cause their disturbances and are given homework assignments to keep track of their "should" and "must" beliefs. They are also given a self-help report form to fill out (Ellis, 1977). They are given other cognitive tools, such as Disputing Irrational Beliefs (DIB) (Ellis, 1974), which supply them with new and better alternatives to their present beliefs. Therapists also use imagery exercises to get them to imagine themselves making new and more effective responses. They may also be taught relaxation techniques to help them overcome anxiety and depression.

CASE EXAMPLE

Rational Emotive Behavior Family Therapy

The following case was described by Ellis (1991) and represents a good example of how rational emotive behavior family therapy works. Only brief segments of the case are presented here.

The family consists of a mother and father, both age 45, two sons, ages 21 and 17, and a daughter, Debbie, age 15. Debbie is the identified patient. She is very bright (140 IQ) but is getting into trouble and doing poorly in school, and this upsets her parents. The key interaction in the first session involves the therapist and Debbie.

Therapist: Do you want to keep getting into the kind of trouble you're in with your parents, with the school, and with your brothers?

Debbie: No.

Therapist: Why do you think you steal?

Debbie: 'Cause I can't control myself.

Therapist: That's a nutty hypothesis! Horse shit! You have difficulty controlling yourself. But that doesn't mean that you can't.

Later in the session Debbie begins to realize how she gets herself in a self-defeating cycle.

Debbie: I guess I do. I keep thinking that I'm really no good. And then things get worse.

Therapist: Right! (therapist reinforces her awareness)

Debbie: But how can I stop that?

(continued)

2. *Emotive techniques.* Attempts are made to get clients in touch with their worst fears and to change them to appropriate feelings. Role playing is used to help clients express and work through their feelings of unworthiness. Also, shame attacking exercises are used to elicit intense shame and self-deprecating thoughts. Humor and paradoxical intention techniques are used to attack an irrational belief or feeling. Finally, clients are given unconditional acceptance by the therapist, which shows them that they can accept themselves even when they have self-defeating behavior.

(CASE EXAMPLE continued)

Therapist: *The best solution is to see very clearly what I said before: that some of your acts are poor or self-defeating but that you are not a worm for doing them. If we could get you to fully accept yourself, your being, your totality, even when you are screwing up and acting stupidly or badly, then we could get you to go back and work on improving your screwups. And you could change most of them.*

Debbie: *I see what you mean. But how am I going to keep seeing that and believing it?*

Therapist: *By damned hard work! By continuing to think about what you say to yourself and do. And by changing your perfectionistic, demanding thinking into preferences and desires.*

The therapist then turned to the parents and said: "She has normal desires, but then she tells herself, I must, 'I must fulfill them!' Now, if I can get all of you, including her, to look for the should, look for the must, which you are all bright enough to do, and if I can persuade you to tackle these absolutes and give them up, you will be able to stop upsetting yourselves, and usually solve the problem of getting along together and living happily in the world."

The therapist closed the session by assigning all three of them to read some REBT literature and to do some behavioral assignments, including keeping track of the times they feel upset during the week and what is happening in the family.

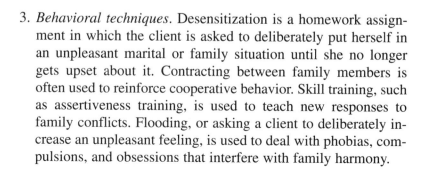

3. *Behavioral techniques.* Desensitization is a homework assignment in which the client is asked to deliberately put herself in an unpleasant marital or family situation until she no longer gets upset about it. Contracting between family members is often used to reinforce cooperative behavior. Skill training, such as assertiveness training, is used to teach new responses to family conflicts. Flooding, or asking a client to deliberately increase an unpleasant feeling, is used to deal with phobias, compulsions, and obsessions that interfere with family harmony.

Goals of Rational Emotive Behavior Family Therapy

The goals of rational emotive behavior family therapy are as follows:

- To help family members learn not to take too seriously what other family members say or do
- To help family members surrender their absolutes (shoulds and musts) about how they would like others in the family to act
- To encourage family members to feel their feelings and use the energy generated by their feelings to help them ask for and get what they want from other family members
- To make family members aware of their irrational beliefs and teach them how to dispute and challenge their own beliefs
- To teach the clients a variety of self-therapy techniques for combating their own irrational beliefs
- To teach the clients more effective conflict resolution skills that can allow them to be happy and effective at getting what they want
- To teach the clients how to handle whatever happens in their family without getting upset or disturbed.

Limitations of Rational Emotive Behavior Family Therapy

Rational emotive behavior therapy does have its limitations. Lyddon (1990, 1992) suggests that REBT may devalue emotion, may not be humanistic, and may not focus on deeper problems. The confrontive and directive style of the therapist may not allow the client to decide what is rational or logical thinking. New beliefs may be pushed on the client, perhaps in a way similar to how the irrational beliefs were first learned. In addition, the therapist is clearly imposing his or her value system on the client in a situation where the client may have very little power. Some critics argue that there is insufficient attention given to the desires of the client and that the therapist may "beat down" clients (Corey, 2000).

Behavioral Family Therapy

Behavioral theory has been a major theory in psychology for about thirty years, but the application of the theory to family therapy is fairly recent (Liberman, 1970). The increased interest in family applications resulted from various research studies on social learning theory demonstrating its effectiveness with a variety of populations, including families (Falloon, 1991).

It had become apparent that the more traditional family therapies were not very effective in cases where family members displayed acting-out and aggressive behaviors. There seemed to be a need for a new theory and new approaches to deal with this kind of behavior problem. Finally, a group of psychologists at the Oregon Social Learning Center, under the direction of Gerald Patterson and John Reid, developed a behavioral treatment approach based on *social learning theory*. Initially, they focused on training parents and others in the acting-out child's environment to act as agents of change. Later, they broadened the approach to work with families with parent-child conflicts. They conducted extensive research, mostly on deviant behavior of children, and developed a number of effective methods for reducing and controlling deviant and disruptive behavior (Patterson, 1976; Patterson, Reid, Jones, & Conger, 1975; Reid & Patterson, 1976). Their later work focuses more on systemic family interaction patterns and avoids overfocusing on the identified patient in a family.

Philosophical Tenets

In this approach, which follows the operant conditioning model of Watson, Hull, and Skinner, the most important source of knowing (*epistemology*) is scientific knowledge discovered through rigorous, repeated laboratory research studies. Some behavioral theorists may not consider clinical judgment to be subjective knowledge reported by the client, and beliefs and attitudes to be valid sources of knowledge. The continuum of ways that humans acquire knowledge in this approach runs from scientific research, objective findings, scientific "facts," and scientific values at the important end—with mental phenomena, phenomenological methods, metaphysical inquiry, subjectivity, and interviewing variables at the less important end.

Behaviorists consider reality (*ontology*) to be the external physical or sensory phenomena that can be measured and counted. This principle clearly follows the earlier philosophical tenets of Descartes, Locke, and Hume. The values (*axiology*) in behaviorism derive from certain truths that emerge as the result of logical and scientific studies.

Informed reason based on the best scientific insights available is considered to be the best source of values (Corey, 2000). We encourage all counselors in training to consider carefully their own *epistemology* (how one knows), their own *ontology* (what is reality and what is the evidence for this), and their own *axiology* (what is good and of value). Considering these points will be extremely helpful in the development of a consistent and congruent counseling theory and supporting interventions.

As behavioral theory has evolved, it has moved from a position that views humans as the product of the environment to one that views humans as both producer and product of the environment (Bandura, 1977). Thus, we are capable of creating our destinies rather than simply being the victim of external reinforcers.

Theoretical Constructs

Theory of Cause

Current behavioral theories including the social learning model, focus on the social reinforcers in a family or other social system. Social learning theorists believe, as did nonbehaviorists such as Bateson, Jackson, and Haley, that dysfunctional behavior is an understandable and logical response to the reinforcement contingencies of the family system. People and the environments in which they live are seen as reciprocal determinants of each other; thus, the concept of reciprocity or *quid pro quo* in families was developed. It was discovered that an improvement or change in one member's behavior was followed by a change in another family member's behavior (Patterson, 1971).

An interactional focus is therefore emphasized to examine the causes of dysfunctional behavior. It is impossible, however, to assign blame solely to a parent for the dysfunctional behavior of a child. The mother may present cues and reinforcers to the child that determine the behavior the child exhibits toward the mother. At the same time, the child is presenting cues and reinforcers to the mother that influence her interaction with the child. In this way, each member of a family influences the behavior and is influenced by other members of the family.

According to this view of a system, if a person or a whole family has not developed adequate positive behaviors, the cause of this problem is a lack of positive reinforcers in the individual or the family.

Gottman et al. (1976) described a model of family interactions based on this premise. These authors used the metaphor that family members each have a bank account where they make deposits or investments and withdrawals analogous to their interactions with the other family members. In functional families, individuals receive a relatively high rate of exchange on their investments of time and energy with other family members because there is a long list of positive equal exchanges. In dysfunctional families, there is more time and energy spent "balancing the books" on a regular basis as each family member attempts to make sure he or she is not treated unfairly.

Patterson et al. (1975) demonstrated the limited value of coercion in creating desired change in families. An escalation of negative behaviors was more likely to occur when coercion was used to attempt to change behavior in another family member. Thus, behavioral family therapists attempt to decrease coercion while increasing reciprocity of positive behavioral exchanges (Falloon, 1991).

Theory of Change

The job of the therapist is to understand the social reinforcement history of an individual, a couple, or a family and begin to help them develop new positive reinforcers. The therapist has to develop a systematic process for observing the antecedents in the environment, the behaviors, and the consequences of the behaviors and then manipulate the reinforcement contingencies to provide opportunities for the clients to learn new behaviors. Any strategy designed to modify the deviant behavior of one family member must be based on changes in the behaviors of other key family members. Parents, spouses, siblings, and children are taught to eliminate their own behaviors that reinforce the deviant member's behavior and to learn and use different behaviors that are incompatible with the deviant behavior (Falloon, 1991).

In developing an understanding of the social reinforcement pattern of a family, it is important to remember a fundamental assumption of behavioral family therapy: Current behavior, no matter how dysfunctional it may seem, is the family's best attempt to deal with their current situation.

Main Therapeutic Interventions

The main tasks of the behavioral family therapist are to analyze the problems, design appropriate interventions, and assess changes in the

CASE EXAMPLE

Behavioral Family Therapy

The following case example was taken from Horne and Ohlsen (1982, pp. 380–384). Only a portion of that case is presented here to illustrate some of the main interventions of social learning family therapists.

Kevin, a sixth-grade boy, along with his parents, was referred for therapy because of his difficulties in school, which included being expelled for fighting and truancy. In addition, Kevin's two younger siblings attended the sessions. Kevin was described as having a chip on his shoulder; he was often aggressive in his responses to teachers and to other students. The family's reaction was to have the therapist "fix" Kevin, and they did not see why they should be part of the therapy. As each member of the family talked, it became evident that the parents had poor parenting skills and tended to ignore the problem behaviors that resulted from their poor skills until some outside agency like the school intervened. The therapist met first with the parents, Dan and Kim.

Therapist: (summarizing the family situation) Kevin has had problems at school for a long time—pretty much ever since he got started—but you have figured that's the school's problem, that they should be able to handle Kevin.

Dan: Damned right, that's what they are there for. I was a lot like Kevin, and they certainly handled me.

Therapist: You pretty clearly have a kid who is more than the school can handle—he's a real expert at what he does, which is messing up.

Kim: We can't go to school and sit by him all the time, and we sure can't beat him all the time for coming home in trouble. That hasn't worked.

Therapist: I'm glad you see that. . . . What we do is teach parents how they can work with the school to get the changes that the school wants. . . . I think we can do that fairly quickly if you are interested in working with us here, but it does involve some real intensive work for awhile, and will require that you put in some time on exercises I'll assign you. It won't be easy and, in fact, will be a nuisance a lot of the time.

Dan: Well, maybe Kim should; she's the one that has the problem around the house, not me.

(continued)

(CASE EXAMPLE continued)

Therapist: *That's a good point, Dan, and I'm glad you brought that up. You see, dads generally have less trouble than moms do. But, as I look at Kim, I see a tired and frustrated lady. She looks like she can use some support, some help. Since you already have pretty good control over how Kevin behaves, would you be willing to work with us to help with the program we have here in order to give Kim the backing she needs, the support she needs? . . . Are you willing to do that?*

Dan: *Well, I'll help out, but I don't see that I need the help.*

Therapist: *As I said, we see that all family members are involved in the welfare of the whole family. . . . We're asking for the family to work as a team with us. Okay?*

The children were then brought into the session, and during the next part of the session, the parents blamed the children for misbehaving and the children blamed the parents for being too lax and ignoring conflicts. Then a co-therapist worked separately with the children while the parents completed several inventories.

In the interview with the children, it came out that Kevin was also having problems with his siblings around the house. The data gathered from the parents showed, among other things, that the marriage was on shaky ground. It was decided that in spite of the marriage problems, working on a behavior management contract with Kevin would help both Kevin and the marriage.

The family agreed to a specified number of sessions, and the members of the family were given homework assignments. Kevin's school was contacted and included in the behavior management program. After three weeks, the program progressed in the family and at school. The treatment then shifted, and conjoint therapy was done with the couple to work on the marital problems. The course of the family treatment was four months. By the end of that time, the home and school conflicts had subsided and more desirable family interactions were occurring. The family required three additional sessions six months later when the new school year began and Kevin reverted to some of his previous behavior. After the three sessions, his behavior changed back to more positive responses at school.

family. The main core skills a therapist using this approach would need are: (1) attending behavior, (2) rapport building, (3) structuring, (4) summarization, (5) interpretation, and (6) reflection of content. In addition, a social learning therapist has to be skilled in behavioral assessment. Behavioral assessment in a social learning model includes:

- Determining which environmental stimulus variables elicit the problem behaviors.
- Discovering what mediating factors exist, such as a person's thoughts and feelings about a problem behavior.
- Finding out how the individual behaves in response to his or her thoughts and feelings about the situation.
- Locating the reinforcers that affect the frequency of the problem behavior.

An important development in behavioral family therapy is the *psychoeducational approach* to family treatment. In this approach, the identified patient and family members are presented with a series of educational seminars that describe the nature of the problem and the strategies for managing the problem. This approach has been especially useful for families with a seriously impaired member (Goldstein & Miklowitz, 1995).

The behavioral family therapist might also teach family members new communication responses using role playing or behavior rehearsal to correct any inappropriate or nonreinforcing responses. Teaching often occurs in two main areas: (1) correctional procedures, and (2) reinforcement procedures. Under the heading of *correctional procedures*, the therapist might teach family members the following skills:

- How to appropriately ignore attention-seeking problem behaviors.
- How to make effective use of natural and logical consequences.
- How to set up behavioral contingency contracts (you must do this before you get to do that).
- How to use the principle of "time out" to temporarily remove a family member from a reinforcing environment to a nonreinforcing environment.
- How to give assigned tasks to family members who don't cooperate.
- How to withhold privileges from family members when the other correctional procedures fail.

The *reinforcement procedures* often taught to family members include:

- How to properly attend to other people. This skill is the same as the nonverbal and verbal attending skills of the therapist.
- How to give social praise, including appropriate ways of demonstrating approval, appreciation, and satisfaction.
- How to give physical attention, such as hugs and touching.
- How to structure activities and spend time together.
- How to provide equal access to family activities and allow children to help plan activities that are agreeable to them and their parents.
- How to use points and other external rewards, which are effective for getting immediate involvement and behavior change but generally not useful for long-term changes.

Limitations of Behavioral Family Therapy

The behavioral model of family therapy has a number of limitations. The method may be manipulative and used to attempt to influence and control behavior. Children, for example, who often do not have equal options or resources, must "go along" with the changes they are asked to make. In addition, this theory may reinforce the idea of the identified patient, although probably not as much as other individual theories do. However, most of the attention of behavioral family therapy is still placed on helping the parents learn to better control the behavior of their acting-out children. Furthermore, the role of the therapist is not always clear. Does the therapist consider herself a member of the family social system, or does the therapist see herself as an objective person removed from the influence of reciprocal interactions with the family?

Social learning theory may be most useful in families with acting-out or disruptive members. It is probably less useful in families where more social inhibition is present. It is also useful in marital therapy as couples work to establish mutually satisfactory *contingency contracts*. Contingency contracts help the couple establish a mutually reinforcing *quid pro quo*. When one partner does something positive, the other partner reciprocates. This is done in ways that have previously been agreed upon in therapy. It is an educational approach and as such avoids looking closely at underlying causes and deals primarily with overt symptoms. The success of this approach is often predicated on the assumption that couples or families are capable of cooperating in a reciprocal, step-by-step effort to improve their relationships. Couples or families who enter therapy, however, may not possess these capabilities.

■ *Summary*

This chapter introduced the reader to two important and fundamental theories for treating individuals, couples, and families. First, we discussed Alber Ellis' Rational Emotional Behavior Therapy (REBT). Ellis emphasized the important function of irrational throughts in producing dysfunctional actions and feelings and demonstrated how the therapist may help the client by teaching techniques for modifying irrational thought.

Then we introduced Social Learning Theory. This theory emphasized the important role our behaviors and actions may play in producing painful thoughts and feelings. We discussed ways to reinforce positive behaviors and eliminate negative behaviors. In the next chapter, we will introduce the reader to three systems-based cognitive/behavior theories.

SUGGESTED READINGS

Ellis, A. (1962). *Reason and Emotion in Psychotherapy.* Secaucus, NJ: Citadel Press.

Ellis, A. (1995). "Rational Emotive Behavior Therapy." In R. J. Corsini & D. Wedding, eds., *Current Psychotherapies,* 5th Ed. Itasca, IL: F. E. Peacock.

Falloon, I. R. H. (1991). "Behavioral Family Therapy." In A. S. Gurman & D. P. Kniskern, eds., *Handbook of Family Therapy*, Vol. II. New York: Brunner/Mazel.

Patterson, G. (1971). *Families: Applications of Social Learning in Family Life*. Champaign, IL: Research Press.

Patterson, G., Reid, J. B., Jonas, R. R., & Conger, R. E. (1975). *A Social Learning Approach to Family Intervention*, Vol. I. Eugene, OR: Castalia Publishing.

Stuart, R. B. (1980). *Helping Couples Change: A Social Learning Approach to Marital Therapy*. New York: Guilford Press.

Cognitive/Behavioral Systems Theories

In this chapter, we will examine three approaches to family systems therapy that have their roots in cognitive and behavioral theory. These approaches are quite distinct from the systems theories with psychoanalytic roots and the systems theories with humanistic/existential roots to be presented later in this book.

The three theories presented in this chapter are structural family therapy as developed by Salvador Minuchin, functional family therapy as developed by Cole Barton, James Alexander, and Bruce Parsons, and brief therapy as developed by the staff of the Mental Research Institute (MRI) in Palo Alto. These three theories have been selected because they are practical, concrete, and relevant and offer concepts that may be of immediate use for counselors and therapists who want to begin using systems theory in their work with couples and families.

KEY CONCEPTS

Subsystems
Boundaries
Homeostasis
Joining
Tracking
Accommodation
Mimesis
Enactment
Restructuring
Symptom focusing

Relabeling the symptom
Conceptual skills
Technical skills
Interpersonal skills
Paradox
Brief therapy
Therapist maneuverability
180° solution
Restraining change

QUESTIONS FOR DISCUSSION

1. According to the structural family therapist, what is the relationship between family structure and family function?

2. What are the major steps the structural family therapist would use to help the family change?

3. What is meant by challenging the current family reality? Do you have any concerns about the use of this technique? Why, or why not?

4. What is the functional family therapist's conceptualization of the purpose of symptoms in the family? Do you agree with this conceptualization? Why, or why not?

5. Describe conceptual, technical, and interpersonal skills in functional family therapy. Why are each of these skill areas important?

6. How are problems identified and solved according to the brief therapy theory of the Mental Research Institute?

7. What is meant by "therapist maneuverability"? What is your reaction to this concept?

8. In the MRI approach, what is meant by "the attempted solutions are the problem"?

$\mathcal{S}$ tructural family therapy (Minuchin, 1974; Minuchin & Fishman, 1981), functional family therapy (Alexander & Parsons, 1982; Barton & Alexander, 1981), and brief therapy as practiced by the staff of the Mental Research Institute (Fisch, Weakland, & Segal, 1982; Segal, 1991; Watzlawick, Weakland, & Fisch, 1974;) have distinct characteristics that distinguish them from other systems theories presented in this book. The characteristics held in common by these theories are: (1) the focus is on discovering a practical solution to the problems presented by the family; (2) short-term tangible results are expected of therapy; (3) the goal is to take action to solve the problems rather than talking about them; (4) action is emphasized over insight; and (5) expression of feeling is viewed as a vehicle to change behavior rather than an end in itself.

Thus, the reader will learn about three of the most action-oriented systems theories in practice. Furthermore, specific techniques associated with these theories will be presented, which will offer specific suggestions for counselors beginning systems therapy with couples and families.

■ *Structural Family Therapy*

Salvador Minuchin was born in Argentina and trained there as a physician with an interest in pediatrics. He served as a physician for the Israeli Army after Israel became a nation in 1948. He then received training in the United States as a child psychiatrist before returning to Israel to work with displaced children. Returning to the United States, Minuchin and his colleagues developed a program for working with delinquent minority children in New York City. These children frequently came from very disorganized families with few rules for conduct and little structure. Minuchin's work with these delinquent children and their families fostered many of the concepts of structural family therapy. A recounting of Minuchin and his colleagues' work with these families at the Wiltwyck School for Boys can be found in *Families of the Slums* (Minuchin, Montalvo, Guerney, Rosman, & Schumer, 1967).

From 1965 through 1975, Minuchin was the director of the Philadelphia Child Guidance Clinic. Under his leadership, it became one of the most highly acclaimed family therapy service and training institutes in the world. During the past several years, Minuchin has worked with psychosomatic families (Minuchin, Rosman, & Baker, 1978) and has written extensively about structural family therapy. He has also presented numerous training workshops and demonstrations of structural family therapy to professional audiences throughout the world.

Philosophical Tenets and Key Theoretical Constructs

According to Minuchin (1974) the function of the family in society is to *support, nurture, control,* and *socialize* its members. "A well-functioning family is not defined by the absence of stress and conflicts, but by how effectively it handles them in the course of fulfilling its functions. This in turn depends on the *structure* and *adaptability* of the family" (Colapinto, 1991, p. 422). Structural family therapy, as its name implies, stresses the importance of the structure of the family system. In other words, how a family organizes itself is important to the well-being and effective psychological functioning of the members of the family (Minuchin, 1974).

Structural family therapists assume that there is an inherent drive toward organization within individuals and other living systems. This organization can be seen at various levels of living systems, from the cellular level all the way to the organization of a large corporation or city. These therapists assume that family *function follows structure.* Thus, structural family therapists understand behavior that occurs within a family as being a product of the *structure of the family.* When certain disturbing behaviors occur within the family, the family therapist will try to help the family reorganize its structure in a way that no longer supports or requires the disturbing behaviors. Adaptable families are those that are able to make the changes necessary to develop a new and more functional structure.

Homeostasis and Disequilibrium

Family systems are evolutionary. They are dynamic and changing. The system passes through periods of *homeostasis*, where change in the family occurs in rather small and acceptable ways that do not alter the current organization or structure of the family. These periods of homeostasis are interrupted by periods of *disequilibrium*, when the changes occurring in the family challenge the current family structure and require that the family structure be modified to accommodate the changes taking place. When the family system fights to retain its old organization instead of adapting to new circumstances, symptoms may develop in one or more family members. The structural family therapist will develop intervention strategies in an attempt to help the family reorganize in a more productive manner that allows for family development and change (Minuchin, 1974).

Subsystems

Each family is composed of subsystems that are parts of the larger family system. In an effort to help clarify the idea that a subsystem is both a whole and a part of a larger system, Minuchin used the term *holon* as a synonym for subsystem (Colapinto, 1991; Minuchin & Fishman, 1981). Each subsystem is identified by *boundaries* and *rules* that define who is in and who is out of the subsystem. For example, a subsystem of father and son may exist when the two go hunting. The rules of this subsystem may exclude mother and sister as well as friends of the father and the son. Thus, the boundaries of this subsystem are clearly defined. Four subsystems are important in a fundamental understanding of structural family therapy (Minuchin, 1974; Minuchin & Fishman, 1981).

1. *The individual subsystem.* Each member of the family is a subsystem of the family. It is important, however, not to view the family's problems as being the result of pathology within an individual. Two or more individuals form larger subsystems in the family. These larger subsystems have boundaries that describe who is a member of the subsystem. In families experiencing problems, the various subsystems are organized in a structural manner that supports the dysfunction. The therapist will seek to help the family adopt a more functional organization through treatment. In any event, all subsystems in the

family are composed of individuals, and the therapist should not lose sight of this fact.

Colapinto (1991) states that "a change in the system consists of individuals changing each other, and therefore requires the detection and mobilization of untapped individual resources" (p. 430). While it is important to conceptualize structurally, it is individuals within the family who will behave in new ways that promote family health.

2. *The spousal subsystem.* The beginning of a new family takes place when a couple decides to unite and the partners begin to share their lives. As the two live together, they develop as a spousal subsystem. As members of the spousal subsystem, the individuals may support each other in times of crisis and indecision. Furthermore, they may work together to formulate decisions on how the family will be started, nurtured, and regulated.

One of the critical functions of the spousal subsystem is to develop boundaries that protect the couple from unwanted intrusions from other subsystems, such as parents, in-laws, or children. A strong, unified, and flexible spousal subsystem contributes much to the success of the larger family. Problems frequently occur in families in which spouses are more committed to another subsystem than to the spousal subsystem. This problem may occur when a husband is married to his work or a wife is overinvolved with her children.

When severe problems develop in the spousal subsystem and go unresolved, the effects reverberate throughout the whole family. Frequently, a child will develop psychological symptoms and may be scapegoated as a troublemaker in the family or be brought into an alliance with one of the parents against the other. An important diagnostic skill of the structural family therapist is to identify a child who is a member of a subsystem to which he or she should not be a member, such as the spousal subsystem. When a child becomes a member of the spousal subsystem, he or she often becomes allied with one parent against the other. This family structure is frequently identified in families that seek therapy.

The spousal subsystem is also known as the *executive subsystem,* as it is the subsystem primarily responsible for the regulatory functions of the family. In single-parent families, a child may be included in this subsystem to assist the parent in regulatory and support functions. This structural form is often effective or may also produce a *parentified child,* one who assumes adult roles too early in life missing many of the developmental tasks of childhood. It is important to understand that structural family therapy does not prescribe functional or dysfunctional family organizations; rather, this therapy attempts to help families develop new and more functional forms when current structures are not working.

3. *The parental subsystem.* The parental subsystem is composed of the husband and wife, or the same members as the spousal subsystem. The members of the parental subsystem have as their primary role the successful rearing of their family. Thus, the parental subsystem is specifically concerned with providing for the needs of the children in the family.

    The parental subsystem differs from the spousal subsystem in an important way. In the parental subsystem, the adults have very flexible roles and boundaries that allow for children to become temporarily parental and for parents to become temporarily childlike. This ability to spontaneously switch roles allows for the playfulness necessary for successful parenting and also allows children the opportunity to learn how to assume responsibility (parental) roles in the family.

    In contrast to the parental subsystem, the spousal or executive subsystem requires that the husband and wife work together to keep the children or other well-meaning friends or relatives from intruding in their activities. When children are regularly involved in the spousal subsystem, it is not unusual to find one spouse allied with the child against the other spouse. The structural family therapist will quickly assess the functionality of both spousal and parental subsystems of the family in therapy to determine whether restructuring these subsystems may be helpful for the family. When families come for therapy, the executive subsystem is frequently weak or nonexistent.

4. *The sibling subsystem.* The fourth major subsystem is composed of the children in the family. In most functional families, communication between the members of the sibling subsystem and the parental subsystem is open and clear. As siblings recognize

that they are excluded from the spousal subsystem, they form a unity, or bond, in the sibling subsystem that works cohesively to influence the adults in the parental subsystem. Although this cohesiveness in the sibling subsystem is certainly not universal and does not occur all the time, it nevertheless is often present in healthy families. Parents are often astounded to hear the therapist say that when their children plot to raid the cookie jar together, it is a sign of a family strength.

Family therapists using the structural approach will come to understand the families they work with in terms of the subsystems represented in the family. The four subsystems identified above are the most common ones noted in structural family therapy literature. It must be remembered, however, that any one of a variety of subsystems may exist within a family, and the functions of these subsystems may be either helpful or problematic for the family. The structural family therapist should be equipped to identify subsystems and their functioning before proceeding with techniques for making family system changes.

Why Families Seek Treatment

As previously described, family systems seek organization and structure defined by the boundaries (rules) of the subsystems within the family. When the system is relatively stable, the family is in a state of homeostasis or equilibrium. When this homeostasis is altered or challenged, the family system attempts to retain its structure by not allowing change to take place. Frequently, the challenges to the family's homeostasis come from natural developmental changes in the family.

For instance, when a daughter was in her early teens, she was most compliant with her parents' rule that she be home by seven each night. However, as she became older, this rule was deemed childish by the daughter, and she rebelled and came home whenever she pleased. The parents tried everything to get their daughter to comply with their wishes. In response to their efforts to gain control, however, she only rebelled more, and the situation became worse.

This couple became angry and confused regarding their daughter's behavior and decided to seek help for her. The family came to a structural family therapist who helped the parents recognize that the current family structure or homeostasis was no longer appropriate for the developmental stage of the family. The therapist helped the family establish a new structural homeostasis with new rules and more appropriate boundaries (Minuchin & Fishman, 1981). As can be seen from this example, families come for therapy when their rules and organization are being severely challenged and all attempts to reestablish homeostasis have failed.

Main Therapeutic Interventions

Structural family therapists assume that family dysfunction occurs because the organization of the family system has been disrupted and the family has been unsuccessful at reestablishing homeostasis or equilibrium. Thus, families come to treatment experiencing a great deal of confusion, anger, and perhaps fear. The confusion arises because they are not able to fix the problem as in the past. Anger arises because, typically, one or more family members are identified as the culprits who have caused the confusion. And fear exists because the family members who come for therapy have little idea of what to expect from the structural family therapist.

Quite naturally, effective therapy will be difficult when members are confused, angry, and afraid. The first task of the structural family therapist is to reduce these affective conditions. This is accomplished by the technique called *joining* (Minuchin, 1974).

Joining

For family therapy to be effective, the therapist has to establish a solid working relationship with the family members. *Joining* is the process of establishing that relationship with each family member. Joining is an especially critical technique in structural family therapy because even though the family members and the therapist share the goal of improving family functioning, the therapist and the family will often differ in their understanding of the locus of the problem, what causes the problem, and what has to be done to resolve the problem (Minuchin & Fishman, 1981).

As the therapist moves toward identifying the problem as one that is structural and involves all family members rather than as a problem with only one of its members, the rules of the family may be violated and the family may retreat in an attempt to preserve homeostasis and avoid change. Under such conditions, helping the family change becomes increasingly difficult. Thus, the family therapist joins with each member of the family, engendering trust so they will allow the therapist to use the knowledge of structural family therapy to assist them in making needed changes.

If the therapist moves too quickly in making changes before successfully joining with the family, the family may resist the therapist's attempts to help. If the therapist has successfully joined with each family member, however, they will generally be receptive to the new ideas, suggestions, and challenges the structural family therapist provides as part of treatment.

Successful joining requires that the therapist become a *significant source of self-esteem validation* for each member of the family. To be in such a position of trust, the family members must experience the therapist as *accurately understanding* the unique perspectives of each individual in the family. The therapist must be able to *communicate* to all individuals in the family that their unique perspectives are indeed understandable and make sense given the current behaviors of the other members in the family system. Thus, the therapist validates each position and, more important, each person in the family.

The specific components of joining are tracking, accommodation, and mimesis (Aponte & Van Deusen, 1981; Minuchin, 1974). *Tracking* refers to the therapist's ability to adopt the family's way of thinking about their situation. The more accurately the therapist uses the family's words, symbols, history, values, and style, the more fully understood the family will feel. The therapist uses *accommodation* in the joining process by relating to the family's current rules and roles. In this way, the therapist shows respect for family members as they are. As they understand this respect for who they are, they will be more willing to look at ways they could be even better. *Mimesis* is the joining technique that refers to the therapist becoming like a family member by adopting the family's style of communication. The therapist adopts similar body language, pace, and other communication behaviors of the family through mimesis.

Techniques for joining will be useless unless the therapist has a genuine interest in the family and is able to provide personal responsiveness. Additionally, the therapist will want to ensure that he or she does not inadvertently become drawn into the family system. If the therapist is *inducted* into the family system, objectivity may be lost as the power of the family's rules organize the session. Induction is *not* joining through accommodation. In the joining process, the therapist intentionally adopts the rules of the family. Induction occurs when the therapist is inadvertently drawn into the family by its rules and loses therapeutic objectivity (Colapinto, 1991).

Activating Family Transaction Patterns and Structural Assessment

To help families through structural family therapy, the therapist must understand and assess the current structure of the family. This process begins during the joining phase of treatment as the therapist notices rules, roles, and subsystems that govern the family's operation. The formal assessment of the family structure begins after the relationship between the therapist and the family has been solidly established. The therapist then learns how the family is structured through the technique of *enactment* (Minuchin & Fishman, 1981).

Enactment occurs when the family functions in therapy sessions as it does in the home, which allows the therapist to understand the family's current structure. Enactment may occur spontaneously in family therapy. However, when it does not, the therapist needs to facilitate the enactment. The therapist may direct certain key subsystems to discuss an acknowledged family problem or situation. As the family members behave in their accustomed ways in the session, the therapist learns how the family currently functions and how it may be able to function more effectively through structural interventions.

Restructuring Family Transaction Patterns

Families come to therapy to relieve stress or symptoms in one of the members. After the structural family therapist has joined with the family, created opportunities for the family to display its current patterns of functioning, and determined how the family functions and how its structure supports this functioning, it is then possible to alter the structure and the functioning of the family.

Structural family therapists have a variety of effective techniques for altering family structure and functioning. Aponte and Van Deusen (1981) have identified three major areas of restructuring: (1) system recomposition, (2) symptom focusing, and (3) structural modification. Each of these areas will be discussed briefly.

System Recomposition Families seeking therapy are often organized rather rigidly into subsystems that may not adequately meet the developmental and emotional needs of the family. When the structural family therapist identifies this as a problem, recomposition of the subsystems becomes one method of treatment. Two major interventions may be used to change the composition of the family system. The first is to identify and *create a new subsystem* in the family. For instance, if a teenage daughter was allied with her mother against her father, the therapist may help create (or strengthen) the father-daughter subsystem by prescribing mutually enjoyable activities for them to do together. The second intervention is to *eliminate subsystems* that are no longer serving a productive function for the family. In the example above, the therapist may seek to eliminate the subsystem of mother and daughter allied against father and replace it with a mother-daughter-father subsystem that works jointly on tasks and issues.

Symptom Focusing Frequently, families seek therapy because of some symptom being displayed by one of the family members. Quite naturally, the family members want to see the symptom eliminated. This view presents a clinical problem for the structural family therapist, who will generally see this presenting problem as a symptom of a dysfunctional family structure rather than as a problem within the identified family member. Thus, the therapist must have a variety of techniques for dealing with the symptom. The following techniques focus on the symptom either more or less intensely. Specifically, the therapist may:

- relabel the symptom,
- alter the affect of the symptom,
- expand the symptom,
- exaggerate the symptom,
- deemphasize the symptom, or
- move to a new symptom (Aponte & Van Deusen, 1981).

When a family begins therapy, it has had months or even years of practice at maintaining the symptom. When the family therapist attempts to deal with the symptom exactly as the family presents it, it may be difficult to help the family change because the family has probably tried most of the reasonable and rational approaches to changing the situation. When the therapist suggests ways to resolve the problem, it is likely that the family will have a "yes, but..." response to the therapist's suggestions for change. *Because the family is the established expert on its problem* it may disqualify the therapist's attempts to help. The therapist has to become the expert on problem resolution.

To accomplish this, the family needs to come to a new understanding of its problem as presented by the therapist. The blinders that allow the family to understand the problem in only one way have to be removed so a new understanding of the problem may occur.

Altering the nature of the symptom redefines the nature of the problem. Through this process, the dynamics of the session are altered in a way that empowers the therapist to help the family make structural changes. When the family accepts the new or revised definition of the problem, the therapist then becomes the established expert on the new problem and is in a position to assist the family in making changes. The family will then rely on the therapist's knowledge about system change and develop a curiosity about how this knowledge may be helpful in resolving the newly defined problem. The family will no longer be limited by its own extensive and unsuccessful experience with the original problem.

Six techniques for altering the symptom are described next.

1. *Relabel the symptom.* This technique is one of the most effective ways to alter tension and affect in the family if implemented correctly. It can also be quite ineffective if the therapist has not accurately assessed the family's readiness for a new understanding of the problem. Relabeling or *reframing* (Minuchin & Fishman, 1981) simply means that the therapist describes the symptomatic behavior in a way that makes it seem understandable and functional given the current circumstances. For instance, when a teenage girl has been consistently ignoring her schoolwork despite her parents' orders that she become more responsible, the family identifies her symptoms as rebelliousness. This definition may even be accepted by the daughter. The effective therapist may relabel the rebelliousness as "the daughter's attempts to establish herself as an autonomous young adult in the family instead of the parents' little girl." If this new label is accepted, the family has a new and potentially manageable problem that the therapist can help the family resolve. The problem becomes "how can we help our daughter become a

responsible young adult" instead of "how can we get rid of her rebelliousness." It is easy to see how the relabeled symptom will require a whole new set of behaviors by the parents and the daughter.

2. *Alter the affect of the symptom.* This technique is closely related to relabeling except that it involves altering the feelings associated with the symptom rather than the definition of the symptom. In the example above, the therapist might relabel the parents' feelings about the daughter's behavior from anger at the daughter to feelings of sadness because they had not been successful in transmitting their values of the importance of education to their daughter. Once again, acceptance of this new label may open doors leading to the productive resolution of this situation.

3. *Expand the symptom.* Usually, the family will have identified one person as "the problem" and will present ample evidence of this person's guilt. In certain cases, the therapist will not be able to relabel the symptom or alter the affect of the symptom. In these cases, the therapist may expand the symptom by specifically identifying behaviors other family members engage in to maintain the symptom. As other members recognize their part in the problem, the identified patient will feel less pressure and may be more likely to change. Furthermore, as other family members begin to understand their roles in maintaining the problem, they may make changes that support change in the identified patient.

   Again, using the example above, the therapist may discover during the enactment portion of therapy that the daughter becomes most rebellious when the mother and father exhibit their disagreement about what would be the best way to get her to study. The therapist then could point out how the parents' disagreement is part of the sequence that could be defined as the symptom. This expansion of the problem takes some pressure off the daughter and encourages the parents to examine their roles in the maintenance of the problem.

4. *Exaggerate the symptom.* This *paradoxical technique* is used when other ways of altering the symptom have not been successful. In this technique, the therapist places an undue amount of emphasis on the symptom and actually suggests that the

family member engage in the symptom more frequently because this may be the only way the member is able to achieve the type of attention needed from the family (Minuchin & Fishman, 1981).

In the case of the teenage daughter cited above, the therapist would say that the problem was indeed a severe one. Because the daughter has no other way of obtaining her parents' attention and concern, she should be certain to avoid her studies even more frequently than she has been. The effects of this type of intervention are twofold. First, it normalizes and relabels the behavior as necessary to gain a positive goal (attention from parents). Second, it puts the daughter in charge of not doing homework and takes parental pressure out of the system. This exaggeration sets the stage for later changes, as the daughter could choose to be in charge of *doing* instead of *not doing* homework.

5. *Deemphasize the symptom.* This technique is designed to draw the family's energy away from the presenting symptom, as intense focus on the symptom often serves to maintain it. Deemphasizing the symptom is generally accompanied by a move to focus on a new symptom of another family member.

6. *Focus on a new symptom.* To decrease the family's intense preoccupation with the presenting symptom, the therapist will often introduce a new symptom (Minuchin, 1974). Introducing this new symptom can remove tremendous pressure from the identified patient and place it on other less vulnerable family members. The therapist is often successful with this technique when it is introduced as follows:

> I can certainly understand your concern about your daughter's poor study habits and difficulty in school. It will be important to deal with that issue as soon as possible. First, however, it is going to be necessary for you and your husband to come to some agreement about what are acceptable study habits for your daughter. If you two are not certain what you want, we can't expect your daughter to be able to please you.

This technique allows the therapist to strengthen the spousal subsystem in the family as the couple discusses the issue, while taking pressure off and allowing change to take place in the identified patient. This technique is effective and often quite reliable in helping families change. However, the therapist must be certain that he or she has joined successfully with the family and that sufficient data has been gathered so the new symptom presented to the family will be recognized and accepted.

Structural Modification When the therapist joins with the family, he or she intentionally becomes part of a system that seeks transformation. However, the family has developed certain rigid and ineffective ways to deal with change. By changing the emphasis on the symptoms, the therapist begins to assist the family in making structural changes. These structural changes are made through a variety of techniques (Minuchin & Fishman, 1981). Those most frequently employed are

- challenge the current family reality,
- create new subsystems and boundaries,
- block dysfunctional transactional patterns,
- reinforce new and adaptive family structures, and
- educate about family change.

These techniques will be described briefly next.

1. *Challenge the current family reality.* Families seeking therapy typically have certain rigid cognitive perceptions of the family and of reality in general. The structural family therapist will challenge those realities, not to convince the family that they are wrong but to show them there are *other ways to be right.* For instance, a family may believe that it is critical for all family members to be home for dinner. When the wife takes a job that does not allow her to be home at dinnertime, the husband may believe she does not value her marriage and family anymore.

   An alternative reality might be that the wife cares so much about her family that she is working difficult hours to help provide the necessities for comfortable living. When the family accepts a different way of thinking about the situation, structural change becomes more likely.

2. *Create new subsystems and boundaries.* This technique is a critical aspect of structural family therapy. When structure determines function and function is ineffective, then structure must

---

CASE EXAMPLE

Minuchin's Structural Family Therapy

A classic example of structural family therapy is provided by reviewing the work of Braulio Montalvo with a family of four at the Philadelphia Child Guidance Clinic. In this example, the presenting problem was a young boy who feared dogs. All of the parents' efforts to help the boy had failed. When Montalvo discovered that the boy's father was a mailman who must have extensive experience dealing with dogs, he took the mother out of the primary role with the son and instructed the father to get the boy a puppy and teach him about dogs. This classic maneuver interrupted the overinvolvement of the mother-son subsystem and established a father-son subsystem, which had previously not existed. Gradually, the boy overcame his fear of dogs. At about the same time, Montalvo discovered that the parents did not have a very solid marriage. The parents were offered the opportunity to look at the marriage in therapy and to strengthen the spousal subsystem. Through the therapy, the parents were able to help their son overcome his fear of dogs and improve their own marriage. The follow-up session confirmed that the changes had been maintained.

---

be altered if family functioning is to improve. To alter family structure, the therapist can highlight relationships in the family that are appropriate for the family's developmental stage and deemphasize subsystem relationships that may be maintaining the current family problems. Typically, the therapist will make behavioral assignments that create new subsystems and provide less opportunity for dysfunctional subsystems to continue. As family members eliminate subsystems that are no longer needed and develop new, more adaptive subsystems, family functioning should be enhanced.

3. *Block dysfunctional transaction patterns.* As the therapist works with the family in the enactment stage of treatment, dysfunctional interaction patterns will be demonstrated by family members. The therapist will note and block the repetitive

and ineffective communication patterns. This goal can be accomplished in several ways. The therapist may simply comment that the previous conversation did not seem to be helpful to the family and ask whether those involved could provide help in understanding what was accomplished.

Once dysfunctional subsystems and communication patterns are identified, the therapist makes assignments that direct other family members to monitor the dysfunctional subsystem and comment when problematic communications occur. This intervention not only alters the dysfunctional communication patterns identified but also alters the subsystem composition as observers become part of the subsystem.

4. *Reinforce new and adaptive family structure.* When the therapist has helped the family develop more effective subsystems and boundaries, these beneficial changes have to be maintained through reinforcement until they become self-reinforcing. To accomplish this, the therapist will enlist the assistance of other family members to report on how well the new subsystem has functioned during the week. In addition, the members of the new subsystems will be asked to evaluate their own performance. Through the positive reinforcement of the new behaviors, the changes made in the family structure can be supported and maintained.

5. *Educate about family change.* Joining, enactment, and restructuring the family may occur fairly rapidly in structural family therapy. However, after structural changes have been made, behavioral reinforcement may be accompanied by education for the family. At this stage of treatment, often only the husband and wife will continue in therapy. During the education phase of treatment, the couple will learn the basic principles of structural family therapy, including how and why some families are able to change and others have great difficulty. This education is designed to help the family develop the skills needed to manage the next opportunity for family growth through appropriate structural change. Some couples are satisfied and terminate therapy when structural changes have been made and family functioning improves. Others are curious about structural family therapy and elect to remain in therapy for the educational phase of treatment.

Strengths and Limitations of Structural Family Therapy

Structural family therapy has a number of strengths. The theory of change is clearly explained, and the techniques closely follow the theory. The special terminology and concepts, such as subsystems and boundaries, have broad applicability to the family therapy field. The theory recognizes the identified patient's symptoms as a manifestation of structural problems in the family. Moreover, the theory focuses on active interventions with the family system to bring about change. An impressive series of studies support the efficacy of this approach (Aponte & Van Deusen, 1981; Gurman & Kniskern, 1981b; Stanton & Todd, 1979).

Structural family therapy also has limitations. The approach may overlook individual distress in searching for problems in the family structure. It minimizes the role of affect in problem resolution. In addition, therapist directiveness may take the initiative for change away from the family and foster dependence. Finally, the use of refocusing and relabeling techniques to remove the pressure from the identified patient may be considered manipulative by some therapists.

■ Functional Family Therapy

Functional family therapy was developed by Cole Barton, James Alexander, and Bruce Parsons and has been comprehensively described in the literature (Alexander & Parsons, 1982; Barton & Alexander, 1981). These family therapists have considerable experience in using behavioral principles when working with families and have conducted important research and published extensively in behavioral family therapy (Alexander & Barton, 1976; Alexander, Barton, Schiavo, & Parsons, 1976; Barton & Alexander, 1977; Parsons & Alexander, 1973). As their ideas became more refined, they began writing about what they have now identified as functional family therapy (FFT).

The principles of FFT were refined for presentation to wider audiences (Barton & Alexander, 1981), and the theory was included in Gurman and Kniskern's (1981b) *Handbook of Family Therapy.* Functional family therapy was later presented in a textbook (Alexander & Parsons, 1982) for use in family therapist training. Since that time,

FFT has been widely accepted as an effective approach to family therapy, largely because of its clear principles and the research that has been conducted that supports the model (Alexander, 1973; Alexander et al., 1976; Alexander & Parsons, 1973; Klein, Alexander, & Parsons, 1977; Parsons & Alexander, 1973).

Philosophical Tenets and Key Theoretical Constructs

Functional family therapy is understood by its developers as an integration of systems theory and behaviorism. This integration is synergistic. FFT is not simply an eclectic blend of systems concepts and behavioral principles; rather, FFT is viewed as a clinical model that emerges from systems theory and behaviorism but is distinct from each. Barton and Alexander (1981) stated that the theory was developed to have both scientific respectability and clinical usefulness. Research studies have been conducted on the effects of FFT, and a series of clinically useful techniques and instruments have been developed to assist the clinician (Alexander & Parsons, 1982).

Functional family therapy differs markedly from most behavioral models in that FFT does not simply attempt to help people change behaviors but is designed to help family members come to understand and change their *subjective conceptual and affective states* as well as their overt behaviors. Functional family therapy not only looks at actual frequencies of behaviors but also attempts to help modify the subjective attitudes family members hold about problem behaviors.

Those who would practice FFT adopt a systems perspective and seek to understand how and why the behaviors of an individual family member make sense given the actions and attitudes of the other members of the individual's family system. Rather than attempting to determine whether the behaviors are functional or dysfunctional, the therapist seeks to understand how and why the behaviors exist and how and why the behaviors are supported and maintained by the other family members. Using FFT, the therapist does not judge whether behaviors are good or bad but only understands how they *function*—thus, the name of the theory, functional family therapy.

Two key assumptions regarding FFT emerge from this perspective. The first assumption is that behavior that may be defined as "bad" is not so defined in functional family therapy. Rather, the therapist using

FFT will seek to understand the behavior as serving a function for the individual and family system and may legitimize what has been defined by others as bad behavior. The second key assumption is that *all behavior is adaptive*. That is, behavior is not good or bad. Instead, behavior is simply a process for creating specific outcomes in interpersonal relationships. Thus, relatively novel assumptions about human behavior must be adopted to understand and treat family problems.

The functional family therapist needs to understand the behavior of individuals from a broader perspective than the therapist working only with individuals and be able to determine how that behavior makes sense given its relational context. Change occurs in FFT when family members are able to reappraise the meaning of specific behaviors in context and come to recognize the function of the behavior and that other family members are supporting the problematic behavior. Another way to understand this concept is to recognize that all family members are doing the best they can with the resources they have available to achieve their goals.

A brief example will highlight these concepts. Assume that a wife nags her husband to the point that he leaves the home. Two immediate solutions to the problem behavior would be: (1) help the wife reduce nagging, or (2) help the husband learn to deal more effectively with the wife's frustration. The functional family therapist would not necessarily move toward either solution. Rather, the therapist would seek to understand the function of the nagging and leaving behaviors. In this case, the function may be to *increase distance* between the spouses. If, in fact, the spouses need distance, are there other ways this might be accomplished? The therapist would believe that the relational outcome of distancing could be accomplished in more effective ways and would seek to help the couple learn to do so.

Main Therapeutic Interventions

To become proficient in functional family therapy and to create conditions for effective intervention, the therapist develops three distinct sets of skills:

- Conceptual skills (how to think about families)
- Technical skills (what to do with families)
- Interpersonal skills (how to apply techniques) (Alexander & Parsons, 1982).

CASE EXAMPLE

Functional Family Therapy

The Talbot family entered therapy with several concerns. Mr. and Mrs. Talbot were recently married, each for the second time. Mrs. Talbot brought her two children from the previous marriage into the home. During the courtship phase, the children seemed to like Mr. Talbot a great deal. Since the marriage, however, Scott, age 13, has been acting out and is defiant toward Mr. Talbot, who becomes angry and frustrated. When this anger and frustration is generated between Scott and Mr. Talbot, Mrs. Talbot enters the situation to defend her son, which angers Mr. Talbot further.

The therapist gained the family's trust by making an assessment and clearly identifying the sequence of behaviors that was disturbing the family. This accurate assessment was critical for developing a trusting atmosphere for the therapy. In the change phase of treatment, the therapist helped the family understand the functions of the behaviors of the three family members. Mr. Talbot wanted to be a good stepfather, which meant providing discipline. Scott felt that Mr. Talbot's attempts to discipline him were undermining his mother, who had provided effective discipline for the past seven years since the divorce. Mrs. Talbot reacted because she was afraid Mr. Talbot no longer valued her son. Therefore, she sought to defend him. As the family came to recognize the functions the problematic behaviors were serving, tension was reduced. Finally, the family entered the education phase of treatment, and members learned effective communication skills, behavior management principles, and information about issues that typical step-families confront. The family left treatment after four months greatly improved and ready to cope more effectively with problems the family situation may present in the future.

Conceptual Skills

Effective therapists need to understand the dynamics of the family's interaction to intervene successfully. To use FFT, the therapist tries to determine what will motivate the family to use identified change strategies to bring about system change. Finally, FFT is based on a distinct conceptual orientation that views the family not as harboring a patient but as a system of interacting parts behaving according to certain principles. Identifying these principles is one of the key challenges for the therapist.

Technical Skills

Technical skills are the basic tools of family therapy used to produce change (Alexander & Parsons, 1982). Techniques are designed and implemented by the therapist to produce change in four areas of family functioning:

1. Perceptions of self and others in family.
2. Specific overt problem behaviors, such as acting-out behavior.
3. Specific psychological states, such as depression and anxiety.
4. Communication among family members that maintains the above conditions.

Beginning family therapists want specific technical skills described in detail. However, functional family therapists must tailor each intervention to respond to the function performed by the behavioral patterns of the family.

Interpersonal Skills

Research completed by Alexander et al. (1976) demonstrated that certain interpersonal skills are necessary to help families change. These skills include: (1) integrated affect and behavior, (2) nonblaming, (3) demonstrating interpersonal warmth, (4) alleviating tension with humor, and (5) appropriate self-disclosure. They also discovered that these skills have little impact in helping families change unless therapists have a solid conceptual framework and well-developed technical skills (Barton & Alexander, 1981). Thus, relationship skills taught in most counseling programs are *necessary* but not *sufficient* to bring about change in client families.

The Process of Therapy in FFT

Before the family therapist can begin helping a family change its problematic behavior, the therapist must understand how the family functions and what has to be changed. Thus, the first stage of therapy is the *assessment* stage. In functional family therapy, the focus is on the function the behavioral sequences serve. Is the behavior creating distance? Is it creating closeness? Or is it regulating distance and closeness among family members? Many functional family therapists view "distance regulation" between family members as one of the key functions of problematic behaviors.

To determine the function, the therapist gathers information from the family. First, the therapist discovers what the family says is occurring. At the same time, the therapist observes the interactions between and among family members to develop an understanding of how the family works and how their behaviors function to regulate intimacy in the family. When the therapist has gathered this information from the family, themes will become evident and important functions of the problematic behaviors can be determined.

Gathering data to make this assessment may present problems for the beginning family therapist if the family is not enacting its usual behaviors in the session. When the family is not providing the necessary information for an assessment, the therapist may use the following three techniques.

1. *The therapist may reflect back to the family* a behavioral sequence that was noted and ask each family member to comment on the sequence. The various perceptions of the family members regarding the sequence may open the door for further data gathering.
2. *The therapist may use the feelings or thoughts of family members* to facilitate discussion. This technique is useful when the therapist is able to pinpoint the feelings of one family member and reflect those feelings back to that member and at the same time observe and comment on the reactions of other family members.
3. *The therapist may focus on key relationships in the family* as a vehicle to gain additional information about the family. In this technique, the therapist deemphasizes the content and affect of what is said and emphasizes the recognized relationship

between the parties involved. As the therapist communicates an understanding of the importance of key relationships in the family, the family becomes more trusting and willing to provide more information for the assessment.

The second phase of therapy is designed to *institute change in the family system.* This phase of therapy is directed toward developing specific interventions to help the family change thoughts, feelings, and behaviors surrounding key family functions identified in the assessment phase of therapy. Specific techniques that may be used in this phase of therapy are:

- Asking questions to clarify relationship dynamics.
- Interrelating the thoughts, feelings, and behaviors of one family member to the thoughts, feelings, and behaviors of other members.
- Offering interpretations of the function of the behaviors of family members.
- Relabeling behavior in a way that removes blame from individual family members.
- Directly discussing the impact that the removal of symptomatic behavior will have on family functioning, as the dysfunctional behavior in one member may serve to stabilize the family by directing attention away from a more critical issue.
- Shifting the focus of treatment from the identified patient to another family member (Alexander & Parsons, 1982).

Each of these specific techniques can serve to help family members think about the family differently, behave differently, and communicate more effectively.

The third phase of therapy is *maintaining change through education.* This phase of treatment begins when family hostility is reduced through the techniques presented previously. Education provides the family with the skills to resolve future issues that may arise. Specifically, during this phase of family therapy, members are taught effective communication skills, behavior management and contracting skills, and other team-building techniques. This phase is especially critical because it is here that families learn skills needed to resolve problems that will inevitably arise in the future.

Strengths and Limitations of FFT

Functional family therapy has a solid base in research and recognizes that all behaviors serve a function. The approach identifies specific therapist interpersonal qualities that are necessary but not sufficient for effective therapy. Moreover, the approach focuses on specific client behaviors and understanding them from a systems perspective.

Functional family therapy is limited in that it may underestimate the intrapsychic function of affect in favor of a systemic interpretation. In addition, it may focus too specifically on overt behavior and not attend sufficiently to cognition and affect. Another danger is that the assessment phase of treatment may distance the family from the therapist. Finally, the approach does not take a stand on the moral value of negative behaviors, such as robbery, because all behavior is viewed as being functional in its context.

▦ *The MRI Approach to Brief Therapy*

In their classic text *The Tactics of Change: Doing Therapy Briefly,* Fisch, Weakland, and Segal (1982) are careful to define the brief therapy approach of the Mental Research Institute (MRI) of Palo Alto, California, as a theoretically complete model for the treatment of a wide range of human problems. They encourage their students not to confuse the MRI approach to treatment with brief crisis intervention or shortened versions of long-term approaches to therapy, made briefer by a lack of time, resources, personnel, or patient finances. MRI brief therapy is an explicit and comprehensive theory that employs innovative techniques for change and focuses treatment on the main presenting problem. Gurman and Kniskern (1991) remind us that "it is essential to keep in mind the distinction between the MRI's Brief Therapy and 'brief therapy' as a much more general reference to a style of practice that includes such diverse forms as brief psychodynamic therapy and brief cognitive therapy" (p. 173).

The history of the Mental Research Institute is closely linked with the application of *cybernetics,* the study of self-regulation to social systems. Famous names in the history of family therapy played a part in the evolution of brief therapy. Gregory Bateson, Don Jackson, Jay Haley, and John Weakland (1971) pioneered the *double-bind theory* of schizophrenia. Moreover, Haley, Jackson, Satir, Weakland, and colleagues studied the effects of *communication* and *paradox* in families (Segal, 1991). Also participating in the development of the MRI model were Milton Erickson, Richard Fisch, Paul Watzlowick, and Heinz Von Foerester. Each of these pioneers "contributed to the understanding of disturbed behavior as a function of an interpersonal system rather than an intrapsychic one, wedding cybernetic epistemology to psychiatry" (Segal, 1991, p. 173).

Philosophical Tenets and Key Theoretical Constraints

The relationship between the theory and practice of brief therapy is critical in that embedded within the theory are the views and premises the therapist holds that govern the identification and description of psychological problems. Moreover, theory will influence what information provided by the client will become the focus of attention and what information will not be the focus. Additionally, theory will predicate what the therapist will and will not do in the treatment of the client and will determine who participates in treatment.

The brief therapist views theory as a map to help treat client problems. Theory is designed to help the therapist move from place to place; for instance, encountering a client's problem and moving to resolution of that problem. Theory should serve as a guide to treatment, as it may be useful in clarifying obstacles encountered in working with human problems. But it is important to remember that theory is only a map, and a map is not the territory. Theory, while quite important, should not become dogma and should never "shortcut" good common sense (Fisch, Weakland, & Segal, 1982).

Defining the Problem

Clearly, defining the problem is critical to successful implementation of brief therapy. According to Segal (1991), a problem is defined in the following ways:

- the client reports experiencing pain and distress,
- the pain/distress is attributed to the behaviors of self or others,
- the client has been trying to change this painful behavior, and
- the client has been unsuccessful at changing.

The client may be an individual or several members of a family. This approach focuses on problem solving and may involve one or several clients. The brief therapist assumes that the complaint is the problem and not the symptom of an underlying pathology. Thus, the goal of brief therapy is to identify and reduce or eliminate the client's pain. The goal may be achieved if the client's behavior changes or the behavior is no longer troubling to the client. Thus, the therapist is responsible for identifying the goals of therapy. Most frequently, the goals of therapist and client overlap, however, in this model it is the therapist who determines what will be useful for the client in bringing about change (Segal, 1991).

How Problems Develop and Persist

Problems result from ineffective handling of ordinary life difficulties. Brief therapy is clear on the point that problems result when behavior deviates from what is desired and that repeated attempts to return behavior to its normal state have failed. In many instances, these attempts to return behavior to its normal state actually make the problem worse. For example, a parent tells her son to go to sleep so he will be well-rested for school. The son refuses to be directed and stays awake. The more the mother attempts to solve the problem by directing him to go to sleep, the more awake the son becomes and the less sleep he gets. In this situation, trying to force the son to rest actually makes him less sleepy, and he gets even less rest. The mother's attempted solution to the problem has made the problem worse.

Segal (1991) describes four clear patterns of mishandling problems:

- forcing correction when normal life difficulties will self-correct,
- seeking a no-risk solution when normal risk is involved,
- insisting on discussion to resolve a dispute when discussion exacerbates the problem, and
- confirming the accuser's suspicion by defending oneself.

An example of forcing correction when it is inappropriate might occur when a student has a writing block over a certain assignment. The more she forces herself to write, the more overwhelming the project becomes. Forcing correction causes an ordinary difficulty to become a serious problem.

An example of seeking a no-risk solution occurs when a shy man works diligently to perfect his opening remarks to a women he wants to meet rather than allowing the conversation to develop naturally. The harder he tries to eliminate risk, the more likely he will be to become tongue-tied and interact inappropriately.

An example of insisting on discussion occurs when a husband and wife are in disagreement. It seems logical that they should talk out the disagreement, but the discussion leads to increased hostility and resentment.

An example of confirming the accuser's suspicions occurs when a teenager accuses his parents of meddling in his affairs and separates himself from the family. Without family support, he becomes depressed and withdrawn. Then the concerned parents attempt to be helpful by talking with their child, and this confirms his position that they are meddlesome.

In summary, two key assumptions underlie brief therapy. First, problems persist only if they are maintained by the actions of the client and other members of the client's family system. The problem will be resolved if those behaviors that maintain the problem are changed or eliminated.

Main Therapeutic Interventions

Segal (1991) operationalizes brief therapy as a series of tasks to be accomplished leading to client improvement. The tasks are:

- identify the family members who are motivated for treatment and arrange for them to attend the initial interview,
- collect specific data about the problem and the ways the family has tried to solve the problem (what has *not* worked in the past),
- set a specific goal for therapy,
- develop a plan to create change in the presenting problem,
- intervene in ways that interrupt the ineffective attempted solutions,
- assess outcome of treatment, and
- terminate.

In the beginning stages of treatment the therapist will notice that the family members take *positions* on such issues as why the problem

CASE EXAMPLE

MRI Approach to Brief Family Therapy

The first author of this text (Fenell) worked with a family who complained that their son was rebellious because he did not go to bed when instructed and, in fact, turned the light on in his room and read Hardy Boys mysteries into the night. All attempts to correct the behavior with verbal warnings and restrictions failed. The parents were becoming increasingly angry and coercive, to no avail. The parents framed the problem (and took the position) that they had a rebellious child who did not respect his parents. The couple was asked what small goal might indicate that things were getting back to normal. They reported that they would like to see their son getting more sleep. The presenting problem was reframed by the therapist. He described the "acting-out" son as a seemingly intelligent young man who loved to read (a positive) and was able to function well with very little sleep (another positive). The parents accepted this reframe because it was "true." It described the original situation with the same facts in a way that portrayed the son's behaviors in positive and different ways. The parents accepted the reframe and the accompanying 180° reversal solution. They were to tell their son each night that they appreciated his intelligence and interest in reading and his ability to function on so little sleep. Further, they were to tell him they trusted him to turn his light off and go to sleep when he was tired.

When the couple returned for the second session, they reported that they had employed the new solution each night for a week. For the first two nights, the boy read into the wee hours, but beginning with the third night, he turned his light out earlier and earlier. In fact, after one week of implementing the new solution, the parents felt the problem was solved.

exists, which family members are helpful and which are not, why the problem is not being resolved, and often times, what the therapist must do to help. The therapist should note these positions and confirm that he or she understands them as well. However, it is critical in this approach for the therapist to maintain *therapeutic maneuverability*. The therapist needs the freedom to intervene in ways that are most helpful for the family and will resolve the presenting problem. If the therapist accepts the positions of the clients, which have not been helpful in bringing about change, the therapist is being compromised and will not have the freedom to maneuver in ways that may be helpful to the family (Fisch, Weakland, & Segal, 1982; Segal, 1991).

Therapy begins with the first phone contact. The therapist attempts to determine if the client is a *customer,* who is genuinely seeking help, or a *window shopper,* who enters therapy at someone else's direction and may not be motivated to change. The brief therapist wants to meet with the family members who are motivated to change. This may mean that the identified patient who does not want treatment will not be seen in the initial interview. Moreover, the identified patient may never enter treatment, but change may still occur as other family members identify their ineffective solutions to the problem and develop new and more effective ones.

Several specific techniques have been developed to bring about change with brief therapy. The most important technique is to understand that the problem is maintained by ineffective attempts to resolve it. The therapist's key function is to help the family implement new solutions.

A second technique is to develop with the family an achievable goal. This goal may not be total change in the problem but a step in the right direction. Segal (1991) manages this therapeutic task by structuring the goal setting in this way: "Since we only have 10 sessions, we need to define a goal of treatment that would tell us you are beginning to solve the problem. You're not completely out of the woods, so to speak, but you'll have found a trail and can find your way on your own. So, what would be the smallest, concrete, significant indicator of this?" (p. 182). Brief therapy is time limited, thus a concrete, achievable goal must be set. Once the family has achieved the goal, therapy is terminated with the expectation that they will continue to implement their new solutions to the old problem and experience relief as a result.

A third technique is for the therapist to avoid the minefield. Avoiding the minefield means that the therapist does not accept the family members' positions and is able to avoid "more of the same" solutions to the problem. If the therapist accepts family members' positions and gives directives that are similar (more of the same) to those already in place, change will not occur, and the problem may be exacerbated. For example, if a family is seeking help in having their son be more involved in family activities, a therapist would be in the minefield with any directive that attempted to command the son to be more involved.

A fourth technique is to seek a 180° shift or U-turn away from the attempted solution and implement a new solution (Fisch, Weakland, & Segal, 1982). In the example above, a 180° shift would be to direct the family to encourage the son to develop autonomy and independence. In so doing, the family could feel good about helping their son develop independence, and the son may well respond by spending more time with a supportive rather than a controlling family. Implementing this 180° shift with the family is often difficult. Such a shift often creates a solution that is counterintuitive to the family and makes no logical sense. "How can we get closer to our son by encouraging him to be distant?" they might wonder.

At this point, clients will need help in performing therapist-initiated directives that appear counterintuitive (Segal, 1991), so the therapist employs a key technique called *reframing*. Reframing is a technique defined by Watzlawick et al. (1974) that "changes the conceptual and/or emotional setting or viewpoint in relation to which a situation is experienced and places it in another frame which fits the 'facts' of the same concrete situation equally well or even better, and thereby changes its entire meaning" (p. 95). For example, the first author of this text (Fenell) worked with a client who insisted that she was powerless to improve her marriage. She complained that no matter what she did to improve her marriage it didn't work because her husband refused to look at his dysfunctional family of origin and his previous problematic marriage.

The more she tried to get him to "do his therapy," the more he resisted. She was extremely angry and depressed. The client believed she was working to improve her marriage by insisting that her husband do family-of-origin work. The therapist reframed the situation as the client's attempt to make it difficult for her husband to demonstrate his unique attempts to improve the marriage by only recognizing one way for him to demonstrate his desire to improve the relationship. The client was surprised and shocked by this reframe and claimed she had no desire to create difficulties for her husband. Thus, she was able to accept the directive that she refrain from trying to make the marriage better for a few weeks "to see what happens." After several weeks of implementing this new solution, the client reported she was less angry and depressed and that her husband seemed to be trying new ways to respond to her needs. In this situation, the reframe worked because it used the same information the client reported and placed it in a different context (trying to improve her marriage was reframed as creating difficulties for her husband). The technique of reframing is essential to prepare the client to accept the 180° shift in the attempted solution.

Brief therapy employs a set of techniques that are considered paradoxical. The 180° solution may be considered an example of *paradox*. Change is created by directing the family to engage in solutions that seem the opposite of what should be helpful. Other examples of paradox include the directive to engage in more of the symptomatic behavior or to engage in it at a specific time. This is called *symptom prescription* and is effective for two reasons. First, if the client follows the directive and increases symptomatic behavior intentionally, he is controlling the symptom. If he can increase the frequency of the symptom, he can also use this control to decrease the frequency of the symptom. Second, if the client resists the directive, as many clients do, and does not increase symptomatic behavior, the symptoms are decreased.

Other paradoxical techniques include the directive to the client to go slowly in changing (Fisch, Weakland, & Segal, 1982). This is known as *restraining change*. This is simply another 180° shift for a client who has been desperately attempting to create change. By going slowly, the client's anxiety may be reduced, and other directives for change may be employed more carefully and with more consideration. Conversely, if the client is not progressing rapidly and is experiencing discouragement, the therapist's directive to go slowly will support the gradual change that may be about to occur or is in the process of occurring. Moreover, the therapist should be prepared to *predict relapse* so clients are prepared to deal with setbacks and do not view these setbacks as failure.

Segal (1991) warns that beginners must not erroneously assume that paradox is the essence of brief therapy. It is more important to understand the usefulness and power of the 180° shift in the attempted solution to the problem and learn to develop and implement effective reframing techniques to support this new solution.

Segal (1991) suggests that termination of therapy occurs when "(1) a small, but significant, change has been made in the problem; (2) the change appears to be durable; and (3) the patient implies or states an ability to handle things without the therapist" (p. 189). The therapist should ensure that the clients feel responsible for making the change rather than crediting the therapist with changing them. It is also important to remind the clients that relapse may occur but that they have the tools to handle future problems. If clients resist termination, the therapist may frame the termination as a temporary break from therapy while the clients consolidate their learning (Segal, 1991).

Strengths and Limitations of Brief Therapy

The MRI approach to brief therapy has several strengths. The most notable is that problem resolution frequently occurs quite rapidly. Additionally, this approach specifically identifies and attempts to change the pattern of ineffective attempted solutions to the problem. As families learn to employ unique and sometime counterintuitive solutions to their problems, rapid change is possible. Finally, brief therapy does not look at individuals as mentally ill. The model looks at problems as the result of ineffective attempts to manage them.

There are several limitations to the approach. Brief therapy is criticized because it does not look at historical aspects of the problem and therefore only focuses on symptoms, not their cause. Others criticize the approach for its use of paradoxical techniques, which they claim are not genuine and are often manipulative.

▇ Summary

In this chapter, we have described three family systems approaches with their roots in cognitive/behavioral theory. Structural family therapy, functional family therapy, and brief therapy seek to help families understand their behavior and employ powerful change techniques to help families function more effectively. All three approaches are readily understood by beginning family therapists because the principles of each theory are clearly explained and the change techniques closely follow the theory. In the next two chapters, we examine individual and systems-based theories with humanistic/existential bases.

SUGGESTED READINGS

Alexander, J., & Parsons, B. V. (1982). *Functional Family Therapy.* Pacific Grove, CA: Brooks/Cole.

Barton, C., & Alexander, J. F. (1981). "Functional Family Therapy." In A. S. Gurman & D. P. Kniskern, eds., *Handbook of Family Therapy.* New York: Brunner/Mazel.

Fisch, R., Weakland, J. H., & Segal, L. (1982). *The Tactics of Change: Doing Therapy Briefly.* San Francisco: Jossey-Bass.

Haley, J. (1976). *Problem Solving Therapy.* San Francisco: Jossey-Bass.

Minuchin, S. (1974). *Families and Family Therapy.* Cambridge, MA: Harvard University Press.

Minuchin, S., & Fishman, C. (1981). *Family Therapy Techniques.* Cambridge, MA: Harvard University Press.

Watzlawick, P., Weakland, J., & Fisch, R. (1974). *Change: Principles of Problem Formation and Problem Resolution.* New York: Norton.

Humanistic, Existential, and Transpersonal Theories in Family Treatment

In this chapter we discuss the application of four humanistic/existential/transpersonal approaches to family therapy: (1) the person-centered approach of Carl Rogers, (2) a Gestalt approach to family therapy developed by Walter Kempler, (3) the psychodrama approach of J. L. Moreno, and (4) transpersonal approaches to family therapy developed by several therapists. These approaches have similar philosophical roots and a common focus on subjective states of being.

Human capacities
Self-awareness
Self-actualization
Self-determination
Subjective experience
Existential death
Search for meaning
Autonomy
Karma
Oneness

Existential aloneness
Phenomenological view
Catharsis
Reflection of content/feelings
Self-disclosure
Unfinished business
Role playing
Family sculpture
Namaste
Universal laws

QUESTIONS FOR DISCUSSION

1. How would a person-centered family therapist communicate unconditional positive regard to a family?

2. What ethical issues might be raised by using a person-centered approach in family therapy?

3. How might a therapist deal with a family member who doesn't want (or is afraid) to take part in an empty-chair Gestalt experiment?

4. How might a Gestalt-oriented family therapist deal with a family member who is avoiding personal responsibility?

5. How might a psychodrama-oriented therapist deal with a family member who is a drug user?

6. What are some of the possible psychological risks associated with using psychodrama techniques with a family?

7. What are the characteristics of someone who has reached the level of self-transcendence on Maslow's hierarchy of needs?

8. What techniques would a transpersonal family therapist use to work with an addictive family?

Humanistic, existential, and transpersonal theories were relegated to separate schools of thought in the past, but because of the similarities of the philosophical underpinnings and a common focus on subjective states of being, they now are often referred to together. In this chapter, we present these theories together as the humanistic/existential/transpersonal approaches. Leaders of this movement include Rollo May, Carl Rogers, Abraham Maslow, James Bugenthal, Viktor Frankl, and philosophers Martin Buber and Jean-Paul Sartre, Carl Jung, Arnold Mindell, and Gay Hendricks.

Because of their common philosophical position, humanistic/existential/ transpersonal therapists can utilize diverse methods to work with families—including cognitive, behavioral, and action-oriented methods. Generally regarded as the "third force" in psychology, the humanistic/existential/ transpersonal approaches to therapy tend to be largely experiential and relationship-centered.

Humanistic/existential/transpersonal theorists argue that human behavior cannot be understood by objective and cognitive methods. For example, a therapist utilizing a humanistic/existential/transpersonal approach with a family that seems to be dealing with conflicts in destructive and self-defeating ways might structure the first session by saying:

> I understand that you have come to therapy because you are not able to resolve the conflicts in your family. I'm pleased that you care enough about yourselves and your family to come to therapy in hopes of finding some solutions to your dilemma. A place to begin the search for solutions is to first see what each of you thinks and feels about the problem. As each of you describes your view of the problem, I want the rest of the family members to listen carefully to what this person is saying rather than thinking of how you will defend or justify your position. Also, each of you might add something about how you would like your family to be different as a result of counseling.

This initial session is designed to have each family member share his or her subjective or phenomenological world. Sharing this world with other family members and the therapist has a therapeutic effect on everybody present, particularly if everyone is really listening to each other.

The four main therapeutic approaches to family therapy covered in this chapter are: (1) the person-centered approach, (2) a Gestalt-oriented approach, (3) a psychodrama-oriented approach, and (4) transpersonal approaches.

Goals of Humanistic/Existential/ Transpersonal Approaches

The basic goal of humanistic/existential/transpersonal approaches is to increase the clients' awareness of their options and potentials as well as to help them make choices and decisions (Watson, 1977). Another goal is to increase autonomy and self-actualization. Rather than to help clients merely adjust to societal norms, they are encouraged to discover how they want to live their lives. Helping clients to accept their own freedom to change and grow along with helping them to accept responsibility for their own existence are other important goals. Because anxiety and uncertainty often accompany the acceptance of freedom and responsibility, another goal of the approach is to help clients face and deal with these anxieties.

The Process of Humanistic/Existential/ Transpersonal Approaches

The helping process in family therapy focuses on what happens *within* individual members and also what happens *between* family members. A brief description of the usual process of family therapy, using a humanistic/existential/transpersonal framework, is as follows.

1. *Milling around.* At first, clients are confused and uncertain about the purpose of the therapy. They ask, "Why are we here? What is going to happen?"
2. *Resisting therapy.* Family members are resistant to share their thoughts and feelings. They wonder if it is safe to do so.

3. *Talking about the past.* Members describe past happenings and their feelings about these events. They are focused on the "there and then."

4. *Negative feelings.* Members begin to share their present negative feelings toward each other or the therapist. They may be testing the safety of the therapy situation. They ask themselves, "Is it safe to be me, even the negative me?"

5. *Expressing and exploring personally relevant issues.* At this stage there is enough trust to permit open expression and exploration of personally relevant material. Family members begin to feel as if they can help change the family to work toward what they want it to be.

6. *Fully expressing feelings in the here and now.* Members express moment-to-moment feelings toward one another. Changes in the family structure begin to take place.

7. *Healing capacity of family members.* Family members begin to turn their attention to helping each other heal the pain and suffering of others in the family. A climate of trust and freedom allows for acceptance and understanding to emerge.

8. *Self-acceptance and change.* Family members begin to accept themselves as they are in the family and as changes in the family take place. Members take responsibility for their actions and are in control of changing their behavior.

9. *Fading facades.* A sense of realness develops among family members, and this becomes a norm. Those who are less real or defensive are challenged to come out with their true feelings and thoughts.

10. *Feedback.* Family members get and give feedback to each other. They even request feedback so they can grow more.

11. *Confrontation.* Any remaining defensiveness is confronted as members drop their politeness and protectiveness. They see each other as being able to deal with confrontation.

12. *Developing the helping family.* By now, reports of helping interactions outside of therapy are common. Family members are more consistently acting as helping agents for each other.

13. *The family encounter.* The family begins to experience itself as a unit, or as a group of interdependent members. Change in one member affects all other members. A family bond develops and is felt by all members.

14. *Fuller expression of closeness.* Family members have warm and genuine feelings toward each other. They have learned to listen to and accept each other's feelings. Disputes are now resolved with less conflict and anxiety.
15. *A changed family.* The members now experience both oneness and separateness in their interactions with each other. They have learned a process by which they can continue to explore and clarify values, examine and make decisions, and challenge issues that come up in the family. They are able to be as open with each other daily as they once were only in therapy sessions (Thayer, 1991).

Advantages and Limitations of the Humanistic/Existential/Transpersonal Approaches

Much has been written to support these approaches. Among the advantages of the overall philosophy are that:

1. It empowers people to take responsibility for their actions and provides a framework for understanding universal human concerns.
2. It presents the positive, hopeful view that humans can continually actualize themselves and reach their potential, and that families have the potential to resolve many of their own problems.
3. It has contributed much to understanding the essential ingredients of the therapeutic relationship.
4. Because the theory emphasizes that techniques should follow understanding, the danger of abusing the techniques is lessened.

The humanistic/existential/transpersonal approach does have several limitations.

1. It uses abstract concepts and language that many clients find difficult to understand.
2. Long-term therapy may be required to complete the process.
3. The theory does not work as well with families that are in crisis.

4. It may focus too much attention on individual development at the expense of family dynamics.
5. There are no set standards for training family therapists to use this approach, leading to wide variance in expertise and training.

Person-Centered Family Therapy

Rogers (1961) discussed the implications of using person-centered therapy with families mostly by translating the principles of individual person-centered therapy to family therapy situations. The approach fits rather naturally with family therapy because of its emphasis on developing effective close relationships (Rogers, 1961). Yet, to most effectively employ the person-centered approach with families requires an expansion of traditional person-centered theory (Anderson, 1989). Rogers theorized that family members will become more trusting of each other if the therapist is able to create the right climate in the therapy sessions. The basic conditions he listed for this climate to develop are genuineness, openness, caring, acceptance, positive regard, and reflective listening.

Some of his followers (Levant, 1978; Van der Veen, 1977) have made advances in the practice of person-centered family therapy. While the *self-concept* is at the heart of person-centered therapy for individuals, the *family concept* is at the heart of person-centered family therapy (Raskin & Van der Veen, 1970). The term *family concept* describes the feelings, attitudes, and expectations a person has toward his or her family of origin and present family. This relatively stable concept organizes and influences much of a person's behavior. According to this theory, for a family to change, the members have to change their family concept.

Philosophical Tenets

Rogers and other person-centered family therapists adopted a *phenomenological view* of human nature. According to this view, the most important source of knowledge (epistemology) is the individual's *experience.* The view does not concentrate on the object of experience or the subject of experience but instead on the point of contact between being and consciousness, which includes both subject and object. The person experiences both the object and the self at the same time, although the focus is usually on one or the other (self or object). In practical terms, a phenomenological approach examines inner space and the client's subjective experience. Understanding and empathizing with clients' views of their experiences is the therapist's best source of knowledge about a client and his or her problems.

According to this approach, the source of reality (ontology) is an individual's subjective perspective of that reality. But there are differences between a purely existential view and a purely humanistic one. The existential position, as stated by Sartre, says that although we learn of our essence through our existence, that essence is largely unknowable. The humanistic view, which is more phenomenological, says that our perception of our essential nature is what we use to guide our behavior. The humanistic theorists are more concerned with discovering this perception than with finding the ultimate truth.

The source of values (axiology), according to this approach, is a set of universal principles that cannot be totally known but is reflected somewhat in the consciousness of each individual. People are seen as essentially good, and as they become more aware or conscious, they are better able to live a life based on these values. Counseling is seen as a way to increase consciousness and allow this natural outcome to emerge.

Theoretical Constructs

Two relevant theoretical constructs are the theory of cause and the theory of change.

Theory of Cause

According to the person-centered approach, people develop emotional problems because they are unable to communicate what they think and feel with others, usually because of fear of punishment or rejection. This fear is a learned adaptation to the way they were treated as a child. They withdraw from people and the world. The most common family problems that person-centered family therapy is best designed to deal with are (Thayer, 1991):

- Lack of realness in dealing with other family members.
- Denial or lack of expression of important feelings in the family.

- Failing to see the individuality of each family member.
- Failing to listen to others or to have much two-way communication in the family.
- Lack of a method or process through which the family can resolve conflicts as they arise. For example, most families have no way to discuss differences in values.
- Lack of awareness of social and cultural effects. These effects include the demands of career, education, peers, television, wars, and world events. Does the family become a dumping ground for frustrations that arise in these other areas? (Thayer, 1991).

Theory of Change

The person-centered therapist sees the individual and the family, rather than the therapist, as the agent of change. The role of the therapist is to create the proper conditions for the untapped potential of the individual and the family to be explored and integrated (Gaylin, 1989). Rogers (1980) believed that individuals have within themselves vast resources for self-understanding and for altering their self-concept, basic attitudes, and self-directed behavior; and these resources can be tapped if a definable climate of facilitative psychological attitudes can be provided. The most important facilitative attitudes, according to Rogers (1961), are *genuineness, empathy*, and *unconditional positive regard.* The therapist teaches these qualities through modeling and helps release untapped qualities in the family members.

Genuineness is a necessary prerequisite to building relationships with family members. Otherwise, they are not likely to let the therapist into their inner family system. Also, genuine responses to the pain or grief of family members can have a powerful effect on the family system. Empathy, when used in family therapy, helps the therapist understand the subtleties of meaning and feelings that family members experience in their relationships with others, rather than just understanding each individual's inner world. Giving unconditional positive regard to family members can be empowering and often helps them feel safe enough to release long-held feelings.

Main Therapeutic Interventions

The basic attitudes mentioned above, plus the following communication skills, are seen as necessary and sufficient for a person-centered therapist. The role of the therapist is to model and thereby teach family members how to utilize these skills.

- *Being attentive* is a way of deepening the therapist's contact with the client (Thayer, 1991). Attending verbal and nonverbal skills are necessary if the therapist wishes to follow the process of the family dynamics.
- *Reflection of content* communicates respect and assures family members that the therapist is really trying to understand their perceptions of the family situation.

CASE EXAMPLE

Person-Centered Therapy

Bob and Joan have been married 6 years. They came to therapy because they were "not getting along with each other." Neither seems to know why, and neither seems to know what to do about it. Using a person-centered approach, the therapist decided to build a relationship with each of them and, in the process, hoped to teach them how to get along with each other. The therapist started with Bob and began by talking to Bob about his job and his interests outside of the relationship with Joan. This formed a good foundation for the breakthrough, which began when the therapist was talking to Joan.

Therapist: Tell me more about your fear of Bob leaving you.

Joan: I'm having another feeling right now, and I think I'm going to cry.

Therapist: You're feeling touched because of what I asked you.

Joan: Yes, it suddenly dawned on me that you really care what happens to me. I don't know if it was what you said so much as it was the way you said it. There was real caring in your voice.

Therapist: Sounds as though you experienced a deep sense of being cared for, something you need very much, and perhaps you are realizing for the first time how much you miss that.

Joan: I think I've wanted Bob to care about me more than he seems to. I didn't know that was behind my loneliness.

(continued)

- *Reflection of feelings* is crucial in communicating empathy and requires the therapist to pay close attention to verbal and nonverbal behavior. Therapists also need to *confront* discrepancies between verbal and nonverbal messages.

- *Self-disclosure* is utilized to model effective communication and is usually a response to something that happens in the moment. For example: "When you say that to John and look away, I feel sad and wonder why you don't look at him when you tell him things that are important to you."

(CASE EXAMPLE continued)

      Bob: *I can see what you mean. I, too, felt the caring in his voice. I do care for you, Joan, but I don't know how to tell you. Please help me.*

    Joan: *You just did. I felt it in my body just now. Usually I'm not open to you this way. I'm guarded when you talk to me, always afraid you're going to tell me I've done something wrong. (long pause)*

Therapist: *Joan, you opened yourself to me and stayed open to what Bob said to you, and our words touched a place deep within you where you have hidden this tender, somewhat fragile need of yours. I'm glad you trusted us enough to let us in. I have warm feelings toward you right now. Bob, how are you feeling toward Joan right now?*

      Bob: *I'm feeling lots of love and compassion. I didn't know you [Joan] felt that way. I think I sensed your fear, and not knowing what it was, I held back saying things to you.*

The relationship the therapist built with each of the clients helped both to lower their barriers to intimacy with each other. By helping family members experience a positive relationship with the therapist, they learn skills to build better relationships with each other.

- *Showing respect* is a skill that person-centered therapists use to demonstrate caring and concern for family members.
- Utilizing *intuitive hunches* is another important therapeutic skill (Thayer, 1991). The therapist has to utilize all of his or her senses and share these "gut reactions" and hunches with family members. Intuitive feelings often help family members reach deeper levels of awareness and growth.

O'Leary (1989) identified the complex role of the person-centered family therapist as twofold.

1. The therapist has to be able to respond to the individual meanings of each family member.
2. The therapist must be able to assess and respond to the objective reality of the family's interactional patterns.

Skills that the person-centered therapist generally does not utilize include *questioning*, which often implies leading and directing, and *interpretation*. The main goals are to reflect and model, leaving the interpretation to each family member.

Limitations of Person-Centered Family Therapy

This approach may work well in the beginning with a family that fears and resists therapy, but it often has to be coupled with other, more action-oriented approaches for significant changes in the family structure to take place. The attitudes and skills required for a person-centered approach are necessary but may not be sufficient to produce lasting change in most family systems.

A second limitation of the approach is that it requires the therapist to be able to tolerate loose structure and ambiguity. This may raise the anxiety of family members more than they can tolerate and also may raise the therapist's anxiety.

Third, being mostly reflectors or mirrors, therapists frequently remain hidden as persons. Thus, therapists can easily become outer-directed and remain cut off from their own feelings and reactions.

In their efforts not to structure the family interview person-centered family therapists often do not provide adequate screening protection or preparation for family members. Sometimes one or more family members are not ready for family therapy or need protection or preparation to make the best use of family therapy. Ethically, family therapists have to prepare people for the possible life changes that might occur and the risks involved. The therapist also must structure the therapy situation to protect weak or defenseless family members.

Finally, some practitioners object to the lack of formal certification or academic training of many person-centered family therapists. The use of minimally trained therapists is supported by research (Carkhuff, 1969b), but this lack of extensive training has led to some other highly trained professionals' reluctance to accept this approach.

Gestalt-Oriented Family Therapy

Nothing in Gestalt-oriented family therapy can be considered original. It is an updated version of what has been known throughout human history. The story of Adam and Eve is based on the same principle of self-awareness that the Gestalt approach uses. It also is seen in Socrates' admonition "Know thyself." Today, the philosophy of Gestalt-oriented family therapy is that direct knowledge of the self is the key to good mental health (Kempler, 1991).

Leaders of this approach are Fritz Perls, James Simkin, Walter Kempler, Irving and Miriam Polster, and Joseph Zinker. Kempler broke away from Perls because he objected to Perls' "one-up, hot seat" approach, in which Perls would frustrate, confront, and confuse clients deliberately to produce behavior change. Kempler believed that Perls kept himself "one-up" and personally removed from the therapy situation and that the therapist should be more personally involved in the therapy as a participant and should share personal thoughts and feelings with clients. Perls did little family therapy or even group therapy.

Gestalt therapy is usually practiced as a one-to-one model of therapy. In 1961, Kempler founded the Kempler Institute for the Development of the Family, near Los Angeles, and continued to focus primarily on family therapy. Besides Kempler's (1965, 1968, 1981, 1991) pioneering works, only a handful of books in the literature deal with Gestalt-oriented family therapy. These include Bauer (1979), Goulding and Goulding (1979), Hatcher (1978, 1981), Kaplan and Kaplan (1978), and Rabin (1980).

The goals of Gestalt-oriented family therapy are:

1. To help individuals within a family structure develop better boundaries between themselves and other family members.
2. To help individuals become more self-aware so they can complete unfinished business and change old, familiar patterns.

There is an attempt to balance individual intrapsychic problems with interpersonal problems that show up in the family interactions. Both types of problems are dealt with in Gestalt-oriented family therapy, so there often is much shifting back and forth from a focus on the individual to a focus on the family.

Philosophical Tenets

Although Gestalt psychology is also a phenomenological approach, it has epistemological differences with person-centered approach. Perls, who was influenced by psychoanalytic theory, placed much more emphasis on the inner or intrapersonal sources of knowledge than the outer or interpersonal sources of knowledge emphasized by the person-centered approach. Both theories share an emphasis on the importance of the phenomenological field of perceptions.

Perls borrowed heavily from an existential framework. His most significant contribution is a focus on the here-and-now, which is existential in nature, as is his belief that people are essentially responsible for their own conflicts and have the capacity to resolve them. He postulated that all unresolved conflicts from our past are with us in the here-and-now and therefore are resolvable in the present situation. Talking about something that happened in the past puts the person in an observer's role removed from the conflict situation; acting it out in the present brings the elements of the original conflict to life.

This approach views awareness as being good and potentially creative in itself. Universal human values are believed to be good, and the more aware people are of their so-called *unfinished business*, the closer they come to these universal values. Gestalt therapy clearly does not try to help people adjust to a set of social values, which are viewed as transitory ways to stay unaware. One of the universal values is to become unified and whole as a person. The Gestalt therapist sees *awareness* as the path to this value. With awareness, people can recognize, face, and reintegrate parts of themselves they have disowned and thus become more unified and whole (Corey, 2000).

Theoretical Constructs

Theoretical constructs include the theory of cause and the theory of change.

Theory of Cause

Gestalt-oriented family therapy is based on the premise that people have the ability and desire to understand and resolve their own problems when they are aware of and take full responsibility for all aspects of their personality and behavior. When this natural desire is blocked, disturbing behavior may result. Anger and sadness are natural reactions to the blockage and are ways of expressing a desire to return to a state of awareness and cooperation as well as frustration at not being there. The causes of these blocked experiences are often forgotten but are present in the here-and-now behavior of each person.

Typically, blocked experiences occurred in a person's encounters with his or her family of origin during childhood. The therapist attempts to help the client bring these experiences back to life in the present moment so the client can begin to gain awareness and discover what was causing the problem and complete its resolution in the present.

Theory of Change

A model called the *Gestalt experience cycle* (Rabin, 1980) shows the main elements of an experience and how to complete an incomplete experience. The cycle begins with *sensations* and *perceptions* that are learned in childhood. These include messages about what we should or should not do and what we can or cannot do. Because of these experiences, we are sensitive to certain stimuli, and when we experience these stimuli, we recall some of the original stimulus events.

Awareness results from the ability to focus on or pay attention to a sensation. If the client is confused about what really happened in his or her childhood, he or she may have trouble bringing this sensation into awareness. Enhancing awareness and helping people understand what really happened during their childhood is central to Gestalt therapy. As

CASE EXAMPLE

Gestalt Therapy

Husband: What can I do? She stops me at every turn.

Therapist: (sarcastically, to provoke him) You poor thing, overpowered by that terrible lady over there.

Husband: (ducking) She means well.

Therapist: You're whimpering at me, and I can't stand to see a grown man whimpering.

Husband: (firmer) I tell you, I don't know what to do.

Therapist: Like hell you don't (offering and at the same time pushing). You know as well as I that if you want her off your back, you just have to tell her to get the hell off your back and mean it. That's one thing you could do instead of that mealy-mouthed apology, "She means well."

Husband: (looks quizzical; obviously is not sure if he wants to chance it with either of us but is reluctant to retreat to the whimpering child posture again.) I'm not used to talking that way to people.

Therapist: Then you'd better get used to it. You're going to have to shape up this family into a group that's worth living with instead of a menagerie where your job is to come in periodically and crack the whip on the little wild animals.

Husband: You sure paint a bad picture.

Therapist: If I'm wrong, be man enough to disagree with me and don't wait to get outside of here to whimper to your wife about how you didn't know what to say here.

Husband: (visibly bristling and speaking more forcefully) I don't know that you're wrong about what you're saying.

Therapist: But how do you like what I'm saying?

Husband: I don't. Nor do I like the way you're going about it.

Therapist: I don't like the way you're going about things either.

Husband: There must be a more friendly way than this.

(continued)

(*CASE EXAMPLE continued*)

Therapist:　Sure, you know, whimper.

Husband:　(with deliberate softness) You're really a pusher, aren't you?

Therapist:　How do you like me?

Husband:　I don't.

Therapist:　You keep forgetting to say that part of your message. I can see it all over you, but you never say it.

Husband:　(finally, in anger) I'll say what I damn please. You're not going to tell me how to talk . . . and how do you like that? (socks his hand)

Therapist:　I like it a helluva lot better than your whimpering. What is your hand saying?

Husband:　I'd like to punch you in the nose, I suppose.

Therapist:　You suppose?

Husband:　(firmly) Enough. Get off my back and stay off.

Therapist:　(delighted to see his assertion) Great. Now, about the rest of them (waving to the family). I'd like to see if there's anything you'd like to say to them.

Husband:　(looks at each one of them and then settles on his wife) He's right. I take an awful lot of nonsense from you, and I hate it (still socking his hand). I don't intend to take any more. I'll settle with the kids my way. If you don't like it, that's too bad.

Source: From Experiential therapy with Families, by W. Kempler, (New York: Brunner/Mazel, 1981), pp. 178–179.

This excerpt from a case study shows how Gestalt-oriented family therapy might be used to help a client re-own something that has been disowned or projected. Unlike the typical empty-chair technique, the therapist acted out the polarity of the client's aggressive side until the client took over the part.

clients become more aware, their bodies are stimulated to action. Clients who are blocked in their awareness may experience tension or pain; others may take ineffective action. The therapist must help the client develop appropriate ways to experience and act out the conflict.

Contact is the next and probably the most crucial stage of the cycle. People who are disturbed resist making genuine contact. Their resistance takes these forms:

- *Projection*—making contact with disowned parts of the self rather than with other people
- *Introjection*—incorporating aspects of the other into the self
- *Retroflection*—turning against oneself
- *Confluence*—confusion in the boundaries between self and others
- *Deflection*—erecting a wall to avoid contact.

In family therapy, the therapist confronts these attempts to avoid contact and helps the client learn new ways to make contact with family members.

The final stage of the cycle is *withdrawal,* which occurs after experiences have been completed. An inability to withdraw and let go of an experience usually results in unfinished business in relationships. The therapist helps the client to let go of an experience and resolve the inner conflict.

Main Therapeutic Interventions

The goals of Gestalt-oriented family therapy are to help family members develop clear boundaries between the self and others and to increase self-awareness so they can break free from stuck patterns and experience themselves and life more completely. As Gestalt therapy is usually an individually oriented approach, it may be useful to see how it could be utilized effectively in a family therapy mode.

There are several differing views as to how to utilize Gestalt therapy with a family. Hatcher (1978) recommended a blend of individual and family therapy. He suggested that a focus on the individual is appropriate when dealing with intrapersonal and boundary issues and that family therapy is appropriate when dealing with interpersonal and transactional issues. He suggested building a contract with a family that permits the shift back and forth within the context of the family therapy session rather than scheduling separate sessions.

Bauer (1979) suggested a similar arrangement using the *empty-chair technique* as a tool for resolving an individual's contact–boundary problems. Although he focused on the family as a whole, Bauer recommended using Gestalt experiments such as exaggeration of problem behavior, making rounds, reversal techniques, and rehearsals.

Kaplan and Kaplan (1978) focused on the process of family therapy to determine whether to intervene with the individual, with a particular subsystem, or with the family as a whole. They described three functions or skills that therapists must have to promote change: observing, focusing, and facilitating.

1. By *observing* the process carefully, the therapist can help the family become more aware of its dynamics.
2. *Focusing* means helping the family better understand specific aspects of its process, which may include use of exaggeration techniques.
3. *Facilitating* is defined as helping the family move toward constructive reintegration. Gestalt experiments are used in this part to help produce a new integration.

The concept of *polarities* is extremely important in Gestalt therapy. Every choice of behavior a person makes has a polar opposite that may be a disowned aspect of the client's personality. Helping clients identify, own, and take responsibility for the polarities in their personality is a significant part of Gestalt therapy (Perls, 1969).

Gestalt-oriented family therapy can be viewed as an eclectic approach. Because it still focuses on individual change, it may be possible to utilize individually oriented techniques drawn from bioenergetics, rolfing, transactional analysis (TA), person-centered, and behavioral approaches.

Limitations of Gestalt-Oriented Therapy

A limitation of Gestalt-oriented therapy is that it involves an anti-intellectual attitude that discounts the importance of cognitive understanding. Practitioners emphasize experience and feelings rather than building cognitive structures with clients. In addition, some Gestalt techniques can be abusive. There is a danger of taking a "one-up" posture with clients. The therapist often is so directive that he or she can create a dependency relationship with the client as underdog. Gestalt therapists may utilize dramatic catharsis and then insist that their clients create personal meaning from the catharsis without helping them work through and integrate the experience. Gestalt therapists can easily hide behind their techniques, and they tend to emphasize a "quick fix" instead of encouraging clients to grow and change over time.

Another problem with Gestalt therapy is the jargon that the therapist and client may use to avoid deeper issues. Phrases such as, "Stay in the here-and-now" or "take responsibility for yourself" can become rigid rules and not just guidelines. Finally, little research has been done on Gestalt therapy, and virtually none has been done on Gestalt-oriented family therapy.

■ *Psychodrama-Oriented Family Therapy*

Psychodrama was created in Vienna in 1921 by J. L. Moreno (1983). In that year, he opened the Theatre of Spontaneity. Those who participated in the theatre were not professional actors, nor did they use scripts. Instead, they acted out in a spontaneous manner the events reported in the daily newspaper or topics suggested by members of the audience. After an event or topic was acted out, the actors and audience were invited to comment on their experiences during the performance. Moreno found that both the actors and those in the audience experienced a catharsis or release of pent-up feelings as a result of being in the play or observing the play. As a result of this experiment, Moreno began to develop specialized therapeutic techniques that became the foundation for psychodrama.

Psychodrama is designed to help people express their feelings in a spontaneous and dramatic way through role playing. Because the work involves many different players, it is good to use in a group setting and lends itself to family therapy as well. Although it is interpersonally oriented, psychodrama is intended to help people explore intrapersonal facets of their lives. Psychodrama recognizes the importance of the social environment and of action methods in the treatment of family problems (Moreno, 1983).

Psychodrama was the precursor of many other action-oriented approaches, including Gestalt, encounter groups, behavioral approaches, bioenergetics, guided fantasy, psychosynthesis, play therapy, and improvisational dramatics. Other family systems approaches, such as family sculpting and role playing, often use psychodramatic techniques originally developed by Moreno.

Philosophical Tenets

Like Perls, Moreno based his ideas on the notion that people are the product of their experiences and are responsible for their actions. This existential position is similar to the philosophies of Camus and Sartre, both of whom emphasized that people are alone in the universe of their experience. This aloneness, however, provides a common experience for all people, a concept that forms the epistemological basis of existentialism. People share the common experience of being as well as the common fear of nonbeing. The belief that death is absolute also frees people to choose to either accept their fate and to enjoy life in the here-and-now or to try to deny or run away from the inevitable and therefore be ruled by fear and guilt.

Like Sartre, Moreno believed that experiences determine a person's essence. People are what they do or experience. Those holding this view do not deny the possibility of preexisting human nature but do not believe it is possible to discover it and therefore ignore its role in human development. The only reality worth considering is a person's experience. According to this view, the source of value is self-awareness and the commitment of the person to take responsibility for himself or herself, as well as exercising his or her ability to respond (responsibility). Evil involves the failure to act according to one's ability.

Theoretical Constructs

Two theoretical constructs are theory of cause and theory of change.

Theory of Cause

Moreno clearly delineated the role of social forces in causing disturbances. Forces of the family, society, occupational groups, and religious groups all shape the personality. Moreno theorized that one of the main results of this socialization process is that most people lack spontaneity and live a sort of "as if" existence, never fully entering into their experiences. Moreno observed that young children are able to enter into spontaneous role playing and fantasy situations and freely express their feelings, but adults have great difficulty in doing so. He saw that people develop limiting scripts for their lives and rigid, stereotyped responses to most situations.

Instead of meeting eye-to-eye and face-to-face, Moreno suggested that parents see in their children only what they want to see and are unable to truly mirror for the child. At the same time, children look at their parents and see omnipotent, perfect gods instead of scared, limited human beings. This condition may cause identity confusion for the child.

With this confusion as a base, most children grow up with distorted views of how the social order works. These distortions are best diagnosed through role playing or action drama. If these distortions are not uncovered and removed before children leave their families, the children's perceptions of the larger cultural milieu also are distorted, which leads to distortion at the universal level.

As a result of all these distortions, people live in a world they hardly even recognize. Most people adapt to their own distortions; they are cut off from their own life force and spontaneity, living life in a bubble, unable to break out, and unable to grow and develop very much without feeling crowded and restricted (Moreno, 1951).

Theory of Change

The cure, so to speak, lies in the client's willingness to risk breaking the bubble through action. In this approach, insight comes as the result of some action. Moreno saw the psychodramatic method as the way to break through the bubble and learn how to be spontaneous. The method uses five instruments: the stage, the client, the director, the auxiliary egos, and the audience.

1. The *stage* provides the client with a living space that is multidimensional and highly flexible. The client's reality is usually much too limited, and the stage allows for a new freedom to emerge. The clients are asked to be themselves on the stage and to portray their own private world. Once they are warmed up to the task, clients are asked to give a spontaneous account of some problem in their daily lives.

CASE EXAMPLE

Psychodrama

Mr. and Mrs. Thomas, their 17-year-old son, John, and their 15-year-old daughter, Ann, came to family therapy because of unresolved conflicts that had beset the family. In the initial interview, the major problem discussed was Mrs. Thomas's criticism of her daughter, comparing her unfavorably with her older brother. Ann was asked to present or role play the way she experienced her mother, and she was happy to show her unexpressed feelings in the safety of the family therapy session as she portrayed her mother's attacks. She said, as her mother, "Ann, you're so lazy. Look at you—you don't do anything but sit around watching TV. John is always busy with his job, school activities, and his friends, and all you do is sit there."

Mrs. Thomas had initiated the family therapy, and it turned out that she also was critical of Mr. Thomas, who she said was always too busy at work. Mr. Thomas defended himself, saying that he stayed away because she was always nagging him.

The therapist attempted to uncover their patterns and help them discover new ways of behaving with each other through role playing. Ann became John, Mrs. Thomas became Ann, and John and Mr. Thomas reversed roles. The therapist helped them all express their feelings toward the rest of the family members. Ann, as John, said, "I feel isolated and alone inside this family. Everyone just expects me to do well, but I don't feel they like me, and I'm always afraid I'll screw up." Mr. Thomas, as John, said, "I'm a lot like Dad. I run away from conflict and just keep busy." Later Mrs. Thomas reversed roles with Mr. Thomas. As Mr. Thomas, she said, "I wish I could bring some order to this family."

The therapist worked with Mr. Thomas to show him what he could say and do to help bring order to the family. Using the double technique, with the coaching of the therapist, he tried out several possibilities. To his surprise, the family members responded positively. The therapist suggested scheduling a regular meeting time during which they could clear their feelings and plan family activities. Mr. Thomas was assigned the role of leading these meetings. The family role played an actual meeting during one session to learn how it might use this type of meeting to resolve conflicts.

2. The *client* is encouraged to become involved with all the people and things present in this problem, which can mean encountering internal parts of himself or herself as well as other people—past, present, and future—who are involved in some way with the problem.
3. The *director* serves as the producer, therapist, and analyst. As the producer, he or she develops the production in line with the client's life script, never letting the production bog down or move too fast. As the therapist, he or she confronts, reflects feelings and content, summarizes, and gives information. The analyst interprets and helps the client integrate the material into his or her life space.
4. *Auxiliary egos* are extensions of the client and are used to portray the actual or imagined personas of their real life drama. They help model and teach the client new ways to act in this and other similar situations.
5. The *audience* is used as a sounding board of public opinion, helping the client see aspects of the drama that he or she overlooked. The client also helps the audience, as people from the audience see aspects of their own life drama being played out on the stage.

Psychodrama has three phases: the warm-up phase, the action phase, and the discussion or sharing phase. The therapeutic element in psychodrama is *catharsis*, or release. This catharsis is produced *only* if a climate fostering spontaneity can be created in the warm-up stage. Such a climate requires that (a) the client feels safe and trusts the direction, (b) the expression of emotions and intuition is permitted, (c) an attitude of playfulness is established, and (d) a willingness to explore novel behavior is encouraged.

During the action phase, the spontaneity of the drama produces a catharsis that enables the client to reexperience repressed feelings and distorted thoughts. This catharsis then can be utilized by a skillful director to enable a new drama to emerge. With the help of the auxiliary egos, the director produces the new drama with the client and allows for new roles and actions to occur within the safety of the therapeutic setting. These new dramas can be properly rehearsed and reinforced by the director, the auxiliary egos, and the audience before the client tries them out in his or her life space.

During the discussion stage, the director protects the client from interpretive or negative feedback because the client is in a vulnerable position. This protection is necessary to help the client integrate what he or she just experienced. The director asks for personal sharing by audience members, asking them how the psychodrama helped them. The catharsis that occurs in members of the audience helps them and the client achieve some integration (Moreno, 1983).

Main Therapeutic Interventions

A number of psychodramatic techniques that lend themselves quite well to family therapy are listed and briefly described next.

1. *Self-presentation.* The therapist lets all family members present how they see themselves in relationship to every other family member. This technique enables the therapist to discover who is enmeshed in the family system and who is an outsider.
2. *Presentation of the other.* The therapist who wishes to know how family members see each other may ask them to present other family members as they see them. The therapist may wish to interview the person who is presenting another family member to get a more complete picture of how he or she sees the other family member.
3. *Role playing.* This is an extension of the "presentation of the other," with a possible role reversal. Two or more family members reverse roles and act out some scene. The therapist encourages maximum expression of feelings in conflict situations. The technique helps to quickly reveal the distortions in the relationships and to correct them, and it can produce new options and much insight into conflict situations.
4. *Double technique.* Sometimes the therapist or another family member has to act as a double for the person to express feelings and content that are blocked or repressed. This technique is often used as a catalyst to get a family member to express feelings or thoughts that have been inhibited. Multiple doubles can be used to help portray mixed or conflicting feelings as well.
5. *Family sculpture.* In this technique, the therapist asks all the family members to sculpt the family the way they see it in relationship to themselves and to each other. This means physically

placing them in postures and having them hold the position as a freeze-frame to examine (Duhl, Kantor, & Duhl, 1973). This technique also can be used to choreograph new patterns by experimenting with different sculpture formations and allowing them to change in ways that members would like. This power-ful intervention can help realign family relationships (Papp, 1980).

Limitations of Psychodrama-Oriented Family Therapy

Although feelings and repressed material can be uncovered quickly using this technique, it requires a sensitive therapist to use the mate-rial effectively. Another problem with the technique is that, like other experiential approaches, this approach does not have a strong research base (Rudestam, 1982). It requires specialized training and supervised experience, yet many practitioners utilize psychodramatic techniques without additional training or supervision.

■ Transpersonal-Oriented Family Therapy

Near the end of his life, Abraham Maslow, one of the founders of humanistic psychology, began to perceive limitations in the somewhat ego-centered humanistic approaches. He believed that there had to be a way to transcend this ego-centered existence and take into account the deeply spiritual, psychic, and paranormal experiences of human beings as legitimate areas of study in psychology. In 1968, shortly before his death, he wrote, "I consider Humanistic, Third Force Psychology, to be transitional, a preparation for a still higher Fourth Psychology, transpersonal, transhuman, centered in the cosmos rather than in human needs and interest, going beyond humanness, identity, self-actualiza-tion and the like" (Maslow, 1971, p. 33).

Maslow had come to realize that the search for transcendence is a higher human need than the search for self-actualization, which is still centered in the self, or ego. Maslow also believed that transcendence cannot be achieved by attempting to avoid development of the ego. Only through mastery of the other ego needs in his hierarchy of needs (physiological, safety/security, love/belonging, self-esteem, and self-actualization) can people recognize and fulfill the deeper need for self-transcendence. Thus, an effective transpersonal therapist has to be able to utilize all the other approaches that work with ego mastery, including psychodynamic, behavioral, and humanistic approaches.

Because most of Western psychology focuses primarily on ego functioning, a transpersonal therapist also must become familiar with Eastern psychology and philosophy, which focuses much more on working with transcendent states of being and so-called altered states of consciousness. As a result, much of transpersonal psychology deals with the study of yoga, meditation, chanting, movement, martial arts, and various body therapies based on oriental and Eastern medical practices and philosophies. In addition, numerous Western approaches have been utilized to help bridge the contrasting philosophies and practices. These techniques include dream work, biofeedback, bioenergetics, guided imagery, visualization, dance and movement therapy, art therapy, and music therapy.

The term *transpersonal* is difficult to define. The term was deliberately left in an undefined state during the first decade of the transpersonal movement. Many of the early leaders feared that giving the word a definition would be limiting. They believed that transpersonal psychology should not be constrained by our present knowledge of human behavior. Nevertheless, some broad definitions have begun to emerge.

In Latin, the prefix *trans* has a number of different meanings. It can mean *connecting,* as in a *transcontinental* flight. It can mean *through,* in the sense of a *transparent* pane of glass, and it can mean *beyond,* as in a *transcendent* experience. The Latin word *personal* has a root word *persona,* which means mask. When we add the prefix *trans* to the word *personal,* the new term means bridging and connecting the parts of the personality or mask, allowing us to see through the mask and to move beyond the mask. Transpersonal theory, then, allows us to look through the persona or ego to get beyond the individual ego and connect with all egos.

The main transpersonal theory in Western psychology is Carl Jung's analytic theory. Jungian concepts such as the collective unconscious, synchronicity, the anima, and the animus point to higher forces that direct or influence our lives and lie beyond the human ego. The center of the personality, according to Jung, is the higher self, as opposed to the lower or ego self.

Arnold Mindell (1987), a practitioner of Jungian analysis, developed his global process work theory to apply Jungian and transpersonal principles in work with families. Mindell looks for the organizing principle or secondary process that is trying to happen in families. By supporting the primary process, the family therapist can discover the secondary process and facilitate its unfolding in the family. Mindell utilizes many nontraditional techniques to uncover the missing pieces in the family process.

Other body-oriented therapists also have developed techniques such as breath work, guided imagery, centering, dance and movement therapy, bioenergetics, and meditation to work with families. Using a variety of body-oriented techniques, Gay Hendricks (Weinhold & Hendricks, 1993) works with family members to help free them from body-armoring and other dysfunctional patterns that show up in their body and breathing patterns. Coming out of a transpersonal framework, Hendricks tries to move family members into transcendent states wherein they can experience the connection with their own core love and be able to connect with family members at the same level.

Theoretical Constructs of Transpersonal Theory

Theory of Cause

Some of the key ideas in transpersonal theory that might be useful for a marriage and family therapist are:

- Oneness
- Unity of mind, body, and spirit
- Expanded context for human behavior
- Validity of spiritual dimensions of life:

  —namaste
  —essence precedes existence
  —karma
  —thought is creative
  —life force and death urge

- Validity of subjective experience and the unconscious
- Validity of core self–ego as a subpart of core self
- Therapist and client are interchangeable
- Everything is possible; acceptance of possibilities
- Therapy is living.

Basic to determining whether a therapist is using a transpersonal approach is whether he or she holds the basic beliefs and attitudes reflected in these concepts. These concepts are described briefly, with suggestions on how a transpersonal therapist may utilize them.

Oneness Transpersonal therapists should see themselves as connected to all other people in a common human experience. From this perspective, most psychological problems in families are seen as denial of or forgetting our basic unity. Parents often react to their children as if they were alien beings and not parts of themselves being acted out.

Projection, in this context, is not a failure to see our own behavior in the behavior of others but, rather, a recognition that what we see in others is really part of us. In families, we project the unintegrated parts of various family members. In addition, the oneness belief allows us to strive to reclaim the disowned parts of ourselves and develop a deeper and more complete sense of inner unity.

Unity of Mind, Body, and Spirit The transpersonal therapist views human behavior from a holistic perspective that focuses on the connections between mind, body, and spirit. A growing body of medical research is clearly pointing to the interrelationship between mental and physical symptoms. Only recently have researchers begun to examine spiritual connections as well. By viewing all behavior as interconnected, the transpersonal therapist often can see connections that are not immediately obvious.

For example, a father described his son as "a pain in the neck," and in a later session the son related a dream in which he was running at "breakneck" speed to avoid a dark figure chasing him. By having the son act out his dream in the session, with his father taking on the part of the dark figure, the son finally realized that he was running away from the unreasonable demands of his father. He turned and faced his father and saw how he was being asked to fulfill the unfulfilled parts of his father.

Expanded Context for Human Behavior The transpersonal therapist adopts an expansionist rather than a reductionist view of human behavior. When trying to understand human behavior, an expansionist view looks for the broadest possible context. For example, when dealing with aggressive behavior, a reductionist view would be to ignore the possibility of an opposite or passive part of that person's behavior and attempt only to extinguish the aggressive behavior as quickly as possible. A transpersonal therapist might look for the opposite, allow that part to be played out, and seek ways to unify the two parts into a larger, more complete whole.

Validity of Spiritual Dimensions of Life   The transpersonal therapist recognizes the validity of certain spiritual principles that can guide our lives. One of these principles *is namaste,* a willingness to see and greet the highest in people. Traditional therapists can easily get bogged down in seeing only the problems and imperfections of themselves and their clients.

Essence precedes existence, another spiritual principle, refers to the transpersonal therapist's ability to wake up and transcend his or her own conditioning and be able to see the spiritual essence of people beyond their social, personal conditioning.

A core belief of most transpersonal therapists is that a human essence is present at birth for most people. This essence has been called the self, peace, love, soul (core self), and cosmic consciousness—our true nature. This true self can be lost or forgotten during childhood if it is not accepted and nurtured by wise and understanding parents and adults. To a transpersonal therapist, *karma* means the unconscious patterns of behavior we have learned from the adults who taught us, mainly the people in our family of origin.

Putting it another way, we could say, "What has been sown, thus shall be reaped." When a person is able to bring to consciousness those unconscious patterns, the person can begin to live under the *law of grace* rather than the *law of karma.*

The concept that *thought is creative* allows the transpersonal therapist to help people see more clearly how their own thoughts can create their reality. If we don't like the reality we have created for ourselves, we have to change our thoughts before a new reality can emerge.

Finally, the transpersonal therapist must recognize the interplay of two basic energy forces in humans: the *life force* and the *death urge.* The transpersonal therapist attempts to see how these two interrelated forces are manifested in himself or herself so he or she can see them in the behavior of others.

Validity of Subjective Experience and the Unconscious   Many therapies teach their practitioners to distrust or disregard the subjective and unconscious experiences of their clients. Transpersonal therapists learn to trust these experiences as having the most validity for themselves and for their clients. A transpersonal therapist does not believe in a definable objective reality. All experiences of reality are projections

CASE EXAMPLE

Transpersonal Family Therapy

Mindell (1987) reported on an interesting family therapy case that illustrates his ideas about primary and secondary processes in families. He believes that the primary process—which usually involves the identified patient and the problem that brought the family to therapy—masks the secondary process that is trying to break through in the family.

In this case, Alex, a teenage son, is the identified patient. Someone stole the cookies his mother baked, and Alex is being accused as the thief. Because he has denied it, his mother is still angry at him for taking the cookies and for his unwillingness to admit it. The therapist asks Alex's mother who she thinks stole the cookies, and why she thinks that way. While she is answering the question, the therapist notices that Alex is turning red.

Then the therapist asks Alex who stole the cookies, and his father burps. The therapist then asks the father the same question, and while he answers, Alex's sister, Marie, begins to fidget.

Finally, the therapist asks Marie to tell him what is going on in the family. Marie answers that she believes everyone in the family is guilty of something they haven't admitted. This gets everyone in the family laughing loudly, so the therapist asks each person to talk about his or her guilt. The family members share a story of something each did wrong, and as a result they all feel closer to each other. They no longer are pointing their collective finger at Alex as the irresponsible thief in the family.

This case illustrates how a family operates as a single unit to keep a secret. If the therapist had only met with Alex, he probably would not have uncovered the secondary process that was trying to happen in this family. Once the secret was revealed and everyone could "come clean," they were all free to share more of themselves in the family. This was the secondary process that was trying to happen in this family, and it led to a deeper level of communication and relationship.

of a subjective experience. The therapist is not an objective observer but, rather, a subjective participant in the therapy process.

Validity of Core Self/Ego as a Subpart of Core Self Transpersonal therapists believe that the ego is not the center of the human personality; it is only a visibly socialized part of us. The core of who we really are is our core self. The ego tends to block our awareness of this core self, and often therapy is a process of "shrinking an inflated ego" so we can make contact with our core self again.

Therapist and Client Are Interchangeable This concept is difficult to grasp and probably runs counter to what most of us were taught about therapy. Yet it is the cornerstone of a transpersonal approach. According to this approach, clients bring the therapist all the therapeutic issues the therapist needs to work on. In giving therapy to a client, the therapist is really receiving therapy from himself or herself and the client. As a client, a person finds out what he or she already knows, and as a therapist, he or she helps remind others of what they already know.

Everything Is Possible; Acceptance of Possibilities This belief is extremely important for the therapist and the client alike. Therapists must believe in themselves as well as the client's ability to transcend limited views of the world. Without a strong belief in change and transcendence, no change or transcendence is possible.

Therapy Is Living Transpersonal therapists have to be willing to work on themselves all the time. No matter what is happening, they have some opportunity for self-improvement and growth in awareness. All experiences in life can be divided into lessons and bliss. Once a person has learned these lessons, more time becomes available to experience bliss.

Theory of Change

Transpersonal approaches usually are based on a set of universal laws or principles that the client and the therapist can move toward. The assumption is that if clients can reorient their lives more in line with these laws, their lives will be more effective. The following laws were assembled by Barry Weinhold (1982) from various esoteric and spiritual traditions.

- *Law of correspondence:* Truth on one level is truth on all levels of reality, and a breakthrough at one level can lead to a breakthrough at all levels.

- *Law of transcendence:* A person cannot move to a higher level of consciousness until he or she fully accepts and integrates all of his or her disowned parts. A person cannot flee to higher consciousness to avoid a part of the ego-self that is unwanted or unclaimed. This is called a "spiritual bypass."

- *Law of grace:* People are never separate from God or the divine. Humanity has a divine essence that may be forgotten but is never lost.

- *Law of cause and affect:* Nothing ever happens by accident or by chance. Chance is merely a cause-and-effect relationship that isn't recognized.

- *Law of rhythm:* Everything in the universe is balanced. All energy expands and contracts in a natural ebb and flow. Ancient people knew how to stay in harmony and balance with the natural rhythms of the earth. In modern times most people have lost this ability.

- *Law of polarity:* Everything in the universe manifests in dual form, and everything has its opposite. All truths are really half-truths, and all paradoxes can be reconciled.

- *Law of oneness:* Everything in the universe is unified and connected. A person who feels separated from the rocks and trees or other people cannot feel at home in the universe.

- *Law of gender:* Everything has masculine and feminine energy. This law helps the universe to evolve. Our job is to balance and harmonize these seemingly competing energies.

- *Law of vibration:* Everything is in a state of motion; everything has a vibrational level. Spirit vibrates so rapidly that it cannot be seen. Matter vibrates so slowly that at its most dense level, it seems motionless.

- *Law of attraction:* People attract relationships and situations that they need to help them solve unresolved problems or conflicts. It is as if "central casting" keeps sending people to us to help us resolve these issues and learn the lessons we are trying to learn.

- *Law of completion:* Any issue, problem, or lesson in a person's life will continue to press for completion until it is completed. A person cannot successfully avoid, ignore, or run away from these issues without some cost to the individual's well-being.

Goals of Transpersonal Therapists

Although some transpersonal therapists might use other terms, the following are the most commonly expressed goals of transpersonal therapists (Walsh & Vaughan, 1980).

1. Teaching themselves and their clients to achieve a daily experience of certainty, liberation, enlightenment, or gnosis, and self-transcendence.
2. Teaching themselves and others to "enjoy the world but not be attached to it, to be of service but not make a pest of oneself" (p. 180).
3. Teaching themselves and their clients the skills they need to handle their own problems as they arise.
4. Teaching themselves and others to increase their tolerance for paradox and ambiguity, as well as not to be satisfied with "easy answers" to life's problems.
5. Teaching themselves and others how to increasingly blend inner and outer experience.
6. Teaching themselves and others to develop compassion, generosity, inner peace, and the capacity for love and relatedness in the world.

The Process of Transpersonal Therapy

The transpersonal process is complex and difficult to define, but we will attempt a brief summary of the stages in this process.

1. *Identification with the ego.* This involves bringing the functioning of the ego in each family member into consciousness. It includes understanding and taking back the ineffective defenses of the ego.
2. *Disidentification with the ego.* After a person has experienced his or her ego as completely as possible, the limitations of the ego become painfully apparent. Frequently, attachment to the ego is so strong that this stage of the process is often experienced as a death of the ego or a fear of physical death itself.
3. *Self-transcendence.* This stage often includes archetypal awareness; the problems that remained insoluble at the ego level are transcended. For example, the fear of death that often surfaces during the previous stage is now transcended, allowing life to become larger than itself. The ordinary reality of "chop wood

and carry water" now is seen in a new, expanded way. Nothing new happens, but an individual's perceptions about everything are changed. The deeper archetypal identities now are actively present as new sources of knowledge and being. The transcendent experience is unique in human existence and deserves a fuller description. Some common characteristics of a transcendent experience are:

- A heightened sense of clarity and understanding of self and others.
- Unique enough to almost defy verbal description; words cannot describe it fully.
- An altered perception of time and space in which everything may seem to slow down or speed up.
- An appreciation of the connected nature of all things and our connections to or with everything.
- An intensely positive feeling or sense of the perfection of everything in the universe.
- The presence of a white or golden light surrounding everything or filling a person's vision.
- All of a person's senses acutely attuned and open to the experience.
- An experience of energy flowing through the body.

4. These deeper identities dissolve into a state of direct knowing, gnosis, or enlightenment. We have few models of this type of existence. Buddhists speak of it as nonattachment or just being awake. Once Buddha was asked by some of his followers, "Who are you? Are you a God? An Avatar?" Buddha answered, "I am awake."

Advantages and Limitations of Transpersonal Family Therapy

A number of advantages might be seen in this approach. It provides the tools for self-therapy and is less dependent on the therapist's having all the answers. The approach focuses on attaining the highest ideals and principles, and it is transformative rather than remedial. It allows for deep, spiritual connections within and without, provides an expanded context for family therapy where there is no blame and everyone is seen as innocent rather than guilty, and frees families from a sense of isolation.

Some disadvantages also can be seen in transpersonal family therapy. One disadvantage is that this approach lacks an inadequate research foundation. Transpersonal therapists tend to engage in "interim over-belief," which means they trust their subjective experience *before* any research is done to confirm their perceptions. They could be wrong, or their perceptions could be distorted. There is now a substantial body of research on meditation and biofeedback, but few of the other concepts and techniques have been examined closely.

Furthermore, success of the therapy is overly dependent on the therapist's personal growth and awareness. Few guidelines have been established for how to train transpersonal therapists not to become a barrier to the client. None of the other approaches requires the therapist to be as "squeaky-clean" as this one does. Moreover, working with subtle energies demands more refined and less intrusive techniques. When people open up to their core, therapists must respect their vulnerability and learn to gently, lovingly assist them in their process of growth. Again, the therapist's sensitivity is key to this issue, and severe psychic damage can occur if the therapist does not handle these issues properly. This danger exists with other therapies as well, but not as clearly as in the transpersonal realm.

SUGGESTED READINGS

Dossey, L. (1989). *Recovering the Soul.* New York: Bantam.

Kempler, W. (1982). *Experiential Therapy with Families.* New York: Brunner/Mazel.

Moreno, J. L. (1946). *Psychodrama.* Boston: Beacon House.

Rogers, C. R. (1951). *Client Centered Therapy.* Boston: Houghton Mifflin.

Rogers, C. R. (1972). *Becoming Partners: Marriage and Its Alternatives.* New York: Dell.

Thayer, L. (1991). "Toward a Person-Centered Approach to Family Therapy." In A. Horne & J. L. Passmore (Eds.), *Family Counseling and Therapy*, 2d ed. Itasca, IL: Peacock.

Weinhold, B., & Hendricks, G. (1993). *Counseling and Psychotherapy: A Transpersonal Approach.* Denver: Love.

Zukav, G. (1990). *The Seat of the Soul.* New York: Simon & Schuster.

Humanistic, Existential and Transpersonal Systems Theories

In this chapter we will present four systems theories of family therapy based in humanistic, existential, and transpersonal thought. Three of these theories—Virginia Satir (1983, 1988), Carl Whitaker (1976, 1981), and Barry & Janae Weinhold (1993, 2000)—emphasize individual differences and the belief in human potential. In addition, we will present the narrative/conversational approach to therapy developed by Michael White and David Epston (1990). This approach includes elements of constructivist theory (Watzlawick, 1984), the human potential movement (Rogers, 1961), and poststructuralism (Parry, 1991); all of which suggest the ability of individuals to re-create themselves and their families through the use of new and more effective language and metaphors.

Self-concept
Family communication
Architects of the family
Family rules
Placater
Blamer
Computer
Distracter
Intrapsychic split
Edges

Battle for structure
Battle for initiative
Co-therapy
Three-generation therapy
Externalization
Therapeutic letters
Reauthored narrative
Developmental trauma
Psychological birth
Surface process

1. According to Satir's communications theory, what is the cause of emotional illness in individuals?
2. Why did Satir believe the personal qualities of the counselor are so important in family therapy?
3. What types of problems are families typically experiencing when they seek treatment from a therapist trained in Satir's communications theory?
4. What major techniques did Satir use to help family members develop self-esteem?
5. What are the characteristics of a healthy family according to Whitaker?
6. What are the battles for structure and initiative? Why are these important in therapy?
7. Why is having a co-therapist important in Whitaker's family therapy?
8. What common errors do family counselors make? How can these errors be avoided?
9. How does narrative therapy employ elements of the historical approach to treatment with elements of brief therapy?
10. How would you use therapeutic letters in your treatment of families? Do you think the time involved in preparing the letters would be justified? Why, or why not?
11. Why is externalization of problems so important in narrative therapy?
12. Why are exceptions so important in narrative therapy?
13. How do you know when you are following a person's process versus taking over a person's process?
14. What do you do if you identify a "double signal" in a family member's report of a problem he or she is having?
15. What are your edges as a family therapist? What issues, problems, or clients can't you deal with in therapy?
16. What is the role of developmental trauma in creating family problems?

$\mathcal{T}$he four systems theories presented in this chapter—those of Virginia Satir, Carl Whitaker, Michael White and David Epston, and Barry and Janae Weinhold—are based in a belief in individual differences and human potential. Humanistic/existential/transpersonal systems therapists believe that individuals and families have a drive toward wholeness and health. Therapy should encourage the family members to identify and come into full contact with their experiences. This process of experiencing is the vehicle for enhanced self-worth and concomitant family improvement. Humanistic/existential therapists are more interested in what is currently occurring in the family than in past memories. Transpersonal therapists, however, are interested in discovering how unresolved past events are directly related to current struggles.

The overall goal of humanistic/existential/transpersonal family systems therapy is to encourage family members to have a corrective experience based on experiencing immediate family issues. Throughout that corrective experience, family members learn how to deal creatively with future issues that will emerge in the family. The discussion of Satir's communications theory is followed by a description of the symbolic-experiential therapy formulated by Whitaker, then the narrative approach used by White, Epston, and others, and finally the developmental process work-approach created by Barry & Janae Weinhold.

Satir's Communications Theory

Born in 1916, Virginia Satir completed her graduate degree in psychiatric social work and began training family therapists at the Illinois State Psychiatric Institute in Chicago in 1955. In 1959 she became one of the founding members of the Mental Research Institute in Palo Alto,

California, where she worked with Don Jackson, Jay Haley, Jules Riskin, and others who were completing research on communication in schizophrenic families. In *Conjoint Family Therapy*, first published in 1964, she put forth her family therapy model. In a revised edition (Satir, 1983), she began to define the humanistic, existential foundation of her communications theory. Satir also had served as director of the residential training program at Esalen Institute, Big Sur, California. She was one of the most widely respected and emulated family therapists, whose genuine warmth and caring for families seemed to be always present. Satir died in 1988 at 76 years of age.

Philosophical Tenets and Key Theoretical Constructs

Satir viewed her theory as a dynamic and evolving concept rather than a set of rigid principles. As such, she considered her model of therapy with families to be constantly in process. She was continually seeking to improve the model by refining her techniques. In her work with families, Satir attempted to identify the processes that occur in all relationships involving human beings. She wanted to help heal those relationships, which then would lead to growth and development of the self-concepts of family members. According to Satir, every relationship is an encounter between two people at a given moment in time. In contrast to the cognitive/behavioral systems theorists, Satir attempted to create genuine encounters between family members, to identify and deal with concealed feelings, and to heal the pain in the family.

Satir (1988) believed that an effective family therapy theory integrated the four basic parts of the self: (1) the mind, (2) the body, (3) the report of the senses, and (4) social relationships. The order of this list suggests that Satir may have placed more emphasis on the functioning of individuals within the family than other systems theorists included in this book. Satir believed that relationships would be stronger and more functional if the persons in the relationships had strong self-concepts. Thus, she placed much emphasis in therapy on development of strong self-concepts in the family members.

In keeping with her fluid and open process approach to therapy, Satir employed principles and ideas obtained from the disciplines of dance, drama, religion, medicine, communications, education, and the behavioral sciences. She believed that effective family counselors do not omit any useful tool to help the family, whether it comes from a discipline typically associated with psychotherapy or not (Satir, 1988).

Satir made three key points concerning therapy and change.

1. The individual needs to observe the self in interaction with significant others, including the family system.
2. The individual needs to recognize how behavior and self-concept are products of the family system itself.
3. All family members need to understand the points above; this understanding may occur in therapy when the process of therapy allows family members to experience each other genuinely and practice new interactional behaviors.

Further, Satir believed that effective therapy, to be most helpful, must be flexible and variable. She may have counseled families for an hour, or she may have worked with them in a marathon session lasting over a weekend. Thus, the *time* of therapy is flexible and variable. Satir may have treated families in her office, their home, at a park, or in their workplace. Thus, the *place* of therapy is flexible. After meeting with the family as a unit and gaining a solid understanding of the situation, Satir would meet with individuals, couples, siblings, spouses, or any other important family subsystem. Thus, *who will be seen* is flexible and variable. She worked alone, with a co-therapist, or with more than one co-therapist. The co-therapist could have been of either gender. Thus the *work of therapists is flexible and variable.*

Furthermore, Satir used techniques she believed would be helpful for the family from virtually any discipline. Thus, *techniques and procedures* for therapy are flexible and variable. This ability to use a wide variety of approaches and therapeutic plans is characteristic of therapists who work from humanistic/existential theoretical orientations. Because of this flexibility and variability of approach, however, duplication of the treatment methods of humanistic/existential therapists like Satir by other therapists and researchers is very difficult (Gurman & Kniskern, 1981b).

Like most therapists, Satir (1983) was interested in effective outcomes for family treatment. She believed that the therapist's answers to the following questions strongly influence the type of therapy provided.

1. What causes illness?
2. What makes illness go away?

3. What makes people grow?

Satir provided answers to these questions, upon which she developed a model of treatment. She believed that illness results when individuals are unable to establish the types of relationships they desire with the people who are most important to them. Specifically, these relationships are dysfunctional because of an inability of the family members to communicate effectively with each other. Illness goes away when people are able to honestly and openly relate to those who are important to them without fear of rejection and threat to their self-concepts. This objective is accomplished through therapy that emphasizes encounters between individuals in the family and the open discussion and resolution of important issues.

As a growth-oriented therapist, Satir did not believe that resolution of a presenting problem is sufficient. She believed that her therapy would be effective only if she were able to create an environment for the family that supported the continued positive growth of the individuals and of the relationships in the family.

Finally, in growth-oriented family therapy, the therapist is particularly important. Satir was willing to risk herself in therapy, to be spontaneous, and to establish intimate contact with family members to support their growth and self-esteem. The use of self in this manner is unique to the humanistic/existential approach to family therapy. The techniques are not designed to achieve specific behavioral outcomes. Rather, therapy and the encounters that occur within the therapy are designed to help individuals become more congruent, genuine, caring, and more capable of taking risks in relationship with others.

Main Therapeutic Interventions

Because Virginia Satir held the optimistic worldview that individuals have within them the potential for growth and wholeness, her techniques and therapeutic interventions were designed to allow people to fully express their potential in relationships with other family members. This approach stresses individual growth and development within the context of the family. It encourages individuals to take risks, to openly express their feelings to those they care about, and to take responsibility for their own behavior. Specifically, Satir believed that growth can take place only when the family communicates effectively and is able to validate and enhance the self-worth of its members.

In her book, *The New Peoplemaking*, Satir (1988) described the family as a factory that is in the business of producing people. More specifically, she focused on the adults in the family as the peoplemakers. Thus, as the *architects of the family*, Satir placed special responsibility on the parents for nurturing their children and maintaining of an effective and loving family environment.

Families that chose Satir for therapy tended to be experiencing problems in one or more of the following ways:

1. The self-worth of family members was too low.
2. The ability of the members to share thoughts and ideas was weak. Communication was vague, indirect, and not really honest.
3. Family rules were autocratically developed, rigidly enforced, and everlasting.
4. The family's link to the societal system was based on fear, acquiescence, and blaming.

Through her therapy, Satir helped the family members develop increased self-worth; clear, direct, and honest communication; flexible and appropriate rules; and open and hopeful links to society (Satir, 1983).

Virginia Satir was a charismatic and deeply caring therapist. She exemplified to her clients the characteristics she hoped to help them develop. Because she was warm and caring, her ability to develop meaningful relationships with family members was outstanding. Thus, she was able to ask important and possibly threatening questions of family members without jeopardizing the relationships she had developed and nurtured.

For instance, Satir might ask each family member how it felt to be a member of the family right now. With this type of question, Satir accomplished at least two goals: (1) She introduced affect, or feeling, to the therapy ("How does it feel?"), and (2) she introduced the importance of the here-and-now ("right now"). Such questions elicit varied responses from family members that provide the therapist with data about the self-worth of members, communication within the family, family rules, and the family's link with society.

In *Conjoint Family Therapy*, Satir (1983) described in detail the role and functions of the therapist. First, the therapist recognizes that the family members coming to therapy will be fearful and unsure whether therapy will help or hurt their situation. They are afraid that they may learn things in therapy that they don't want to know, and they are afraid to ask questions. *Because the family is afraid, the therapist must be unafraid.* The therapist has to be confident of his or her ability to help the family.

The therapist creates a setting in which the family members may first take the risk of looking clearly at themselves and their behaviors and then make changes in these behaviors. The confident therapist asks the questions necessary to allow the family to experience this openness. The therapist is sensitive to the risk the family members are taking as they disclose their feelings. Because all families are idiosyncratic, the therapist checks out all assumptions, including those made by family members and those of the therapist. The therapist gains the family's trust by being unafraid to help the family explore itself and the thoughts, feelings, and behaviors of its members. The therapist gives the family confidence by showing that therapy has direction and purpose and by asking questions that elicit the information the therapist and family members need to bring about family growth and change.

Once the therapeutic relationship has been established, the therapist continues to help family members look at themselves more objectively and talk to one another about what they are learning. Thus, the therapist *encourages feedback among the family members* about how each member may look to others. This feedback must be given in a helpful and nonjudgmental way. In daily living, most people do not get this type of feedback. Clients appreciate feedback from the therapist and other family members when it is provided in a sensitive manner. In addition, the therapist provides specific information about communication to family members and models effective communication through nonjudgmental feedback.

Central to effective therapy is the ability to help family members *develop positive self-esteem.* For the family members to be able to relate effectively to others and present their own points of view, they must feel good about themselves and their thoughts and feelings. The therapist assists each client in the development of self-esteem using these techniques:

1. Making "I value you" comments to the client.
2. Identifying client strengths and reporting these to the client.

3. Asking the client questions that are in his or her area of expertise. Thus, the client feels competent.
4. Emphasizing that the client may ask for clarification if the therapist's communication is not clear.
5. Asking each family member what he or she can do to bring happiness to other members (Satir, 1983).

Building self-esteem is critical to the therapy. Satir's communications theory emphasizes the idea of the therapist and the family working together as a team to solve family problems. The therapist must be perceived as a knowledgeable expert who works at the same level as members of the family, cares for them, and helps them along rather than tells them how they should proceed.

The therapist also needs the ability to structure the therapy sessions. The therapist sets rules for therapy that encourages clients to listen to each other and respect the opinions of other members. For instance, a therapy rule might be that each person must speak for himself or herself or that the family members do not engage in disruptive activities in therapy. By providing this structure, family members will feel secure and will begin to explore their issues in therapy.

The core of Satir's theory is the development of effective communication skills for all family members. Once these skills are developed, they may be used to maintain and enhance self-esteem, negotiate family rules, and connect the family with the external social system. Satir (1988) developed a creative description of the types of dysfunctional communication patterns or styles that family members may adopt.

1. *Placater:* attempts to keep others from getting upset. The placater says, "Whatever you want is fine with me," but in reality feels that he or she is of no value and is helpless to change.
2. *Blamer:* communicates in a way that makes the other person believe he or she is at fault and that the communicator is strong. The blamer always seems to say, "You can't do anything right" and finds fault with others. In reality, the blamer feels unsuccessful and lonely.
3. *Computer:* communicates in a logical and overly-reasonable way that takes the emotion out of any situation. He or she establishes self-worth by out-reasoning others. These "super-reasonable

computers" appear calm and in control but use their style to cover the vulnerability they feel in life.

4. *Distracter:* attempts to move the focus of attention away from a potentially threatening issue to some irrelevant or tangential situation. Distractors use themselves to deflect attention from family problems. Distracters often seem flighty and scatterbrained, but inside they feel they are not valued and cared about.

The therapist teaches family members about these communication styles and encourages them to identify which styles they and others in their family use. The therapist then works with them on ways to eliminate these ineffective styles and replace them with open, congruent, and direct communication.

Satir (1983) believed treatment should terminate when:

1. Family members can complete transactions and seek clarification without threat.
2. Members can recognize hostility from others and reflect this interpretation to the sender.
3. Members become able to understand how others view them.
4. Members can provide nonblaming feedback to others about their behavior.
5. Members can openly share hopes, fears, and expectations.
6. Members can disagree.
7. Members can make choices.
8. Members can learn through practice.
9. Members are no longer bound by past models and inappropriate rules.
10. Members can be congruent in communication with a minimum of hidden messages.

Satir helped families develop these characteristics so the family environment became a haven where children were nurtured and developed as responsible persons with high self-esteem. She believed that effective communication is critical in this process and parents, as architects of the family, need to take responsibility for ensuring that these conditions exist in the family. Many acclaim her warm, humanistic approach to treatment as a breath of fresh air in a profession dominated by technique-oriented theories.

Strengths and Limitations of Satir's Communications Theory

Satir's approach to family therapy is one of the most widely accepted by therapists who are trained in individual psychotherapy because it has the stated goal of increasing the self-worth of the individual family members. Increased self-worth is often one of the chief goals of individually oriented counseling theories. Thus, a major strength of this approach is that it is readily accepted by therapists working with individuals and is an excellent first theory for counselors to employ in family therapy. Other strengths of the approach are:

- It emphasizes the therapist's personhood. Family therapists are more than well trained technicians. They are warm, caring, and empathic to the needs of the family.
- It recognizes and deals with the feelings of individual members of the family in treatment. Identification and exploration of feelings is recognized as an important component of the therapy.
- It recognizes the importance of excellent communication skills in dealing with family members' feelings. By openly recognizing and dealing with feelings using healthy communication patterns, family members gain more respect from others and a heightened sense of self-worth. This increased self-worth through effective communication leads to a healthier family.

The major limitation of Satir's approach to family therapy is that, although her charismatic style of treatment has attracted thousands of students, the approach remains uniquely Satir's. Satir's ability to connect with each family member in her own warm, loving, and nurturing way had a major influence on the family's ability to change in treatment. Because the success of treatment relies heavily on the therapist's personality, training therapists in this approach may be difficult. Thus, the major limitation of Satir's growth-oriented approach to family therapy is that it is not a systematic method for family treatment that other therapists can easily replicate (Gurman & Kniskern, 1981b).

CASE EXAMPLE

Satir's Communication Theory

Mr. and Mrs. Smith sought family therapy because their daughter was experiencing feelings of hopelessness about her future. The therapist requested that the entire family come for the initial sessions. At the first session all members were present. Mr. Smith was a successful systems analyst for a data-processing firm. Mrs. Smith was a homemaker with numerous interests and talents in the arts. Debby, the identified patient, was 15 years old and had average grades as well as a tremendous drive to play basketball, which her parents did not support. John was 7 years old. The family members viewed him as being very cute and not part of the problem.

The therapist began by gathering information about the family and how it resolved issues. During the information-gathering period, the therapist worked to develop the self-concept of each family member by identifying the strengths of the members. The therapist introduced the concept of communication styles and asked the family members to evaluate their styles. Dad was found to be a super-reasonable computer; Mom was a placater trying to make everyone else happy at her own expense; Debby was a blamer who was angry at Dad for not encouraging her in her sports activity; and John was a distracter who could be counted on to be cute whenever family tensions increased.

Once the therapist helped the members recognize their communication styles, work began on developing effective communication patterns. As communication improved, Mom, Dad, Debby, and John expressed their hidden feelings and Debby's symptoms of depression lifted. Mom became less concerned with making the family run smoothly and began to develop her artistic interests. Dad became more playful and had less need to analyze the feelings of family members. Finally, John remained cute, but his cuteness no longer was needed to distract family members from emerging issues in the family.

■ Whitaker's Symbolic–Experiential Family Therapy

Carl Whitaker (1918–1995), a psychiatrist, had been active in family therapy before its formal recognition in the early 1950s. He developed and refined his model of family therapy, called symbolic–experiential family therapy (Whitaker & Keith, 1981), through collaboration with several colleagues, including David Keith, Augustus Napier, and John Warkentin. Previously trained as an obstetrician/gynecologist, Whitaker was board-certified in psychiatry during World War II. His early experience was as a psychiatric administrator at a small hospital, and he later received training in child guidance and play therapy. He treated family members separately, as was the practice in those days.

Whitaker said he began to formulate ideas about mental illness and its treatment because of what he learned from these experiences. In his work with patients, Whitaker noticed that his interventions were most effective when he acted spontaneously and genuinely in a situation presented by a patient rather than when he attempted to intervene based on some theoretical construct. Thus, Whitaker began to hypothesize that change is the result of client experiences rather than therapeutic education.

A classic example is when Whitaker used a baby bottle left by a previous patient's child for nurturing subsequent adult patients. This "technique" was effective for patients with all sorts of problems as long as Whitaker was invested in the notion of mothering the patient. As he began to move on to other ideas about treatment, the baby-bottle intervention was no longer effective.

In a second classic example, Whitaker dozed off during an interview with a client and then shared his dream with the client as a part of the therapeutic process. This technique proved valuable when it was a spontaneous and experiential part of treatment. But when it became a therapeutic technique to be taught to others, it lost its effectiveness.

As with many of the family therapy pioneers, Whitaker began to formulate ideas about family interaction in psychopathology based on work with schizophrenic patients and their families. His most widely recognized work began at Emory University in Atlanta, Georgia, and was continued when he accepted a position at the School of Medicine at the University of Wisconsin in 1965. One of the senior members of the family therapy profession, Whitaker was a sought-after speaker and conducted numerous workshops throughout the country and the world.

Philosophical Tenets and Key Theoretical Constructs

Some professionals question classifying symbolic–experiential family therapy as a humanistic/existential theory. Whitaker believed that theory itself can be harmful to clients because it allows the therapist to remain removed from the intimate contact he believed is necessary for therapeutic change (Whitaker, 1976). Thus, Whitaker's approach to family therapy may be viewed as a moment-to-moment encounter with the family based on the therapist's own experience as well as caring for the family members. This moment-to-moment nature of symbolic–experiential therapy, coupled with the importance Whitaker placed on the therapist's ability to become genuinely involved with the family, leads us to classify this "nontheory" in the humanistic/existential grouping.

Key tenets of symbolic–experiential family therapy are developed with caution because therapists using this approach do not want to establish a set of rules for therapy. Rather, this theory is constantly open to change and depends ultimately on the therapist's intuition and understanding of family problems. Whitaker and Keith (1981) identified key tenets of the theory in their description of the healthy family. Therapy is designed to help families develop the following characteristics:

- Family health is a process of perpetual becoming.
- The healthy family is able to use constructive negative input to improve functioning.
- A healthy family is composed of three generations that maintain healthy separation and autonomy.
- Family roles are flexible, and members are encouraged to exchange roles and explore various family roles.
- The distribution of power in a family is flexible.
- Healthy families develop an "as if" structure that allows tremendous latitude in behaviors tolerated in the family.
- Family members are free to behave temporarily in "crazy" ways without being viewed as permanently deviant by the family.
- The healthy family continues to grow despite adversities.
- The healthy family develops a functional reality about itself that is evolutionary and changes as necessary.

- Healthy families are not symptom-free; rather, they are able to deal with symptoms as part of family growth and development.
- Problems with children are opportunities for parents to look at themselves and determine how they will grow from the challenge. Whitaker would say, "We get the children we need to help us develop as parents" (Whitaker & Keith, 1981).
- Healthy families are aware of the stresses each member experiences and do not focus the stress and concomitant problems permanently in one member. The identified patient in a healthy family moves from person to person rather than remaining fixed on one member.
- Healthy families change through crisis.
- Healthy families encourage expression of both positive and negative feelings. Children and parents should know they are loved and hated.
- In a healthy family, intimacy and separateness go hand in hand. Members are free to be both intimate and distant as required to meet individual needs.
- The healthy family encourages and supports outside relationships for its members.

In summary, Whitaker's followers support maximum autonomy so individuals can experience a full range of behaviors in family life. They encourage individuals to be serious as well as crazy, to know that they can choose to be either, and to know that this ability to choose is healthy. They encourage families to experience both pain and joy in family living and to grow from those experiences. Families who do not grow and change based on their experiences are most likely to seek or need therapy at some point in their development.

Main Therapeutic Interventions

The major goals of symbolic–experiential family therapy are to increase members' sense of belonging to the family and at the same time create the opportunity for the members to individuate from the family. This objective can be accomplished by developing and exercising the creativity of the family in dealing with problems. To achieve these goals with a family in distress, certain therapeutic techniques may be employed. *Mediating goals* and *ultimate goals* are part of this theory. Mediating goals create a therapeutic environment, and ultimate goals are selected by the therapist and the family to be attained through treatment (Roberto, 1991).

The Battle for Structure and Initiative

Two battles are typically waged as family treatment begins (Napier & Whitaker, 1978). The first, the *battle for structure,* begins when the family attempts to tell the therapist what is wrong in the family as well as what should be done about it and who should be treated. The battle for structure begins with the first telephone contact between the therapist and a family member. To be effective, the therapist must control the structure of therapy. If the therapist gives up this role and loses this battle, the family will bring the same ineffective structure to therapy that currently is creating problems in the family.

The symbolic–experiential therapist should set the unit of treatment, which almost always is the entire family. If the client resists this requirement for therapy, the therapist must be prepared to stand firm and be willing to refer the client to another therapist if the client refuses to agree to the proposed structure. Until the battle for structure is resolved, further therapeutic work cannot be accomplished, as the therapist and family will be engaged in a struggle for control. Therapy cannot be effective until the family has decided to trust the therapist and give responsibility for structuring the therapy to the therapist. Winning the battle for control is paradoxical, however, because when the therapist has won the battle, he or she will frequently defer to the family members' wishes about what they want to do to help improve the family.

The second battle to be fought is the *battle for initiative.* This battle must be won by the family. Any initiative for change must come from and be supported and maintained by the family. The therapist cannot ultimately be responsible for the choices the family members make. Initially, members will want to lean on the therapist and become dependent on the therapist's leadership. The therapist rejects this type of leadership and instead supports family members in their decisions to change the way they deal with problems in their family.

These two critical battles are the keys to an effective outcome in therapy. The therapist must be in charge of therapy, and the clients must be in charge of the changes they will or will not make.

Co-Therapy

Because symbolic–experiential family therapists become involved so intensely in their relationships with family members, a co-therapist is essential for effective therapy. The therapist is often reacting at a gut level with the family, and this reaction more often than not is therapeutic. On occasion, however, the therapist becomes inappropriately involved and is not able to withdraw from the intensity of the interaction.

At this time, the co-therapist intervenes and directs therapy while the other therapist regains perspective on what occurred. The co-therapist in this situation might ask the other therapist and the family member involved in the exchange to describe what happened and use that interaction for growth for the family and the therapist alike. Using the "experience" of the moment in the therapy is a necessary element of the change process. Families (and therapists) have to be able to learn and make changes based on their life and therapeutic experiences (Napier & Whitaker, 1978).

Another reason to use co-therapy, according to Whitaker, is that healthy interactions between co-therapists are a model for family members. Co-therapists can support each other, disagree, be confused, teach each other, and engage in many functional behaviors. Observing this behavior is almost always helpful for the family (Whitaker & Keith, 1981).

Six specific techniques for therapy, described by Whitaker and Keith (1981), are presented next. Techniques are useful only insofar as they function to create a learning experience in the therapy for the family members.

1. *Redefine symptoms as efforts for growth.* Family members enter therapy with complaints about the other members. The therapists redefine these behaviors in some way that points out the need for the family to grow and that these behaviors are attempts to tell the family that this growth is necessary. For instance, the father may report that his son is neglecting his chores and behaving rudely at home. The therapist might suggest that the son is merely trying to get the husband and wife to grow in their relationship and work together in their efforts to discipline him.

2. *Teach family members to use fantasy alternatives rather than real-life behaviors.* For example, if a rebellious adolescent

reports wanting to kill his "perfect" older sister, the therapist might ask the youth how he would do the deed and how it would help his situation. Thus, the youth's thought would not be considered abnormal, and he would not be criticized, or even hospitalized, because of his thoughts. Instead, by accepting the thoughts and encouraging the expression of fantasy, the need to turn the thought into action is dissipated.

3. *Assign homework that directs family members to change roles and, most important, not to talk about the family interviews between sessions.* As family members change roles, they experience increased autonomy and flexibility in the family. Role changes break up rigid patterns in the family, allow the family to experience itself differently, and support changes based on that experience. Talking about the session between meetings will drain some of the emotional intensity from the family members. For symbolic–experiential family therapy to be most effective, this intensity has to be present in the therapy session. Along the same line, co-therapists are advised not to talk about the family during the week, as doing so might drain the therapists' energy from the session that would be better used there.

4. *Augment the despair of family members.* When the therapists heighten the despair a family member feels, the others will rally to provide support that was not present before. Despair is a part of family life, and it must be acknowledged and respected. Denial of negative feelings leads to intensified family problems. Support is often lacking in troubled families, and development of a supportive climate eliminates many family problems.

5. *Engage in affective confrontation.* At times, the therapist will feel genuine affect toward family members based on their behaviors. The symbolic–experiential therapist confronts the family with his or her affective reaction. For example, a child may begin dismantling the therapist's office and the parents may be ineffective in stopping the child's behavior. The therapist may say angrily, "Stop destroying my property and sit in your chair, now!" The child—and, perhaps more important, the parents—would experience and assimilate this affective confrontation, which could lead to the parents and child choosing to change their behavior patterns.

6. *Treat children as children and not as peers.* This important principle clarifies that generational differences and boundaries must be acknowledged and respected at certain times. By recognizing generational differences, the spouses may win a "battle for structure" in their own family and develop a sense of order based on appropriate and flexible parental authority.

Symbolic–experiential family therapy has employed these specific techniques. The co-therapy team, however, is by no means limited to these techniques. Frequently, spontaneous reactions and corresponding interventions create experiences that foster new awareness in the session and may be what is needed to facilitate family change.

Whitaker and Keith (1981) listed principles designed to help the therapist avoid errors, including the following:

- Do not become so much a part of the family that it affects your ability to help.
- Do not become so aloof from the family that you operate from only a technical perspective.
- Do not pretend that you don't feel stress or feelings of inadequacy.
- Do not employ a technique for change if it will only create another serious problem in another family member.
- Move at the appropriate pace for the family.
- Do not expect insight to produce change. Therapists often move too fast and expect insight to produce change.
- Do not expect the family to operate from your value system.
- Do not revere your intuitive leaps. Intuition is only intuition, and it may not be appropriate for the family. If the family resists, back off quickly.
- Recognize when you have the family's trust. If you don't, you may waste time in the relationship-building phase when the family is ready to work.
- Do not create a new scapegoat in the family. Help the family understand that each person has a part in the problems within the family.
- Realize the benefits of not treating someone. Not all families need therapy, and not all families will benefit from therapy.

Three-Generation Therapy

When therapy reaches an impasse, the symbolic–experiential therapist may attempt to break the impasse by inviting the older generation to participate in therapy to help unlock the process (Napier & Whitaker, 1978). The grandparents are not invited to therapy as clients but, rather, as consultants to help the co-therapists and family members break the impasse that has developed. The insights the grandparents bring to therapy frequently uncover a whole new arena of experience for the parents and the children and lead to other areas of family growth and development.

Strengths and Limitations of the Symbolic–Experiential Approach

Symbolic–experiential family therapy as practiced by Whitaker and his colleagues has several important strengths. First, it fully recognizes the power of a family in maintaining its dysfunctional behavior patterns and the necessity for using a co-therapy team for work with families. Furthermore, Whitaker recognized the importance of the therapist's winning the battle for structure so the therapist and not the family is in charge of how therapy shall proceed. Finally, this approach, more than any other, encourages the therapist to be spontaneous and creative in introducing new experiences to bring about family change.

The major limitation of this approach is that it lacks a systematic theoretical base for replication of the interventions in treatment. Because treatment in symbolic–experiential therapy is based strongly on the experiences and immediate reactions of the co-therapy team to the family members, no specific treatment interventions are suggested to intervene in specific situations. Thus, the ability of other therapists to replicate this treatment approach is questionable. At best, therapists may attempt to develop their own version of this approach.

As another weakness, this approach suggests ineffective treatment would be unlikely to do lasting harm to a family. Gurman and Kniskern (1978a, b) have indicated that exacerbation of the family's problems may indeed result from family therapy and that therapists should be cognizant of this fact. A third criticism is that, although much has been written about symbolic–experiential family therapy, the claims of this approach have little empirical support in the literature.

CASE EXAMPLE

Whitaker's Symbolic–Experiential Family Therapy

Mrs. Green called to set up an appointment for her 12-year-old son, who was regularly truant from school. She wanted the therapist to work with her son for a while, and then she wanted to join the process. The therapist stated that he would need to see the entire family for his initial evaluation. Mrs. Green protested, and the therapist offered to give her the names of some therapists who would see the boy alone. Mrs. Green said she wanted to work with this therapist because he had been highly recommended by a trusted friend, so she would comply with his desire to see the whole family.

The first few sessions were devoted to learning about the family and the problems with the son, James, and winning the battle for structure. When the family began to trust the co-therapy team to direct therapy, the next phase of treatment began.

In this second phase of treatment, the therapists began to challenge the family's reality of James being the problem and suggested that the entire family seemed to be experiencing a problem. James's behavior was defined as his attempt to point out to the entire family that growth and changes were needed. The rest of this phase of therapy was devoted to helping the family members discover what they needed to change about themselves to increase family intimacy while allowing and encouraging autonomy. As therapy progressed, James's truancy stopped and the family began redefining what members of the family should reasonably be expected to do. This process was handled with little assistance from the therapists, who suggested that the family was doing well on its own and that termination was in order.

White and Epston's Narrative Therapy

Many family therapists have heralded narrative therapy as the answer to the question, "How can we do in-depth therapy with clients under the constraints of short-term managed care regulations?" Narrative therapy, developed primarily by Australians Michael White and David Epston, may hold the key to dealing with difficult family problems based on past experiences and injunctions using brief therapy.

Philosophical Tenets and Key Theoretical Constructs

The tenets of narrative therapy are simple, yet, like most therapies, it is difficult to implement without training and practice. The narrative therapist establishes a warm, caring relationship with the client family and facilitates the clients' telling of their story, which will contain the precipitating elements of the problem situation within it. Embedded in the client's story will be explanations rooted in the past for the client's present symptoms and current difficulties with life. Through a series of steps that will be described in detail later, the narrative therapist assists the client in *externalizing the problem* so the problem, not the client, is understood as the reason for treatment. Moreover, the narrative therapist helps the client reauthor his or her life by retelling this life story in new ways that identify the client's positive characteristics and strengths. As the client comes to accept the reauthored narrative, significant life changes become possible and often occur.

Narrative therapists have great respect for the client's past. By telling their history, clients begin to realize they have the power to reshape their lives and to begin to live in new and more productive ways. Unlike psychodynamic theories, which assume that problems are the result of internal personality difficulties, narrative therapy helps the client look at the larger system consisting of all forces, past and present, that have shaped the individual's attitudes and behaviors.

Narrative theory assumes that clients adopt identities and behaviors based on numerous life influences. These influences define the client's problem-focused identity because clients assume that societal norms, family members' rules and opinions, and influences from other important relationships have the power and authority to define what is good or bad and what is a psychological problem. Narrative therapy helps clients understand the forces that have affected them over the years and make conscious choices to reshape and redefine their responses to these influences.

The key to successful narrative therapy is the fundamental understanding that the "person is never the problem; the problem is the problem" (O'Hanlon, 1994, p. 23). Through the therapy process, clients come to recognize that they are not the problem but that some external forces are influencing them to behave, think, and feel in ways that are unproductive. Externalization (White, 1986) of the problem gives clients a sense of their own personal worth as well as an active force to fight against—the externalized problem.

For example, a client may enter therapy believing she is a depressed person. The narrative therapist works with the client to help her understand that she has been influenced by societal messages to believe she is a depressed person and that she is the problem. In reality, however, the "forces of depression" are working on the client, and these forces of depression are the problem, not the client herself.

When clients realize that they are not the problem, they come to understand that they need to develop new responses to combat the problem. Once they gain this important insight, powerful and creative responses are possible. Externalization puts clients in the position of being responsible and accountable for the choices they make responding to the problem. In the example above, the client might be asked how depression has been controlling her life. Then the therapist might ask what the client could do to fight depression and keep it from ruling her. This type of narrative questioning empowers the client and shows respect for the client's ability to respond in effective ways to the problem (O'Hanlon, 1994). In summary, the key element of this theory is the ability to separate, *through the use of language,* the problem from the client's personal identity.

O'Hanlon (1994) listed the following fundamental steps in the narrative approach.

1. Establish collaborative relationship with the family, and have all members mutually agree upon a name for the problem. For example, a depressed father might name the depression "Agony."
2. Personify and externalize (give its own identity) the problem, and attribute oppressive characteristics to it. For example, Agony is identified as a powerful entity that steals the client's pleasant memories and time with family members.
3. Investigate how the problem has been disruptive, dominating, and discouraging for the client and the family. For example, ask family members to describe how Agony has disrupted their lives and been a demoralizing factor for the family. This description encourages the family to mobilize resources to combat Agony. Do not suggest that the problem "causes" client

behaviors. The force of the problem only influences, tricks, confuses, or tries to recruit the client into certain unproductive actions, thoughts, or feelings. The language used in narrative questioning must *highlight the client's choices* in response to the problem.

4. Discover, through narrative questioning, moments when the problem has not dominated or discouraged the family members. For example, ask the client in this situation to describe the longest period he has not been influenced by depression. By identifying times when he is symptom-free—which are *exceptions* to the rule of being depressed—the client begins to understand that he has power over the problem in certain situations. Next, seek ways to help the client develop power over the problem in most situations.

5. Discover historical evidence to support and reinforce the view that the client is competent enough to have stood up to, defeated, or escaped from the dominance of the problem. In this stage of the therapy, the client begins to *rewrite his life story through narrative*. The therapist and the client discover a reality very different from the one that brought the client to therapy. In this newly discovered reality, the client is competent and powerful and able to respond effectively to the problem. The therapist might ask: "As you continue to overcome the forces of depression, tell me how your life will be different from the one that Agony had planned for you?"

6. Ask family members to speculate on their future in a family with a strong, competent person who is able to overcome the forces of the problem. This speculating becomes a *reauthoring of the family reality* and reinforces the identified patient's reauthoring of his life.

7. *Establish an audience for the client* that will support and reinforce the new life story and new identity created by this story. Problems develop in social contexts. Ensure that the client will be in a context that supports the reauthored life script. Involving family members is one way of developing the new audience. Discussing with family members how they will continue to live according to their new life story is an important part of the termination phase of the narrative approach.

The Use of Therapeutic Letters

Epston (1994) found that narrative conversations with clients may be extended by the use of therapeutic letters to the clients that may be reread days, weeks, months, or years after the therapy has terminated, to reinforce the new narrative. Epston (1994) suggested that therapists use a letter to the family after most sessions. In addition to reinforcing the new narrative explored in therapy, the letter provides clients and the therapist with a record to work from in future sessions and clarifies what took place in previous sessions. Although letters initially are time-consuming, with practice and effective in-session note-taking, most therapists can write a meaningful letter in about 30 minutes (Epston, 1994).

Nylund and Thomas (1994) conducted research concerning the efficacy of therapeutic letters. In a survey of 40 clients on the usefulness of the letters, 37 respondents found them to be "very useful" and 3 found them to be "useful." The "average worth" of one letter was 3.2 sessions. The clients believed that more than 50% of the gains in therapy were a result of the letters alone. The average length of therapy was 4.5 sessions. These results strongly suggest that therapeutic letters are powerful tools and clients as a whole support the use of letters in narrative and other therapies.

Nylund and Thomas (1994) proposed a format for therapeutic letters to help the novice begin using this powerful tool. They suggested the following four areas to be covered in the letter.

1. In an introductory paragraph, join with the clients and reconnect them to the therapy process.
2. Record statements that define how the problem is influencing the client and reinforce the concept of *externalization* of the problem.
3. Ask questions that might have been asked in the session but were not. For example: "I wish I had asked which of your friends will be most likely to support the changes you have made in resisting the influence of depression."
4. Document and reinforce elements of the session that show the client as competent and able to resist the influences of the problem. This focus on client strengths in the session often helps the client maintain the change by rereading the letter between sessions.

Obviously, letters to clients are not a panacea. But they offer the therapist an additional avenue of intervention and support for client change.

Strengths and Limitations of Narrative Therapy

Narrative therapy offers an answer to the therapist's dilemma of how to attend to the client's past and yet focus on present change. Through the use of narrative and reauthoring client life stories, significant changes may be made in relatively brief therapeutic encounters. The therapist is able to work with the client as a colleague in this process and does not

---

CASE EXAMPLE

Narrative Therapy

The Albertson family entered therapy because their son was anxious and fearful in most situations and was unwilling to go to school or to other places where he would be with strangers. The therapist used standard techniques in joining with family members. In the joining process, he had the family members come up with a name for the anxiety. The family called the anxiety "Mr. Fear." This personalization of the anxiety began the process of externalizing the problem.

In the next phase of treatment, the therapist asked family members questions demonstrating that the problem, Mr. Fear, was oppressive and was creating havoc for the identified patient and family members. Next, the therapist investigated with the family the many ways in which the problem was disruptive to the family. All members were able to list several ways the externalized problem had adversely affected the family, and all agreed that the forces of Mr. Fear were great and very disruptive.

In the next phase of the narrative, family members were asked to identify times when Mr. Fear had not been influencing the family and the client had been able to withstand the power of the problem. This created a situation in which the identified patient and family members

(continued)

have to take a more powerful and directive position in the therapy. The use of letters to clients is viewed as a powerful adjunct to therapy.

Criticisms of the narrative approach suggest that by externalizing problems, therapists may minimize the feelings that clients have about their problem situations and about themselves. Fish (1993) suggested that White and Epston engage in therapy that "denies the existence or relevance of differences in power at an interpersonal level" (p. 228). Moreover, Fish suggested that this theory does not deal with the realities of interpersonal power and power politics. Moreover, the reauthoring of life stories cannot exist outside the sphere of political, social, and economic realities.

(CASE EXAMPLE continued)

began to focus on times when the client and the family had been able to function in the face of the problem. If the problem had been successfully defeated in the past, perhaps this could be done again in the future. The family was asked to record specific instances in their history when Mr. Fear was not in control and to discuss how the family worked to make such times happen.

Continuing the narrative approach, the therapist asked family members to speculate on how the family's life would be different without the power and influence of Mr. Fear. The family responded quickly to ways they would be more productive and able to focus their energies on projects that up to now were impossible to contemplate.

Finally, the therapist and the family searched for ways to create a context that would support the newly developed narrative suggesting that the client and the family could make choices that would defeat the influence and tricks of Mr. Fear. This context or audience is crucial to reinforcing and maintaining the new narrative.

A few weeks after termination of therapy, the therapist sent the family a letter outlining the process of the therapy and specifically reminding the identified patient and family members what they did to overcome the powers of the externalized problem, Mr. Fear.

■ Developmental Process Work: A Transpersonal Family Therapy

Developmental systems theory (DST), described fully in Chapter 11, and its application, developmental process work (DPW), is a transpersonal systems theory. As an emerging approach to marriage and family therapy, DPW goes beyond the psychodynamic, behavioral, humanistic, and family systems models of therapy to include metaphysical and transpersonal elements, creating an integrative approach that bridges individual and family systems theories.

Transpersonal family therapists use both objective and subjective information and stay personally involved in the therapeutic process. For this reason, this theory is described by Barry and Janae Weinhold, who created this therapeutic approach.

Utilizing developmental process work techniques with our clients, we found that many transpersonal processes are present in family and relationship problems. Once we learned to follow these processes as they emerged out of presenting problems, we often encountered relationship and family problems involving spiritual abandonment, intrapsychic structures, transcendent experiences, traumatic reenactment, and other transpersonal phenomena. Through these experiences we have learned to trust the "rightness" of whatever process is emerging. We believe that openness to and acceptance of a wide range of psychological and spiritual experiences are necessary to do this kind of work. Working with people at these deep levels does require spiritual courage on the part of client and therapist alike.

This kind of work also can produce a spiritual emergency in therapists if they have not done their own deep work. Your clients will challenge you to do your own deep work. You need to trust that your clients will bring you exactly what you need to work on and that only the clients you are ready to help will appear for therapy. Also, you have to know your limitations and be ready to refer a client you don't feel ready to deal with. If this happens, you should regard it as a "sign" that the client's issue is touching an important area of personal work for you.

Philosophical Tenets of Developmental Process Work

Developmental process work builds on the transpersonal paradigm outlined in the previous chapter and the various assumptions presented there. It adds numerous principles that apply directly to the therapeutic process and support the client in emerging from therapy through a more whole, individuated process. The main philosophical tenets are these:

1. The goal of developmental process work is to help family members develop an intimate relationship with their own soul and with their spiritual realm.

2. To develop spirit/soul intimacy, family members have to reclaim the parts of themselves that split off during childhood. At the core of each split-off part is some unmet developmental need that must be met before that part can be integrated.

3. The process of reclaiming split-off parts includes doing trauma-reduction work to reduce clinical or subclinical symptoms of post-traumatic stress. Untreated trauma and unexpressed core feelings related to trauma keep dysfunctional patterns recycling.

4. Developmental trauma occurred in our primary family relationships from childhood. Healing these developmental traumas in adulthood requires safe, committed family relationships. These may be committed love relationships or relationships between friends who are committed to helping each other get their unmet developmental needs met.

5. Each family member has an innate drive to individuate and is striving in his or her best way (albeit unskilled) to become whole. Every behavior, whether it is effective or not, is an attempt to reach the essential wholeness with which we were born.

6. Each family member enters therapy carrying a "healing process in progress." This healing is expressed in relationship interactions and unconscious body language. The therapist's task is to discover this self-healing process and help the family member become aware of it so he or she may do it more consciously. The therapist must always see the family as evolving in this process, rather than as people who are stuck in a particular psychological state. This requires "process-oriented" thinking rather than the "state-oriented" thinking associated with most medically oriented psychological models.

7. The family is always in charge of the therapy and dictates the speed at which the process moves. This puts the power back in the hands of the client and removes the therapist from a role that

can be invasive or dominating. Hurrying clients along often makes them skip important pieces of their learning process that then requires that they "cycle" the issue again.

8. Unmet developmental needs from childhood are carried along as "excess baggage" until they get met. They recycle again and again, particularly during conflict, always pressing to be met.

9. All current conflicts and problems are the result of unresolved conflicts from childhood. By following the client's process, the sources of these conflicts will be revealed.

10. Therapists tend to draw families who have the same issues they have. The law of attraction can help both complete their unfinished business.

11. Family members' problems and body symptoms have a "rightness" about them. Looking for the rightness of all problems and symptoms is a way of helping family members reframe their experiences. This removes judgment and avoids shaming.

12. It is never too late to get childhood developmental needs met. Human development is a life-long process that can get stunted or have gaps, but it never stops.

13. The therapist serves as a protector. The therapist's first and foremost task is to do no harm and to provide a safe and sacred space in which the client may open up his or her most vulnerable parts. Invasion, perpetration, and abuse of any kind in such a space might justify the label of "sin."

Major Therapeutic Interventions of Developmental Process Work

In DPW, the goal is to help family members achieve wholeness as a system. Any therapeutic "doorway" can be used to access parts of the psyche that were split off during childhood because of trauma or developmental disruptions. These split-off or un-integrated parts usually exist in opposition to other parts of the psyche that are owned or more integrated. The first step in applying the principles of DPW is to discover the conflicting parts of the psyche that usually operate at an unconscious level.

The second step is to help the family member or the family as a whole discover how the conflict between these two parts contains unmet needs or unresolved issues from childhood. The third goal is to help family members get these needs met and integrate this new learning in such a way that it helps the family become more whole, more interdependent, and more able to access transpersonal or spiritual realms.

How to Follow the Multiple Processes of the Family and Its Members

To discover the conflicting parts of the psyche created by traumatic experiences, to identify the unmet developmental needs that are keeping them split off, and to help the client meet these needs, the therapist has to follow the client's process through his or her verbal and nonverbal language. Each family member is seen as a subsystem that constantly emits information through verbal and nonverbal communication. Following this process can be a challenge for a therapist. It may take the therapist through a confusing maze that can make him or her feel lost and out of control. For this reason, we always work as co-therapists when we do couples or family therapy. To follow the family member through this winding journey, a guiding structure is necessary. The following concepts help create a structure that allows therapists to follow the process more effectively.

1. *The surface process:* what the client is identified with at any given moment. It may be called the *ego self;* for example, "I am unemployed." Statements that begin with "I am" are indicators of the client's surface process.
2. *The deep process:* what the client is not identified with in the given moment. The client describes this as something that is happening to him or her. For the client who is unemployed, the deep process might be, "No one wants to hire me." The deep process often is associated with an unwanted or an un-integrated aspect of the personality that carries repressed feelings such as shame. Moving into the deep process with its unconscious material can be frightening to a client. It is important to move slowly and respectfully into this unconscious material.
3. *The edge:* the point of conflict between the surface and the deep processes. The edge is also the edge of awareness between the known and unknown parts of the psyche. The edge often can be identified by statements that begin with, "I can't . . . ." In the

above example, the edge might be, "I can't get a job." Because it often is frightening to move into the deep process, it is important to work as long as necessary at the edge of it. At the edge, the client will learn many valuable things. He or she may learn about unmet developmental needs, about dysfunctional patterns of behavior, or about spiritual lessons. The edge is the place where old feelings are stored that need to be released. The edge also is the place where people can build important intrapsychic structures that are needed to close the developmental gaps and ultimately repair the damage to their soul.

4. *Channels:* the ways in which information passes through a person's system. The channels we use are *auditory, visual, kinesthetic* (movement), *proprioceptive* (a combination of emotions and body sensations), *relationship* (between two people), and *family* (between three people or more). The therapist's task in DPW is to follow the flow of information, as it winds its way through the client's information channels, without interrupting, perpetrating, violating, or disturbing the client and his or her process until it is appropriate to make an intervention. When the information is flowing through a channel, the channel is "occupied." When a channel has no information or has unconscious information in it, the channel is "unoccupied." Terms such as these are simply tracking mechanisms for the therapist to use while watching the information flow.

When information flows simultaneously through two channels and the information is not congruent, this is a "double signal." An example is a woman saying, "I'm in love with my husband" while she also is shaking her head from side to side, which may be saying, "I don't think my husband loves me." Double signals are a quick way of helping the therapist identify the surface process ("I'm in love with my husband") and the deep process ("I don't think my husband loves me") so the work at the edge of the deep process can begin ("I can't face finding out that he may not love me").

5. *Amplification of signals:* involves deliberately increasing or decreasing the strength of a signal to help the therapist and the client determine the actual meaning of the signal. For example, a therapist might ask a client who is shaking a foot while talking to shake it more or to stop shaking it altogether. Either

approach may open up some new information that could be hidden in the movement.

6. *Mirroring:* involves the therapist showing the client how his or her behavior looks from the outside. This technique can be useful for clients who cannot see their own behavior. To do this, the therapist must be good at observing and acting out the observation.

7. *Taking over a signal or part:* requires that the therapist act out or role play an unwanted part that exists in an unoccupied channel so the client can learn more about it. It is important that the therapist give the part back to the client during the therapy so the client can integrate it and so the therapist does not continue to carry it after the session is over.

8. *Interpretation:* Little interpretation is done in DPW. Again, the client determines what is meaningful and useful. The therapist intervenes or interprets only when the client needs cognitive information, mirroring, or help in completing some developmental task.

9. *Resistance:* DPW has no such concept as resistance. If the therapist suggests an intervention and the family doesn't respond favorably, this is considered negative feedback. The family is indicating that this is not the correct approach, or it is not the right time for the intervention. The family should never be forced to follow the therapist's agenda or program.

How to Conduct a DPW Therapy Session

The following steps show clearly how to conduct a therapy session using developmental process work.

1. *Begin therapy by creating a contract with the couple or family members.* This may consist of a general therapy contract regarding number of sessions, cost of sessions, and goals for therapy, as well as specific desired outcomes for each session ("What do you want to accomplish in your session today?"). The initial contract is for a specific number of sessions, usually three to six. The contract is important for three reasons. First, as much power as possible should be placed in the hands of the couple or family. Reclaiming personal power and making clear and

healthy agreements are important parts of the therapy process. Second, having a contract helps the therapist and the couple or family members have some measure of outcome both for the initial therapy contract and the session contract. Third, the initial series helps the therapist determine whether the therapist and the couple or family members can work together effectively.

2. *Support the couple's or family's surface process* by using reflective listening and clarifying statements, by supporting the feelings (expressed directly or indirectly), and by validating the experiences (often by naming, for example, "That sounds like abuse"). During the first few minutes or hours of rapport building, the couple or family members will reveal through the conversation a number of doorway opportunities. The client may show movements in the hands or feet, lower the head, look up or to the side, or describe a strong relationship or family conflict. Many such simultaneous signals can confuse the therapist. By waiting patiently, the therapist eventually will be able to sort these signals into a pattern.

3. *Keep the spiritual component of DPW in the forefront.* When the unconscious material—the traumatic wounds—of a family member appears, the therapist absolutely must assume a position of protector. When some aspect of these wounds appears after a long period of hiding, it can be assumed that some overwhelming experience was associated with its disappearance. When encountering this reemerging part, it is appropriate to assume an attitude of reverence, of sanctity such as that associated with the birth of an infant. The therapist may harm the family member by moving too quickly into the unconscious material in an attempt to get them through it rapidly. It is better to discover the client's rhythm and follow it.

4. *Look for something that identifies the emergence of the deep process.* This might be the expression of an intense feeling, a strong verbal statement, or dramatic physical gesture or movement.

5. *Amplify the signal* by asking the person to do it more, or by forbidding the signal all together. For example, with the previous person, the therapist might say, "Just close your eyes and let yourself feel that sadness" or, "What would happen right now if you stopped rubbing your finger?" Either statement could help her change channels (from kinesthetic into proprioceptive).

6. *Changing channels* usually happens spontaneously and brings a release of information from the unconscious to the client's conscious mind. If the change involves moving into the proprioceptive channel, it also can lead to release of old feelings. A primary goal of the therapist is to facilitate the client in changing channels as many times as needed to help him or her access new information or repair traumatic memories.

7. *Work at the edge between the surface and deep processes* if a family member or the family as a whole is not able to shift into the deep process. Here at the intersection of these two processes, the client will learn valuable emotional, mental, physical, and spiritual lessons that indicate the real nature of the problem as well as the course of action needed to remedy it. Working at the edge also is a sacred space and requires the therapist's most respectful and attentive attitude. To let the client work at the edge without pushing him or her requires patience. Most therapy time in DPW involves working at the edge. Some techniques for working at the edge are:

   ■ Have the client explore options about going into the deep process to make sure he or she has adequate intrapsychic structures for going over the edge without precipitating a psychotic break. This is particularly important when working with clients who have a personality disorder.
   ■ Amplify or forbid the act of going into the deep process.
   ■ Role play or have another family member role play, going into the deep process for the client.
   ■ Have the client fantasize what going into the deep process might be like.
   ■ Help the client find a way around the edge separating the surface and deep processes.
   ■ Have the client ask for the kind of support from other family members the client needs into the deep process.

8. *Integrate to achieve wholeness.* The last step in a session of DPW is integration. The purpose of integration is to help the couple or family system find more wholeness by using the new information, insights, perceptions, and awarenesses gained during the session. The most effective way for couples or family members to anchor new learning is to help them return to the

channel that they occupied at the beginning of the session. For example, if the person's presenting issue or problem emerged in the form of a dream or in a series of internal pictures, the occupied channel was visual. To integrate the session's learnings, the person needs to return to the visual channel. The therapist can help the client do this by asking, "How do you see yourself using what you learned in this session, especially with regard to the issue you began with?" The person then would have to create a new series of pictures related to the presenting issue and develop new behaviors congruent with the new learning.

This aspect of DPW is very important for several reasons.

1. It provides a vision of the next steps in the couple's or family's process. Without a vision, we have found that it is almost impossible for people to develop new behaviors.
2. It asks the couple or family members to take information and experiences that may be of a transpersonal nature and translate them into practical, day-to-day behaviors or goals.
3. It returns the couple or the family and the therapist to the goal stated at the beginning of the session. This aspect of integration provides a sense of completion and sets up closure for the session. It also provides an opportunity for the couple or the family members and the therapist to evaluate the therapy experience, and it can provide productive feedback to the therapist.

Therapeutic Goals of DPW

In DPW, therapeutic interventions are appropriate during a couples or family therapy session when the therapist discovers evidence of developmental traumas or incomplete developmental tasks emerging in a family member's process. These incomplete tasks may be related to incomplete bonding, separation, autonomy, or cooperation issues from the first five years of a family member's life. They also can be related to incomplete tasks of the parents in their couple relationship or incomplete tasks in the family system or all of the above.

The therapist must be able to recognize the nonverbal signals indicating that memories of developmental trauma may be emerging in the therapeutic process. Signals that often appear include rocking movements, a childlike tone of voice, curling up or lying down, and crossed feet. Therapists should know the specific developmental needs and tasks of the four stages of development: co-dependent (bonding), counterdependent (separation), independent (autonomy and mastery), and interdependent (cooperation). Each stage will leave characteristic behaviors that indicate exactly what must be completed. For example, an adult with incomplete bonding often has one or more addictions to substances (food, drugs, alcohol), sex, or people. Adults with incomplete separation issues often have addictions to work or exhibit compulsive behaviors.

We have developed a series of skill-building exercises designed to help people complete these developmental stages; they are contained in our recent books (Weinhold & Hendricks, 1993; Weinhold & Weinhold, 1989, 1992, 1994, 2000). We give these handouts to couples and family members to help them take charge of their own healing process. These exercises include:

- How to identify unmet developmental needs
- How to get these needs met as an adult
- How to express feelings appropriately
- How to validate the client's childhood experiences and feelings
- How to resolve old conflicts with members of the client's family of origin
- How to resolve current conflicts in partnership ways
- How to develop a vision of life beyond dysfunction
- How to conduct a family meeting.

Limitations of Developmental Process Work

Use of DPW in couples or family therapy may be problematic in some cases because a long-term commitment might be required to break intergenerational family patterns. We usually recommend about one month of therapy for every year of life, but we have found that when a couple or a family works together to create a therapeutic milieu in the family, the time in therapy is greatly reduced. Finally, this type of therapy requires the couple or family to transcend the conventional wisdom and look at their problems and issues from an expanded perspective. Some couples or families are just not ready or willing to do that and therefore are not good candidates for this type of therapy.

Developmental Process Work

A couple recently came to us for therapy in the midst of an intense relationship crisis. The woman had just discovered that her husband was having an affair with another woman. She said she was angry enough to kill him. She claimed that a demon inside her was telling her to kill him and that she was afraid this demon would take over her behavior.

After getting her to agree that she would use nonviolent means to resolve her conflict with her husband, we asked her to draw a picture of her demon and conduct a dialogue with it. She placed the picture of the demon she drew on a pillow in front of her and then carried on a Gestalt-like dialogue for about 15 minutes.

Much to her surprise, she discovered through the dialogue with this demon that it served a useful purpose in her life. When she asked the demon what it was, he replied, "I've been waiting 900 years for you to work on this issue." When she asked what the issue was, it said, "You need to learn how to give up control. It was your need to control that led your husband to have an affair." The demon added, "I'm here to help you let go, and I'm very patient." Eventually, she asked the demon to help her work on her control issue. Later she began working on this issue in therapy. She also saw that her husband's affair provided her with another opportunity to learn to give up the illusion of control over him that was pushing him away.

We wondered how more traditional therapists might have handled this client. We saw that she was, in effect, having a "spiritual emergency" precipitated by her husband's affair. Even though she looked and sounded psychotic, we knew it was important not to try to take her out of this state until we all better understood the purpose of her "demon" process. We trusted that there was something "right" about this process and decided to invite her to discover more about the so-called demon part of herself. A more medically oriented therapist probably would have medicated and even hospitalized her to get her out of her "crazy" thinking process and through her emergency.

■ *Summary*

This chapter explored four systems-based theories of family therapy that will be of particular interest to therapists who believe family treatment must consider and emphasize the uniqueness of the individual within the family context. The theories of Virginia Satir, Carl Whitaker, Michael White and David Epston, and Barry and Janae Weinhold all place a premium on the genuine encounter between the therapist and the family members and seek to bring about family change through these humanistic/existential/transpersonal encounters.

SUGGESTED READINGS

"The Legacy of Virginia Satir." (1989). *Family Therapy Networker, 13*(1), 26–56.

Napier, A. Y., & Whitaker, C. A. (1978). *The family crucible.* New York: Harper & Row.

"The Promise of Narrative." (1994). *The Family Therapy Networker, 18*(6), 18–49.

Satir, V. M. (1982). "The Therapist and Family Therapy: Process Model." In A. M. Horne & M. M. Ohlsen, eds., *Family counseling and therapy.* Itasca, IL: Peacock.

Satir, V. M. (1983). *Conjoint family therapy,* 3rd ed. Palo Alto, CA: Science and Behavior Books.

Satir, V. M. (1988). *The new peoplemaking.* Palo Alto, CA: Science and Behavior Books.

Weinhold, B. K., & Hendricks, G. (1993). *Counseling and psychotherapy: A transpersonal approach.* Denver: Love.

Weinhold, B. K., & Weinhold, J. B. (1989). *Breaking free of the co-dependency trap.* Walpole, NH: Stillpoint.

Weinhold, J. B., & Weinhold, B. K. (1992). *Counter-Dependency: The flight from intimacy.* Colorado Springs, CO: CICRCL Press.

Weinhold, B. K. & Weinhold, J. B. (2000). *Conflict resolution: The partnership way.* Denver, CO: Love.

Whitaker, C. A., & Keith, D. V. (1981). "Symbolic–Experiential Family Therapy." In A. S. Gurman & D. P. Kniskern, Eds., *Handbook of family therapy.* New York: Brunner/Mazel.

White, M., & Epston, D. (1990). *Narrative means to therapeutic ends.* New York: Norton.

PART THREE

Special Issues in Marriage and Family Therapy

■ **CHAPTERS**

Conflict Resolution in Family Treatment

In this chapter we present a two-part vision for resolving conflicts in couples and families. The first part presents an optimal model for couples and families with an aim of preventing developmental trauma. The second part of the vision focuses on the **Partnership Way,** a method of resolving conflicts developed by Barry and Janae Weinhold. The chapter will show how to use this innovative approach in therapy to alleviate developmental traumas, particularly those that appear in conflict situations in couples and families.

Partnership way
Developmental trauma
Dominator families
Developmental tasks
Meta-theory
Developmental systems theory
Regression-progression
Prenatal and perinatal psychology
Partnership families
Interdependent stage of development
Drama triangle
Co-dependent stage of development
Independent stage of development
Counter-dependent stage of development

QUESTIONS FOR DISCUSSION

1. In the description of optimal development in this chapter, what developmental tasks do you think are you still attempting to complete in your adult relationships?

2. According to the **Partnership Way,** what is the cause of intractable conflicts in couples and families?

3. What are the main assumptions of this approach to conflict resolution, and how do they differ from the assumptions of more traditional approaches?

4. What characteristics of dominator relationships and families do you think are the most prevalent? Why?

5. What do you think are the main barriers to people using the Partnership Way of resolving their couple and family conflicts?

6. How do you see the drama triangle interfering with the resolution of conflicts in couples and families?

Because of research in prenatal and perinatal psychology (Chamberlain 1996; Klaus, Kennell, & Klaus, 1993, 1995; Verny 1981), we now are able to present an optimal model of development in which parents conceive, gestate, give birth, and parent consciously. They prepare themselves for these tasks prior to conception by consciously clearing any major unresolved conflicts from their own childhood. This becomes the basis for a new paradigm, the Partnership Way.

Optimal Model of Development

During all phases of their child's development, the parents must focus their attention on the child's needs. They are able to provide loving encouragement, take the needs of the child seriously and set limits in a loving and supportive way without harming the child mentally, emotionally, physically and spiritually. If these parents find themselves unable to provide constancy in their parenting or experience conflict between them, they use adult resources such as therapy or parent support groups to help them deal with these issues.

Around this optimal nuclear family unit is a secondary ring of support that comes through an extended family network. The function of this group of individuals, couples, and families is to support the parents so they can parent the child. This group provides emotional, spiritual, physical, and mental sustenance for the couple so they can provide constant and consistent attention to the child's needs. A tertiary ring of help for the nuclear family unit comes through community resources. This ring provides aid via social programs and policies designed to foster strong family units and make the needs of children a priority.

Buoyed by assistance from these multitiered support systems, the child is able to complete the first crucial stages of psychological development without lasting trauma. By age 3 the child is sufficiently self-reliant, self-confident, and capable of getting his or her needs met without having to whine, cry, get angry or act violently. Able to instinctively trust his or her intuition and natural ways of knowing, the child grows in wisdom and understanding about how the world works.

The parents, who accept the child's natural curiosity and impulses, allow the child to master the tasks of daily living and delight with the child in his or her growing competencies. The child continues to refine his or her skills in getting needs met by direct negotiation and learns to resolve conflicts of wants and needs naturally in cooperative "win/win" ways. The parents model respectful interpersonal behaviors and honor differences of all kinds.

School experiences are structured so the child expands his or her skills in living interdependently. Cooperative learning replaces competition and rewards and punishment. Teachers model respectful, cooperative behaviors and reinforce kind, compassionate, humane and benevolent behaviors. As the child moves into adolescence, the adults in his or her life support the healthy, safe exploration of adult roles and responsibilities and the child becomes more mature in his or her choices.

Children who experience a strong developmental foundation grow up to become mature adults capable of directing their lives in responsible ways. They know how to get their needs met in healthy, responsible ways and can effectively resolve their conflicts.

This prevention-based vision of birthing and rearing peaceful children in a peaceful world is currently within the realm of possibilities. Frederic Leboyer (1975), one of the pioneers of this vision, discovered that gently birthed babies were developmentally advanced for their ages, were happier, better adjusted and were more loving and peaceful (Russell, 1979). The significance of the birth experience has been repeatedly correlated with the overall quality of a person's life (Grof, 1985). This research is now influencing public policymaking. After a lengthy investigation into the "roots of crime," the Commission on Crime Control and Violence Prevention in Sacramento, California recommended, among other things, childbirth with parental involvement, family intimacy and a natural delivery (Jones, 1995).

The vision of remedying the effects of traumatic births and early childhood traumas is equally attainable. Research findings on optimal childhood development provide us with practical guidelines and interventions, coupled with new trauma-reduction therapies. These breakthroughs allow us to develop a comprehensive model for emancipating adults and children from their residue of developmental trauma. This chapter deals with how to utilize this vision to resolve conflict in couples and families.

When President John F. Kennedy announced his vision of sending a man to the moon by the end of the decade of the 1960s, the technology to accomplish this task did not exist. Because his vision caught people's imagination, the scientific world quickly created the technology and accomplished the task.

Now sufficient scientific information and psychological technologies are available to make the vision of a peaceful world a reality. The next step is to inspire the imagination of this vision at a collective level. As technology has shrunk the world, the need for cooperation and peaceful interdependency is an evolutionary necessity. The peaceful resolution of conflicts becomes unequivocally linked to our survival as a species.

A New Paradigm

Realizing the limitations of existing models of conflict resolution to address the growing evolutionary crisis, we set about developing a new paradigm for resolving conflicts. Through field research and a meta-analysis of the research on existing models of conflict resolution, the authors have identified a number of critical components for creating a new paradigm in the field of conflict resolution that will teach people how to:

- simplify the context of conflict
- simplify the resolution of conflict
- reframe conflict from a negative to a positive experience
- utilize the strong feelings that often emerge during conflict situations
- unify opposites that appear in conflict situations
- develop reciprocity in relationships
- infuse conflict situations with compassion and kindness
- resolve intractable conflicts at their source.

The *Partnership Way* (Weinhold & Weinhold, 2000) represents a new paradigm of conflict resolution that teaches couples and families the psychological skills they need to effectively resolve intractable conflicts of all kinds in a cooperative, peaceful manner. The Partnership Way focuses on helping couples and families resolve conflicts of wants and needs, values and beliefs, and intractable conflicts at their source. Specific therapeutic and psychoeducational interventions have been developed for resolving each kind of conflict.

The term *partnership way* is used for three basic reasons.

1. It advocates embracing or partnering with both the experience of the conflict and the people with whom you have the conflict. The goal of embracing conflict is *self-discovery.* Information discovered during the process of resolving a conflict can be used as an opportunity for personal growth.
2. It advocates building partnership relationships in couples and families that facilitate reciprocity, interdependency, unity, mutuality, and cooperation.
3. It facilitates moving people beyond polarized "us versus them" splits in thinking into the "both/and" thinking essential for partnering.

The theoretical foundation, for the Partnership Way is called *developmental systems theory,* (DST), described briefly below. The therapeutic application of this theory, developmental process work (DPW), was described in Chapter 10. This treatment modality focuses specifically on resolving conflicts at their source through a systemic approach that applies the principles of individual development and dysfunction to the development of larger and more complex human systems, such as couples and families.

DST identifies seven systemic levels of development, as well as the developmental tasks to be completed at each level and the developmental needs that must be met to complete these tasks. The seven systemic levels of development are:

1. Individuals
2. Couples (intimate partners, friends, and co-workers)
3. Families
4. Organizations
5. Cultural subgroups
6. Nation–states
7. Humans as a species

Within each systemic level are four developmental stages through which the system must evolve:

1. *Co-dependent stage*
2. *Counter-dependent stage*
3. *Independent stage*
4. *Interdependent stage.*

The theory also identifies the common dysfunctional behaviors and conflicts that appear at each systemic level if the needs are not met and the tasks not completed, causing a degree of "stuckness" at each stage.

■ *Assumptions of the Partnership Way*

The Partnership Way has certain critical assumptions that address some of the limitations and deficits in other existing approaches. These philosophical assumptions create a specific lens through which we began to view conflict.

- *The natural state of the universe is peaceful interdependence.* The main premise in this approach is that *peace is inevitable.* This new paradigm in the field of conflict resolution transcends the prevalent paradigm that conflict is inevitable and all we can do is learn to manage it. The next leap in evolution for the human species is one that will help people learn to live peacefully and interdependently.
- *All conflict as an unskilled, ineffective attempt by humans to prove their worth and get their needs met.* This approach identifies unmet developmental needs as a primary cause of humans' competitive, aggressive nature. It shows how the lack of proper parental support during the first 3 years of life produces individuals with undiagnosed developmental trauma that leaves them unable to get their needs met in peaceful, cooperative, nonviolent ways.
- *Conflict presents an opportunity for growth and intimacy.* Many people avoid conflict because they fail to see the inherent opportunities for growth and increased intimacy in conflict situations. Resolving conflicts effectively brings people closer together and helps them work more cooperatively.

- *Individual initiative is critical* in resolving the conflict. Each person is responsible for identifying and addressing his or her contribution to the conflict situation.
- *Unidentified and untreated developmental trauma is a major force in the creation of conflict.* Unresolved effects of early developmental traumas and conflicts cause intrapsychic splitting (dissociation), polarization, and other symptoms of post-traumatic stress that later give rise to intractable, recycling conflicts in relationships, families, organizations, and nation–states.
- *The ability to feel compassion and express kindness helps people bring together polarities* both inside and outside themselves.

Theoretical Foundations of the Partnership Way

Supporting the Partnership Way is a meta-theory, *developmental systems theory* (DST), which combines the elements and tools from cognitive–behavioral theories, humanistic theories, psychodynamic theories, systems theories, transpersonal theories, and chaos theory in addressing conflict resolution. Rather than attempting to compare the theories, the gem of information or tools was extracted from each theory and synthesized into this meta-theory.

Developmental systems theory is a *systematic eclectic* theory. This means that certain key elements of various theories and various intervention strategies have been integrated in a systematic way to create a new theory. Much of the theory building in psychology has followed this model: Previously existing theoretical material is reshaped and combined in a unique way to create a new theory. This is how most practitioners operate as well. During their training as therapists, they may have learned or been exposed to a variety of theories, but when they attempt to apply the theories, they have to adapt them to fit their own personality and the population with whom they work.

The theoretical foundations of developmental systems theory mentioned here are general systems theory, transactional analysis (TA), the psychoanalytic work of Alice Miller, the developmental theories and research of Eric Erikson, Robert Havighurst, and Margaret Mahler, the Jungian-based global process work approach of Arnold

Mindell, family systems theories, and various transpersonal and meta-physical theories.

Contributions From General Systems Theories

General systems theory originated in the early 1940s as mathematicians, physicists, and engineers searched for functional and structural rules that could describe all physical (nonhuman) systems. Norbert Weiner (1954) first applied these principles to develop the Norden bombsight during World War II. He coined the term *cybernetics* to describe this emerging field of study. Pioneers Buckley (1967) and von Bertalanffy (1968) attempted to apply systems concepts to human systems. Finally, in 1978 James Miller wrote a book that laid out a more complete application of the concepts of general systems theory to human systems.

Contributions From Transactional Analysis

In 1970, Jacqui Lee Schiff published *All My Children,* this book described a revolutionary new therapy approach called "corrective parenting," which grew out of Eric Berne's work on transactional analysis. The book reported the work that Jacqui Schiff and her husband did with schizophrenics no one else wanted to work with. Their treatment approach involved a residential treatment program. Many patients became successfully functioning adults, some becoming therapists themselves.

As the concept of corrective parenting grew in the 1970s, many practitioners began to experiment with it in an outpatient format. From this early experimentation, practitioners were able to detail the kinds of interventions that produced lasting changes in their clients. Jacqui Schiff and her colleagues followed with a sequel book, *The Cathexis Reader* (Schiff, 1976), which described a set of passive or discounting behaviors that served to keep people stuck in symbiotic or co-dependent relationships.

Schiff also outlined effective therapeutic methods for confronting these dysfunctional behaviors. For example, she found that passive people often discount their own needs and focus on the needs of others, hoping to "win" some attention or approval from them. Passive people discount their ability to ask directly for what they want. Teaching them to ask directly to get their needs met was an effective intervention for dealing with this problem. As Schiff and her colleagues studied passivity and discounting, they discovered that it wasn't just part of the pathology of schizophrenics but also was very much a part of everyday life for most people. These therapists estimated that as many as two in every five "transactions" or interactions between people involve some discounting or passivity.

TA practitioners Dorothy Babcock and Terry Keepers (1976) combined the passivity/discounting information with script analysis in a book for parents called *Raising Kids OK*. Others adapted this material in other types of TA therapy, such as redecision therapy (Goulding & Goulding, 1978).

With the onset of the co-dependency movement, the corrective parenting treatment modality again began to appear in the recovery literature. Jon and Laurie Weiss (1989), in their book *Recovery from Co-dependency,* described corrective parenting techniques they used in treating co-dependency. Jean Illsley Clarke and her colleagues (1978, 1989) wrote several books applying this evolving theory to parenting. Pam Levin also wrote several books that further developed corrective parenting theory, including *Becoming the Way We Are* (1988a) and *Cycles of Power* (1988b). Other books, *Breaking Free of the Co-dependency Trap* (Weinhold & Weinhold, 1989) and *Counter-dependency: The Flight from Intimacy* (Weinhold & Weinhold, 1992), further developed aspects of this theory. *Breaking Free of Addictive Family Relationships* (Weinhold, 1991) describes the process of breaking dysfunctional transactions in present relationships using many concepts from corrective parenting.

Psychoanalytic Contributions of Alice Miller

Much of the revival of interest in the corrective parenting approach grew out of the work of Swiss analyst Alice Miller. Her pioneering books (1981, 1983, 1986, 1988, and 1991) helped rekindle interest in how early narcissistic wounds affect later development. Miller's work showed clearly some of the adverse effects of what might be called "standard parenting practices," as well as documenting the process of how the same dysfunctional behavior patterns repeat from one generation to the next.

Developmental Contributions of Eric Erikson, Robert Havighurst, and Margaret Mahler

The work of Erikson (1950), Havighurst (1972), and Piaget (1951) identified the normal stages of physical development and the cognitive and emotional tasks that have to be mastered at each stage. In addition, the research of Margaret Mahler (1968) and her colleagues (Mahler et al., 1975) were able to chart the course of early childhood development from the early *bonding stage* (birth to 9 months) through the *separation stage* (9 to 24 months). Kaplan's book, *Oneness and Separateness* (1978), based on Mahler's research, provides a clear narrative description of these two stages, including what might prevent the successful completion of each stage.

Global Process Work Approach of Arnold Mindell

Dr. Arnold Mindell, a Jungian analyst, developed a new adaptation of Jungian theory called *global process work,* formerly known as process-oriented psychology (see Mindell, 1983, 1985a, 1985b, & 1987). Expanding on Jung's ideas about dreams, Mindell began to realize that most people are dreaming all the time. Their waking dreams, according to Mindell, are often ways to avoid unpleasant realities or unpleasant memories, while their sleeping dreams provide an outlet for unconscious material to emerge.

The real genius of Mindell's theory, however, was his expansion of information theories such as *neurolinguistic programming* (NLP) into six main channels for inputting and outputting information and the use of Taoist principles in his therapy. This information theory provided a mechanism the therapist could use to track information as it presented itself through the client's symptoms and problems. Mindell's use of Taoist principles provided a context for understanding the "rightness" of all symptoms and problems, as well as the use of client-centered techniques for "following" the client's process.

In addition, he used the principles of unified field theory from quantum physics to show how problems move from one "field" or system to another. For example, according to his theory, an internal conflict that is not resolved at the individual level will move out into the relationship "field" and emerge there as a conflict. If the conflict is not resolved at that level, Mindell hypothesized, it will move out into the next level of system, the family. Using this theory to examine national and international conflicts, he began to hypothesize about how unresolved global conflicts can be the collective manifestation of many unresolved individual, relationship, family, and organizational conflicts.

Contributions From Family Systems Theories

As early as the late 1950s, the Palo Alto group led by Gregory Bateson began applying cybernetics to the study of family therapy. The work of the Palo Alto group eventually led to the major paradigm shift in the field of family therapy that now views the individual and each successively more complex social group as systems interacting with each other. This provided a new perspective in family therapy so that the family could be treated as a system containing various subsystems. Developmental systems theory utilizes both the systems language and the concept of a family as a dynamic system that is constantly changing and evolving.

Developmental systems theory also borrows from several of the established family systems theories. The work of Bowen and Framo forms a useful model for helping individuals and families sort out family-of-origin issues that are recycling in their current family dynamics. Bowen also was the first to emphasize the importance of family therapists' doing their own family-of-origin work as part of training to become family therapists.

Structural family therapy has contributed useful definitions of the boundaries and rules present in each subsystem in a family. This helped create three interrelated subsystems used in DST: the individual, the couple, and the family.

The work of Don Jackson (1965) and Sager and his associates (Sager et al., 1971) showed how to bring together intrapsychic and family systems concepts. The basic assumption of their model is that unconscious and conscious aspects of family members' inner lives form an important part of the systemic feedback loop that can be observed in their interaction, communication, and behavior patterns. Taub–Bynum (1984) extended the family communication system developed by Jackson and others to include transpersonal aspects such as telepathy and extrasensory perception as ways by which the family's unconscious is communicated.

Like the strategic approaches, DST focuses on resolution of the presenting family problem. The belief is that following the family's process is going to be the therapist's most useful route. Also, in the application of DST, paradox is utilized much the same way it is used by the strategic family therapist.

Transpersonal and Metaphysical Contributions

Ken Wilber (1980) described the transcendent and spiritual aspects of developmental psychology. His concepts of the transegoic stages of human development, as well as the superconscious levels of awareness, helped integrate the spiritual and transformative elements of human development into this emerging theory.

The work of Frederick LeBoyer (1975), a French obstetrician; Igor Charkovsky, a Soviet physician; Michel Odent of France (Johnson & Odent, 1995); and the American midwifery movement helped develop therapeutic methods to assist people in re-creating an ideal birth. Prenatal and perinatal psychology helped develop a variety of ways to link many adult problems to prebirth and birth traumas as well as early childhood trauma.

▇ Stages of Development

The stages of development theory divides childhood and adolescence into four main stages of development:

1. *Co-dependent stage* (pre-birth to 9 months)
2. *Counter-dependent stage* (10–36 months)
3. *Independent stage* (3–5 years)
4. *Interdependent stage* (6–18 years).

In each stage, the person has to master certain key developmental tasks. If these tasks are not met at their proper time, they become excess baggage that gets dragged along to the next stage and interferes with the overall flow of development. These key tasks can be completed later only through effective interventions. This discovery led to the creation of developmental process work to provide parents, teachers, and therapists with the skills to make effective interventions that help children and adults complete these tasks (Weinhold & Hendricks, 1993; Weinhold & Weinhold, 1992).

Co-dependent Stage

The main developmental task of the *co-dependent stage* is *bonding.* If a child grows up in a child-centered family where the child's needs are attended to with respect and nurturing, he or she will develop a solid foundation. The child will feel secure and will be ready to begin exploring his or her world at around 6 to 9 months. This ensures that he or she will develop a "love affair with the world" and continue to grow and learn into the next stage of development.

In addition to having basic physical needs met, the fully bonded child needs to be touched, sung to, talked to in loving ways, and have his or her essence mirrored by patient and loving parents and other significant adults. Children who experience democratic parenting practices like these will likely grow up to create a similar loving and nurturing family of their own.

Unfortunately, with the increasing number of single-parent families and families in which both parents have to work outside the home, many children do not receive secure bonding. In their book, *High Risk: Children Without a Conscience,* Magid and McKelvey (1987) pointed out that poorly bonded children often become the sociopaths and psychopaths of society. These are the kids who join gangs, become criminals, or are unable to hold steady jobs. Research also has confirmed the connection between poor bonding and child abuse. When maternal and paternal infant bonding is strong, there is almost no child abuse.

Counter-dependent Stage

The *counter-dependent stage* requires that the child complete two important developmental tasks:

1. To successfully separate from the constraints of the symbiotic relationship with mother to form a separate, autonomous identity.
2. To learn to manage feelings of frustration and anger in response to normal limits imposed by the world in general and parents in particular. Parents must handle temper tantrums and other forms of emotional outbursts gently, giving clear limits without using shame or physical punishment.

If parents punish the child severely for these emotional outbursts by using physical punishment, shame, or humiliation, the child will suffer narcissistic wounds and experience the punishment as an attempt to annihilate the self. Anger and rage then become protective mechanisms against this fear of annihilation. Alice Miller (1983) wrote, "Contrary to popular opinion, the injustice, humiliation, mistreatment and coercion a person has experienced (while growing up) are not without consequences" (p. 247).

One of the consequences Miller alludes to is activation of the deepest and most primitive of human defenses, called the *talionic response.* This is the response behind the Biblical statement, "An eye for an eye and a tooth for a tooth." If during the counter-dependent stage children are not trained by understanding and sensitive parents to manage this primitive impulse effectively, these children likely will develop violent or aggressive means for handling frustrations and conflicts. This becomes the basis for intergenerational patterns of child and spousal abuse, sometimes called "the vicious cycle of cruelty" (Weinhold, 1991). This is why older kids pick on younger kids on the playground or attempt to bully or intimidate other children, and it is likely that it plays a big part in all the youth violence (Weinhold, 2001).

Independent Stage

The developmental tasks of the *independent stage*—mastery and autonomy—are impossible to complete if the child did not successfully complete the developmental tasks of the previous stages. If the child doesn't receive enough bonding during the co-dependent stage or receives abusive or neglectful parenting during the counter-dependent stage, it is almost impossible for that child to develop as a separate, autonomous individual. The "psychological birth" of the individual is the important outcome of successfully completing these crucial tasks. The independent stage is the time when the child learns to play independently, dress, feed, and nurture himself or herself. The child also asks questions to find out how everything works and learns to ask directly for what he or she wants and needs from others. Finally, the child learns to trust his or her own intuition and inner wisdom to guide his or her life.

Without the proper foundation from the previous stages, the child is trapped in an endless web of self-doubts and insecurities. He or she may decide that becoming a separate person is too frightening and, instead, will turn away from himself or herself and learn how to be dependent on others to direct his or her life. This tragic decision makes it impossible for the child to think freely, feel all of his or her feelings, dream, or function later as an effective parent charged with the responsibility of guiding and directing the lives of his or her children.

Interdependent Stage

The *interdependent stage* relies on the foundation created during the previous stages. The main developmental tasks here are to learn how to cooperate with others and to resolve conflicts in nonviolent win-win ways. Again, if the foundation is weak, the child has great difficulty developing cooperative behaviors and resolving conflicts in win-win ways. The task also becomes more difficult because most schools operate on a competitive model rather than a cooperative one. By the time they enter school, children with a poor foundation tend to fluctuate between giving themselves up to get along with others or aggressively or narcissistically demanding that others do what they want. This is why youth gangs have replaced families: Gangs allow children to give themselves up to the code of behavior in the gang (a distorted form of bonding), and they can band together to bully others into giving them what they want (a distorted form of autonomy).

Translating the Stages Into Couples Therapy

Developmental Systems Theory presents a systemic approach to recovering the self through couples and family therapy. One of the main goals of the family therapist using this approach is to create a therapeutic milieu in the couple relationship and in the family so people can help each other complete these vital tasks that hold them back from being effective parents and adults.

The theory posits that the same developmental stages that the individual system goes through are present in couple relationship systems and in family relationship systems. With the aid of this information, the family therapist can begin to locate the developmental "holes" in the couple system. By skillfully following the processes and the presenting problem of the couple, the therapist can design interventions to help fill those holes and move the system to a higher level of functioning.

Developmental Stages of Intimate Relationships

The Partnership Way can be applied to relationships between two people, whether they are two friends, two co-workers, or a committed couple. A "committed relationship" also can consist of two sisters, a parent and a child, a boss and an employee, or two friends. The commitment is that both people will stay involved during a conflict and attempt to find a resolution. This kind of commitment is essential for resolving intractable relationship conflicts. When two people can work cooperatively to resolve their conflicts, they can develop a tremendous amount of intimacy in their relationship, resolve their own internal conflicts, and deepen their relationship between them.

The evolution of intimate relationships follows a developmental sequence similar to the path individuals take. As the relationship and the people involved grow and mature, relationships undergo a series of predictable changes. When you enter an intimate relationship, you carry with you the residue of your unrecognized and unhealed developmental traumas. Any unmet developmental needs and issues related to incomplete psychosocial tasks eventually will surface during conflicts in the relationship. Generally, these issues will surface in an intimate relationship when it is safe enough for conflicts to erupt. Many couples avoid conflicts to maintain some false sense of harmony.

Experiences in a couple relationship provide opportunities for completing the psychosocial tasks of your relationship and also the tasks related to individual development. Intimate relationships are an ideal crucible for helping the couple move to a higher stage of development. The four stages of relationship development are: *co-dependent, counter-dependent, independent,* and *interdependent.* The psychosocial tasks of each stage and methods for completing these tasks are listed in Table 11.1.

When people seek therapy, they usually are in conflict, and they often relate similar stories. Although their stories have various versions, the main theme is, "We had wonderful relationship in the beginning. We got along so well. Then we started to get on each other's nerves and began having fights." Sometimes the two people have been in conflict long enough to create a "reservoir of ill will" between them by holding grudges and resentment.

TABLE 11.1

Four Stages of Relationship Development

Stage of Development	Psychosocial tasks of Intimate Relationship	Methods for Completing These Tasks
Co-dependent	• Bonding with each other • Establishing primal trust in the relationship • Creating a relationship identity • Establishing parameters regarding expression of sexual energy	• Establishing friendship as a quality of the relationship • Recognizing and acknowledging each other's spiritual essence • Exchanging nurturing touch and talk • Respecting and validating each other's needs and feelings • Giving and receiving unconditional love • Creating common interests, values, beliefs, and goals
Counter-dependent	• Separating psychologically from each other • Resolving internal conflicts between needs of self and needs of other	• Exploring interests outside of the relationship • Separating nurturing touch from sexual touch • Establishing individual goals, values, and beliefs within the relationship • Establishing and receiving respect for individual boundaries • Identifying self-needs versus other needs • Negotiating directly to get needs met
Independent	• Mastering self-sufficiency within the relationship • Establishing an equal, egalitarian form of autonomy within the relationship • Achieving object constancy as a couple	• Achieving equality in the relationship (financial, professional, educational, and spiritual) • Achieving a balance between individual and relational needs and interests • Maintaining individual goals, values, and beliefs within the couple relationship • Experiencing mutual constancy in spite of conflicting needs and/or wants
Interdependent	• Partnering with each other • Developing an experience of synergy in the relationship • Utilizing couple synergy in service to the community or world	• Using win/win conflict resolution methods • Sustaining a spiritual dimension in the relationship • Utilizing the relationship as a tool for individuation and mutual spiritual evolution • Mutually affirming spiritual values and goals and acting from them • Identifying situations in which couple devotion can be extended to others outside the relationship

This dramatic change in the course of the relationship indicates that the relationship is maturing, that it is moving from the co-dependent stage to the counter-dependent stage of development. In the co-dependent stage, also known as the "honeymoon stage," potential conflicts usually are ignored to preserve the good feelings and harmony. Some relationships remain in this stage for a long time, particularly if the individuals involved are skilled at avoiding conflict.

When the relationship moves into the counter-dependent stage, the disharmony once ignored or avoided comes to the forefront. This may be frightening at first, as it activates fears that the relationship might end. As in individual development, the shift from the co-dependent stage to the counter-dependent stage of development often is triggered by the desire for more autonomy by one member of the relationship.

In a relationship, this typically does not happen simultaneously. One person usually wants to become more autonomous and seek out individual activities before the other person is ready to do so. This creates an imbalance between one person's need for separateness and the other person's need to maintain oneness. The shift into the counter-dependent stage of relationship development may erupt innocently and end up as a conflict that feels catastrophic. For example, he wants to take a long trip without her, or she decides to enroll in night classes to get an advanced degree. These kinds of relational changes may activate the other person's fears of abandonment or suffocation and undiscovered symptoms of post-traumatic stress related to developmental trauma and unmet developmental needs.

Major Therapeutic Interventions

In addition to the major therapeutic interventions described in the previous chapter some therapeutic interventions work particularly well with couples and families. Below is a synopsis of these.

Reframing Relationship Conflicts

If your relationship reaches the counter-dependent stage of development before you are ready for this change, you may feel angry, depressed, or ashamed. When a couple seeks therapy, they need feedback to reframe the problems in their marriage. The counselor might say, "Congratulations! Your relationship is maturing. It is now strong enough and safe enough for conflict to emerge." This kind of feedback may seem strange and confusing and the couple might reply, "This is the dumbest thing we ever heard of."

But when couples understand that relationships go through developmental stages, they often can reframe their perceptions and see their conflict as a sign of growth, challenging though it may be. Working from a developmental perspective also can help the partners understand that the source of the conflicts was present from the beginning of the relationship and the couple needed time together and feelings of safety for them to surface.

Most relationships, too, contain invisible elements that can cause conflict. You may become aware of subtle differences between you and your partner related to energy levels; the need for change, freedom or novelty; and contrasting levels of perceptiveness and sensitivity. These kinds of subtle differences can cause imbalances in the levels of awareness, and they can affect the sense of "timing" and different styles of expression that can complicate communication patterns.

If you are a sensitive person, for example, you may be able to perceive a potential conflict when it is just a spark, whereas your partner may not be able to perceive the potential conflict until it ignites into flames. A person who needs more freedom or wants to change the relationship may feel controlled by a partner who wants to maintain the status quo. The control issue could be expressed in subtle messages that say, "I'm scared that you will leave me or abandon me." If the partner feels afraid of being left behind has any unresolved abandonment traumas or conflicts, the desire for more freedom eventually will activate these issues.

These subtle elements in a relationship often create more disruption than obvious differences such as age, religion, parenting styles, or basic values and beliefs. It is important to recognize the potential power of these subtle differences and to look for them as possible sources of relational friction.

Reaching the counter-dependent stage of development is an important milestone for couples. This passage truly is an affirmation of the strength of the relationship and can be a source of empowerment to help the partners see the positive aspects of this shift. What couples need most to help them through this crisis is a cooperative context for understanding the nature of their conflicts and tools for resolving with them.

Developing a Partnership Relationship

A cooperative framework is essential for redefining the context of a relationship into one that is "transformative." It provides opportunities for reframing negative perceptions into more positive perceptions that are essential for the partners' mutual growth and development. If a couple agree that they want to develop a partnership relationship, the therapist can utilize the following guidelines to help the couple achieve their goal.

1. Recognize and acknowledge each other's unmet needs. At the beginning of a romantic relationship the two usually are on their best behavior, trying to impress the other person with their lovable and capable nature. It takes spiritual courage to reveal necessary weaknesses to the other person, after working so hard trying to impress him or her with one's strengths. Acknowledging that both bring unfinished business to the relationship carries an element of truthfulness to the relationship that prevents posturing, denial, and other defense mechanisms. More empathic and compassionate responses to each other are required when weaknesses and unmet needs surface.

Without a framework for helping each other heal the wounds from the past, exposing vulnerabilities and deficits can be risky. Including this higher purpose in a relationship enables the two to develop a partnership relationship. The sooner you risk acknowledging to your partner that you bring unmet needs to your relationship, the better chance you have of getting them met.

2. Help each other meet unmet needs. This step, which calls for sense of understanding and compassion, can create a larger context for the relationship. It can shift the relationship from a competitive model to a cooperative model, where real healing can happen. Then the partners each remove projections and see the wounded child inside.

3. Be willing to ask for what you want and need 100% of the time. Rather than being indirect or complaining, the partners must be willing to ask each other directly for what they want. This doesn't mean they must ask 100% of the time, only that they are *willing* to ask. This agreement is essential if they are going to break through the old unresolved conflicts and the ineffective ways of resolving them.

4. Tell the truth about your behavior, feelings and needs 100% of the time. Telling the truth frees a person mentally, emotionally, physiologically, and spiritually and also removes the barriers to intimacy. But this requires taking big risks. The best policy, although not the easiest, is to tell the truth even if it creates a conflict. Only when couples do this will they develop the kind of trust in each other that allows the relationship to evolve.

5. Close all the exits. When the partners are encountering a lot of conflict, they must agree to stay together during the counter-dependent stage of the relationship. A no-exit agreement can help hidden fears surface, as it eliminates responses such as running away or blaming the partner. Neither person can threaten to end the relationship in the middle of a conflict or to avoid the issues by escaping into addictions or by seeking another relationship. If a partner refuses to accept a "no-exit" agreement, it really is not safe for the other partner to attempt to resolve his or her deepest conflicts. In such situations, the one partner can only work alone on his or her part of the conflict or with a trusted friend or therapist. He or she is not dependent on the partner's cooperation to learn more about himself or herself and to resolve conflicts from the past.

6. Practice equality of power, opportunity, and responsibility. A couple can mutually evolve only if they have a firm foundation of sharing at all levels in the relationship. Relationships with equality as a component create a spirit of cooperation, as well as mutual trust and respect. In a world with economic, social, political, and psychological inequalities, equality is difficult to achieve without a conscious commitment. The partners also must commit to using cooperative partnership conflict resolution methods.

7. Redefine intimacy. A couple has to choose to define everything they do as intimacy: the intimacy of re-creation, the intimacy of regressing and having posttraumatic symptoms, the intimacy of being separate, the intimacy of yelling, the intimacy of holding and comforting, the intimacy of being sexual, and the intimacy of mutual healing.

8. Respect each other's boundaries. A couple can inspire a great deal of freedom and respect for each other's space if they agree to identify their boundaries and to negotiate clear agreements about sharing their psychological space. This is where the agreement to tell the truth 100% of the time is essential.

9. Develop common spiritual practices. Spiritual practices can take many forms, from formal activities such as prayer, meditation, or church attendance to informal practices involving walks in the park together or exercising together. Moments of quiet, deep connection can become important islands of intimacy. While the outer world stops, they are in touch with each other in that place of timeless connection and eternal love. Moments such as these nourish the soul and offer support in coping with the stresses of daily living.

10. Keep all relationship agreements and negotiate any changes. Whenever circumstances around an agreement change, the partners have to go back and renegotiate a new agreement. Broken agreements quickly undermine the trust and good will of a relationship, especially if they are broken unilaterally without direct negotiations with those involved.

11. Work together to help each other resolve conflicts at their source. One of the most powerful and affirming parts of a partnership relationship is when they can help each other resolve their conflicts at their source. This cooperative work brings tremendous intimacy to the relationship. It is what people want but are afraid to ask for.

▉ Differences Between Dominator and Partnership Relationships

One of the factors that fosters *drama triangle* dynamics in couples and families is a dominator relationship with its inequities in power. The drama triangle involves three revolving roles: The persecutor, the rescuer, and the victim. The most dominant or most powerful person or family member often acts out the persecutor role, the second most dominant person or family member acts out the rescuer role, and the weakest person or family member(s) acts out the victim role.

Dominator relationships involve splitting and polarization, such as dominator/dominated, passive/aggressive and win/lose, to create hierarchical structures. Partnership relationships involve interdependent actions based on unity, mutuality, and cooperation, to create non-hierarchical structures. A comparison of the two kinds of relationships is presented in Table 11.2.

From the comparison in Table 11.2, you can see some of the basic differences in philosophy and practice of the dominator and the partnership relationships. Most relationships do not exhibit all of either set

TABLE 11.2

Characteristics of Dominator and Partnership Relationships

Dominator Relationships	Partnership Relationships
• Use force or threat to enforce domination	• Use the vision of higher consciousness to encourage linking for common good
• Create inequalities in power and decision making	• Create equal opportunities and use knowledge as shared power for joint decision making
• Utilize rigid gender roles	• Utilize flexible gender roles
• Value violence and exploitation	• Value negotiation and harmony
• Are competitive	• Are cooperative
• Use fear to create separation	• Use hope and high ideals to create unity
• Are materially oriented	• Are spiritually oriented
• See women and children as property or chattel	• See women and children as equal and unique individuals
• Support co-dependent and counter-dependent behaviors	• Support independent and interdependent behaviors
• Follow a path of fear and protection	• Follow a path of learning and discovery
• Use control, manipulation, and deception in communicating	• Use truth, empathy, and directness in communicating
• Value either the needs of the individual or the needs of the relationship	• Value both the needs of the individuals and the needs of the relationship

of characteristics, but the dominator form of relationship is still by far the most prevalent form of relationship in the world today.

Stages of Family Development

The evolution of family relationships follows a developmental model similar to that for individual and couple relationships. Adult members of a family carry with them into the family system all the unresolved conflicts and issues related to developmental trauma from both the individual and the couple stages of development. This "baggage" eventually surfaces in the same way as it does during drama triangle conflicts within the family system.

The principles of the family component of the Partnership Way apply to relationships of three or more people, whether this consists of two parents and a child, three friends, or three co-workers. Most people do not understand that a dramatic shift takes place in the relational dynamics when the system shifts from two people to three people. The word "dramatic" contains the word "drama." This is no coincidence. As soon as a relationship has three people, it has sufficient players to fill all the roles in the drama triangle. These dynamics appear only after sufficient trust and intimacy have been established over a period of time. Once this foundation of security is in place, the unfinished business of all three people will surface. For this reason, conflicts involving relationships of three or more tend to be some of the most intractable.

Staying conscious and clear in a family can be difficult, as cues from members' unprocessed trauma can effortlessly trigger conflict. The success of family or three-way relationships depends on the extent to which each person has resolved any developmental trauma, is able to abstain from the dynamics of the drama triangle, and has completed the "splitting" phase of the counter-dependent stage of development. For the same reasons, trained professionals have difficulty in navigating relationships with two or more people.

The evolution of families follows a developmental model similar to that of individuals and couples, and the stages are the same: *co-dependent, counter-dependent, independent,* and *interdependent*. The psychosocial tasks for each stage are illustrated in Table 11.3. As a family provides effective methods to help each member of the system and the parents complete their psychosocial tasks of their couple relationship, the family can evolve to a higher stage of development.

TABLE 11.3

Stages of Family Development

Stage of Development	Psychosocial tasks of a Family	Methods for Completing These Tasks
Co-dependent	• Establish bonding between parents and children • Establish primal trust in the family • Establish an identity as a family	• Establish a constant environment for parenting the children • Recognize and acknowledge each other's spiritual essence • Exchange nurturing touch and talk between parents and children and between siblings • Give and receive unconditional love between parents and children and between siblings • Create common interests, values, beliefs, and goals among family members
Counter-dependent	• Achieve psychological separation between parents and children • Resolve conflicts between needs of parents and needs of children	• Explore interests outside the family • Recognize the unique character-istics and life path of each child • Build appropriate boundaries between children and parents • Identify parent needs versus children's needs • Seek partnership solutions to conflicts between children's needs and parents needs
Independent	• Develop individual initiative • Develop individual and couple autonomy within the family structure • Achieve object constancy as a family	• Provide children with independence training in managing time, money, school, extracurricular activities • Develop a consequence-based method of discipline for children • Maintain boundaries between adult/parent activities and interests and parenting activities • Achieve balance between adults' and children's needs • Experience constancy of family relationships and structure during times of stress and/or conflict
Interdependent	• Build consensus in decision making • Develop equitable and equal relationships • Develop each member's fullest potential as a human being	• Manage family affairs through family meetings • Value and keep agreements between family members • Use power equitably between adults and adults, between adults and children, and between children and children • Provide a high level of physical, mental, emotional, and spiritual resources for all members

■ *Sources of Family Conflict*

The birth of the first child usually precipitates the shift from couple to family dynamics. The change in dynamics becomes more visible when the child begins separating from the mother or primary caregiver during the counter-dependent stage of development. This stage, characterized by a lot of conflict, is the time when adults often use "reverse psychology" on the child to cope with the frustration of splitting exhibited by the child's oppositional and defiant behaviors. When a parent is directive and authoritative, the child will become oppositional and set off a power struggle between them. The child's independent behaviors can trigger the parents' unresolved drama triangle dynamics.

Family conflicts are complicated because two parallel levels of dynamics are happening simultaneously. The first level is occurring between the child and parents in present time. The second is occurring inside of each of the parents in past time. Psychodynamic psychology recognizes that adults often unconsciously regress to the chronological age of their child and reenact unprocessed feelings, and traumas (deMause, 1982, p.135). This psychological phenomenon, known as *regression–progression,* stimulates an unconscious restaging of the parents' own developmental trauma. This restaging provides the parents with a venue where they unconsciously reprocess the trauma related to same-age experiences from their own childhood. In essence, these parent–child conflicts function as an unconscious "therapeutic" process for the parents.

Parents can be expected to replay their own developmental trauma through each stage of their child's development, particularly during the counter-dependent stage of development. Each parent becomes psychologically vulnerable to regression during family conflicts, especially when the other parent or caregiver is in conflict with the child. The parents' symbiotic bond and strong identification with the child trigger their symptoms of post-traumatic stress disorder (PTSD), activating latent feelings and behaviors related to their own struggle for separation.

In short, the boundaries between the parent's experiences of the past and the present become blurred. Similar to a post-traumatic flashback experience, the past feels as though it is still happening in the present. Parents experience exaggerated feeling states that relate more to their past than their present. For example, when the mother is in conflict with the child, the father may identify with the child as the *victim* and perceive the other parent as the *persecutor*. This symbiotic identification with the child triggers *rescuer* behavior in the father and activates the dynamics of the drama triangle between the two parents and the child.

In another common parent–child drama, a parent sees the child as an enemy. For example, the father perceives that the mother is more attentive to the child than to him. This triggers the father's memories of developmental trauma related to sibling rivalry, stimulating him to criticize the mother for "spoiling" the child. Unable to identify his own unmet needs for nurturing, the father attempts to diminish the strong bond between the mother and the child. Parenting provides a stage upon which both parents can unconsciously seek resolution to their unresolved developmental trauma. The recycling of trauma through family dramas is a major cause of intractable family conflicts.

One of the most fascinating aspects of family conflict is *regression–progression*. While it sits on a foundation of love-based symbiosis between parent and child, it can suddenly be transformed into a hate-filled situation in which the parent perceives the child as an enemy. The realization that a young child could appear threatening to an adult indicates the presence of *projection*. Projections involve splitting between past/present, self/other, and us/them are prevalent in family conflicts. The adults' inability to separate the past from the present and self from other can suddenly transform a small conflict in the present into a life-threatening episode of family violence involving the parents' deepest emotions. The parents' loss of reality indicates symptoms of PTSD, a critical factor in causing intractable family conflicts.

The problem with *regression–progression* is that it allows adults to unconsciously use children as projective or "therapy" objects to purge themselves of their feelings related to unresolved developmental trauma. Rather than working consciously on these issues through counseling or parenting classes, parents simply reenact their trauma with their children. This reenactment creates intergenerational patterns of child use and abuse. The solution to regression–progression is conscious parenting that encourages adult family members to use external resources such as therapy or support groups to clear themselves of their unresolved developmental trauma. This recommendation applies not only to parents rearing children but to all adults who provide custodial

care for children, such as daycare personnel, school teachers and officials, athletic coaches, and church supervisors and teachers.

Parents who are learning to stop the practice of *regression–progression* typically have done extensive personal work via therapy and support groups that have helped them heal their developmental traumas.
Most significantly, however, these parents learn to redefine the nature
of their wounds. Rather than seeing themselves as "broken," they
reframe their problems as a "developmental delay." This helps them to
depathologize their dysfunctional behaviors and to accept their projections and episodes of emotional overreactions as cues regarding their
own traumas. This reframing helps to create a vision for complete healing of developmental traumas and the full realization of their potential.

Acting out of *regression–progression,* some parents lay traps, lie,
threaten violence, manipulate, withdraw their love, humiliate, distrust,
scorn, ridicule, coerce, terrorize, and commit violence against their
children. Doing these things to their children is a way of proving that
their parents really did love them. This denial and repression of abusive
and traumatic experiences is a major force in the replay of conflictual
family patterns. The best way to break the cycle is to:

- Reexamine childhood experiences from an "optimal parenting"
  perspective to determine the developmental needs that remain
  unmet since childhood
- Look for symptoms of unhealed developmental traumas from
  childhood
- Identify and plan ways to meet these unmet developmental needs
- Express any and all feelings not expressed as a child
- Repattern relationship dynamics to eliminate trauma-related
  distortions.

Psychoeducational Interventions With Family Conflicts

Often the first step in stopping the *regression–progression* family
dynamic is psychoeducation. After adults come to understand the
nature of the *regression–progression* phenomenon, they have to decide
not to participate any longer in drama triangle dynamics. These adults
commit to redefining themselves and reframing their life experiences.

Breaking free from the *regression–progression* dynamic requires that adults become totally responsible for their residue of developmental trauma. Making this shift might mean having to shift their whole reality base.

Psychoeducational interventions can be initiated by the therapist or by a class or support group. The primary goal of psychoeducation for family members is to help everyone develop an internal sense of "object constancy" and "I'm okay, you're okay" thinking. This allows them to retain their sense of worth even when they feel rejected or unworthy during family conflicts. When family members are not able to do this, it indicates the presence of unresolved issues from the "splitting subphase" of the counter-dependent stage of individual development, which can best be resolved through individual therapy.

Resolving Conflicts of Wants and Needs

Family members can be taught how to resolve the most common source of family conflicts—wants and needs. What follows is an eight-step method for resolving conflicts of wants and needs that can be taught to all family members in therapy or in a class that is an adjunct to family therapy.

1. Describe objectively your perception of the problem or behavior. Begin with "I statements." Avoid using harsh or judgmental language, "you statements," threatening body language, and a strident voice. For example, you might begin, "I noticed that you didn't clean up your dishes after you ate last night."

2. Share the way you feel toward the person or problem. Keep your focus internally, specifically on your inner experience of the conflict to help you stay centered so you do not escalate or lose your objectivity. Continuing with the above example, you might say, "I felt angry with you when I saw the dishes sitting there. "

3. Describe the tangible effects or results of the problem or issue on you and/or your relationship. Speak authentically in a way that helps the other person realize that his or her behavior has created a consequence that affects the bond or connection between you. Using the example, tell the other person how what he (she) did affected you by saying, "When I had to clean up your dishes to use the sink, I didn't feel close to you and I didn't look forward to being with you tonight."

4. State directly what you want from the other person. Formulate this request ahead of time in your mind so you can speak precisely. Be prepared to enter into a negotiation process, if necessary, to get your need met by having a series of options or solutions that might be acceptable. Emphasize how much you value and care for the other person. In the example, say, "What I want is to be able to feel close to you, and to do that, I want you to keep your agreement to clean up your dishes after you eat."

5. Ask the person directly for what you want. Asking directly gives the other person a choice. When people have choices, they are more likely to act cooperatively and be willing to negotiate if the initial suggestion is not acceptable to them. You need to ask directly, "Are you willing to do that?"—then be prepared for a refusal of cooperation with the question, "Well, what are you willing to do?"

6. Use reflective listening. At this point the other person will likely give an explanation for his or her behavior. Repeat what you hear him or her say so the partner feels heard and understood before going on to the next step. Avoid getting bogged down here by defending yourself, blaming the other, complaining about him or her, or escalating by bringing in other issues. Focus on your feelings of compassion and caring for the partner as you reflect what you think he or she is feeling. You can say, "When I get angry about these things, you look like you're feeling hurt and angry. Is this true?" Once you have reflected the statement, you may want to return to your original question: "Would you be willing to do that?"

7. Negotiate if there are differences between what you want and what the other person is willing to give or do. If the other person refuses to cooperate with your initial request, ask, "What would you be willing to do?

8. If you are unable to negotiate the differences, look for other sources of the conflict. In this case, you may have to agree to disagree and invite the other person to join you in exploring the conflict further.

You might say, "I see that we just don't agree on this issue, and I accept our disagreement. Would you also agree that we can't find a partnership solution at this time?" Or you might say to the other person, "Would you be willing to explore our differences further, looking for possible conflicts of values or beliefs or look for other possible sources of this conflict?"

Resolving Conflicts of Values and Beliefs

Conflicts of values and beliefs are usually more complex and more difficult to resolve than conflicts of wants and needs. They require a different set of skills and have to be directed more on developing mutual understanding and respect for differences than trying to change the other person's values and beliefs. A seven-step process for resolving conflicts of values and beliefs follows.

1. Take turns listening to each other's views of the conflict using reflective listening. Identify the feelings as well as the content. Agree not to state your own opinion or position until you agree that you have reflected what the other person has said. For example you might say, "You seem to be saying that you think I'm trying to control you, and you also seem a little angry and scared to me. Do I understand accurately what you're saying and feeling?" When the other person indicates feeling heard, move to Step 2.

2. Take turns finding the sources of the value or belief conflict. Each person talks about personal experiences that may have led to the formation of this value or belief. You might ask your partner, "What other experiences have you had in your life where you've felt that people were trying to control you?" Again, listen and back the feelings and content for each other before moving forward to the next step.

3. Take turns finding the sources of the feelings. Focus on the feelings and reflect what you hear from the other. Ask, "What other times in your life have you felt this way?"

4. Determine any shifts in awareness. Take turns restating any new perceptions. You might say, "Based on your exploration of the sources of your values or beliefs and your feelings, do you have any new perceptions of your value or belief? Are you feeling kinder or more compassionate toward my views?" Again use reflective listening.

5. Explore areas of agreement and disagreement. One way to do this is to say, "I think we can now agree that what we originally identified as control was really a desire for more directness in our relationship. Because of our past history, where other people tried to control us, we're indirect in our communication with each other. Do you agree that this could be a problem for us?"

6. Make plans to handle any areas of disagreement. This might take the form of saying, "If either of us feels controlled by the other in any way, can we agree to bring it directly to the other so we can talk about it again?"

7. Make plans to handle any strong feelings or reactions. If this conflict brings up strong feelings and reactions in either of you, you will have to look deeper to locate the source of these strong feelings and reactions. You may have hidden developmental traumas that prevent you or the other person from completely listening and communicating respect and understanding. If both parties are willing, the therapist may utilize the process below for resolving intractable conflicts at their source.

Resolving Intractable Conflicts at Their Source

Intractable conflict is obviously the most difficult kind of conflict to resolve and usually involves developmental trauma and unmet developmental needs. To do this conflict resolution in a couple or family, you first need a mutual commitment to work cooperatively on these kinds of conflicts. Then you can proceed to the step-by-step process for resolving intractable conflicts at their source.

1. Ask your partner to role play the person with whom you had the original unresolved conflict. Ask your partner to participate by saying something like, "Would you be willing to play my father and listen while I express the anger I felt toward him when he divorced my mother and left our family?"

2. Identify the element in the conflict that is unfinished or unresolved. To inform your partner about what you will be needing, you can set the stage by saying something like, "I never got to express my anger at my father and to hear him acknowledge and accept my feelings."

3. Make a specific contract with your partner. The request must be specific: "Will you role play my 'functional father' and accept my feelings of anger and really hear my feelings? After I've expressed my anger, I want you to tell me that I have a right to be angry and that you still love me and won't abandon me. Will you do that?"

4. Complete the contract. Sit across from your partner and complete the contract. You will need to express your anger at your "father." Your partner, who is role playing your father, replies, "You have a perfect right to be angry at me. What I did changed your life and made life difficult for you. I'm glad you have the courage to tell me how you feel. I still love you and won't abandon you."

5. Allow yourself to feel the full impact of the role play. The impact of the role play may be dramatic or subtle, so allow enough time to fully feel the changes in awareness that might result. You might report, "I'm feeling much lighter and freer. My jaw seems looser, and I notice I'm feeling a little sad. I must be grieving the loss of my dad's presence in our family for the first time since he left. My anger must have blocked me from feeling the sadness."

6. Ask for any additional support. If you need support or feedback from your partner after completing this risky contract, ask for it: "Will you hold me or comfort me while I experience my sadness and grief?" If you do want to be held, clarify whether it is your father or your partner who is doing the holding. If you need to be held by your father, you must renegotiate with your partner to role play the father. The roles and relationships always must be clear and separate.

7. Allow your partner to leave the role. Use a direct statement to acknowledge that your partner has completed the role play so you can reenter the present. Say to your partner, "I feel complete now in our role play. We can return to present time." Thank your partner for helping you complete this unfinished business with your father.

8. Return to the current conflict. After completing the unresolved elements from your past conflict, return to the current conflict to see if it now can be resolved. It usually is easy to resolve the current issues once the issues from the past have been resolved.

Family Meetings

Family meetings can be an important way to implement partnership relationships within a family structure. Here, children learn to participate in group decision making, to negotiate to get their needs met, to solve problems, and to resolve conflicts effectively. Children who learn skills in family meetings can apply them outside the family setting. Emphasizing this learning can make implementing family meetings easier, as some members may not see the significance of family meetings.

Couples who are transforming their family structures into a partnership system often notice that their children resist their parents' attempts at reform. These children, who have learned how to function in a dominator family with secrets, triangulation, power plays, and other forms of dirty fighting, may fear losing their position of power in the family hierarchy. Once a new partnership structure is operationalized, the children usually find that family meetings support them in getting their needs met more directly.

Strengths and Limitations of the Partnership Way

Like the other theories described in this book, the Partnership Way of resolving conflicts has strengths and limitations. Major strengths of this approach are:

1. This approach offers therapists a family systems perspective for understanding conflicts in couples and families.
2. The developmental framework allows the therapist to support couples and families as they help each other to heal developmental traumas that may be causing their conflicts.
3. This approach enables couples and families to develop a deeper understanding of the causes of their conflicts and thereby helps

them have more compassion and empathy toward each other; it assists couples and families in finding more cooperative ways of resolving their conflicts.

4. This approach gets to the underlying causes of intractable conflict, which is the most common form of conflict brought to therapy. Most therapies just help couples and families learn to do a better job of "managing their conflicts."

5. This approach enables a skilled therapist to get to the source of the problems rather quickly and may require less therapy time than many of the other family therapies. This is an advantage to those who are applying this theory in a managed care setting.

Limitations of the Partnership Way are:

1. Therapists who use this approach have a high risk of developing counter-transference. To reduce the risk of counter-transference, the therapist has to have dealt with his or her own developmental traumas.

2. Therapists who use this approach must have "researched" their own family of origin and determined the effectiveness of their own personal theory of conflict resolution.

3. Therapists who use this approach typically need in-depth training beyond what they normally get in their graduate training programs.

4. This theory is new and has little research behind it to date. Although it has been shown to be effective in a variety of clinical settings, its suitability may be limited to higher-functioning couples and families.

SUGGESTED READINGS

Weinhold, B., & Weinhold, J. (2000). *Conflict resolution: The partnership way.* Denver: Love Publishing.

Weinhold, B., & Weinhold, J. (1993). Building partnership families: A psychosocial approach. *Family Counseling and Therapy, 1,* 1–20.

Weinhold, B., & Hendricks, G. (1993). *Counseling and psychotherapy: A transpersonal approach* (2d ed.). Denver: Love Publishing.

Weinhold, J., & Weinhold, B. (1992). *Counter-dependency: The flight from intimacy.* Colorado Springs, CO: CICRCL Press.

Weinhold, B., & Weinhold, J. (1989). *Breaking free of the co-dependency trap.* Walpole, NH: Stillpoint.

CASE EXAMPLE

A 38-year-old businessman was awarded physical custody of his seven children, ages 4 through 15. They all lived together in a large house he had rented. He hired a live-in nanny to help care for the children. After about a year he began to observe a number of problems in the children. Several had bed-wetting problems, problems of aggressiveness toward each other, and some school problems. The father sought family therapy with us to find better ways to help the children. After a few family sessions, we suggested that the father begin to hold regular family meetings to create an orderly weekly ritual to help him handle the logistics of rearing seven children. We offered to visit the home and observe the family meetings and coach him on how to run them effectively.

At one of the meetings, he began by berating some of the children for not doing their chores and for continual fighting. He felt overwhelmed and discouraged by what seemed to him uncooperative behavior. He said, "You don't care for me or this family. I'm working as hard as I can, and all you're interested in is the money I bring home to buy you what you want and need. I just can't keep doing this without more help and appreciation from all of you. "

We saw that the father was feeling unseen, unappreciated, and unloved by his children. When he confirmed that this indeed was the way he was feeling, we suggested that he do a "perception check" with them to see if that actually was what was happening. We asked each child, starting with the oldest, to stand in front of him, look him in the eyes, and tell him the truth about how they saw him and how they felt toward him.

(continued)

(CASE EXAMPLE continued)

Each child stood in front of the father and began to tell him how much they loved him as a person and how they appreciated his efforts to create a better family. By the time the third child stood before him, he began to melt. He finally broke down and started sobbing. He said, "All my life I've worked hard to please others, and I never felt that the people close to me really loved me for who I am, but more for what I did for them. That's how I grew up—always trying to please my parents, hoping they would love me and see who I was. They never did, so I guess I just kept trying harder to be good enough to earn love from others I was close to. I finally see that my children do love me for who I am and I'm crying because I'm so happy that my need has finally been met. Thank you for helping me heal that old conflict inside of myself. "

Following the father's emotional confession, all the children came and surrounded him, climbing on his lap, hugging him, and telling him how much they loved him. Later, as we debriefed the session with the family, we commented on the apparent breakthrough in this family. They all agreed and talked about the positive effects of the session on them. Shortly after that session, family therapy was terminated with the understanding that they continue to work together through their family meetings and, if needed, they could schedule additional family therapy sessions in the future.

Although the family still had some conflicts, the father did not request any further family therapy to help the family resolve conflicts. Several family members, including the father, continued with individual therapy to get ongoing support. This is an example of the regression–progression phenomenon and showed how parents can easily get triggered into regression by what is going on with their children. This parent, with therapeutic support, was able to utilize incidents of regression–progression for further personal healing.

Treating Families With Special Needs

Family therapy originally was developed as a method for working with individuals with schizophrenia and their families. Later, these theories and techniques were used with families exhibiting a variety of problems. More recently, family systems theories have been applied to specific family constellations, including blended families, ethnically diverse families, families with children with disabilities, alcoholic families, abusive families, families experiencing divorce, families with a member who is HIV-positive, families with a depressed or suicidal member, military families, and rural families. Each of these family situations is discussed briefly in this chapter.

Blended families
Alcoholic families
Abusive families
Divorcing families
Rural families
Military families

Families with a depressed member
Families with children with disabilities
Ethnically diverse families
Gender issues in family therapy
Families with an HIV-positive member

1. What important issues should a couple remarrying a different partner resolve prior to the marriage?
2. What is the best way for the family therapist to prepare to work with ethnically diverse families?
3. In what ways are the dynamics of families with children with disabilities similar to those of families that do not have any children with disabilities? In what ways do the dynamics of these family types differ?
4. What special problems should the family therapist be aware of when treating a family with an alcoholic member?
5. What are the critical issues to consider when treating a family with an abusive member?
6. What are the significant steps in the divorce process?
7. How can depression in one family member be maintained by the behaviors of other family members?
8. How would you treat a family with a suicidal member?
9. How might gender stereotyping affect the process of family therapy?
10. What are your thoughts concerning power differentials between males and females in marriage? What do you recommend as an alternative if one is needed?
11. What would be your concerns when working with a family with an HIV-positive member? What skills would be most important?
12. What are important issues to consider when working with military families?
13. What are key family therapist skills needed to work with rural families?

As family therapy has matured and gained respect from the mental health community, new responsibilities have emerged for the profession. Clinical research has increased, and information has emerged that suggests certain strategies for treating families with specific problems. In this chapter we will discuss treatment for several of these special situations.

■ *Blended Families*

Blended families are created when one or both partners bring children from a previous marriage into a new marriage. Divorce and remarriage occur frequently. Glick (1989) reported that an estimated 69% of children in the United States lived with both parents, and for children born in the 1980s, 59% could expect to live with only one parent for a period of time and 35% could expect to live with a stepparent before the age of 18.

One of the most common problems in the remarried or blended family is that family members attempt to reconstitute as a traditional nuclear family (Visher & Visher, 1979). Frequently, the stepparent will attempt to assume the role of the "real" mother or father and quickly engage the stepchild in an escalating battle to determine who will define the adult–child relationship. As this situation escalates, the biological parent frequently enters the fray on the side of the child, intensifying the problem by creating a division between the parents.

When this type of family enters therapy, the therapist should quickly join with each member by understanding the frustrations inherent in each person's role. After establishing credibility as an expert on stepfamilies, the therapist identifies the "myth of the nuclear family," which suggests that stepfamilies will be similar in all respects to traditional families (Visher & Visher, 1979). Once the family recognizes this myth, it no longer will drive the family's behavior and the family will stop attempting to replicate the traditional family. At this point, members can discuss and negotiate how they would like their blended family to function. This intervention gives stepparents the opportunity to hear directly from the stepchildren how they would like the relationship to develop. Therapy should also provide an opportunity for the parents to discuss how they wish their children to be treated by the stepparent as well as ways the couple will support each other when dealing with stepchildren.

Therapy with a blended family can be an extremely positive experience after the family releases some of its idealistic notions concerning how blended families function. Structured premarital counseling (Fenell, Nelson, & Shertzer, 1981; Fenell & Wallace, 1985) can help couples prepare for certain problems associated with blended families and is advised whenever possible.

■ *Ethnically Diverse Families*

Most family therapists will have the opportunity to work with client families of diverse ethnic backgrounds. This can be challenging, as different ethnic groups value and respond to therapy in their own unique ways (McGoldrick, Pearce, & Giordano, 1982). When a therapist meets a client family from a different ethnic background, how should he or she respond? Each person and, indeed, each family is unique, and the therapist must value that uniqueness. If the therapist is open to the process of learning about, understanding, and respecting the values and behaviors of *all* families—because, indeed, all families are unique—that therapist is likely to take the time to understand the uniqueness of any ethnically diverse family that he or she encounters in the therapy room. This ability to relate to families is the key characteristic of therapists who are effective with a wide range of ethnically diverse families.

An alternative point of view contends that the effective family counselor must be familiar with the fundamental characteristics of a variety of ethnic groups to be able to respond effectively to them in therapy. This point of view maintains that understanding a variety of ethnic groups and the characteristics of these groups better prepares the therapist to work effectively with all groups. A major criticism of this approach is that the therapist may form stereotypical ideas about members of certain ethnic groups that, while valid for the majority of members of the group, may not apply to the specific individuals who are in family therapy. Thus, the therapist might believe that he or she understands the context of the family before actually learning from the family what that context is. This is a recipe for ineffective therapy regardless of the family's ethnic background.

All counselors must remember that an ethnic group may have as much diversity *within* the group as it does when compared to another ethnic group. To assume knowledge that has *not been validated* through conversation with the family members is bad therapy indeed. For example, the *within-ethnic group differences* between an African–American born in Nigeria and educated in England and an African–American born in poverty in New Orleans is likely to be as significant as the *between-group differences* of an Asian–American and a Hispanic American.

The key is to let the family educate *you,* and as you come to know the family, you will be better able to develop interventions that are consistent with the family's ethnic values. This is really no different that what *any* effective family counselor does with *any* family he or she may encounter in treatment.

McGoldrick, Preto, Hines, and Lee (1991) contend that the best preparation for a family therapist who will work with ethnically diverse clients is for the therapist to thoroughly study his or her own ethnic identity. By so doing, the therapist will come to understand the unique characteristics of the group and recognize that the values of the group, while understandable and useful for its members, might not be useful for other groups. The therapist comes to understand that the values of each ethnic group are born out of the context and experiences of each group's members and are clearly understandable when the therapist realizes the forces that have shaped the group. Further, it is critical that the effective multicultural therapist recognizes when he or she is operating out of a personal, ethnically based value in therapy. If the therapist is able to transcend ethnic identity, a multiethnic perspective develops, and the therapist no longer feels the need to convince clients to adopt his or her values.

The effective therapist knows how to think about ethnic differences and how these differences could have an impact on therapy rather than possessing a wealth of specific knowledge about a variety of ethnic groups. Specifically, various ethnic groups may have different responses toward suffering; different attitudes about helping professionals; a more formal or informal interactional preference with strangers; or differing attitudes about the appropriateness of childrens' expressiveness. The therapist will have to be sensitive to each of these and numerous other possible conditions in therapy.

While well aware of the problems associated with stereotyping members of ethnic groups and with no intention of doing so, McGoldrick and Rohrbaugh (1987) conducted a study that characterized differences among groups to help clinicians become aware of the range of values brought to therapy experience. Some of the most striking modal characteristics of several groups identified in the study are:

- Jewish families
  marry within group
  value success and education
  encourage children
  talk out problems
  have shared suffering
  use guilt to shape children's behavior

- WASP families
  are expected to be strong and make it alone
  are independent
  have self-control
  suffer in silence
  hide conflicts

- Italian families
  hold nothing more important than family
  are expressive and enjoy a good time
  follow traditional sex roles
  relate through eating
  accomplish tasks through personal connections
  tend to have male-dominant roles

- African–American families
  exhibit strength to survive
  are religious
  are able to make it alone
  see women as strong
  want children to succeed

- Asian families
  always have time for family members
  respect elders for their wisdom
  believe that bad behavior reflects on the whole group
  worry about children doing well in school
  want children to succeed

- Hispanic families
  take responsibility for care of elderly
  always have time for family members
  have defined roles: men protect and women nurture
  respect elders for their wisdom
  consider "losing face" as catastrophic

Again, we emphasize that these characteristics come from a preliminary study; they are based on average behaviors and should not be used to stereotype any group. Understanding the uniqueness of each family remains one of the most important tasks of the family therapist in dealing with ethnic minority families, or any family for that matter.

Families With a Child With a Disability

Fenell, Martin, and Mithaug (1986) described therapy with a family having a child with a disability. They suggested that once the initial shock of dealing with the reality of a child with a disability subsides and the family accepts the reality of the situation, the parents begin working to provide the best possible environment for the child. At this point, two problems may arise.

1. The parents may focus so much of their energy on the child that they neglect their own relationship and perhaps the needs of their nondisabled children.
2. The family may do so much for the child with the disability that the child does not learn what he or she is able to accomplish without assistance.

The first problem often precipitates the need for therapy, as the marriage partners begin to experience the void in their own relationship or a nondisabled child begins to act out.

The therapist's first task is to communicate that he or she understands and appreciates the sacrifices each member has made for the child with a disability. Then the therapist points out that the family has not been able to make time for other members because the family members have organized their lives around the child with a disability (Berger, 1982). Helping the family find time to reestablish other relationships requires patience and understanding on the therapist's part.

When the child with a disability is the identified patient, the situation differs from most family therapy in that the child often is physically or mentally unable to make the improvements that a nondisabled identified patient could. Thus, only small improvements by the child with a disability are likely, as the child is usually not the symptom-bearer for the family.

Although the family may devote considerable energy to the child with a disability, the child's behaviors typically are not a result of a stressed family environment. The therapist should take this factor into consideration when working with a family with a family member who has a disability. Therapy should devote considerable effort toward helping the *other family members* create an environment for the child with a disability that will allow the child to fully develop his or her potential, regardless of how limited that might be, and permit other members to lead their lives as normally as possible.

This objective is accomplished while strengthening the key subsystems in the family, especially the spousal subsystem and the subsystems between parents and nondisabled children. Frequently, parents do not know what resources are available in the community to help them with their child. Furthermore, they may feel guilty placing the child in short-term care so the family can enjoy some time away from the problems the child presents.

The therapist should be ready to help the family in both of these areas by providing necessary information about available support systems and by normalizing the parents' concern about leaving the child in short-term care. The parents and the child both need to spend time away from each other.

When the parents begin taking their focus off the child, they may experience deficits in their own relationship. They may need support and training in communication to begin to relate to each other as individuals in meaningful ways. As the family begins to balance its time and energy better, the child with a disability often is able to accomplish many things the parents and siblings had previously done for him or her. This change has a systemic effect on the parents and siblings, who then begin to encourage further appropriate autonomy for the child.

▆ Families With an Alcoholic Member

Families with alcoholic members often are treated with family therapy (Edwards & Steinglass, 1995). Many professionals consider alcoholism a disease, and others believe it is a behavioral problem. Regardless of the therapist's definition of alcoholism, the alcoholic member clearly affects the family system and the individuals in the family and also is affected by the family (Kaufman & Kaufman, 1979; Pattison, 1982).

Family therapists have criticized treatment of the individual alcoholic member outside of the family context, and many drug and alcohol therapists have criticized family therapists for assuming that alcoholism can be cured by eliminating dysfunctional family patterns. All but the most minor problems of alcoholism may be treated most effectively by a combination of interrupting the drinking cycle through therapy with the individual and employing family therapy. The purpose of family therapy is to modify the family environment so the family does not precipitate and reinforce old drinking patterns.

Pattison (1982) identified four themes in the interaction of the alcoholic member and the family.

1. The alcoholic member places significant stress on the family system. Members may have to adopt roles to cope with the alcoholic member that are not in their own best interests. For instance, a young son may have to assume a parental role and care for an infant sibling because his mother is frequently drunk.
2. Therapists must understand the effect the family has on the alcoholic member. Conflict in the marriage or with children may precipitate excessive drinking and maintain the drinking pattern. Thus, alcoholism may serve as (a) a symptom of family dysfunction; (b) a method for coping with family stress; (c) a consequence of dysfunctional family rules, roles, and structure; or (d) a combination of these functions.
3. Alcoholism is a family disease. It may be transmitted from one generation to the next. If one generation has an alcoholic

family member, the chances increase that the next generation also will have an alcoholic member. Nonalcoholic sons or daughters of alcoholic individuals frequently marry an alcoholic person and keep the intergenerational cycle functioning.

4. Family participation in the treatment of an alcoholic member improves the prognosis. Pattison (1982) reported that family participation in aftercare greatly enhances the positive outcome of treatment. He believes it is critical that family members be included in the treatment of alcoholism.

However helpful it may be, family therapy alone is rarely sufficient in treatment. The alcoholic person suffers from major physical, emotional, social, and vocational impairments. These problems often must be treated with specific rehabilitation methods, which may include inpatient therapy to break the drinking cycle (Pattison, 1982).

When couples and families with alcoholic members seek family therapy, they rarely present their problem as being based in alcoholism. Rather, some other symptom almost always precipitates the decision to enter therapy. As a result, family therapists too often do not explore the possibility of an alcohol problem in the family and many alcoholic families remain untreated. Usher and Steinglass (1981) encouraged family therapists to explore the possibility of an alcohol problem in the family. If an alcohol problem is detected, those authors maintain that the problem with alcohol must be dealt with before any other symptoms may be effectively treated.

Initial treatment of the family requires diagnosing the alcoholism as a *family problem*. All family members must understand that each of them has a role to play in resolving this family problem. The therapist's diagnosis of alcoholism will not be helpful unless the family members accept the diagnosis. Thus, the therapist must carefully gather and present data to support the diagnosis sensitively and firmly.

The first requirement of treatment is to interrupt the drinking pattern. The therapist will prepare the family members for "slips" so their expectations are not too high. Participation in Alcoholics Anonymous, Alanon, and Alateen are often useful adjuncts for the family while the drinking cycle is being stopped.

After the drinking has stopped, the therapy focuses on reestablishing intimacy in the family that is not built around alcohol but, rather, on the genuine caring and respect of family members for one another.

When alcohol is removed from the family system, this may leave an intense void. Members no longer know how to act or what to do. Family therapy can help the members move through this confusing and frightening phase to more productive family functioning. Although family therapy is no panacea in the treatment of alcoholism, it often is useful (Edwards & Steinglass, 1995).

■ Gender Issues in Marriage and Family Therapy

The feminist critique of family therapy was one of the most powerful trends in the field during the past decade. Feminist family therapists questioned the notion of circularity in assessing families and the resulting conclusion that all family members are equally involved in maintaining a pattern of behavior (Goodrich, Rampage, Ellman, & Halstead, 1988). The feminists insisted that many family systems are unequal, with males having significantly more power than the women. Moreover, those writers condemned critics who conceptualized systematically at the expense of an individual within the family, often a woman (Sprenkle, 1990).

In response to this criticism, family therapists have looked closely at the role of gender in family treatment. In the past, to assume that a family held traditional gender roles might have been safe. Not so anymore. Therapists now need to spend time with males and females within families, attempting to understand how each person would like the family to function and how each person expects to be treated.

Therapists also have to examine client family patterns to determine if those patterns are maintained by family hierarchical structures supported by implicit or explicit threat to other members. If such structures are identified, clarifying the effects of this way of functioning with all family members present is essential. Helping families develop alternative and more equal structures would be a goal of treatment.

In a special section of the *Journal of Marital and Family Therapy,* several authors commented on the role of men in marriage (Doherty, 1991). Doherty (1991) warned that moving men from the pedestal to the mud and women from the mud to the pedestal will not solve the gender problems. Doherty's concern was that we have moved from a model that recognized women as men with deficits to an equally problematic deficit model of recognizing men as women with deficits.

Berg (1991) criticized the movement to make men more like women and women more like men. She challenged the assumption that obliterating the differences between men and women will solve gender problems. Rather, Berg suggested an intervention that asks the question: How can this particular woman learn to get what she wants in life using her strengths and talents? How can this particular man learn to get what he wants from life using his unique assets? How are we the same and different? Let us make these commonalties and differences work for us separately and together (pp. 311–312).

How do mental health professionals develop a more gender-sensitive approach to our work? Storm (1991) suggested that therapist training is crucial to this shift. She developed a training module placing gender at the heart of the training program. Although this approach to family therapy training emphasizes the importance of systems theory in treatment, it challenges the axioms and assumptions of systems theory throughout the training program. In order to determine if modified training programs have an effect on family therapists' behaviors and attitudes, Black and Piercy (1991) developed a research scale for assessing students' attitudes toward a feminist-informed perspective on therapy.

Families With a Member Who Is HIV-Positive

The AIDS epidemic has created many issues for counselors. The Centers for Disease Control and Prevention has reported 665,000 cases of AIDS and 99,000 cases of HIV infection in the United States (Serovich & Mosack, 2000).

When a family member has AIDS, the information may or may not be disclosed to other family members. Because of the ignorance about the disease as well as reactions to an HIV-positive diagnosis, the impact on family members is likely to be difficult and disrupt typical family functioning (Serovich & Mosack, 2001). The presence of a skilled family therapist to help the family members openly discuss and begin to deal with the issues involved can be critical in maintaining family stability and support for the infected member.

To deal effectively with this issue, the therapist must be educated about the disease and be aware of the most recent information available.

Information on HIV changes rapidly, and the counselor must remain current to provide the help these families need. Moreover, the therapist must be skilled in working with emotionally laden topics such as death, discrimination, and sexuality. Involvement of all immediate and extended family members may be useful in understanding the disease and its implications and in developing effective support for the patient and those who love him or her.

Ethical issues involving the treatment of AIDS patients and their families arise when an infected client discloses that he or she is engaging in unprotected sexual relationships. Pais, Piercy, and Miller (1998) and Serovich and Mosack (2000) have offered guidelines for therapists when this situation arises. The American Counseling Association addressed infectious diseases in the ethical standards published in 1999. The standards state that the counselor is justified in breaking confidence and warning prospective partners. Other professional associations are wrestling with the issue. Members of the American Medical Association encourage the patient to disclose to sex partners. If they will not, the physican is to report to the local health department and finally to those at risk if the health department does not act (Serovich & Mosack, 2000).

Families With an Abusive Member

Violence in families has long presented a difficult problem for mental health professionals to treat. It is especially difficult because physical abuse frequently is a violation of the law as well as a threat to the family structure of those involved (Margolin, 1987). When abuse or neglect involves a child, therapists should be aware that they have a legal obligation to report the abuse in most states (Huber, 1994). Because abusive adults often were abused as children, their self-concepts are frequently low. Their ability to control their impulses and consider alternatives in a potentially violent situation is limited.

From a family systems perspective, physical abuse of a spouse or a child is considered to be part of a pattern of behavior that involves several family members. Unlike most other types of presenting problems, however, the family therapist should not attempt to take the focus off the abuser, as this approach serves only to lead family members and community service agencies to believe that the therapist is excusing the violent acts. Families often enter treatment shortly after an abusing incident has taken place. At this time, the abuser usually feels badly about the violent actions and is ready to work at improving the family situation and eliminating the abuse. Other family members typically are hopeful that therapy will eliminate the abusive situation.

When the family enters treatment, the therapist has two basic goals. *First,* the therapist helps the abusive member learn to delay acting on impulses. *Second,* the therapist helps the abused client and the abuser develop the ability to recognize and consider several alternatives to potentially violent situations. The abuser must learn to recognize and select alternatives other than violence (Hatcher, 1981).

The first session is often a crisis intervention. The therapist might be the first person outside the law enforcement system with whom the family has been able to discuss the problem. Therefore, the therapist must talk with each family member and allow all unexpressed feelings to be presented *without* allowing those feelings to escalate. At this point in treatment, escalation of feelings could precipitate abusive motivations that the family is not yet ready to handle.

As the therapist discusses family members' feelings with them and does not allow them to escalate, the members develop a sense of control. Perhaps for the first time, they are able to discuss what has happened without escalation. The sense of control that develops is the first step toward impulse control. As they begin to share their feelings, the therapist reinforces the aspects of the discussion that demonstrate control of their behavior. This initial process sets the stage for the family to deal with anger within controlled limits—a characteristic that violent families need to develop.

Davidson (1978) proposed a domestic violence cycle that therapists have to understand to be helpful to families in treatment. The stages of the cycle are:

1. Tension builds in the family.
2. A violent incident occurs.
3. The violent member is remorseful and seeks sympathy and understanding.

From a systems point of view, the violent incident can be understood through the provocation–response cycle (see Figure 12.1). When the victim senses the tension building and realizes that a violent incident is going to occur, he or she may precipitate the incident to speed

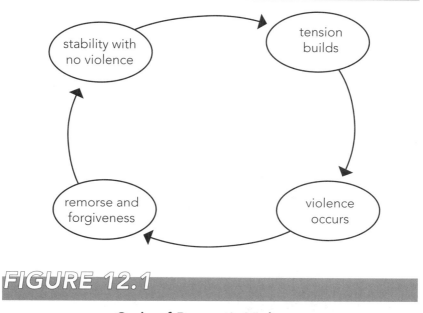

FIGURE 12.1

Cycle of Domestic Violence

movement through the violence stage to the remorseful stage. If this behavior is occurring, it should be identified in a way that does not remove the responsibility of committing violence from the abuser. Again, the therapist must ensure that all family members understand that the abusive behavior is not acceptable while helping each member recognize his or her role in maintaining the behavior. Furthermore, the therapist must ensure that the family knows that if the abuser does not learn to manage the violent behavior, the police and courts will intervene. The therapist and family members all must agree that the behavior is unacceptable (Hatcher, 1981).

A contract should be developed with the family (Hatcher, 1981). In this contract family members agree that when tension is building and violence is likely, the victims will leave the home. The contract should specify that the family will be in a "safe house" for an agreed-upon length of time and that a call will be made to the home before the family considers returning home. The place where the family will go should be arranged in advance but should not be known to the violent member. If this is not possible, the person agreeing to help the victims must be prepared to contact the police if the violent member precipitates a potentially dangerous situation at the safe house.

After the situation deescalates, each family member involved is instructed to call the therapist to describe how he or she managed the situation. These calls to the therapist are important because they reinforce that the leaving behavior on the victims' part is appropriate and that the victims have helped the violent member by leaving. Actual physical violence does not occur then, and this is a positive step. The abuser must understand that when the family leaves the home, this is *good behavior,* designed to strengthen the family relationships, and not abandonment. The therapist plays an important role in helping the abuser recognize and accept these facts.

In the first session therapists should attempt to develop a basic contract with the family. Refinements take place in later sessions. If the family cannot agree on the contract or if a contract is not finalized, the therapist may suggest that a temporary separation is needed if the welfare of the family members is of concern.

After the family has been in therapy for several sessions, the members may be establishing a pattern for impulse control and considering options other than violence. At this point, the family members might benefit from attending support groups. These support groups for victims and abusers help the family members know that they are not alone in their struggle and that they have the understanding and support of those who have been in similar circumstances. Furthermore, these groups provide support for the changes the family is making in therapy.

One of the major contributors to long-term success with violent families is to help the violent member gain self-esteem. Accomplishing this objective may require working individually with key family members in counseling sessions designed to enhance their self-esteem, too.

A final caveat for the therapist working with an abusive family is the potential threat to the therapist. If a threat is made or implied, the therapist should take the threat seriously and deal with it in a matter-of-fact manner. If the threatening client is not appropriately responsive, the therapist should not be reluctant to discontinue treatment and take other appropriate protective measures (Benedek, 1982).

The need to provide treatment to families with an abusive member is unquestionably crucial. But outcome studies on the effects of treatment have been discouraging (Hamberger & Hastings, 1993). We have no conclusive studies to suggest effective intervention other than the permanent separation of the conflictual parties.

Families With a Depressed or Suicidal Member

Depression in Families

All therapists encounter depressed clients several times during their careers. Olin and Fenell (1989) completed a study suggesting that when one spouse in a marriage is depressed, the other may be depressed as well. They suggested marital therapy as an effective treatment for depressed marriages. Often, the depression becomes severe and life-threatening and the depressed family member contemplates suicide.

As in other life-threatening situations, the systems therapist should focus treatment initially on the presenting problem, the potential suicide. Although a systemic conceptualization might be helpful in understanding the family dynamics that support the suicidal ideation, to attempt to defocus the presenting problem is usually a mistake until it has been explored thoroughly and steps have been taken to remove the immediacy of the suicide threat.

Thus, in the first phase of therapy, the therapist should attempt to learn from the family members what has occurred in the past to lead to the depressed and suicidal feelings in one member. Frequently, the therapist discovers that because of intense worry about the suicidal member, the family is overloading the identified patient with love and concern, which paradoxically can cause the person to feel more depressed and hopeless. The therapist can help family members learn to express just the right level of concern to the depressed member. This change in the family's behavior tends to take some of the pressure off the identified patient and alleviate the depression and hopeless feelings.

Because depression and suicidal thoughts frequently occur together, the therapist should assess the client's life situation and explore the history that has precipitated the depression. Individuals who perceive their family-of-origin experiences to be positive are less likely to experience depression or other health problems than those who perceive their family-of-origin experiences to be problematic (Canfield, Hovestadt, & Fenell, 1992).

When a longstanding history of depression is identified, the client may be referred for an examination by a psychiatrist to determine whether antidepressant medication may be helpful in stabilizing the hopeless and helpless feelings that accompany depression. If medication is indicated, it often helps to stabilize the client's mood and enable more effective work to take place in family therapy (Conye, 1987). The therapist should caution the family that antidepressant medication is dangerous if taken in excessive amounts. The family should be instructed to monitor the patient's use of the medication, especially during the early weeks of treatment when effects of the medication may not be evident and when the depression is severe (Conye, 1987).

Suicidal Family Member

Nothing brings family therapy to a screeching halt faster than the statement by one of the members that he or she is contemplating suicide. All the systemic goals and creative conceptualizations are "out the window" and the focus shifts from system reconstruction or individual growth to keeping the person alive (Jurich, 2001). Suicidal behavior exists on a continuum from a thought about self-destruction to a carefully conceptualized plan. The therapist must determine as accurately as possible the client's point on the continuum.

Most people have suicidal thoughts from time to time when life is not going well and they are in emotional pain. But the vast majority of these individuals recognize that the alternative is not a good one and they do not become overtly suicidal. A few clients, however, do reach a point at which they prefer death to their currently painful life.

Five major dimensions should be assessed to determine the significance of the situation.

1. The therapist should assess the *physical factors* affecting the client. Does he or she have health issues that seem to be out of control and have left the client feeling helpless and hopeless?
2. Is the client experiencing any personal crises that he or she cannot meet successfully?
3. Have family issues such as divorce or an affair by the spouse left the client feeling hopeless and rejected?
4. Does the client have problems with peer relationships? Does the client have any friends and support systems?

5. Are there factors stressing the individual such as legal proceed-
    ings or the inability to provide food and shelter for him- or her-
    self and family?

The therapist must assess the problems in each of these areas and
determine the magnitude of the stress created by the demand and the
client's resources to respond to that stress. When stressors on the client
are greater than the resources available to meet them, the therapist must
consider how to best support and keep the client alive until the suicidal
impulse passes (Jurich, 2001).

Jurich (2001) uses the information gained in interviewing the client
to answer four questions:

1. Is the client's level of pain and isolation high enough to move
    suicidal ideation into action?
2. Does the client have the resources and family support to over-
    come the suicidal impulses?
3. What are the client's perceptions that support death over life,
    and what might the family or therapist do to modify these
    perceptions?
4. If the client has a plan for suicide, how lethal is that plan, and
    how can the therapist ensure that the plan is not implemented?

In addition to the interview with the client and family, the therapist
can employ brief assessment instruments such as the Beck Depression
Inventory to lend support or perhaps to disconfirm the initial diagnosis
of lethality.

The behavior of family members toward the suicidal member is
important. The therapist and family members must provide the client a
forum to openly discuss the pain and isolation that he or she feels.
When the client feels that those close to him or her are aware of the
pain, the intensity of the impulse subsides. The therapist must be able
to facilitate this process and prevent family members from attempting
to "correct" the client's perceptions. Acceptance of the suicidal person's feelings and thoughts is critical at this stage of treatment.

All those involved in the treatment must be concerned and attentive,
but in a way that communicates to the person that the helpless feelings
are understandable and that, with the help of therapy as well as changes
in the family system, the feelings can be managed. Their attitude
should communicate respect for the client's ability to work through the

situation. In situations in which the family cannot develop the appropriate level of concern, the therapist may begin sessions with only the depressed individual present and gradually integrate the family into the sessions as the suicidal thoughts become less intense.

The family should become involved in treatment as soon as possible because, as is the case when the therapist chooses to focus on the presenting problem, the family may label the identified patient as the sick one. This attitude validates the family's perceptions that it does not need to change; only the patient has to do so.

One of the most effective ways to begin treatment of a family with a depressed or suicidal member is to develop a *no suicide contract* with the family. In this contract the suicidal member agrees not to attempt suicide while involved in treatment. Whenever possible, other family members should identify in the contract specifically what they will and will not do to assist the suicidal member in getting back to normal. By including all family members in developing the contract, a systemic base is established that begins to broaden the family's understanding of the problem as a family problem that the behaviors of all its members may be maintaining and supporting.

The contract is helpful for the suicidal member because it formally offers a way for the person not to take his or her own life. Agreeing to a contract not to commit suicide often removes a tremendous burden from the suicidal member. A caution is in order, however: A contract will not stop a person who is determined to take his or her own life. If the therapist suspects that the client will attempt suicide despite a contract, hospitalization or some other type of inpatient treatment should be arranged.

Once the immediate threat of suicide has subsided, more traditional family therapy should begin. Rather than keeping the focus on the suicidal member, the focus may shift to other members and their impact on the family's overall health.

Therapy With Divorcing Families

Divorce is a widespread phenomenon in American society. Most therapists will deal with divorce-related problems in their practices, and the effects of divorce will touch the majority of adults and children in the United States in some way (Everett & Volgy, 1991). As many as one-half to two-thirds of marriages contracted in 1990 may end in divorce (Kitson & Morgan, 1990). Fenell (1993b) reviewed the literature suggesting the potential harmful impact of divorce on children, extended family members, and the divorcing couple themselves. Despite the potential pain associated with divorce, it remains common.

The process of divorce is developmental, and the therapist may be brought in at various points in the process and with various clients. For example, a therapist may work with:

- a couple in marriage counseling who discover that they do not want to stay together.
- a spouse whose partner has informed him or her that the marriage is to end and is devastated by the news.
- an acting-out child who is responding to the recent divorce of his or her parents.
- a couple who intends to divorce and wants the process to be as positive as possible for all concerned.

Everett and Volgy (1991) developed a framework for the divorce process to help therapists understand and treat the various aspects of divorce with specific interventions. They postulated a series of steps and suggested that therapists be prepared to intervene at any of the steps. The most important steps in the divorce process as identified by Everett and Volgy are described here.

1. *Heightened ambivalence.* The couple begin to have serious doubts about the marriage. It is during this stage that children usually become aware that a problem exists. The therapist may be involved here, or the couple may let the relationship deteriorate without seeking help.

2. *Distancing.* The marriage relationship begins to be characterized by both physical and emotional distance. This distancing also may occur with extended family and some friends. During this phase, the couple may become aware that outside help is essential if the relationship is to improve.

3. *Preparation fantasies and actions.* Here the partners begin to imagine that they will have their needs met by a return to the family of origin or by living a less restricted life after the divorce.

4. *Physical separation.* At this point the reality of the divorce begins to have an impact on the children and may be a time when the children enter therapy.

5. *Pseudoreconciliation.* Events such as problems with the children or financial settlements sometimes bring the couple back together. Although this coming together has signified a reconciliation, it usually is not the case. Moreover, this phase fuels children's fantasies that the parents will get back together, which can be devastating when the reconciliation is short-lived. After the temporary reconciliation, old problems resurface and reconfirm for the spouses why they want a divorce. At this stage, they often become more open with others about their plans. As children recognize this parting of the parents, they may develop symptoms or problems that slow the divorce process. At this point therapy often is sought to help the children, as well as to smooth the divorce process.

6. *Decision to divorce.* During this stage the legal system becomes actively involved and the therapist must consult with a network of family law specialists.

7. *Recurring ambivalence.* This stage resembles the earlier attempt at reconciliation. This time the overwhelming forces of the legal process lead one or both spouses to reconsider the decision to divorce. During this stage children's hopes for reconciliation are renewed, and in a few cases, these hopes are rewarded as the divorce process is discontinued.

8. *Dealing with potential disputes.* The divorcing couple may choose to deal with disputes through the use of mediation or through adversarial methods. If they choose the adversarial method, the therapist must be aware of the possibility of being called into court to testify concerning the case.

9. *Postdivorce co-parenting.* Once the divorce is finalized, the couple with children begins to establish clearly defined rules and responsibilities—essential for the sake of the children. When co-parenting problems arise, therapy may be of great value.

10. *Remarriage.* Most couples who divorce eventually will remarry. More than 65% of women and 70% of men are likely to remarry after divorce (Norton & Mooreman, 1987). Many of these

remarriages will require intervention by the family counselor to help the new family define roles, rules, and responsibilities.

11. *Dual family functioning.* In the final stage, if both partners from the former marriage are remarried, share children, and assume new parenting roles for the new spouse's children, a therapist can be helpful. This is indeed a complex undertaking that requires skill and perseverance.

Glang and Betis (1993) developed the following list of suggestions to help children through the divorce process.

- Both parents tell the children, with care and concern, about the plan to divorce.
- The parents give children advance warning before one parent moves out.
- The parents both ensure that their children do not feel they are being divorced from either parent and they spend individual time with each child.
- The parent with whom the child spends the most time usually will be the "anchor" parent, the parent who most likely will experience most of the child's anger and sadness.
- The parents should explain the divorce to kids in words they will understand, reassuring them that the divorce is the result of the adults' shortcomings, not the child's.
- Children should see the parents' emotions and know that the parents are human. Too much emotionalism, however, may lead children to believe they have no adult to rely on and consequently may feel overwhelmed and frightened.
- Neither parent should criticize the former spouse in front of the children. The children will find fault with both parents. The kids, not the parents, should be able to bring up these faults.
- The kids should see a parent's new home as soon as possible and be assured some space of their own. They may have a room, a closet, or perhaps only a chest of drawers, but it must be their own private space.
- Children often wish their parents would reconcile, even years later. Parents should be aware of this and accept their children's feelings even though reconciliation is out of the question.
- The parents should help kids look forward to the stay with the other parent. These transitions can be difficult and stressful for the children, and parents should help smooth the process.

Counselors' awareness of the stages of divorce and of ways to intervene during these stages can be useful in helping families through these most difficult times.

■ *Therapy With Military Families*

The attacks on the World Trade Center and the Pentagon of September 11, 2001, sent a call to arms to active duty and reserve military personnel throughout the United States. These military personnel are members of families, and these families often experience considerable stress associated with the military lifestyle, which consists of frequent moves and separations of the military member from the rest of the family. Moreover, some of the separations may place the military member in harm's way. Because the military lifestyle has such a tremendous impact on the family, a meeting of the entire military family with a family therapist skilled in military issues can be a useful source of support for the family.

When working with military families, several common themes emerge. First, Military personnel frequently are concerned that they will be stigmatized if they seek any type of counseling. The first job of the family counselor, then, is to assure the family members of confidentiality in the sessions and, rather than demonstrating weakness, to assure them that seeking counseling is a sign of strength and a valuing of the family unit. Further, the family must be assured that the "Command" will not be made aware of the request for treatment. Military personnel believe that if "Command" knows they are in treatment, it may affect their progress in the military. Whether this concern is valid or not depends on many factors including the values of the commanders regarding counseling. Nonetheless, the perception of those in need of help must be acknowledged.

A second major issue is the disruption to the lives of the spouse and children caused by frequent moves. The spouse frequently is unable to secure a job commensurate with her (or his) abilities because employers know that the individual will not be a permanent employee. This can create frustration and resentment for the nonmilitary spouse. These feelings can often be expressed more productively if they are raised openly in the safe environment of a family counseling session.

Issues with children transferring from one school to another can be stressful for the children. Although some military children thrive in the environment of frequent moves, others are set back socially, academically, and in their pursuit of success in extracurricular activities.

The issues created by frequent school changes by military children are the focus of the Military Coalition on the Family (Working With Military Children, 2001). This organization is attempting to form a coalition of school districts that serve large military populations around the nation. The coalition would develop policies and procedures so that transferring students would not lose academic credits, would be able to participate in extracurricular activities of interest, and would be invited to join groups to facilitate entry into the new school. Again, the family's ability to be able to discuss these concerns openly with a skilled family counselor can help the family deal effectively with the challenges of frequent moves.

The dedication of military personnel to their country and their fellow soldiers sometimes creates serious issues for the family. The military member spends long hours at the job and frequently is part of a tight team, almost a second family. When that second family is perceived to be more important than the real family, serious conflicts emerge. The family counselor helps the spouse, children, and military member express their feelings about the situation and discover ways to meet family responsibilities and duty alike. Research has shown that military personnel who have solid families perform better on the job.

In a related issue, some military members have jobs that involve classified information. This creates a situation in which open communication about work is impossible. The family counselor can help the couple find ways to be open without breaking laws concerning classified information.

Finally, deployments create long periods of time when the service member is away from the family. Family members might fear harm to the service member, especially if deployed to a combat zone. Open discussions of these fears in family counseling helps make them manageable. When fears are not discussed and are repressed, they can become overwhelming or can lead to other displaced dysfunctional behaviors in the spouse and children.

Another serious problem for some families is the concern about sexual fidelity during the deployment. When one or both spouses are unfaithful, all of the other concerns of the family are exacerbated.

Immediate support from a family counselor may prevent anger and hurt from turning to violence if the indiscretion is discovered. The bottom line is that when military families have problems, a deployment will usually make them worse. Thus, predeployment counseling with a trained and military-sensitive counselor may prevent many future problems for the military family.

When the military spouse returns, issues of reentry may surface. The nonmilitary spouse has been taking care of all the family business while the military member is away. Now the military member wants things to be the way they were before she (or he) left for deployment. Moreover, sometimes children have grown distant emotionally and need time to reconnect with the military parent. Family counseling sessions can assist the military family in speeding its return to a more normal state.

▓ *Rural Family Therapy*

Rural families have unique needs that are consistent with their lifestyle. Problems in rural communities are frequently magnified because of the relative lack of privacy. The closeness characteristic of rural communities is one of the strengths of communities but at the same time can generate problems. Closeness can be a blessing when rural families support each other through times of crisis. Closeness can be a curse when the entire community knows about a family's private issues.

As social and economic pressures mount throughout the United States, rural communities, used to a conservative and low-stress lifestyle, feel them uniquely. With urban demands impinging on the lifestyle and economic uncertainties, rural communities are experiencing significant mental health problems that frequently are treated best in a family context (Fenell, Hovestadt, & Cochran, 1985).

Providing mental health services to families in rural communities offers unique challenges to the family counselor. Hovestadt, Fenell, and Canfield (2002) have identified several important skills of effective family therapists working in rural communities. First is *appreciation and understanding of the rural community.* This characteristic simply states that the therapist enjoys rural life, appreciates the people, and understands the workings of the community.

Rural values often are more conservative that those of the typical family therapist. If the therapist has strong value differences with the dominant community values, the therapist will be isolated and marginalized. But the therapist truly appreciates the community, people, and values, joining the community will be relativly easy and the therapist can anticipate acceptance and the possibility of doing much good.

A second key ability is the therapist's *knowledge of systems theory* and the skill to apply this knowledge to the rural community. The rural community is a large system with key subsystems that the therapist must acknowledge and join if the community is to accept him or her. If the Lions Club is the place where key community members meet, the therapist will want to join the club and come to be accepted and valued by members of the community.

Successful counselors in rural communities do much more than work with families. They must be *generalists*—a third key ability. Although some work in rural communities is family-related, the ability to do individual and group therapy is essential, as is the ability to consult with community organizations. Mental health services are few and far between in rural communities, and the therapist must be skilled in a variety of interventions to provide the most assistance.

A fourth characteristic of effective therapists in rural settings is the ability to be comfortable meeting clients in social and other community settings. In a small community the ability to see clients only during sessions is not possible. The therapist will encounter clients in the hardware store, at church, and in restaurants. If the therapist is not comfortable *meeting clients socially,* the rural setting probably is not a good fit.

If the family therapist is able to develop each of these key skills, he or she is likely to be effective in helping rural families and individuals resolve many of the issues that are emerging as urban values begin to subsume the rural way of life.

Summary

For marriage and family counselors to be best able to serve clients' divergent needs, they must have specific knowledge about numerous family-related problems. In this chapter, we have introduced and briefly discussed several specific family problems the family counselor will frequently encounter in clinical practice. We suggest that the reader use this chapter as an introduction and springboard to a more comprehensive study of these important issues, as well as other specific problems not covered here.

SUGGESTED READINGS

Ammerman, R. T., & Hersen, M., Eds. (1992). *Assessment of Family Violence: A Clinical and Legal Sourcebook.* New York: John Wiley.

Barnard, C. P. (1981). *Families, Alcoholism and Therapy.* Springfield, IL: Charles C. Thomas.

Beck, A. T. (1976). *Cognitive Therapy and the Emotional Disorders.* New York: International Universities Press.

Beck, A. T., Rush, A., Shaw, B., & Emery, G. (1979). *Cognitive Therapy of Depression.* New York: Guilford Press.

Fenell, D. L., Martin, J. E., & Mithaug, D. E. (1986). The Mentally Retarded Child. In L. B. Golden & D. E. Capuzzi, Eds., *Helping Families Help Children: Family Interventions With School-Related Problems* (pp. 87–96). Springfield, IL: Charles C. Thomas.

Goodrich, T. J., Rampage, C., Ellman, B., & Halstead, K. (1988). *Feminist Family Therapy: A Casebook.* New York: Norton.

Margolin, G. (1987). The Multiple Forms of Aggressiveness Between Marital Partners: How Do We Identify Them? *Journal of Marital and Family Therapy, 13*(1), 77–85.

McGoldrick, M., Pearce, J. K., & Giordano, J. (1982). *Ethnicity and Family Therapy.* New York: Guilford Press.

Visher, E. B., & Visher, J. S. (1979). *Stepfamilies: A Guide to Working With Stepparents and Stepchildren.* New York: Brunner/Mazel.

Wallerstein, J. (1989). *Second Chances: Men, Women and Children After Divorce.* New York: Ticknor & Fields.

Research in Marriage and Family Therapy

Because of the complexity involved in identifying system change, much of the research in family therapy has focused on individual change—changes by the identified patient. This research has demonstrated that family therapy is effective in working with a variety of presenting issues, which shall be addressed throughout this chapter. Although much of the research has shown that family interventions are effective, evaluating change at the individual subsystem level loses sight of the unique change potential of the systems therapies.

Future researchers have to develop methodologies appropriate for systems therapy rather than trying to "shoehorn" systems therapies into a linear, cause-and-effect research model. This chapter presents an overview of the research on psychotherapy, followed by more specific information about the research in marriage and family therapy.

Meta-analysis
Marital satisfaction research
Effects of divorce on children
Family therapy effectiveness
Gottman's research
Randomized studies

QUESTIONS FOR DISCUSSION

1. Why is research important in marriage and family therapy?

2. Why is family therapy research so difficult?

3. How does divorce affect the children involved? Do you agree with Wallerstein's findings? Why or why not?

4. What marital or family area do you believe is in need of research? Why is this important?

5. What professional journals are most useful to you? Why do you enjoy them?

Family therapy research is difficult for several reasons. First, if the client is considered to be the family system, what assessment instrument can be used to demonstrate change in the system? Compared to research on the symptoms of an individual, family research outcomes are complex and difficult to operationally define. For instance, two families may come to therapy, each with a rebellious child. One family might adjust its rules and roles and normalize the rebelliousness. This family has improved and therapy has been successful. In the second family the parents learn to become more united and confront the rebellious child directly. This family, too, has improved, but in a very different way. How does the researcher show that changes in two very different systems lead to more successful and productive families? It is important for the reader to understand how system changes can look quite different, yet still contribute to successful therapy.

■ *Early Studies*

In 1952 Hans Eysenck shook the world of psychotherapy with the results of his research on the effectiveness of psychotherapy. Eysenck (1952) reported that, according to his analysis, about 67% of neurotic patients improved within 2 years whether they received therapy or not. Eysenck challenged psychotherapists to demonstrate the effectiveness of their approaches or to concede that these approaches were not useful.

Bergin (1967, 1971) was one of the first researchers to respond to Eysenck's criticism. His reevaluation of Eysenck's data revealed that psychotherapy was at least moderately effective with neurotic patients, as 65% improved within 2 years with psychotherapy, while 43% of untreated neurotic patients improved within 2 years.

Despite Bergin's findings, the challenge to demonstrate the effectiveness of psychotherapy remains. As ethical practitioners, psychotherapists seek to provide the most beneficial treatment to clients. How can we know what kinds of treatment are most beneficial unless effective research is conducted to demonstrate the results of various approaches? As ethical therapists, we want to know, within the limits available, whether the treatment works (Levant, 1984).

Paul (1967) phrased a question that described what psychotherapy research attempts to discover. His question clearly identified the complexities involved in conducting psychotherapy research. He asked: "What treatment, by whom, is most effective for this individual with that specific problem, and under what set of circumstances?" Attempting to respond to Paul's question has been, and will continue to be, a major challenge for psychotherapy researchers.

Following the publication of Bergin's (1967, 1971) findings, investigators began to identify deterioration in clients as a result of psychotherapy (Lambert, Bergin, & Collins, 1977). Deterioration means that the client becomes worse as a result of therapy. It was discovered that deterioration occurred in less than 10% of the clients treated, and the rate was higher for more disturbed clients.

Several research projects investigated the effects of the level of therapist empathy, warmth, and genuineness on the outcome of therapy (Mitchell, Bozarth, & Kraft, 1977; Rogers, 1957; Truax & Carkhuff, 1967; Truax & Mitchell, 1971). Although the results of these studies consistently suggested that these therapist qualities are important to client change, the mechanism for these results, as well as how widely the findings can be generalized, has been questioned (Mitchell et al., 1977). Nonetheless, when various theories of counseling are compared, the results indicate that one approach is generally just as effective as another (Luborsky, Singer, & Luborsky, 1973; Smith & Glass, 1977; Strupp & Hadley, 1979). Thus, researchers have not been able to conclude precisely what it is about psychotherapy that brings about improvement. These studies lend indirect support to the researchers who have concluded that the therapist qualities of *empathy, warmth,* and *genuineness* are factors that facilitate change.

Subsequent studies by Bergin and Lambert (1978) suggested that short-term therapy lasting 6 months or less was effective in providing symptom relief for the client. Smith and Glass (1977) completed a meta-analysis of 375 controlled-outcome studies, which suggested that the typical client in therapy is better off than 75% of individuals with similar problems who are not treated. Thus, a fairly solid body of research has been compiled suggesting that psychotherapy is effective.

This summary of some of the important findings in psychotherapy for individuals sets the stage for a review of the research in marriage and family therapy. The same problems that exist in research with individual clients are found in family therapy research, but with additional complications. In marriage and family therapy research, change is more difficult to assess. Are we looking for change in the identified patient? Other family members? Family subsystems? The family system itself? Without knowing what to look for or where to look, it is difficult to assess change (Gurman & Kniskern, 1981b). Olson, Russell, and Sprenkle (1980) stated that, to evaluate family therapy, researchers need ways to identify and measure family system changes. A significant amount of work remains to be completed before researchers are able to reliably identify and accurately measure system change.

Major Reviews

Five major reviews of the research concerning the outcome of marriage and family therapy have been conducted by DeWitt (1978), Gurman and Kniskern (1978a), Pinsof & Wynne (1995a, b), Olson, Russell, and Sprenkle (1980), and Wells and Dezen (1978). Of these, the Gurman and Kniskern and Pinsof and Wynne reviews are cited most often in the marriage and family therapy literature. Specific findings based on these comprehensive reviews indicate the following conclusions.

- Improvement rates in marriage and family therapy are similar to improvement rates in individual therapy.
- Deterioration rates in marriage and family therapy are similar to deterioration rates in individual therapy.
- Deterioration may occur because:
  - The therapist has poor interpersonal skills;
  - The therapist moves too quickly into sensitive topic areas and does not handle the situation well;
  - The therapist allows family conflict to become exacerbated without moderating therapeutic intervention;
  - The therapist does not provide adequate structure in the early stages of therapy; and
  - The therapist does not support family members

- Conjoint marital therapy (with both partners present) is the treatment of choice over individual therapy for couples experiencing marital problems. Lower improvement rates and higher deterioration rates are found when couples are treated separately for marital problems (Gurman & Kniskern, 1978b).
- Family therapy is just as effective as individual therapy for problems involving marital and family conflict and even for treating an individual's problems.
- Brief therapy, limited to about 20 sessions, seems to be as effective as open-ended therapy.
- Participation of the father in family therapy increases the probability of a successful outcome.
- Co-therapy has not been shown to be more effective than one-therapist family therapy.
- Therapist relationship skills have an influence on the outcome of therapy. Good relationship skills produce positive outcomes, and poor relationship skills may produce deterioration.
- When the identified patient has severe diagnosable psychological problems, a successful outcome is less probable.
- Modified structural family therapy has been used to successfully treat psychosomatic problems (Minuchin, Rosman, & Baker, 1978) and drug and alcohol problems (Stanton, 1978; Stanton & Todd, 1979, 1981).
- Family type, family interaction style, and family demographic factors have not been demonstrated to be related to the outcome of family therapy (Gurman & Kniskern, 1981b).

A special issue of the *Journal of Marital and Family Therapy* (1995) reviewed outcome studies on the effectiveness of marital and family therapy. A meta-analysis of 163 randomized studies was completed by Shadish et al. (1995). A meta-analysis takes the results of a number of related studies and quantifies the results to determine any significant overall effects. The results of this study demonstrated that marital and family therapy with a variety of presenting problems works. But no orientation was shown to be more effective than another, and individual therapy was as effective as marital and family therapy. Moreover, the authors concluded that marital and family therapies are conducted in different ways and are difficult to compare in meta-analyses. More specific findings concerning the efficacy of family therapy are presented next.

Family Therapy With Schizophrenic Disorders

Goldstein and Miklowitz (1995) reviewed research conducted on families therapy with a member with schizophrenia. The authors challenged early theories (Bateson et al., 1956; Bowen, 1960) suggesting that the family climate and relationships precipitate the onset and maintenance of the illness. More recent research presents an almost exclusive biological basis for the disorder. Nonetheless, the authors found that family therapy interventions, coupled with appropriate medications, are most helpful in treating schizophrenic disorders. Specifically, *family psychoeducation* was found to be far more effective than routine care in preventing relapse.

The unit of treatment for the psychoeducational family therapy included (a) the family and the patient, which encompassed skill-building, problem-solving, case-management and crisis-intervention strategies; (b) the family without the patient in sessions focusing on providing support and developing approaches to cope with the disorder; and (c) multi-family support groups that also did not include the patients.

Goldstein and Milkowitz (1995) suggested common ingredients in an effective psychoeducational family therapy intervention program. They reported that it is important that the family be engaged early in treatment and that the family treatment does not imply that the family is responsible for the patient's illness. The counselor also should present factual information on schizophrenia—including causal factors, prognosis, and the reasons for various treatments. Moreover, the program must include recommendations for coping with the disorder and problem-solving techniques. Finally the sessions should help the family members communicate effectively and deal effectively with crises if they occur. Goldstein and Milkowitz believe that psychoeducational family therapy can be used effectively with disorders other than schizophrenia.

Family Therapy With Affective Disorders

The largest and most comprehensive study to date of the effects of individual therapy on depression is the NIMH Collaborative Depression Study (Shea et al, 1992). This study compared cognitive therapy, interpersonal therapy and pharmacotherapy. Even though initial results for all forms of treatment were promising, some 40% of the clients relapsed. This result led Prince and Jacobson (1995) to conclude, "Individual treatment may be overlooking some critical factors in the etiology, maintenance and resolution of affective disorders" (1995, p. 378). This hypothesis suggests that marital and family therapies might provide the contextual focus that is missing from individual treatments.

Prince and Jacobson (1995) reviewed three well designed studies comparing individual therapy and conjoint marital therapy for depressed couples in which the woman was diagnosed with unipolar depression. Results of the studies suggested that conjoint marital therapy is as effective as well tested individual therapies for treating depressed women in distressed marriages, and that conjoint treatment is more effective than individual treatment in alleviating marital distress. Even with these results, the authors noted that success requires improvement in both (a) reduced depression and (b) enhanced marital quality. Unfortunately the authors discovered that, even with notable success for many couples, a number of couples did not improve significantly on these dimensions.

▨ *Marital Therapy for Conflict and Divorce*

After reviewing the literature on the effects of marital therapy on marital conflict and divorce Bray and Jouriles (1995) concluded that marital therapy is effective in the short run for resolving marital conflict. Long-term follow-up studies, however, suggest that marital therapy is less effective for the long run. One of the reasons for this may be that couples do not return for periodic "booster shots" of therapy that might help them maintain the early gains of treatment.

Moreover, no type of marital therapy treatment has been shown to be more effective than another. Most of the research has been conducted on behavioral marital therapy (BMT), and this therapy is not used much outside the academic environment. On a more positive note, Bray and Jouriles (1995) found that marital therapy is successful in preventing divorce. They reported that even though treatments are statistically successful, about 50% of those treated in marital therapy are not helped in the long run. So, again, a way to reach those not helped through traditional therapies is desperately needed.

■ *Family Therapy in Treating Alcoholism and Drug Abuse*

Edwards and Steinglass (1995) did a modified meta-analysis of 21 studies examining the effects of family interventions on alcoholism. They found that the spouse's involvement led to alcoholics (especially men) entering treatment significantly more often than alcoholics whose spouse did not participate. Studies evaluating outcome found that at 6-month follow-up, alcoholics treated with family therapy did better than those treated individually or not at all. This gain, however, did not hold up over longer periods. Finally Edwards and Steinglass found that family involvement in aftercare was related to continuing abstinence for up to 2 years after treatment began.

Liddle and Dakof (1995) reviewed 18 studies dealing with adult and adolescent drug abuse and found overwhelming support for family treatment in engaging adolescent drug abusers and their families in therapy and the concomitant reduction in drug use. The findings considering family therapy for adult drug abusers are not as compelling. Results of the studies are mixed. Though some show family therapy to be as effective in engaging families in treatment, others suggest that family therapy is no better than other treatments—which often are not very effective. Liddle and Dakoff (1995) remind the reader that many of the family interventions used in the studies they reviewed are imbedded in a broader treatment approach, so it is impossible to determine if the family component is uniquely responsible for the change.

■ *Family Therapy With Disorders of Childhood and Adolescence*

Estrada and Pinsof (1995) reviewed the research on the use of family therapy in treating selected behavioral disorders of childhood, using the age of 14 as the cutoff between childhood and adolescence. They concluded that most so-called family therapy studies for the treatment of behavioral disorders were some form of parent management training (PMT). This training typically was behavioral, and the family component was part of a larger treatment protocol. Thus, isolating the change-producing factors is impossible.

Nonetheless, Estrada and Pinsoff did find evidence to support the efficacy of family therapy as described in the treatment of childhood conduct disorders, phobias, anxiety, and autism. Their review of the data did not support the superiority of brief PMT for ADHD children when compared to treatment with Ritalin.

Chamberlain and Rosicky (1995) extended the research on the treatment of adolescent conduct disorders by reviewing seven studies published since 1988 that used specific, manualized independent variables (treatment variables), a control or comparison group, and some form of family treatment that targeted adolescent conduct disorders. Independent variables that have been described in detail in treatment manuals are applied consistently according to a documented procedure. Changes resulting from manualized treatments are more reliable than changes that have not used standardized treatments.

Treatments in the studies reviewed were based on social learning theory with families, structural family therapy and a multimodal family therapy. Results of the seven studies suggested that family therapy interventions seem to decrease conduct problems when compared to standard individual therapy and no treatment. The researchers caution that even though these results are promising, several families participating in the studies were not satisfied with the outcome of the family treatment.

Research on Marriage

Next we examine whether marriage is a positive experience and how divorce impacts children and we report on the characteristics of successful long-term marriages. In preparing this discussion, we reviewed empirical studies, descriptive studies, and case-study research.

Advantages of Marriage

In their comprehensive review on marriage, Waite and Gallagher (2000) reported that, on the average, married men and women live longer, are healthier, happier, more solvent financially, and are more satisfied sexually than their unmarried counterparts. While the research often shows men benefiting more than women from marriage, husbands and wives alike are better off than their unmarried peers.

Coombs (1991) reported that married persons generally have lower incidences of alcoholism; lower rates of suicide; longer lifespan, lower incidences of mental illness, and greater happiness than unmarried persons. Coombs cautioned that the benefits of marriage are likely predicated on the positive qualities of the marriage. It is hard to imagine a person in an extremely unhappy marriage leading a pleasant and satisfying life.

Divorce and Its Consequences

Divorce can have devastating negative consequences to the partners and children involved. Morgan (1990) and Wallerstein, Lewis, and Blakeslee (2000) have described the multiple consequences of divorce. Divorce contributes to poor physical and mental health, economic problems, and problems in social adjustment as a single person. Coombs (1991) reported higher suicide rates among divorced individuals than married individuals. Wallerstein and her colleagues' landmark longitudinal study of children of divorce reported that, contrary to much of today's conventional wisdom, divorce often does have devastating effects on children. Children of divorce on the average are less physically and mentally healthy, less well-educated, and less successful in their careers and own relationships than children from intact marriages (Waite & Gallagher, 2000; Wallerstein et al., 2000). Although divorce is necessary in certain situations, many researchers believe that couples willing to work together with integrity can resolve many of the issues that otherwise would result in divorce (Fenell, 1991, 1993a; Gottman, 1999; Wachtel, 1999; Weiner-Davis, 1992).

Fenell Study on Successful Marriages

Fenell (1993a) conducted a survey of 147 couples in satisfactory first marriages of longer than 20 years in duration. These couples were middle class, were from an urban/suburban environment, and ranged in age from 39 to 65 years of age. One of the criticisms of previous research on characteristics of long-term marriages is that the studies often examined marital duration without considering marital quality (Glenn, 1990; Lewis & Spanier, 1979). The Fenell (1993a) study responded to this criticism by administering the Dyadic Adjustment Scale (Spanier, 1976) to all participants to ensure the presence of marital quality. People who were not in satisfactory marriages as identified by the scale were eliminated from the study.

A survey was developed through a modified Delphi process that resulted in a questionnaire listing 59 potential marital strengths. Each of the 59 items was a potential strength that could contribute to a successful, long-term relationship. The survey was administered to each of the 294 participants in the study to determine the major characteristics of long-term marriages. A key finding of this study was that men and women in successful marriages demonstrated considerable congruence in what they believed contributed to their successful long-term relationships. The top 10 characteristics contributing to the long-term and high quality marriages, as identified by the participants, are described below.

1. *Lifetime commitment to marriage.* The most frequently endorsed characteristic contributing to the successful and long-term marriages in this study was a lifetime commitment to marriage. The participants believed that this commitment was the glue that held the marriage together during the inevitable bad times. When marriage partners do not feel committed to each other and to the institution of marriage, their marriage is likely to suffer. Couples with less commitment to the institution of marriage might be more prone to leave the marriage during troubled times.

2. *Loyalty to spouse.* The second most frequently endorsed characteristic was *loyalty to spouse.* This quality suggests the importance of standing with and supporting the other, especially during rough times in the marriage.

3. *Strong moral values.* Although the values held by each couple in the study varied, the importance of value congruence in successful marriages is noted throughout the literature (Murstein, 1976, 1987). The moral values referred to here were not made explicit by the study participants. Nevertheless based on couple-congruent responses to the questionnaire, some of these values may be inferred from the other characteristics reported in this study.

4. *Respect for spouse as a best friend.* This characteristic is important as the marriage endures and the initial passions fade (Flowers,

2000; Rowe & Meridith, 1982; Swensen, Eskew, & Kohlhepp, 1984). Couples with solid friendships enjoy each other and sustain their relationships at a high level. Good friends are self-disclosing—revealing their feelings to each other—and are empathic and understanding. Both self-disclosure (Hansen & Schuldt, 1984; Hendrick, 1981; Knapp & Vangelisti, 1991) and empathic understanding (Mackey & O'Brien, 1995) have been identified as important characteristics in successful relationships. Moreover, a good friendship can serve as a buffer for the marriage when the stress levels are high (Shapiro, Gottman, & Carrere, 2000).

5. *Commitment to sexual fidelity*. Without trust and sexual exclusivity in the relationship (Mackey & O'Brien, 1995), it rarely is possible to attain marital quality and, thus, divorce becomes more likely. Although an affair does not automatically lead to divorce, the pain the affair causes may make repair of the relationship quite difficult (Bader, Pearson, & Schwartz, 2000).

6. *Desire to be a good parent*. Although a body of research suggests that the transition to parenthood can cause the relationship to decline in quality (Glenn, 1990; Shapiro, Gottman & Carrere, 2000), participants in this study believed that their shared desire to be good parents was an important contributor to the success of their marriages.

7. *Faith in God and spiritual commitment*. This finding is identified in numerous other studies (Abbot, Berry, & Meridith; 1990; Olson, Sprenkle, & Russell, 1983; Schumm, 1985; Stinett & Saur, 1977; Thomas & Rogharr, 1990) and is not surprising given the religious nature of many of the populations selected for study. Nonetheless, the religious faith of couples in the long-term marriages served as a guide for behaviors and feelings during difficult times in the marriage. This religious or spiritual dimension of long-term marriages strongly emphasizes preservation of marriage over divorce when possible. Married couples who have differing views on the role of religion in marriage may leave the marriage during difficult times and when their deeply held values clash. In contrast, couples with religious or spiritual convictions encouraging marital preservation may "weather the storm" of marital difficulty and later move to a period of marital happiness and marital stability (Robinson & Blanton, 1993; Schumm, 1985; Weiner–Davis, 1992).

8. *Desire to please and support the spouse.* This characteristic encourages successful marriage by recognizing the importance of appreciating the partner, identifying the partner's needs, and having the desire and ability to respond to those needs. Winch (1958) developed the theory of complimentary needs in marriage and postulated that when those needs were met for both partners, the relationship was strengthened. A spouse who engages in behaviors that please and support the spouse also must be the recipient of pleasing and supporting behaviors from the partner. Reciprocity of positive behaviors is important in successful marriages. If one spouse does all the giving and the other all the taking, marital problems are likely (Jacobsen, 1978).

9. A *good companion to the spouse.* This characteristic is similar to the fourth characteristic, respect for spouse as a best friend. It differs, though, in its emphasis on companionship—being with the spouse physically, emotionally, and with deeper commitment to the partner and the marriage. As partners spend more enjoyable time together as companions, their appreciation of each other increases and strengthens the marriage.

10. *Willingness to forgive and be forgiven.* The couples in this study were in successful, long-term marriages. These happy couples, however, did encounter significant problems in their marriages that could have, but did not, result in divorce (Fenell, 1991). The couples in this study emphasized the importance of being able to forgive the partner for real and perceived transgressions during the long-term marriages. Equally important was that the spouse who had committed the relationship–threatening act recognized how it hurt the partner and the relationship, was apologetic, and was able to receive the partner's forgiveness. Without forgiveness and the ability to receive forgiveness, marriages labor with unspoken resentments and guilt—qualities that do not support successful marriage.

Fenell (1993a) used the results of this study to develop a Marriage Characteristic Worksheet and has used the worksheet in his work with couples experiencing marital difficulties for the past eight years.

Other Studies on Successful Marriages

Other marital researchers have identified characteristics of successful marriages. Berger and Kellner (1977) suggested that, based on their study of numerous couples, an *existential shared meaning creation* is the hallmark of successful marriages. They believe that couples construct a shared reality as they redefine the individual realities that each brings to the marriage. The shared reality provides meaning to the relationship.

To the extent that the shared meaning encompasses the most salient personality traits of each partner, the relationship is strengthened. If the shared meaning excludes the critical individual traits, consensus and cooperation become difficult. Thus, a successful marriage must develop a mutually reinforcing shared reality in which the couple values the characteristics that each partner possesses and believes are important to the sense of self.

Wallerstein and Blakeslee (1995) conducted a longitudinal study of 50 couples married from 9 to 40 years. They found no single model of marital success and discovered that no marriages were free from conflict, tragedy, and other hardships. Results of the study showed that successful marriage partners were *good friends, respected each other,* and *enjoyed each other's company.* The couples believed that their marriages were works in progress, not finished products. Many of these findings are similar to those of Fenell (1993a), Flowers (2000), and Robinson and Blanton (1993).

Robinson and Blanton Study

Robinson and Blanton (1993) conducted a study of 15 couples in long-term marriages, using an unstructured interview format. They interviewed each spouse separately and asked each to report the strengths of the spouse, strengths of the relationship, and strengths of the individual being interviewed. In addition, the participants were asked to discuss times when they felt close to their spouse, difficulties in the relationship, and the most important things one should know about marriage.

Results of the Robinson and Blanton (1993) study revealed several key characteristics of these successful marriages.

1. *Intimacy.* Defined as closeness to one's spouse, intimacy was the central concept identified by the participants in this study. The elements of intimacy they reported include: shared interests, activities, thoughts, feelings, values, pains, and joys; involvement through good times and

bad; and interdependence. Although the couples reported high levels of connectedness, the authors concluded that this was a healthy and mutual intimacy rather than fusion (Bowen, 1978), which is a way of completing an incomplete sense of self and may be dysfunctional and stressful in a marriage. In addition, the participants reported that strong friendships (Fenell, 1993a; Flowers, 2000) were a component of intimacy and that time spent together was mutually enjoyable.

2. *Commitment.* Defined as an expectation by the partners that the marriage would endure, commitment was a second key characteristic of these long-term marriages. The participants reported that the influence of an external commitment—an expectation by society to remain in the relationship (Lewis & Spanier, 1979)—and internal commitment—a deeply held personal value—were equally important to the success of their relationships. In addition, the couples reported feeling a deep level of commitment to the spouse and to the marriage (Fenell, 1993a; Lauer & Lauer, 1986; Weishaus & Field, 1988).

3. *Communication.* In this study, communcation was defined as an emotional transparency or a sharing of thoughts and feelings, discussing problems, and listening to the other's point of view. These couples used their communication skills to resolve many of the problems they experienced in their marriages. Communication was important in facilitating shared decision making and conflict resolution. Effective communication also enabled participants to interact effectively and minimize negative feelings. Couples who reported higher intimacy levels also had stronger communication abilities. Noler & Fitzpatrick (1990) reviewed the literature on communication in marriage, and this review further supported the relationship between good communication and marital quality.

4. *Congruence.* The married couples in the study identified similar strengths in their relationship. The spouses had strong congruence in their perceptions of communication, commitment, intimacy, family orientation and religious orientation. The couples also expressed congruence in certain areas of relationship weaknesses.

Partners who share congruent and positive perceptions of the relationships are more likely to be in well-adjusted and satisfactory marriages (Robinson & Blanton, 1993; Fields, 1983; Sporakowski & Hughston, 1978). In his study of long-term, successful marriages Fenell (1993a) found that the marital strengths identified by the husbands and wives were highly correlated and congruent. Future research might investigate whether congruence in happy marriages was present in the beginning of the relationship, whether it evolved over time, or whether it was some combination of these.

5. *Religious orientation.* Research by Schumm (1985) suggested that religious orientation is the key characteristic in successful relationships that influences all others. Robinson and Blanton (1993) and Fenell (1993a) concur that religion is an important variable in enduring relationships, but their research did not identify religion as the main factor influencing all others. All 15 couples in the Robinson and Blanton research were affiliated to some extent with a specific religious denomination, so this finding is not surprising. A majority of participants indicated that they received social, emotional, and religious support from their faith. Commitment to the marriage and an expectation for family togetherness were reinforced through the values of religion. Moreover, religious faith helped the couples deal with adversity in their marriages and provided a common value base for marital and family decision making.

Robinson and Blanton (1993) did not find a strong relationship between religiosity and marital quality in their subjects. Although religious orientation was an important characteristic, some of the less religiously involved couples seemed to have stronger marriages than some couples who were more involved in their religion.

The importance of religious orientation, though controversial, appears in much of the research on long-term marriages (Abbott, Berry, & Meridith, 1990; Fenell, 1993a; Schumm, 1985; Stinett & Saur, 1977; Thomas & Rogharr, 1990) and merits consideration along with other qualities in contributing to successful marriages. Critics have suggested that the relationship between religious orientation and successful marriages is a spurious one based on marital "conventionalization." A number of the long-term studies on marriage obtained their samples from predominantly religious populations and, thus, the participants' reports of the importance of religion to their successful marriages makes sense.

Lewis and Spanier Model

Finally, Lewis and Spanier (1979) developed one of the most compre-hensive models for successful marriage. They examined premarital variables, marital variables, and external contingencies that lead to suc-cessful marriages. Their model considered the couple's *similarity, pre-marital resources*; exposure to *adequate role-models* and support from *significant others* as key premarital predictors. The most important marital variables were found to be:

1. *Satisfaction with lifestyle*, including employment roles, eco-nomic adequacy, community support, and optimal family size.
2. *Rewards from spousal interaction,* including positive regard, emotional gratification, communication, role-fit and amount of interaction

The two *external contingencies* that impact marriage are (a) *alter-native attractions*, such as an emerging affair or significant workplace involvement, and (b) *pressures to remain married*. This pressure includes factors such as family approval and sanctions from church and society. Any dissatisfaction with the marital variables gives weight to the power of alternative attractions from the marriage. Satisfaction with the marriage adds strength to external pressures that couples feel to remain married.

Research by Gottman and Colleagues

Gottman (1999), one of the most prolific and respected researchers in the field of marriage and family therapy, has conducted an extensive series of longitudinal studies on marriage quality, involving nearly 700 couples. These studies have been based on the careful observation, cod-ing, and analysis of actual couple behaviors recorded in his Couples Laboratory at the University of Washington. Based on an exhaustive review of the outcome research on marital therapy, Gottman contends that most marriage counseling interventions are not effective in enhancing marital quality. Even with marriage counseling, only between 11% and 18% of the couples in therapy maintain the initial gains achieved in treatment. After reviewing the research on relapse rates in marital therapy, Gottman estimates that 35% of the couples treated experience positive changes in the relationships and an improved marriage. But his review of available studies suggests that 30% to 50% of the couples who initially improve then relapse after a year.

Based on his review of the marital therapy research, Gottman's analysis of marital treatments led to his conclusion that many widely used approaches to the treatment of marital problems have not been successful. Moreover, to be successful in the future, effective marital interventions must be based on demonstrated empirical studies that clearly define what is functional and what is dysfunctional in marriages. To accomplish this, he designed an elaborate research laboratory to observe, record, and evaluate the actions, communication, and physiological responses of hundreds of married couples and identified research-based conclusions on what contributes to satisfactory and enduring marriages.

Some of Gottman's findings are controversial, as they contradict much of the "shared wisdom" of the profession of marital therapy. The findings reported, however, are based on the highly controlled observations of marital couples and extensive follow-up of those couples. Gottman (1999) believes that his research has provided a picture of what leads to divorce and the characteristics that couples possess that make them resistant to divorce. He offers a model that identifies the marriage style that couples develop, the four major causes of divorce and several keys for improving marriage.

Gottman (1993, 1999) found that conflict was present in happy and distressed marriages alike and that the *process of resolving the conflict* was a key predictor in whether the marriage was successful or ended in divorce. Couples in happy marriages had the ability to *repair* the relationship, whereas couples in unhappy marriages did not. Gottman points out that repairing the relationship does not imply resolving all the conflict. His studies found that most couples had ongoing conflicts that were never fully resolved. The happy couples possessed the mechanisms in their relationships to repair the conflicts but not necessarily resolve them.

Specifically, Gottman's research found that couples in happy, stable marriages had an *overall level of positive affect*. Based on observations of couples in happy marriages, he found that the ratio of positive to negative affective exchanges in their marriages were at least 5 to 1. This means that happily married couples engaged in at least five affirming affective behaviors for every negative behavior recorded. Examples of positive affect are showing interest, showing caring, being affectionate, being empathic, being appreciative, showing concern, being accepting, using appropriate humor, and sharing joy.

A second key ability found in couples in happy marriages was the ability to *reduce the negative affect during conflicts*. Couples in distressed marriages established a pattern of escalating negative affect in their conflicts. Moreover, couples in unhappy marriages held perceptions of the partner's hurtful behavior as *unchangeable and an internal part of the personality*. In contrast, couples in happy marriages viewed the partner's hurtful behavior as *temporary and a result of external causes* such as a bad day at work.

Gottman (1994, 1999) has been able to predict with a high degree of accuracy the marriages that will endure and those that will end in divorce. Based on behavioral, self-report, expert observation and physiological data recorded from participating couples, he predicted with 95% accuracy which couples' marriages would strengthen and which would deteriorate (Gottman, 1991, 1999). He identified three styles of conflict and conflict resolution. Many therapists think that two of the three styles often contribute to the deterioration of marriage. The research, however, discovered that all three styles can result in happy marriages. They are:

1. *Validating style.* This is the style that most marriage therapists encourage couples to develop during therapy. The communication is clear and direct; a moderate amount of affect is expressed; and support is provided for each partner.
2. *Volatile style.* This style has high levels of affect, frequent arguments, and lots of bickering. Most marital therapists consider this to be a dysfunctional marital style. Gottman agrees that it presents more potential for problems than the validating style but can produce happy marriages.
3. *Conflict-avoiding style.* This style is characterized by low affect and by minimizing marital problems. The partners are eager to compromise, see the other's point of view readily, and are willing to suppress their own thoughts and feelings to preserve the marriage. Minimizing the conflict is their strategy for dealing with controversial issues that emerge in the relationship. Many therapists consider this style as dysfunctional because it lacks

the openness and disclosure believed necessary for happy marriages. Yet this style also produces happy marriages.

Gottman (1999) discovered that all three styles may produce happy marriages. What is most important in each style is the partners' ability to interact in ways that present positive affect in a ratio of at least five positive messages for each negative message. Moreover, the happy couples are able to initiate repair mechanisms in their arguments and to reduce the negative affect the arguments generate. Gottman discovered in his research that not all problems will be resolved and that some become perpetual issues that recur. The ability to repair the relationship by *soothing the negative affect* expressed by the partners when perpetual issues are negotiated is one of the key characteristics that differentiate happy and unhappy marriages.

To understand how to make marriage successful, Gottman (1999) believes it is important to understand what occurs when the marriage is in difficulty. His observational research identified four specific characteristics of marriages in trouble: *criticism, defensiveness, contempt,* and *stonewalling.* These characteristics occurred in sequence. First one partner criticized the other. Then the criticized partner became defensive and escalated the conflict. This portion of the sequence exists in happy and distressed marriages alike. In distressed marriages, however, the conflict escalates and contempt for the partner emerges. Finally, the couple stonewalls, or closes off interaction, and negativity increases.

In Gottman's (1999) research, criticism, defensiveness, and stonewalling were found in both happy and distressed marriages. But contempt was identified only in distressed marriages. In happy marriages couples were able to institute the repair mechanism discussed previously and did not move into the contempt phase. Unhappy couples were not able to institute repair mechanisms, and their fighting escalated to the contempt phase. Contempt is such a strong predictor of marital unhappiness that Gottman encourages marital therapists to "label contempt as psychological abuse and unacceptable" (p. 47) in the treatment of couples trying to improve their marriages.

Other important findings concerning successful marriages emerging from Gottman's (1999) research are that in successful marriages, wives, beginning early in the marriage, are better able to identify negativity in the relationship. Moreover, in happy marriages, wives were more likely to raise the negative issues for consideration. In more troubled marriages, wives often adjusted their "negativity threshold," adapting to increasing negativity by the husbands. This adaptation by the wives often was a precursor to marital distress and divorce. Wives who identified the negativity rather than increasing their threshold levels were more likely to be in happy marriages.

Another of Gottman's important findings was that couples with higher expectations for their marriages tended to have better marriages than couples with lower expectations. Thus, couples who expected much from marriage were more likely to get it and to be in happy marriages. Still another important finding (Gottman, 1999) was that husbands who are able to self-soothe and lower their levels of anger during conflict were more likely to be in happy marriages.

Even though the Gottman (1994, 1999) research has provided a new view of the causes of marital happiness and distress and new ideas about what are successful and unsuccessful marriages, many of his specific techniques for maintaining happy marriages are similar to those identified by other researchers. Developing skills to repair disagreement and conflict in marriage is seen as essential to happy relationships. The techniques to accomplish this are similar to those that others identified. For example, Gottman believes, like Berger and Kellner (1977), that happy couples create a shared meaning and that, to maintain a happy relationship, the partners need to communicate more positives than negatives (Jacobsen, 1978) to each other. Moreover, Gottman concurs that couples learn to communicate (Robinson & Blanton, 1993) complaints clearly rather than criticize; express genuine caring and validation to the partner; use nondefensive listening and speaking skills; and identify thoughts that perpetuate the problem and redesign these thoughts.

Gottman (1994) identified four strategies for maintaining and improving a marriage.

1. Identify emotional reactions to a situation and make an effort to *calm down*.
2. *Speak nondefensively* using good communication skills.
3. Use *validation* to let your spouse know you understand and are empathic. Gottman believes this is especially important for men, who can become hyper-rational.
4. *Overlearn* the previous skills. Use the skills again and again so they become automatic for use in conflicts that inevitably arise.

Summary of the Research

The research reviewed in this chapter suggest that marital and family therapy may be useful in a variety of problem situations including the following:

- Family psychoeducation with schizophrenic disorders (Goldstein & Miklowitz, 1995)
- Family therapy with affective disorders (Prince & Jacobson, 1995)
- Family therapy with selected behavioral disorders of childhood (Estrada & Pinsof, 1995)
- Family therapy with adolescents with conduct disorders (Chamberlain & Rosicky, 1995)
- Family therapy for the treatment of alcoholism (Edwards & Steinglass, 1995)
- Family therapy for the treatment of drug abuse (Liddle & Dakof, 1995)
- Family therapy in the treatment of physical illness (Campbell & Patterson, 1995).
- Family therapy in the treatment of marital dysfunction (Fenell, 1993a; Gottman, 1999).

Pinsoff and Wynne (1995) summarized what we know based on recent family therapy research. They reported that the research on family therapy in its many forms is more effective than no treatment at all and does not seem to have negative effects on clients. They reported that family therapy is more efficacious than standard/individual treatment for depressed outpatient women in distressed marriages, adult schizophrenia, marital distress, alcoholism and drug abuse, anorexia in young women, and in the treatment of several medical problems. Although not all studies confirm these findings, many do. Moreover, family involvement is an important ingredient but was not sufficient by itself to bring about change in the studies reviewed. Finally, no one type of family therapy has been found to be superior to any other.

Future research efforts should address a series of issues.

1. The disorder and the symptoms of the problem being treated should be clearly operationalized and the severity of the symptoms controlled.

2. The independent variables, or treatment variables, have to be clearly defined. Research using manualized treatments are attempting to address this issue.

3. Future research should be methodologically sound with control groups, larger sample sizes, assessments with standardized, reliable and valid instruments appropriate for the treatment being employed, and assessment should be made for both short-term and longer-term outcomes.

These findings reflect the synthesis of numerous studies conducted over the past 20 years. Psychotherapy research is still in a relatively primitive state, and the findings should be considered with this limitation in mind.

Foremost of the professional journals reporting the results of marital and family therapy research are:

American Journal of Family Therapy
Family Journal: Counseling and Therapy for Couples and Families
Family Process
Family Systems Medicine
Family Therapy
Family Therapy Networker
Journal of Family Psychology
Journal of Marital and Family Therapy
Journal of Marriage and the Family
Journal of Sex and Marital Therapy
Journal of Strategic and Systemic Therapies

Future research should focus on evaluating specific aspects of treatment on specific targets in the family system. Because specific therapist behaviors to produce change may have little relation to the theory of family therapy being practiced, identifying these specific, change-producing, theory-neutral factors will be important for all practitioners.

Further, future research designs should use a control group so findings can be generalized as much as possible. In addition, findings should be useful in practical ways to clinicians as well as statistically significant to researchers. Another need is for researchers to conduct follow-up evaluations of their subjects to determine the long-term effects of treatment (Gurman & Kniskern, 1981b).

In addition to providing practicing clinicians with information about the efficacy of certain treatment approaches, research in psychotherapy provides a continuous flow of information to the increasingly critical public concerning the effects of treatment for psychological difficulties.

■ *Summary*

This chapter has introduced the reader to the complexities involved in conducting research on therapy outcomes. The problems are especially complex when attempting to isolate the variables in family systems theories that are change producing. While the available research suggests that for most problems treatment is preferable to no treatment, researchers still are in the primitive stages of determining what therapeutic interventions are best for treating a variety of family problems. If the family therapy profession is to advance in the future, more high quality controlled studies will be required to determine efficacy of the treatments provided.

SUGGESTED READINGS

Fenell, D.L. (1993a). Characteristics of long-term first marriages. *Journal of Mental Health Counseling, 15,* 446–460.

Coombs, R. H. (1991). Marital status and personal well-being: A literature review. *Family Relations, 40,* 97–102.

Gottman, J. M. (1999). *The marriage clinic: A scientifically-based marital therapy.* New York: W.W. Norton.

Professional Issues & Ethics

The discipline of marriage and family therapy has emerged from the clinical experience and research of several older disciplines including psychology, psychiatry, social work, group therapy, and others. Thus, marriage and family therapy has developed as both a separate discipline and as a specialty area of other established mental health professions. In this chapter we will discuss several key issues influencing and confronting marriage and family therapy and its continued development. We also will discuss the ethical standards of marriage and family therapists, with a focus on some of the ethical issues that may occur when the client is a family rather than an individual.

Professional organizations in family therapy
Clinical member, AAMFT
Confidentiality
Privilege
Informed consent
Preparation of MFTs
Diagnosis in family therapy

QUESTIONS FOR DISCUSSION

1. Do you think marriage and family therapy is a profession in itself, or is it a subspecialty of several mental health professions? Support your answer.

2. Why should a counselor use a professional disclosure statement?

3. What type of professional training do you think a counselor should undergo before beginning work with couples and families?

4. What are some unique ethical problems a therapist might encounter when providing marriage and family therapy?

5. What are the advantages and disadvantages of diagnosis in family therapy?

The professional practice of marriage and family therapy grew tremendously during the 1980s and early 1990s. To represent the interests of the increasing number of professionals practicing marriage and family therapy, several professional organizations with a focus on marriage and family therapy have emerged.

Professional Organizations

Three professional organizations specifically represent the professional interests of therapists who work with couples and families:

- American Association for Marriage and Family Therapy (AAMFT)
- International Association of Marriage and Family Counselors (IAMFC), a division of the American Counseling Association (ACA)
- Division of Family Psychology, American Psychological Association (APA)

American Association for Marriage and Family Therapy (AAMFT)

The oldest and most widely recognized of the professional organizations is the AAMFT, which was established in 1942. Originally, this organization was called the American Association of Marriage Counselors because the focus of the membership was on treating marriage problems. In 1970 the organization was renamed the American Association of Marriage and Family Counselors because of the growing interest of its members in family therapy. In 1978 it was renamed the AAMFT because the term "counselor" was not believed to accurately represent the thrust of the practice of most members in the organization, and the

Board of Directors believed that the new title would be more effective in representing the profession to insurance companies that might approve third party payments for family therapists (Broderick & Schraeder, 1991).

The AAMFT has served as a professional association and as a credentialing agency for its membership. AAMFT has three levels of membership, described below (from AAMFT, 2002):

1. Clinical Membership

   Clinical Members meet the full set of requirements established by the AMFT for the independent practice of marriage and family therapy. These requirements include:
   - a graduate degree in marriage and family therapy or a related mental health discipline from a regionally accredited institution
   - 11 courses in theory, practice, human development, research, ethics
   - a minimum of 300 hour supervised clinical practicum during graduate program
   - 1000 hours of direct client contact and 200 hours of supervision
   - the applicant's agreement to abide by the AAMFT Code of Ethics

2. Associate Membership

   Associate Members have completed a graduate degree in marriage and family therapy or a related mental health field and are in the process of earning the clinical experience necessary for AAMFT Clinical Membership and/or licensure as a marriage and family therapist. Associate Membership requirements include:
   - a graduate degree in marriage and family therapy or a related mental health discipline from a regionally accredited institution
   - 8 of the 11 courses in theory, practice, human development, research, ethics
   - a minimum of 300 hour supervised clinical practicum during graduate program
   - the applicant's agreement to abide by the AAMFT Code of Ethics

3. Student Membership

   Student Members are currently enrolled in programs leading to a graduate degree or post-graduate certificate in marriage and family therapy or a related mental health field. Student Membership requirements include:

- enrollment in a graduate degree or post-graduate certificate program in marriage and family therapy or a related mental health discipline in a regionally accredited institution
- the applicant's agreement to abide by the AAMFT Code of Ethics

In addition to the membership categories outlined above, in 1983 the AAMFT designated approved supervisors, who have advanced training and experience in supervising the clinical work of prospective marriage and family therapists seeking clinical membership. Approved supervisors have submitted their credentials for careful review and have met the highest standards of clinical education and experience (Huber, 1994). AAMFT created the Commission on Supervision (now the supervision committee) in 1983 to administer the approved supervisor designation.

Furthermore, AAMFT has developed rigorous standards for accrediting graduate and post-degree marriage and family training programs. In 1978 the Commission on Accreditation for Marriage and Family Therapy Education was recognized by the U.S. Office of Education, Department of Health, Education, and Welfare, to establish standards for training programs in marriage and family therapy education. This recognition was continued under the U.S. Department of Education.

Until 1978, AAMFT was the only professional organization specifically designed to recognize and support mental health service providers specializing in marriage and family therapy. Other organizations have emerged on the professional scene offering alternatives for professional affiliation for marriage and family therapists.

International Association of Marriage and Family Counselors (IAMFC)

The inaugural meeting of the IAMFC was held at the 1987 Annual Convention of the American Association for Counseling and Development (now the American Counseling Association). The purpose of the meeting was to approve bylaws and identify potential members so the IAMFC might petition the American Counseling Association for inclusion as a division of that larger organization.

The ACA has an accrediting body called the Council for Accreditation of counseling and Related Academic Programs (CACREP). This body accredits programs in community counseling, school counseling, marriage and family counseling/therapy and colleges student services. CACREP has accredited 165 university counselor training programs in the United States. Only 23 universities have CACREP accredited counselor training programs in Marriage and Family Counseling/Therapy (MFC/T). The universities with the MFC/T accredited programs are listed below. Many counselor training programs offer marriage and family courses (Gladding, Burggraf, & Fenell, 1987). So few are accredited in MFC/T because of the ongoing debate within the counseling profession about whether marriage and family counseling should be separately accredited from community counseling programs or whether marriage and family counseling should be considered a sub-specialty of community counseling. Those programs that view MFC/T as a sub-specialty of community counseling rather than a unique profession are not likely to seek a separate accreditation in MFC/T even though they may be eligible to do so. For a discussion of the politics surrounding this issue, read the Fenell and Hovestadt (1986) treatment of the problems involved.

The IAMFC membership consists mostly of ACA members with a primary identity as professional counselors but who also identify themselves as marriage and family counselors. Graduates of CACREP-based programs are eligible for licensure as Licensed Professional Counselors in most states but rarely are eligible for licensure as a Marriage and Family Therapist. State laws, however, usually do not preclude LPCs from providing marriage and family therapy services as long as they have been properly trained and supervised in marriage and family counseling and provide ethical and effective treatment to their client families and couples. Specific information regarding licensure as a professional counselor or a marriage and family therapist is available from the various state licensing boards.

The IAMFC was created to meet the needs of individuals with professional training in mental health disciplines other than marriage and family therapy. Professionals trained in other disciplines are often unable to meet the stringent—and some from professional training programs other than marriage and family therapy would say exclusionary—academic requirements to obtain clinical membership in AAMFT and state licensure as a marriage and family therapist. Thus, a need for professional affiliation for family counselors who are not eligible for clinical membership in AAMFT has been met through creation of other marriage and family therapy professional organizations. Whether this diversity of professional organizations will have a beneficial effect on the training, practice, and regulation of marriage and family therapy remains to be seen.

CACREP-accredited academic programs in MFC/T are available at:

California Polytechnique State University
California State University–Fresno
California State University–Los Angeles
California State University–Northridge
San Francisco State University
University of Colorado–Denver
University of Northern Colorado
Barry University (FL)
University of Florida
Governor's State University (IL)
Southern Illinois University at Carbondale
Lindsey Wilson College (KY)
University of Louisiana at Monroe
Our Lady of Holy Cross College (LA)
Mississippi College
Montana State University–Bozeman
University of Nevada–Las Vegas
University of North Carolina at Greensboro
University of Akron (OH)
Duquesne University (PA)
University of South Carolina
Southwest Texas State University
Texas Women's University

Division of Family Psychology

Because of rapidly growing interest by psychologists in marriage and family therapy, the Division of Family Psychology of the American Psychological Association was created in 1984. This division is composed mainly of professionals whose primary identity is that of psychologist but who have special interests in marriage and family issues and therapy. In 1989 Family Psychology was recognized as the seventh diploma specialty area by the American Board of Professional

Psychology. A stringent application process must be completed to gain this recognition (Huber, 1994).

Licensure of Marriage and Family Therapists

As demonstrated in the previous discussion of professional associations, marriage and family therapy is practiced by a wide array of licensed professionals, including professional counselors, psychologists, psychiatrists, social workers, and marriage and family therapists. The practice of marriage and family therapy is licensed as a distinct professional practice in these 44 states, as of May 2002:

Alabama	Kentucky	North Carolina
Alaska	Louisiana	Oklahoma
Arizona	Maine	Oregon
Arkansas	Maryland	Pennsylvania
California	Massachusetts	Rhode Island
Colorado	Michigan	South Carolina
Connecticut	Minnesota	South Dakota
Florida	Mississippi	Tennessee
Georgia	Missouri	Texas
Hawaii	Nebraska	Utah
Idaho	Nevada	Vermont
Illinois	New Hampshire	Virginia
Indiana	New Jersey	Wisconsin
Iowa	New Mexico	Wyoming
Kansas		

Because the content of these state laws differed in substantial ways and did not define the practice of marriage and family therapy consistently, the AAMFT developed a model for states that are pursuing marriage and family therapy licensure to use in defining the profession. Individuals interested in licensure should contact the regulatory board of the state for which licensure is sought to determine specific requirements for the license. Graduate students are advised to seek this information early in their programs to ensure that appropriate courses are completed. An alternate route to clinical membership in AAMFT is available to professionals licensed by their state to practice marriage and family therapy.

■ *Professional Status of Marriage and Family Therapy*

The issue of whether marriage and family therapy is or is not a distinct profession is loaded with controversy (Gurman & Kniskern, 1981a). As the descriptions of the three professional organizations illustrate, the various professional organizations do not agree on the status of marriage and family therapy. Fenell and Hovestadt (1986) gave four possible descriptions of the status of marriage and family therapy (see Figure 14.1):

1. An independent profession
2. A profession that partially overlaps with another mental health profession
3. A professional specialty area within a specific mental health profession
4. An area of elective study within a specific mental health profession.

Thus, family therapy is conceptualized on a continuum from an independent profession to an area of elective study within a specific mental health profession.

The AAMFT and IAMFC support the notion of marriage and family therapy as an independent profession (AAMFT) or as a clearly definable professional area developed in conjunction with another mental health profession (IAMFC). Clinical membership in AAMFT is awarded to those who meet the rigorous academic and supervised experience requirements of that organization. Some members of other mental health professions, such as professional counseling, psychology, and social work, believe that their training programs, while possibly not meeting AAMFT requirements, adequately prepare graduates to work with people who are experiencing marriage and family problems.

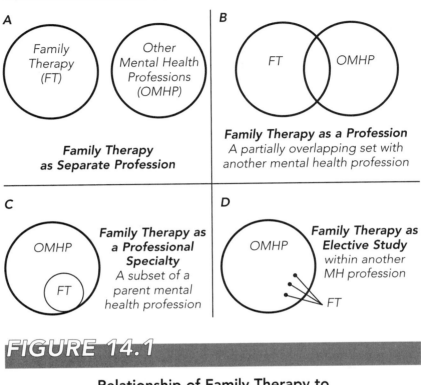

FIGURE 14.1

Relationship of Family Therapy to Other Mental Health Professions

Others, however, would argue that marriage and family therapy graduate education should be conducted by institutions accredited by the Commission on Accreditation of Marriage and Family Therapy Education of the AAMFT or by the Commission on Accreditation of Counseling and Related Academic Programs (Marriage and Family Therapy specialty).

Nevertheless, many non-accredited mental health graduate and postgraduate programs are training individuals from a variety of mental health professions to work with marital and family problems. These therapists are providing marital and family services as licensed counselors, psychologists, social workers, psychiatric nurses, and pastoral counselors. Thus, the question of the status of the profession of marriage and family therapy remains unanswered. Will the field emerge as a distinct mental health profession? Or will it be recognized as a specialty area within other established professions, such as professional counseling, psychology, and social work (Fenell & Hovestadt, 1986)? Because many therapists from other professions do practice marriage and family therapy, the field seems to exist both as a profession in itself and as a professional specialty, depending on the background, training, professional affiliation, and perspective of the mental health professionals involved.

Diagnosis and Family Therapy

Clinical diagnosis in the field of family therapy has emerged as a controversial issue in the new millennium and is directly related to the professional identity of family therapists. Family therapy emerged in the 1950s as a reaction to the ineffectiveness of the medical model and diagnosis in resolving certain types of psychological problems. On the one hand, family therapy has traditionally conceptualized the entire family as the unit of treatment. Currently, there are no recognized diagnostic criteria identifying family systems patterns. Thus, family therapy purists do not diagnose. These therapists contend that diagnosing one member of the family serves to confirm the family's perception that it has within it a disturbed member and undermines the assumption that the acting-out member is part of a disturbed family system. Therefore, systems interventions will not be consistent with the diagnosis and the stated reason for therapy, that being curing the problem of the diagnosed individual.

On the other hand, many insurance companies will not recognize the work done by a family therapist unless treatment is coded with a diagnosis from the *DSM IV.* Family therapists know that the work they do is often helpful and want to ensure they are able to receive payment for their services. Proponents of diagnosis claim that they are able to effectively apply systemic interventions even though one of the family members is identified as having a psychiatric diagnosis. Ethical and perhaps legal issues emerge when a therapist makes a diagnosis of a family member for insurance purposes but does not treat that member as the focus of therapy. Other family therapists take the approach that diagnosis does serve a purpose of creating a unifying understanding of client behaviors and is helpful in this regard. These therapists treat the diagnosed individual in a family context, relying on the other family members to serve as reinforcers for altered behaviors by the identified and diagnosed patient.

Denton (2002), a psychiatrist and family therapist with a Ph.D. from Purdue University, has written extensively about the use of diagnosis and family treatment. He believes that diagnosis is important and useful, but that a new diagnostic category must be developed that considers systemic family functioning. The Global Assessment of Relational Functioning (GARF) Scale, an earlier attempt at this diagnostic process, was included as an appendix to *DSM IV* as an area for further study. As work is proceeding on *DSM V,* Denton and other family therapists who support diagnosis are hopeful of a major change that acknowledges relational problems and provides appropriate systems-based diagnostic categories.

Lyman Wynn, also a physician and family therapist, in an interview with Shields (2002), stated that family therapy students need to have a working knowledge of individual *DSM* diagnoses. Further, Wynn encourages training programs to ensure that students can conceptualize at all levels of systems, especially including the individual system level. That means family therapists must be able to diagnose with the *DSM.* Wynn agrees with Denton that the mental health community needs to develop ways to diagnose at the larger family systems level. However, Wynn is not optimistic that the current psychiatric macrosystem will support this process.

The preponderance of support in the recent literature seems to favor including individual diagnosis as a part of family therapy practice as well as keeping a systems perspective to employ when that is the best way to resolve the presenting problem. In some ways, this begs the issue of how problems develop. The problem formation question is at the heart of the debate. How do problems form? Are they intrapsychic and individually based and thus amenable to diagnosis, or do they emerge as a symptom of a larger family systems problem, in which case diagnosis of the symptomatic individual becomes counterproductive? This question remains to be resolved.

Haley (1963) said, "The system is powerful." He was, of course, referring to the power of a family to induct the therapist into their patterns of thought and behavior. The quote may also ring true for other systems. The medically dominated mental health care system may possess the financial and political power to incorporate family therapists into the individually based diagnostic treatment model that it is founded upon. Some call it the "coming of age" of family therapy and others call it the "selling out" of family therapy. The next few years will be critical in the evolution of the profession and may determine whether family therapy remains a unique alternate paradigm for the treatment of psychological problems or whether it becomes another player in the individually based mental health treatment system.

Ethical and Legal Issues in Marriage and Family Therapy

The ethical guidelines developed by the American Counseling Association (ACA) and the American Psychological Association (APA) primarily address the therapeutic relationships between one client and one therapist and the relationship between one therapist and an unrelated group in group therapy. These ethical guidelines do not directly address many of the issues that face the marriage and family therapist. The marriage and family therapist may encounter specific legal issues surrounding confidentiality, child custody, and divorce. To communicate effectively with clients who are dealing with legal issues in the family, marriage and family therapists must be familiar with the laws in their state (Margolin, 1982).

Ethical Considerations

Margolin (1982) identified six areas of specific ethical concern to the marriage and family therapist:

1. Therapist responsibility
2. Confidentiality
3. Client privilege
4. Informed consent and right to refuse treatment
5. Therapist values
6. Training and supervision.

These areas of concern will be discussed briefly, with suggestions for how the marriage and family therapist might respond to each.

Therapist Responsibility

The therapist working with individuals is responsible for the client's welfare. In marriage and family therapy this issue becomes more complex. Who is the client in marital therapy? Is it each of the two individuals involved in treatment, or is it the marital system? What may be in the best interests of the husband may not be in the best interests of the wife.

Consider the following example. Mr. North has decided he wants to leave his marriage. He is unwavering in this decision, yet has agreed to join his wife in marriage counseling to see if something can change his mind. Mrs. North is a homemaker with no career and is terrified of going it alone. She pleads with the therapist to help restore the marriage. Over the course of several sessions, the scenario does not change. Mr. North still plans to leave the marriage. What is the ethical responsibility of the therapist, and to whom does the therapist owe allegiance? Should the therapist:

- support Mrs. North during the divorce process?
- support Mr. North as he extricates himself from the marriage he no longer wants?
- continue to treat the couple and hope to save the marriage?

What is good for one family member is not always good for another. The therapist must be able to help the family system change in some manner that ultimately is reasonably satisfactory for all concerned. The therapist must attempt to balance the responsibility to help each individual while also working to help the marital and family system adjust to a more satisfactory condition—an often difficult position to reach.

Confidentiality

The confidentiality of the relationship between client and counselor has long been an ethical hallmark of psychotherapy. Except in cases of child abuse, potential physical harm to the client, or potential physical harm to others by the client, the therapist is bound to maintain client confidentiality. Maintaining confidentiality may become a problem for the marriage and family therapist when individuals share secrets with the therapist. Suppose a couple is in therapy to attempt to rebuild the marriage because the wife has had an affair. The husband agrees to remain in the marriage if the wife agrees to stop her affair. In a private call to the therapist, the wife reveals that she is still involved in the affair but that she does not want her husband to know. How should the ethical marriage and family therapist respond to this situation?

Helping family members learn to communicate openly is one of the typical goals of therapy. A serious problem may arise in therapy when a family member creates a situation that does not allow the therapist to communicate openly with all family members. The problem is especially complex when the other members might need the information to make responsible decisions.

Some marriage and family therapists respond to this problem by informing the family members before beginning therapy that the therapist will not keep secrets. This stance, however, may keep a family member from divulging information that could be essential to the therapy. But therapists who agree too readily to maintain confidentiality often find themselves unable to intervene in a productive manner. A potentially productive middle ground for the therapist is to clearly articulate a position to the family at the beginning of therapy stating that, in the interest of helping to resolve presenting issues, the therapist may use any information provided by a client. If information received in a private conversation would not be helpful to the therapy, the therapist probably would choose not to use it in a session.

Whatever course of action the therapist takes regarding confidentiality, the family members must clearly understand the policy from the start. In addition to being a legal requirement in many states, a *disclosure statement* signed by the clients, describing the therapist and the therapy process including information on confidentiality, is an effective way to communicate this information to clients.

Some family therapists find a one-way mirror useful in family treatment. Therapists who use the mirror as an adjunct to therapy often have a team of one or more colleagues observe the session and provide suggestions to the therapist during and after the session (Fenell, Hovestadt, & Harvey, 1986). In addition to the observation team, sessions can be videotaped for later review by the therapist, the team, and, in some cases, the family.

Involvement of these additional persons in the therapy process also creates issues of confidentiality. Family members should be fully informed about the mirror, video recorder, and observation team. Again, a disclosure statement signed by the clients will ensure that clients are informed and agree to the process. Family members must be told how the therapy process works with the amount of detail they care to know. Furthermore, members of the observation team and family members alike should be reminded of the need for confidentiality regarding information revealed in the session.

Client Privilege

Closely related to the issue of client confidentiality is the issue of *privileged communication*. Privileged communication protects the client from a situation in which confidences from therapy are revealed on the witness stand in court. Privilege belongs to the client. But when working with a family or couple, who is the client? When one family member seeks testimony from a therapist about another family member, courts typically have respected the client privilege and therapists have not been required to testify. This is not always the case, though. Herrington (1979) reported a case in Virginia in which the judge stated that when a husband and wife are in therapy together, there is no privilege because the statements were not made in private to a professional counselor, but in the presence of a third party.

Marriage and family therapists may be able to avoid giving this type of testimony by claiming that the unit of treatment is the entire family rather than any one individual. Thus, as Gumper and Sprenkle (1981) suggested, testimony about any part of the family system would violate the privilege of the family. Nonetheless, courts still may order therapists to testify regarding information obtained in multiperson therapy sessions. Therapists are advised to determine what the laws of their own states require concerning client privilege in marriage and family therapy situations.

Informed Consent and Right to Refuse Treatment

It is becoming increasingly important that clients be clearly informed concerning their rights and responsibilities in therapy, as well as the therapist's responsibilities. Many therapists have developed disclosure statements to obtain informed consent from clients and advise them of their right to refuse treatment. Before families enter therapy, they should be adequately informed concerning the nature of therapy and important aspects of the process. Many states now have laws requiring therapists to use disclosure statements. Points of important consumer information, as described by Gill (1982), are to:

- Describe the purpose of psychotherapy.
- Describe what you believe helps people lead more satisfying lives.
- Describe what clients should expect as a result of therapy.
- Describe the responsibilities of clients in therapy.
- Describe your primary therapeutic approach and the techniques that emerge from this approach.
- Describe the problems you have been most effective in helping clients resolve.
- Describe the conditions that might precipitate referral to another therapist or agency.
- Describe the limits of confidentiality in the therapeutic relationship.

The marriage and family therapist will want to ensure that all family members have agreed to participate in therapy and that all have signed the informed consent form. Clients engaging in marital and family therapy also will have to be informed of possible negative outcomes of therapy. When working with multiperson systems such as families, the outcome of therapy may be viewed as undesirable by one or more of the family members (Gurman & Kniskern, 1978b, 1981a; Wilcoxon & Fenell, 1983, 1986).

Finally, therapists who provide treatment only to whole families should not simply refuse treatment to a family that does not agree to have all members present. Rather, the therapist should be prepared to refer these families to other therapists who do not have this restriction on treatment (Margolin, 1982).

Therapist's Values

One of the most critical ethical issues confronting marriage and family therapists concerns their values. With the tremendous plurality of family styles, effective therapists carefully examine their values and ensure that these values do not adversely affect the client's goals for the treatment. When therapists encounter family values in certain clients that are opposed to their own values, a therapist sometimes forms biases against these clients and aligns with the other family members who hold values similar to the therapist's own values. According to Margolin (1982), specific values that may cause problems for the therapist include attitudes toward divorce, attitudes toward extramarital affairs, and attitudes toward sex roles in the family, especially as they pertain to women.

Attitudes Toward Divorce

Concerning attitudes toward divorce, counselors should be well aware of their own values. Divorce frequently is a painful option, but at times it may be in the best interests of family members. Counselors must be certain that they are not pushing couples either to stay together or to divorce. The therapist's role is to help the couple identify issues in the marriage to be resolved and to help the partners make a joint decision about whether to stay in the marriage or to divorce. When couples ask a counselor about his or her biases regarding marriage and divorce, the counselor should be honest with the clients. If clients are not comfortable with the counselor's values, the counselor should offer referrals.

Attitudes Toward Extramarital Affairs

The counselor's attitude toward extramarital affairs can hinder therapy when it conflicts with the attitudes of one or both spouses. If the therapist believes that affairs are acceptable and one or both of the marriage partners do not, clients may perceive the counselor as advocating behaviors that may be destructive to a marriage in need of help. If the counselor believes that affairs are harmful to the relationship, he or she must be careful not to side too heavily with the spouse who was faithful. This attitude could create the perception that the marriage problems are entirely the fault of the person who had the affair, a nonsystemic conceptualization. A counselor who employs systems theory will seek to discover how each partner engaged in behaviors that created marital problems and resulted in the affair. It usually is most beneficial to discover how the spouses share responsibility for the marital problems in any attempt to restore the marriage.

Attitudes Toward Sex Roles

Concerning attitudes toward sex roles, some family systems therapists have stereotyped women and encouraged them to stay in unsatisfactory marriages. Therapists should be careful not to pay less attention to a woman's career, perpetuate the notion that children's problems are the result of poor mothering, exhibit a double standard that views the wife's extramarital affairs more severely than the husband's affairs, or place more emphasis on the husband's needs in a relationship. When a counselor has certain values that may have a significant impact on the therapy, the therapist should inform the clients so they can make a responsible choice concerning the appropriateness of treatment with the therapist (Corey, Corey, & Callahan, 1993).

Training and Supervision

Marital and family problems are widespread. Therefore, most mental health practitioners have frequent opportunities to treat these problems. But not all therapists are adequately trained to treat marital and family problems. Gurman and Kniskern (1981b) suggested that, if treatment is to be successful, family therapists might need more forceful intervention methods than therapists who treat individuals are typically trained to use. Furthermore, Margolin (1982) reported that adequate preparation in marriage and family therapy is the exception rather than the rule among mental health service providers. Thus, therapists who work with couples and families must be careful not to exceed the bounds of their competence.

Fenell and Hovestadt (1986) developed a three-level model of clinical training for marriage and family therapists and suggested that therapists should evaluate their ability level and limit their practice to marital and family problems they are appropriately prepared to handle. Therapists must have access to clinical supervision by marriage and family therapists for assistance in evaluating couples and families who may need referral to a professional with more training and experience in family systems therapy.

■ *Ethical Standards for Marriage and Family Therapy*

Most professional organizations have ethical standards for practitioners. The American Association for Marriage and Family Therapy (AAMFT, 1991) has developed a revised set of standards specifically for marriage and family therapists. This set of standards, entitled the *AAMFT Code of Ethics,* addresses the following major points:

1. *Responsibility to clients.* Marriage and family therapists advance the welfare of families and individuals. They respect the rights of anyone seeking their assistance and make reasonable efforts to ensure that their services are used appropriately.
2. *Confidentiality.* Marriage and family therapists have unique confidentiality concerns because the client in a therapeutic relationship may be more than one person. Therapists respect and guard confidences of each individual client.
3. *Professional competence and integrity.* Marriage and family therapists maintain high standards of professional competence and integrity.
4. *Responsibility to students, employees, and supervisees.*
5. *Responsibility to research participants.*
6. *Responsibility to the profession.* Marriage and family therapists must respect the rights and responsibilities of professional colleagues and participate in activities that advance the goals of the profession.
7. *Financial arrangements.* Marriage and family therapists make financial arrangements with clients, third-party payors, and supervisees that are reasonably understandable and conform to accepted professional practices.
8. *Advertising.* Marriage and family therapists engage in appropriate informational activities, including those that enable laypersons to choose professional services on an informed basis.

The complete *AAMFT Code of Ethical Principles for Marriage and Family Therapists* is presented in Appendix A.

When a violation of the *AAMFT Code of Ethical Principles for Marriage and Family Therapists* is suspected, the AAMFT Ethics Committee is contacted and procedures are set in motion to determine if the complaint is against an AAMFT member, to determine if the complaint has validity, and to determine action by the Ethics Committee and the association. Complaints may proceed in three ways.

1. The complaint may be dropped and no charges filed.
2. The charged member and the AAMFT may settle the complaint by mutual agreement.

3. The Ethics Committee may recommend that action be taken against the member. Actions taken may include:

   a. request to cease and desist,
   b. censure of member,
   c. probation of member,
   d. required supervision for member,
   e. required therapy or education for member,
   f. suspension or termination of Approved Supervisor designation, or
   g. suspension or termination of membership in AAMFT.

A thorough appeals process is provided for members who believe the process has been managed improperly. (A booklet specifying the details for handling ethical complaints may be requested from the AAMFT, or information may be obtained from the AAMFT Web site at www.aamft.org) Understanding and employing ethical principles for marriage and family therapists is critical in providing ethical services to clients and in maintaining a solid reputation for integrity in the profession.

The IAMFC (1993), too, has also developed ethical standards identified as the *Ethical Code for the International Association of Marriage and Family Counselors.* These standards cover the following key points:

■ client well-being,
■ confidentiality,
■ competence,
■ assessment,
■ private practice,
■ research and publications,
■ supervision, and
■ media and public statements.

The entire IAMFC ethical code is presented in Appendix B. The reader will note the similarities between the IAMFC code and the AAMFT code.

■ *Family Therapy Training*

Family therapy claims to be more than another set of techniques for helping families change. Experienced practitioners believe that family therapy is a different way of thinking about problems that people encounter. Because of the distinctions between the practice of individual and family therapy, training approaches have evolved for family therapists that differ from typical approaches used in training individual therapists (Fenell & Hovestadt, 1986; Fenell, Hovestadt, & Harvey, 1986; Liddle, 1991).

Academic Preparation

Professionals who identify themselves as marriage and family therapists come from a wide range of academic training programs. Family therapy, for example, is taught in graduate departments of counselor education, family studies, psychiatry, psychology, social work, nursing, and pastoral counseling (Fenell & Hovestadt, 1986; Hovestadt, Fenell, & Piercy, 1983). Many graduates of these programs seek clinical membership in the AAMFT. To be eligible for clinical membership, therapists must have completed an accredited graduate training program, be licensed as an MFT by their state, or complete a graduate degree meeting the following requirements or their equivalent (AAMFT, 2001):

> *Theoretical Knowledge*: Content in this area will address the historical development, theoretical and empirical foundations, and contemporary conceptual directions of the field of marriage and family therapy and will enable students to conceptualize and distinguish the critical epistemological issues in the profession of marriage and family therapy. The materials presented will provide a comprehensive survey and substantive understanding of the major models of marriage, couple, and family therapy. The content presented in this area will be related conceptually to clinical concerns.

> *Clinical Knowledge*: Content in this area will address, from a relational/systemic perspective, psychopharmacology, physical health and illness, traditional psychodiagnostic categories, and the assessment and treatment of major mental health issues. The material presented will address couple and family therapy practice and be related conceptually to theory. The content will also address contemporary issues, which include, but are not limited to, gender, violence, addictions, and abuse, in the treatment of individuals, couples, and families from a relational/systemic perspective. The coursework will address a wide variety of presenting clinical problems to include issues of gender and sexual functioning, sexual orientation, and sex therapy as they relate to couple, marriage and family therapy theory and practice. Moreover, the content will include significant material on diversity and discrimination as it relates to couple and family therapy theory and practice.

Individual Development and Family Relations: Content in this area will focus on individual development across the lifespan and include material on family development across the lifespan.

Professional Identity and Ethics: Content will include professional identity, including professional socialization, scope of practice, professional organizations, licensure, and certification and will focus on ethical issues related to the profession of marriage and family therapy and the practice of individual, couple, and family therapy. A generic course in ethics will not meet this standard. The coursework will focus on the AAMFT Code of Ethics, confidentiality issues, the legal responsibilities and liabilities of clinical practice and research, family law, record keeping, reimbursement, and the business aspects of practice. The content of the materials presented will inform students about the interface between therapist responsibility and the professional, social, and political context of treatment.

Research: Content in this area will include significant material on research in couple and family therapy. It will focus on research methodology, data analysis and the evaluation of research including quantitative and qualitative research.

Additional Learning: Additional learning will augment students' specialized interest and background in individual, couple, and family therapy. Additional courses may be chosen from coursework offered in a variety of disciplines.

Clinical Experience Requirements: Students will complete a minimum of 500 supervised, direct client contact hours. At least 400 of these hours must be in face-to-face (therapist and client) therapy with individuals, couples, families, and/or groups from a relational perspective. Up to 100 hours may consist of alternative therapeutic contact that is systemic and interactional. At least 250 hours (of the required 500 hours of client contact) will occur in clinical sites for which the training program has broad, but not necessarily sole, responsibility for supervision and clinical practice of individual, couple and family therapy as carried out by program students. The facilities will offer these services to the public. At least 250 (of the required 500 hours of client contact) will be with couples or families present in the therapy room. Students will work with a wide variety of people, relationships, and problems. The program will publish and adhere to criteria for determining when students are prepared for clinical practice. Clinical work will not be interrupted for arbitrary student, administrative, or didactic scheduling reasons, when interruption would be harmful to clients. Programs will provide students the opportunity to work with clients who are diverse in terms of age, culture, physical ability, ethnicity, family composition, gender, race, religion, sexual orientation and socioeconomic status.

Supervision: Students will receive at least 100 hours of face-to-face supervision with at least one hour of supervision provided for every five hours of direct client contact. Supervision will occur at least once every week in which students have direct client contact hours with individual supervision occurring at least once every other week. Students will receive at least 50 hours of supervision based on direct observation, videotape, or audiotape. Students should be given opportunities to observe their supervisors' clinical work. In this context, "clinical work" includes therapy in progress, clinical evaluation in progress, and role playing. Group supervision is required.

Clinical membership in the AAMFT is a highly regarded credential. In recent years the AAMFT has developed policies to assist potential members who are interested in clinical membership. These new policies attempt to recognize the qualifications of professionals who are competent MFTs but may not have had the opportunity to attend an AAMFT-prescribed graduate program.

In addition to these academic training requirements, the AAMFT requires prospective clinical members to complete 2 years of postdegree clinical experience under the supervision of an approved supervisor recognized by the AAMFT or a supervisor acceptable to the AAMFT Membership Committee. At least 1,000 hours of direct client contact must be completed during the 2 years of supervised experience, and at least 200 hours of supervision must be completed, of which at least 100 hours must be in supervision involving therapy with individuals.

Clinical Training and Supervision

One of the features of marriage and family therapy that sets it apart from most treatment approaches for individuals is the focus on the family as a system. This emphasis is taught in the academic portion of the therapist's training program and is practiced in the supervised clinical experience. Many family therapy training programs have on-campus clinics where graduate students practice therapy under supervision. In most of these clinics a one-way mirror allows the therapist to be observed working with the couple or family. Often, a supervisor and a team of the trainee's colleagues will observe the therapist working in the session. This observation permits the supervisor to obtain an accurate impression of the work the therapist is doing and to offer immediate feedback to the student regarding the session.

Family therapy supervisors and trainees generally have an understanding that when the supervisor detects a way the therapist could be more effective, the session may be interrupted to inform the therapist of the possible intervention that could be used. Because family therapists can easily become emotionally engaged with the family system, having a supervisor and team of observers behind the glass offers a unique opportunity for feedback on what may be going on in a session that is outside the therapist's awareness. Initially trainees may believe they are being judged and become defensive to in-session suggestions. Over time and through their own participation in observing other trainees, however, they come to value the *metaperspective* of the supervisory team and learn to use the feedback effectively to improve their family therapy skills.

Although much has been written about family therapy supervision (Fenell & Hovestadt, 1986; Liddle, 1991; Liddle & Halpin, 1978), little research has been attempted to demonstrate the effectiveness of family therapy supervision over traditional case-presentation supervision (Kniskern & Gurman, 1979). One study using a small sample compared family therapy supervision with traditional supervision. The results showed no correlation between the acquisition of family therapy skills and the supervision method used (Fenell, Hovestadt, & Harvey, 1986). Liddle, Davidson, and Barrett (1988) discovered that live supervision could lead to excessive dependence on the supervisor, especially early in the training process. These authors suggested that assumptions regarding effective family therapy clinical training should be examined.

The AAMFT established the Commission of Accreditation for Marriage and Family Therapy Education (COAMFTE) as the agency for accreditation of clinical training programs in marriage and family therapy at the master's, doctoral, and postgraduate levels. COAMFTE accreditation is recognized by the U.S. Department of Education and the Council for Higher Education Accreditation (CHEA, formerly CORPA) and is a requirement for obtaining eligibility for participation in Federal programs. Further information on specific standards for accreditation candidacy and a complete listing of COAMFTE training programs and addresses are available online at http://www. aaamft.org/resources/Online_Directories/coamfte.htm

SUGGESTED READINGS

Fenell, D. L., & Hovestadt, A. H. (1986). Family Therapy as a Profession or Professional Specialty: Implications for Training, *Journal of Psychotherapy and the Family, 1*(4), 25–40.

http://www.aamft.org/Resources/lrmplan/Ethics/ethicscode 2001.htm (for latest version of ethics statement)

http://www.iamfc.org/ethicalcodes.html (for latest version for text)

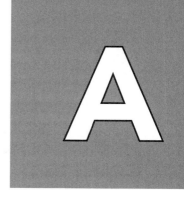

AAMFT Code of Ethical Principles for Marriage and Family Therapists

Reprinted by permission of the American Association for Marriage and Family Therapy. This revised code was approved—effective July 1, 2001. The AAMFT can make further revisions of the code at any time the association deems necessary.

▩ *Preamble*

The Board of Directors of the American Association for Marriage and Family Therapy (AAMFT) hereby promulgates, pursuant to Article 2, Section 2.013 of the Association's Bylaws, the Revised AAMFT Code of Ethics, effective July 1, 2001.

The AAMFT strives to honor the public trust in marriage and family therapists by setting standards for ethical practice as described in this Code. The ethical standards define professional expectations and are enforced by the AAMFT Ethics Committee. The absence of an explicit reference to a specific behavior or situation in the Code does not mean that the behavior is ethical or unethical. The standards are not exhaustive. Marriage and family therapists who are uncertain about the ethics of a particular course of action are encouraged to seek counsel from consultants, attorneys, supervisors, colleagues, or other appropriate authorities.

Both law and ethics govern the practice of marriage and family therapy. When making decisions regarding professional behavior, marriage and family therapists must consider the AAMFT Code of Ethics and applicable laws and regulations. If the AAMFT Code of Ethics prescribes a standard higher than that required by law, marriage and family therapists must meet the higher standard of the AAMFT Code of Ethics. Marriage and family therapists comply with the mandates of law, but make known their commitment to the AAMFT Code of Ethics and take steps to resolve the conflict in a responsible manner. The AAMFT supports legal mandates for reporting of alleged unethical conduct.

The AAMFT Code of Ethics is binding on Members of AAMFT in all membership categories, AAMFT-Approved Supervisors, and applicants for membership and the Approved Supervisor designation (hereafter, AAMFT Member). AAMFT members have an obligation to be familiar with the AAMFT Code of Ethics and its application to their professional services. Lack of awareness or misunderstanding of an ethical standard is not a defense to a charge of unethical conduct.

The process for filing, investigating, and resolving complaints of unethical conduct is described in the current Procedures for Handling Ethical Matters of the AAMFT Ethics Committee. Persons accused are considered innocent by the Ethics Committee until proven guilty, except as otherwise provided, and are entitled to due process. If an AAMFT Member resigns in anticipation of, or during the course of, an ethics investigation, the Ethics Committee will complete its investigation. Any publication of action taken by the Association will include the fact that the Member attempted to resign during the investigation.

1. Responsibility to Clients

Marriage and family therapists advance the welfare of families and individuals. They respect the rights of those persons seeking their assistance, and make reasonable efforts to ensure that their services are used appropriately.

1.1 Marriage and family therapists provide professional assistance to persons without discrimination on the basis of race, age, ethnicity, socioeconomic status, disability, gender, health status, religion, national origin, or sexual orientation.

1.2 Marriage and family therapists obtain appropriate informed consent to therapy or related procedures as early as feasible in the therapeutic relationship, and use language that is reasonably understandable to clients. The content of informed consent may vary depending upon the client and treatment plan; however, informed consent generally necessitates that the client: (a) has the capacity to consent; (b) has been adequately informed of significant information concerning treatment processes and procedures; (c) has been adequately informed of potential risks and benefits of treatments for which generally recognized standards do not yet exist; (d) has freely and without undue influence expressed consent; and (e) has provided consent that is appropriately documented. When persons, due to age or mental status, are legally incapable of giving informed consent, marriage and family therapists obtain informed permission from a legally authorized person, if such substitute consent is legally permissible.

1.3 Marriage and family therapists are aware of their influential positions with respect to clients, and they avoid exploiting the trust and dependency of such persons. Therapists, therefore, make every effort to avoid conditions and multiple relationships with clients that could impair professional judgment or increase the risk of exploitation. Such relationships include, but are not limited to, business or close personal relationships with a client or the client's immediate family. When the risk of impairment or exploitation exists due to conditions or multiple roles, therapists take appropriate precautions.

1.4 Sexual intimacy with clients is prohibited.

1.5 Sexual intimacy with former clients is likely to be harmful and is therefore prohibited for two years following the termination of therapy or last professional contact. In an effort to avoid exploiting the trust and dependency of clients, marriage and family therapists should not engage in sexual intimacy with former clients after the two years following termination or last professional contact. Should therapists engage in sexual intimacy with former clients following two years after termination or last professional contact, the burden shifts to the therapist to demonstrate that there has been no exploitation or injury to the former client or to the client's immediate family.

1.6 Marriage and family therapists comply with applicable laws regarding the reporting of alleged unethical conduct.

1.7 Marriage and family therapists do not use their professional relationships with clients to further their own interests.

1.8 Marriage and family therapists respect the rights of clients to make decisions and help them to understand the consequences of these decisions. Therapists clearly advise the clients that they have the responsibility to make decisions regarding relationships such as cohabitation, marriage, divorce, separation, reconciliation, custody, and visitation.

1.9 Marriage and family therapists continue therapeutic relationships only so long as it is reasonably clear that clients are benefiting from the relationship.

1.10 Marriage and family therapists assist persons in obtaining other therapeutic services if the therapist is unable or unwilling, for appropriate reasons, to provide professional help.

1.11 Marriage and family therapists do not abandon or neglect clients in treatment without making reasonable arrangements for the continuation of such treatment.

1.12 Marriage and family therapists obtain written informed consent from clients before videotaping, audio recording, or permitting third-party observation.

1.13 Marriage and family therapists, upon agreeing to provide services to a person or entity at the request of a third party, clarify, to the extent feasible and at the outset of the service, the nature of the relationship with each party and the limits of confidentiality.

2. Confidentiality

Marriage and family therapists have unique confidentiality concerns because the client in a therapeutic relationship may be more than one person. Therapists respect and guard the confidences of each individual client.

2.1 Marriage and family therapists disclose to clients and other interested parties, as early as feasible in their professional contacts, the nature of confidentiality and possible limitations of the clients' right to confidentiality. Therapists review with clients the circumstances where confidential information may be requested and where disclosure of confidential information may be legally required. Circumstances may necessitate repeated disclosures.

2.2 Marriage and family therapists do not disclose client confidences except by written authorization or waiver, or where mandated or permitted by law. Verbal authorization will not be sufficient except in emergency situations, unless prohibited by law. When providing couple, family or group treatment, the therapist does not disclose information outside the treatment context without a written authorization from each individual competent to execute a waiver. In the context of couple, family or group treatment, the therapist may not reveal any individual's confidences to others in the client unit without the prior written permission of that individual.

2.3 Marriage and family therapists use client and/or clinical materials in teaching, writing, consulting, research, and public presentations only if a written waiver has been obtained in accordance with Subprinciple 2.2, or when appropriate steps have been taken to protect client identity and confidentiality.

2.4 Marriage and family therapists store, safeguard, and dispose of client records in ways that maintain confidentiality and in accord with applicable laws and professional standards.

2.5 Subsequent to the therapist moving from the area, closing the practice, or upon the death of the therapist, a marriage and family therapist arranges for the storage, transfer, or disposal of client records in ways that maintain confidentiality and safeguard the welfare of clients.

2.6 Marriage and family therapists, when consulting with colleagues or referral sources, do not share confidential information that could reasonably lead to the identification of a client, research participant, supervisee, or other person with whom they have a confidential relationship unless they have obtained the prior written consent of the client, research participant, supervisee, or other person with whom they have a confidential relationship. Information may be shared only to the extent necessary to achieve the purposes of the consultation.

3. *Professional Competence and Integrity*

Marriage and family therapists maintain high standards of professional competence and integrity.

3.1 Marriage and family therapists pursue knowledge of new developments and maintain competence in marriage and family therapy through education, training, or supervised experience.

3.2 Marriage and family therapists maintain adequate knowledge of and adhere to applicable laws, ethics, and professional standards.

3.3 Marriage and family therapists seek appropriate professional assistance for their personal problems or conflicts that may impair work performance or clinical judgment.

3.4 Marriage and family therapists do not provide services that create a conflict of interest that may impair work performance or clinical judgment.

3.5 Marriage and family therapists, as presenters, teachers, supervisors, consultants and researchers, are dedicated to high standards of scholarship, present accurate information, and disclose potential conflicts of interest.

3.6 Marriage and family therapists maintain accurate and adequate clinical and financial records.

3.7 While developing new skills in specialty areas, marriage and family therapists take steps to ensure the competence of their work and to protect clients from possible harm. Marriage and family therapists practice in specialty areas new to them only after appropriate education, training, or supervised experience.

3.8 Marriage and family therapists do not engage in sexual or other forms of harassment of clients, students, trainees, supervisees, employees, colleagues, or research subjects.

3.9 Marriage and family therapists do not engage in the exploitation of clients, students, trainees, supervisees, employees, colleagues, or research subjects.

3.10 Marriage and family therapists do not give to or receive from clients (a) gifts of substantial value or (b) gifts that impair the integrity or efficacy of the therapeutic relationship.

3.11 Marriage and family therapists do not diagnose, treat, or advise on problems outside the recognized boundaries of their competencies.

3.12 Marriage and family therapists make efforts to prevent the distortion or misuse of their clinical and research findings.

3.13 Marriage and family therapists, because of their ability to influence and alter the lives of others, exercise special care when making public their professional recommendations and opinions through testimony or other public statements.

3.14 To avoid a conflict of interests, marriage and family therapists who treat minors or adults involved in custody or visitation actions may not also perform forensic evaluations for custody, residence, or visitation of the minor. The marriage and family therapist who treats the minor may provide the court or mental health professional performing the evaluation with information about the minor from the marriage and family therapist's perspective as a treating marriage and family therapist, so long as the marriage and family therapist does not violate confidentiality.

3.15 Marriage and family therapists are in violation of this Code and subject to termination of membership or other appropriate action if they: (a) are convicted of any felony; (b) are convicted of a misdemeanor related to their qualifications or functions; (c) engage in conduct which could lead to conviction of a felony, or a misdemeanor related to their qualifications or functions; (d) are expelled from or disciplined by other professional organizations; (e) have their licenses or certificates suspended or revoked or are otherwise disciplined by regulatory bodies; (f) continue to practice marriage and family therapy while no longer competent to do so because they are impaired by physical or mental causes or the abuse of alcohol or other substances; or (g) fail to cooperate with the Association at any point from the inception of an ethical complaint through the completion of all proceedings regarding that complaint.

4. *Responsibility to Students and Supervisees*

Marriage and family therapists do not exploit the trust and dependency of students and supervisees.

4.1 Marriage and family therapists are aware of their influential positions with respect to students and supervisees, and they avoid exploiting the trust and dependency of such persons. Therapists, therefore, make every effort to avoid conditions and multiple relationships that could impair professional objectivity or increase the risk of exploitation. When the risk of impairment or exploitation exists due to conditions or multiple roles, therapists take appropriate precautions.

4.2 Marriage and family therapists do not provide therapy to current students or supervisees.

4.3 Marriage and family therapists do not engage in sexual intimacy with students or supervisees during the evaluative or training relationship between the therapist and student or supervisee. Should a supervisor engage in sexual activity with a former supervisee, the burden of proof shifts to the supervisor to demonstrate that there has been no exploitation or injury to the supervisee.

4.4 Marriage and family therapists do not permit students or supervisees to perform or to hold themselves out as competent to perform professional services beyond their training, level of experience, and competence.

4.5 Marriage and family therapists take reasonable measures to ensure that services provided by supervisees are professional.

4.6 Marriage and family therapists avoid accepting as supervisees or students those individuals with whom a prior or existing relationship could compromise the therapist's objectivity. When such situations cannot be avoided, therapists take appropriate precautions to maintain objectivity. Examples of such relationships include, but are not limited to, those individuals with whom the therapist has a current or prior sexual, close personal, immediate familial, or therapeutic relationship.

4.7 Marriage and family therapists do not disclose supervisee confidences except by written authorization or waiver, or when mandated or permitted by law. In educational or training settings where there are multiple supervisors, disclosures are permitted only to other professional colleagues, administrators, or employers who share responsibility for training of the supervisee. Verbal authorization will not be sufficient except in emergency situations, unless prohibited by law.

5. *Responsibility to Research Participants*

Investigators respect the dignity and protect the welfare of research participants, and are aware of applicable laws and regulations and professional standards governing the conduct of research.

5.1 Investigators are responsible for making careful examinations of ethical acceptability in planning studies. To the extent that services to research participants may be compromised by participation in research, investigators seek the ethical advice of qualified professionals not directly involved in the investigation and observe safeguards to protect the rights of research participants.

5.2 Investigators requesting participant involvement in research inform participants of the aspects of the research that might reasonably be expected to influence willingness to participate. Investigators are especially sensitive to the possibility of diminished consent when participants are also receiving clinical services, or have impairments which limit understanding and/or communication, or when participants are children.

5.3 Investigators respect each participant's freedom to decline participation in or to withdraw from a research study at any time. This obligation requires special thought and consideration when investigators or other members of the research team are in positions of authority or influence over participants. Marriage and family therapists, therefore, make every effort to avoid multiple relationships with research participants that could impair professional judgment or increase the risk of exploitation.

5.4 Information obtained about a research participant during the course of an investigation is confidential unless there is a waiver previously obtained in writing. When the possibility exists that others, including family members, may obtain access to such information, this possibility, together with the plan for protecting confidentiality, is explained as part of the procedure for obtaining informed consent.

6. Responsibility to the Profession

Marriage and family therapists respect the rights and responsibilities of professional colleagues and participate in activities that advance the goals of the profession.

6.1 Marriage and family therapists remain accountable to the standards of the profession when acting as members or employees of organizations. If the mandates of an organization with which a marriage and family therapist is affiliated, through employment, contract or otherwise, conflict with the AAMFT Code of Ethics, marriage and family therapists make known to the organization their commitment to the AAMFT Code of Ethics and attempt to resolve the conflict in a way that allows the fullest adherence to the Code of Ethics.

6.2 Marriage and family therapists assign publication credit to those who have contributed to a publication in proportion to their contributions and in accordance with customary professional publication practices.

6.3 Marriage and family therapists do not accept or require authorship credit for a publication based on research from a student's program, unless the therapist made a substantial contribution beyond being a faculty advisor or research committee member. Coauthorship on a student thesis, dissertation, or project should be determined in accordance with principles of fairness and justice.

6.4 Marriage and family therapists who are the authors of books or other materials that are published or distributed do not plagiarize or fail to cite persons to whom credit for original ideas or work is due.

6.5 Marriage and family therapists who are the authors of books or other materials published or distributed by an organization take reasonable precautions to ensure that the organization promotes and advertises the materials accurately and factually.

6.6 Marriage and family therapists participate in activities that contribute to a better community and society, including devoting a portion of their professional activity to services for which there is little or no financial return.

6.7 Marriage and family therapists are concerned with developing laws and regulations pertaining to marriage and family therapy that serve the public interest, and with altering such laws and regulations that are not in the public interest.

6.8 Marriage and family therapists encourage public participation in the design and delivery of professional services and in the regulation of practitioners.

7. *Financial Arrangements*

Marriage and family therapists make financial arrangements with clients, third-party payors, and supervisees that are reasonably understandable and conform to accepted professional practices.

7.1 Marriage and family therapists do not offer or accept kickbacks, rebates, bonuses, or other remuneration for referrals; fee-for-service arrangements are not prohibited.

7.2 Prior to entering into the therapeutic or supervisory relationship, marriage and family therapists clearly disclose and explain to clients and supervisees: (a) all financial arrangements and fees related to professional services, including charges for canceled or missed appointments; (b) the use of collection agencies or legal measures for nonpayment; and (c) the procedure for obtaining payment from the client, to the extent allowed by law, if payment is denied by the third-party payor. Once services have begun, therapists provide reasonable notice of any changes in fees or other charges.

7.3 Marriage and family therapists give reasonable notice to clients with unpaid balances of their intent to seek collection by agency or legal recourse. When such action is taken, therapists will not disclose clinical information.

7.4 Marriage and family therapists represent facts truthfully to clients, third-party payors, and supervisees regarding services rendered.

7.5 Marriage and family therapists ordinarily refrain from accepting goods and services from clients in return for services rendered. Bartering for professional services may be conducted only if: (a) the supervisee or client requests it, (b) the relationship is not exploitative, (c) the professional relationship is not distorted, and (d) a clear written contract is established.

7.6 Marriage and family therapists may not withhold records under their immediate control that are requested and needed for a client's treatment solely because payment has not been received for past services, except as otherwise provided by law.

8. Advertising

Marriage and family therapists engage in appropriate informational activities, including those that enable the public, referral sources, or others to choose professional services on an informed basis.

8.1 Marriage and family therapists accurately represent their competencies, education, training, and experience relevant to their practice of marriage and family therapy.

8.2 Marriage and family therapists ensure that advertisements and publications in any media (such as directories, announcements, business cards, newspapers, radio, television, Internet, and facsimiles) convey information that is necessary for the public to make an appropriate selection of professional services. Information could include: (a) office information, such as name, address, telephone number, credit card acceptability, fees, languages spoken, and office hours; (b) qualifying clinical degree (see subprinciple 8.5); (c) other earned degrees (see subprinciple 8.5) and state or provincial licensures and/or certifications; (d) AAMFT clinical member status; and (e) description of practice.

8.3 Marriage and family therapists do not use names that could mislead the public concerning the identity, responsibility, source, and status of those practicing under that name, and do not hold themselves out as being partners or associates of a firm if they are not.

8.4 Marriage and family therapists do not use any professional identification (such as a business card, office sign, letterhead, Internet, or telephone or association directory listing) if it includes a statement or claim that is false, fraudulent, misleading, or deceptive.

8.5 In representing their educational qualifications, marriage and family therapists list and claim as evidence only those earned degrees: (a) from institutions accredited by regional accreditation sources recognized by the United States Department of Education, (b) from institutions recognized by states or provinces that license or certify marriage and family therapists, or (c) from equivalent foreign institutions.

8.6 Marriage and family therapists correct, wherever possible, false, misleading, or inaccurate information and representations made by others concerning the therapist's qualifications, services, or products.

8.7 Marriage and family therapists make certain that the qualifications of their employees or supervisees are represented in a manner that is not false, misleading, or deceptive.

8.8 Marriage and family therapists do not represent themselves as providing specialized services unless they have the appropriate education, training, or supervised experience.

This Code is published by:
American Association for Marriage and Family Therapy
112 South Alfred Street, Alexandria, VA 22314
Phone: (703) 838-9808 — Fax: (703) 838-9805
www.aamft.org

Ethical Code for the International Association of Marriage and Family Counselors

Reprinted with permission from the International Association for Marriage and Family Therapy. This draft of the code was approved by the board and published in 2002. IAMFC can make further revisions of the code at any time the association deems necessary. Final approval is pending.

Preamble

The IAMFC (The International Association of Marriage and Family Counselors) is an organization dedicated to advancing the practice, training, and research of marriage and family counselors. Members may specialize in areas such as: premarital counseling, intergenerational counseling, separation and divorce counseling, relocation counseling, custody assessment and implementation, single parenting, stepfamilies, nontraditional family and marriage life-styles, healthy and dysfunctional family systems, multicultural marriage and family concerns, displaced and homeless families, interfaith ad interracial families, and dual career couples. In conducting the professional activities, members commit themselves to protect and advocate for the healthy growth and development of the family as a whole, even as they conscientiously recognize the integrity and diversity of each family and family member's unique needs, situations, status, and member's unique needs, situations, status, and condition. The IAMFC member recognizes that the relationship between provider and consumer services is characterized as an egalitarian process emphasizing co-participation, co-equality, co-authority, co-responsibility, and client empowerment.

This code of ethics promulgates a framework for ethical practice by IAMFC members and is divided into eight sections: client well-being, confidentiality, competence, assessment, private practice, research and publications, supervision, and media and public statements. The ideas presented within these eight areas are meant to supplement the ethical standards of the American Counseling Association (ACA), formerly the American Association for Counseling and Development (AACD), and all members should know and keep to the standards of our parent organization. Although an ethical code cannot anticipate every possible situation or dilemma, the IAMFC ethical guidelines can aid members in ensuring the welfare and dignity of the couples and families they have contact with, as well as assisting in the implementation of the Hippocratic mandate for healers: Do no harm.

Section I: Client Well-being

A. Members demonstrate a caring, empathic, respectful, fair, and active concern for family well-being. They promote client safety, security, and place-of-belonging in family, community, and society.

B. Members recognize that each family is unique. They strive to respect the diversity of personal attributes and do not stereotype or force families into prescribed attitudes, roles, or behaviors. Family counselors respect the client's definitions of families, and recognize diversity of families, including two-parent, single parent, extended, multigenerational, same gender, etc.

C. Members respect the autonomy and independent decision-making abilities of their clients. When working with families with children, counselors respect the parent's autonomy in child-rearing decisions.

D. Members seek to develop working, collaborative relationships with clients which are egalitarian in nature. Counselors openly disclose information in sessions, including theoretical approach to understanding behavior, and processes for decision-making and problem-solving.

E. Members assist clients to develop a philosophy on the meaning, purpose, and direction of life. Counselors promote positive regard of self, family, and others.

F. Members do not impose personal values on families or family members.

   Members recognize the influence of worldview and cultural factors (race, ethnicity, gender, social class, spirituality, sexual orientation, educational status) on the presenting problem, family functioning, and problem-solving skills. Counselors are aware of indigenous healing practices and incorporate them into treatment when necessary or feasible. Members are encouraged to follow the guidelines provided in Multicultural Competencies (cf. Arredondo, P., Toporek, R., Brown, S., Jones, J., Locke, D.C., Sanchez, J., & Stadler, H. (1996). Operationalization of the multicultural counseling competencies. Alexandria, VA: American Counseling Association)

G. Members do not discriminate on the basis of race, gender, social class, disability, spirituality, religion, age, sexual orientation, nationality, language, educational level, marital status, or political affiliation.

H. Members do not engage in dual relationships with clients. In cases where dual relationships are unavoidable, family counselors are obligated to discuss and provide informed consent of the ramifications of the counseling relationship.

I. Members do not harass, exploit, or coerce current or former clients. Members do not engage in sexual harassment. Members do not develop sexual relationships with current or former clients.

J. Members must determine and inform all persons involved that the primary client is the family. Members must be sure that family members have an understanding of the nature of relationships, and the nature of reports to third parties (schools, teachers, managed care companies, etc.).

K. When a conflict of interest exists between the needs of the clients and the counselor's employers, family counselors must clarify commitments to all parties. Counselors recognize that the acceptance of employment implies agreement with policies, and therefore monitor their place of employment to make sure that the environment is conducive to the positive growth and development of clients. If after utilizing appropriate institutional channels for change, the counselor finds that the agency is not working toward the well-being of clients, the counselor has an obligation to terminate institutional affiliation.

L. Members should pursue the development of clients' cognitive, moral, social, emotional, spiritual, physical, educational, and career needs, as well as parenting, marriage, and family living skills, in order to prevent future problems.

M. Members terminate relationships if the continuation of services is not in the best interest of the client or would result in an ethical violation. If a client feels that the counseling relationship is no longer productive, the member has an obligation to assist in finding alternative services.

N. Members inform clients (in writing if feasible) about the goals and purpose of counseling, qualifications of the counselor(s), scope and limits of confidentiality, potential risks and benefits of the counseling process and specific techniques and interventions, reasonable expectations for outcomes, duration of services, costs of services, and alternative approaches.

O. Members refrain from techniques, procedures, or interventions that place families or members at risk of harm. Counselors should refrain from using intrusive interventions without a sound theoretical rational and full consideration of the potential ramifications to families and members.

P. Members maintain accurate and up-to-date records. They make all file information available to clients unless the sharing of such information would be damaging to the status, goals, growth and development of clients.

Q. Members are urged to consult with supervisors and consultants when facing an ethical dilemma. Counselors may contact the IAMFC executive director, president, executive board members, or chair of the ethics committee at any time for consultation or remedying ethical violations.

R. Members have the responsibility to confront unethical behavior conducted by other counselors. Counselors should attempt first informally to resolve the unethical behavior with the counselor. If the problem continues, the members should then use the procedures established by the employing institution. Counselors should also contact the appropriate licensing or certification board.

Section II: Confidentiality

A. Nature of confidentiality
   1. Members recognize that the proper functioning of the counseling relationship requires that clients must be free to discuss secrets with the counselor, and counselors must be free to obtain pertinent information beyond that which is volunteered by the client. Absent exceptions, this protection of confidentiality applies to all situations, including initial contacts by a potential client, the fact that a counseling relationship exists, and to all communications made as part of the relationship between a counselor and clients.
   2. Members protect the confidences and secrets of their clients. Counselors do not reveal information received from clients. Counselors do not use information received from a client to the disadvantage of the client. Counselors do not use information received from a client for the advantage of the counselor or of any other person.
   3. Unless alternate arrangements have been agreed upon by all participants, statements made by a family member to the counselor during an individual counseling or consulting contact are to be treated as confidential and not disclosed to other family members without the individual's permission.
B. Integration of legal and ethical limits on confidentiality
   1. Members make reasonable efforts to be knowledgeable about the legal status of confidentiality in their practice location.
   2. Members recognize that ethical standards are not intended to require counselors to violate clearly defined legal standards in their practice location.
   3. Members support professional activity to establish legal protection for confidentiality of communications between counselors and clients.
C. Exceptions to confidentiality
   1. Members may reveal a client's confidences with the consent of that client, but a counselor first makes reasonable efforts to make the client aware of the ramifications of the disclosure.
   2. Members may disclose confidences when required by a specific law such as a child abuse reporting statute.
   3. Members may disclose confidences when required to do so by a court of competent jurisdiction.

4. Members may disclose an intention of a client to commit a crime, and may also disclose such other confidences as may be necessary to prevent the commission of the crime.
5. Members may disclose confidences in order to prevent clearly identified bodily harm to the client or to some other clearly identified person.
6. Members may reveal a client's confidences to the extent necessary to establish or collect a fee from that client.
7. Members may reveal a client's confidences to the extent necessary to defend the counselor and/or associates against a charge of wrongful conduct brought by that client.

D. Informed consent about confidentiality
1. Members inform clients about the nature and limitations of confidentiality, including the separate but related status of legal and ethical standards regarding confidentiality.
2. Members use care not to explicitly or implicitly promise more protection of confidentiality than that which exists.
3. Members use care to get informed consent from each family member concerning limitations on confidentiality of communications made in the presence of a family or other group.
4. Members clearly define and communicate the boundaries of confidentiality agreed on by the counselor and family members prior to the beginning of a family counseling relationship. As changing conditions might necessitate a change in these boundaries, counselors get informed consent to the new conditions prior to proceeding with the counseling activities.
5. Members terminate the relationship and make an appropriate referral in cases where a client's refusal to give informed consent to the boundaries of confidentiality interferes with the agreed upon goals of counseling.

E. Practice management concerning confidentiality
1. Members assert the client's right to confidentiality when the counselor is asked to reveal client confidences.
2. Members notify the client when the counselor receives a subpoena which might lead to the counselor having to disclose the client's confidences.
3. When a member receives a subpoena to go to court, the counselor makes a reasonable effort to ask the court to recognize the value of the counseling relationship and the importance of confidentiality to that relationship, and consequently to excuse the counselor from disclosing confidential information.
4. When members are not excused from giving testimony, they exercise caution not to disclose information or relinquish records until directed to do so by the court.

5. Members exercise care in planning and monitoring their practices in order to assure that the counselors, their associates and staff, and the clients avoid any behavior that might be construed as a waiver of confidentiality.

6. Members make reasonable efforts to teach their clients to avoid any behaviors, such as disclosing secrets under conditions which do not lead to an expectation of confidentiality, which might be construed as a waiver of confidentiality.

7. Members exercise professional judgment and discretion in deciding whether an exception to confidentiality applies in particular cases. In cases where the decision is not apparent, counselors utilize advice from consultants and the professional literature in making a decision.

8. When members make a good faith decision to disclose confidences based on one of the exceptions listed above, the amount and kind of information disclosed, the person(s) to whom the disclosure is made, and the method of communication all are limited to what is necessary to discharge the duty created by the exception.

9. Members get informed consent from all clients prior to making an electronic recording of a counseling session.

10. Members recognize that the normal operation of a counseling practice exposes confidential information to certain other counselors and to non-counseling staff, but counselors exercise care to limit access only to that which is necessary.

11. Members use care in screening, training, and supervising all paid and volunteer staff in order to assure that the staff members protect confidentiality in their role as an extension of the counselor.

12. Members use care in creating and maintaining office practices which protect confidentiality. For example, client reception areas are separate from counseling offices and work stations where confidential files are handled, and clients are not allowed to have access to areas where they might hear or see other clients' secrets.

13. Members use care to assure that clients' records are produced, stored, and disposed of in a way that protects confidentiality. Written records should be kept in a locked and secure location, and computerized record systems should use appropriate safeguards to prevent unauthorized access.

14. Members create a system to protect the confidentiality of client records in the event of the death or incapacity of the counselor.

15. Members who disclose certain client information in order to get consultation from another counselor use care not to reveal the identity of the client or any other information beyond that which is necessary to get effective consultation. Members seek consultation only from

other professional counselors who recognize their obligation to keep all shared information confidential.

16. Members who use client data for research, teaching, or publication purposes must use care to disguise the data in order to protect clients' privacy rights and confidentiality rights.

▓ *Section III: Competence*

A. Members have the responsibility to develop and maintain basic skills in marriage and family counseling through graduate work, supervision, and peer review. An outline of these skills is provided by the Council for Accreditation of Counseling and Related Educational Programs (CACREP) Environmental and Specialty Standards for Marriage and Family Counseling/Therapy. The minimal level of training shall be considered a master's degree in a helping profession.

B. Members recognize the need for keeping current with new developments in the field of marriage and family counseling. They pursue continuing education in forms such as books, journals, classes, workshops, conferences, and conventions.

C. Members accurately represent their education, areas of expertise, credentials, training and experience. They make concerted efforts to ensure that statements others make about them and/or their credentials are accurate.

D. Members do not attempt to diagnose or treat problems beyond the scope of their abilities and training. While developing new skills in specialty areas, marriage and family counselors take steps to ensure the quality of their work through training, supervision, and peer review.

E. Members do not undertake any professional activity in which their personal problems might impair their performance. They seek assistance for problems, and, if necessary, limit, suspend, or terminate their professional activities.

F. Members do not engage in actions that violate the "standards of practice" of their given professional counseling community.

G. Members are committed to gaining cultural competency, including awareness, knowledge, and skills to work with a diverse clientele. Members are aware of their own biases, values, and assumptions about human behavior. They employ techniques/assessment strategies that are appropriate for dealing with diverse cultural groups.

H. Members take care of their physical, mental, and emotional health in order to reduce the risk of burnout, and to prevent impairment and harm to clients.

▦ Section IV: Assessment

A. Members have the responsibility of acquiring and maintaining skills related to assessment procedures and assessment instruments that promote the best interests and well being of the client in clarifying concerns, establishing treatment goals, evaluating therapeutic progress, and promoting objective decision making.
B. Members provide clients with assessment results, interpretation, and conclusions drawn from assessment interviews and instruments. Members inform clients of how assessment information will be used.
C. Members use assessment methods that are current, reliable, valid, and germane to the goals of the client, including computer-assisted assessment. Members do not use inventories and tests that have outdated test items or lack normative data.
D. Members use assessment methods that are within the scope of their qualifications, training, or statutory limitations. Members using tests or inventories have a thorough understanding of measurement concepts.
E. Members are familiar with any assessment instruments prior to its use, including the testing manual, purpose of the instrument, and relevant psychometric and normative data.
F. Members only use instruments that have demonstrated validity in custody evaluations and do not make recommendations based solely on test and inventory scores. Members conducting custody evaluations recognize the potential impact that their reports can have on family members and use instruments that have demonstrated validity in custody evaluations.
G. Members strive to maintain the guidelines in the Standards for Educational and Psychological Testing, written in collaboration by the American Educational Research Association, American Psychological Association, and National Council on Measurement in Evaluation, as well as the Code of Fair Testing Practices, published by the Joint Committee on Testing Practices.

▦ Section V: Private Practice

A. Members in private practice have a special obligation to adhere to ethical and legal standards, because of the independent nature of their work.
  1. Members keep informed of current ethical codes and ethical issues of the profession.
  2. Members maintain a working knowledge of legal standards in the geographical area and areas of specialty in which they work, abiding by these standards in their practice.

3. Members continue professional growth and knowledge through consultation, supervision.
B. Members practice within the scope of their training.
　1. Members promote themselves only within the areas of their professional training, supervision, and experience.
　2. Members refer to other practitioner's clients who would benefit from services outside of their own areas of expertise.
C. Members in private practice are responsible and respectful of client needs in their setting and collection of fees for service.
　1. Members provide a portion of their services at little or no cost as a service to the community.
　2. Members appropriately refer clients who are unable to afford private services and cannot be seen pro bono by the private practitioner.
　3. Members do not share or accept fees for offering or accepting referrals.
　4. Bartering is discouraged because of the inherent potential for erosion of professional boundaries and introduction of dual relationships. If unavoidable and considered the standard of practice in the community, fair value for services/items exchanged should be included in a contract and reported as income.
D. Members do not terminate counseling with established clients that would benefit from further counseling without referring them to an appropriate practitioner or agency.
E. Members enter into professional partnerships only with others that adhere to ethical standards of the profession. Implicit in this standard is that members should not share or accept fees for accepting or offering referrals.

▣ *Section VI: Research and Publications*

A. Members shall be fully responsible for their choice of research topics and the methods used for investigation, analysis, and reporting. They must be particularly careful that findings do not appear misleading, that the research is planned to allow for the inclusion of alternative hypotheses, and that provision is made for discussion of the limitations of the study.
B. Members safeguard the privacy of their research participants. Data about an individual participant are not released unless the individual is informed about the exact nature of the information to be released and gives written permission for doing so.
C. Members safeguard the safety of their research participants. Members receive approval from, and follow guidelines of, any institutional research committee. Prospective participants are informed, in writing, about any

potential risk associated with a study and are notified that they can with-draw at any time.

D. Members make their original data available to other researchers.

E. Members only take credit for research in which they make a substantial contribution, and give credit to all such contributors. Authors are listed from greatest to least amount of contribution.

F. Members do not plagiarize. Ideas or data that did not originate with the author(s) and are not common knowledge are clearly credited to the original scores.

G. Members are aware of their obligation to be a role model for graduate students and other future researchers and so act in accordance with the highest standards possible while engaged in research.

H. Family counselors should be cautious when assessing culturally diverse clients. Family counselors include cultural factors when assessing behaviors, functioning, and presenting symptoms of clients. Counselors are careful to use assessment techniques that have been appropriately formed and standardized on diverse populations. Counselors are also careful to interpret results from standardized assessment instruments in light of cultural factors.

■ *Section VII: Supervision*

A. Members who provide supervision demonstrate advanced skills in marriage and family counseling, and receive appropriate training and supervision-of-supervision prior to providing supervisory services. Members provide supervision only within the limits of their professional competence. Additionally, they accept supervisory responsibilities only for counselors they can appropriately and adequately oversee.

B. Members who provide supervision respect the inherent imbalance of power in supervisory relationships. Thus, they actively monitor and appropriately manage multiple relationships. They refrain from engaging in relationships or activities that increase risk of exploitation, or that may impair the professional judgment. Sexual intimacy with students or supervisees is prohibited.

C. Members who provide supervision regard content of supervisory sessions as confidential. They provide the same level of security for documentation related to supervisees as they do for clients.

D. Members who are supervisors educate supervisees about professional ethics and standards of practice. Supervisors provide service to professional organizations and work to improve professional practices. They also encourage supervisees to participate in professional organizations.

E. Members who are supervisors provide accurate and complete information (e.g., areas of expertise, credentials, philosophy and approaches to supervision, procedures for evaluation, responses to client emergencies, ethical guidelines to which they adhere, etc.) to assure that potential supervisees engage in supervisory relationships with clear understanding of the supervisory arrangements. They articulate expectations surrounding skill building, knowledge acquisition, and the development of competencies. Members also provide ongoing and timely feedback to their supervisees.

F. Members who provide supervision are responsible for protecting the rights and well-being of their supervisees' clients. They monitor their supervisees' counseling on an ongoing basis, and create procedures to protect the confidentiality of clients whose sessions have been electronically recorded.

G. Members who provide supervision assure that supervisees' clients receive information about supervisees' level of training and credentials, parameters of supervision, the counseling processes and purposes, benefits and risks they may encounter, and limits of confidentiality prior to establishing contracts for counseling.

H. Members who provide supervision endorse for practice only those supervisees who demonstrate expectations for competency and professional judgment.

I. Supervisors assure that supervisees are knowledgeable about professional ethics and standards, and that they practice within those parameters.

J. Members who provide supervision strive to reach and maintain the guidelines provided in the Standards for Counseling Supervisors adopted by the ACA Governing Council and the Code of Ethics established by the Association for Counselor Education and Supervision.

K. Members understand the influence of cultural issues in the supervisory relationship, including issues of oppression and power structures within the relationship.

L. Members who provide supervision discuss cultural issues in the work of supervisees and clients, and promote cultural sensitivity and competence in the supervisees.

Section VIII: Advertising and Other Public Statements

A. Members accurately and objectively represent their education, training, professional qualifications, skills, and functions to the public. Members do not use membership in a professional organization to suggest endorsement of their competency.

B. Members ensure that all advertisements, announcements, or other public statements they make regarding their professional services are not false or misleading, either by commission or omission. Such public statements should focus on objective information that allows clients to make an informed decision about seeking services. Providing information such as highest relevant academic degree earned, training and experience, professional credentials, types of services offered, office hours, fee structure, and languages spoken can help clients decided if the advertised services are appropriate for their needs.

C. Members advertise themselves as specialists within marriage and family counseling only in those areas in which they can demonstrate evidence of training, education, and supervised experiences in the area of specialization.

D. Members who engage others to advertise or promote their professional services remain responsible for all forms of public statements made. Members strive to make certain that statements about their professional services made by other persons are accurate. In addition, members do not ask for or accept testimonials from current or former clients regarding the uniqueness, effectiveness, or efficiency of counseling services.

E. Members promoting counseling-related products for commercial sale make every effort to ensure that advertisements and announcements are presented in a professional and factual manner. In addition, announcements and advertisements about workshops or training events should never contain false or misleading statements. Members make certain that advertisements and announcements regarding products or training events provide accurate and adequate information for consumers to make informed choices.

F. Members have the responsibility to provide information to the public that enhances marriage and family life. Such statements should be based on sound, professionally accepted theories, techniques, and approaches. When presenting information to the public, members only address issues for which they are adequately qualified and prepared. Due to the inability to complete a comprehensive assessment or provide follow-up, members do not give specific advice to an individual through the media or other public venues.

Glossary

AAMFT American Association for Marriage and Family Therapy. Largest professional organization for couple and family therapists.

Abuse Misuse or excessive use, such as spouse abuse and substance abuse.

ABC theory Model for disputing irrational beliefs in rational emotive behavior therapy.

ACA American Counseling Association. A professional organization for counselors.

Accommodation The counselor's adjusting to the family's style; useful in the joining process of family therapy.

Behavioral family therapy Treatment mode that focuses on specific actions of family members and uses reinforcement to increase or decrease the frequency of those actions.

Blended family A family formed by uniting members from two previously married families; stepfamilies.

Boundaries Rules determining who is in and out of various family subsystems.

Brief therapy A solution-focused, short-term approach to treating families.

CACREP Council for Accreditation of Counseling and Related Educational Programs. Accrediting agency affiliated with the American Counseling Association; accredits marriage and family counseling/ therapy.

Certification Designation of competence awarded by a certifying body such as Clinical Membership in AAMFT.

Circular causality Actions in a feedback loop that view any cause as a reaction to a prior cause.

Circumplex model A framework for assessing families based on the dimensions of adaptability and cohesion.

Co-dependency Two or more people who depend on each other in a way that is not healthy; one member over-functions while the other underfunctions.

Conceptual skills The ability to think about and understand family functioning and family patterns.

Confrontation Directly facing or being required to face personal shortcomings, attitudes, and how one is perceived by others.

Congruence The interaction of actions, attitudes, and feelings all being honest and consistent.

Contracting Making a formal agreement, usually in writing, that stipulates what changes the members involved in family therapy will make.

Couples' group therapy A treatment group composed of couples in committed relationships to work on improving those relationships.

Co-therapy Two therapists working together with a couple or family; brings varied therapeutic perspectives into the session.

Cybernetics The concept of self-regulation of machines that has been extended to living systems; the mechanisms by which families and other living systems regulate their behaviors.

Differentiation The application of learning to emotional experiences that leads to mature choices and actions; opposite of fusion.

Disengaged Describes a family that has little real emotional contact with other members or those outside the family.

Disequillibrium Absence of emotional and behavioral stability within the family system.

Division of family psychology The group within the American Psychological Association for family psychologists.

Divorce therapy Treatment to help a couple end their marriage without bitterness or other hard feelings.

Double-bind A message with two incompatible parts; the responder is wrong no matter what the choice.

DPW Developmental Process Work, a transpersonal systems theory.

Ego states Parent, adult, and child dimensions of transactional analysis.

Escalation of stress Counseling technique that puts pressure on the family system to cause disequillibrium, offering the opportunity for change.

Emotional cutoff Withdrawing from one's family of origin, believing the cutoff will alleviate emotional pain.

Empathy Awareness of another's thoughts and feelings and their possible meanings.

Enactment A counseling term referring to the family interacting with each other in usual ways, allowing the counselor to gain an understanding of the family's problems and dysfunctional interaction patterns.

Enmeshment Blurring of boundaries between family members overinvolvement in each other's activities, making autonomy impossible.

Executive subsystem In structural family therapy, the husband-wife subsystem that ultimately is responsible for the welfare of the family.

Externalizing problems A technique in narrative therapy that labels the problem as outside the individual, permitting the client to mobilize resource to overcome it.

Family life cycle Stages families go through with unique tasks that must be accomplished at each stage.

Family of origin A person's original family, parents, and siblings.

Family of origin therapy Treatment that works with an adult client and his or her parents to resolve past hurts and unresolved differences.

Family projection process Playing out unresolved emotional issues of the parents with their families of origin through dysfunction in one or more of the children.

Fusion An individual's emotions overpowering reason, leading to a loss of individuality and autonomy; opposite of differentiation.

Genogram A diagram of one's family tree over three generations or more, allowing the client and counselor to identify recurring themes over the generations.

Homeostasis A balanced state of equilibrium in the family; living systems adjust themselves to attempt to remain in this state at all times.

IAMFC International Association of Marriage and Family Therapist, a division of ACA.

Identified patient The family member who bears the symptoms of a dysfunctional family system.

Internal family systems An intrapsychic model used to apply system concepts to change internal dynamics.

Interpersonal skills Critical relationship skills needed in functional family therapy and other treatment models.

Intrapsychic Competing forces within the mind as opposed to competing forces in the environment.

Irrational beliefs Cognitions that are not valid and lead to self-defeating behaviors.

Joining Forming a working relationship with each family member.

Licensure Legal recognition by the State of professional competencies, rights, and obligations.

Linear causality A cause-and-effect model of the etiology of behaviors.

Live supervision A procedure in which the supervisor observes the counseling session and provides feedback during and immediately after the session.

Maneuverability A quality that family therapists try to maintain that permits the therapist to access the full range of intervention possibilities without threatening the family.

Marital dysfunction Problems in the relationship between husband and wife.

Meta-analysis Statistical technique that merges the quantitative results of several studies to produce an overall effect of the treatment; used in studies to determine if therapy is effective.

Multigenerational transmission process Murray Bowen's concept of emotional illness being transmitted from one generation to the next.

180-degree solution In brief therapy, a solution to a presenting problem that is opposite of what the family currently is doing to resolve the problem.

Object relations theory A concept that emphasizes the resolution of attachment and differentiation issues as the key elements of psychological health.

Paradigm shift A change in basic assumptions about problem formation necessary to use systems theories effectively.

Paradoxical intervention A command given to a client that creates a situation in which compliance or refusal leads to improved functioning; normally the command is to continue the symptom, thereby demonstrating control of it or resisting and having the symptom become less frequent.

Partnership Way A developmental systems theory used in conflict resolution.

Pseudomutuality A family condition that shows a façade of harmony while actually experiencing distress.

Quid pro quo A behavioral exchange intervention of "something for something" used in many family therapy theories.

Reauthoring A narrative therapy intervention in which the client composes a story about how he or she would like life to be; the therapist helps the new narrative become reality.

Reframing Attributing positive motives to a situation that has been perceived to be negative.

Reinforcement A behavioral event that increases the frequency of a specific response.

Restructuring A technique that changes subsystem composition and power within the larger family system to create a more functional family.

Restraining change A technique to overcome resistance by suggesting that family members not change; by resisting, they do change.

Rules Repetitive patterns of family behavior that regulate family functioning in a predictable way.

Schizophrenic mother Early family therapy concept, later shown to be incorrect, holding that schizophrenic offspring were the product of a family with an overinvolved, double-binding mother and a disengaged, ineffectual father.

Sculpting A nonverbal family therapy technique in which family members position themselves in a room to represent how each experiences significant aspects of the family.

Self-worth Virginia Satir's term for the most important gift parents can give their children; parents without their own sense of self-worth cannot give it to their children.

Single-parent families Families with only one adult to provide and care for the children.

Subsystems Smaller units of the family with their own organization and functions; may be determined by age, gender, interests, and other factors.

Therapeutic letters A narrative therapy technique in which the counselor writes a letter to the client documenting how the client has overcome the forces of the externalized problem.

Transference The client's projection of unconscious and unresolved issues onto the therapist; often the therapist is imagined as being like someone in the client's family of origin.

Triangulation Stabilizing a conflictual relationship between two persons by bringing a third person into the relationship.

Unit of treatment In family therapy, the family of various subsystems of the family.

References

Abbott, D. A., Berry, M., & Meridith, W. H. (1990). Religious belief and practice: A potential asset in helping families. *Family Relations, 39,* 443–448.

Ackerman, N. W. (1958). *The psychodynamics of family life.* New York: Basic Books.

Adler, A. (1927). *The practice and theory of individual psychology.* New York: Harcourt, Brace, Jovanovich.

Alexander, J. F. (1973). Defensive and supportive communications in normal and deviant families. *Journal of Consulting and Clinical Psychology 40*(2), 223–231.

Alexander, J. F., & Barton, C. (1976). Behavioral systems therapy with families. In D. H. Olson (Ed.), *Treating relationships.* Lake Mills, IA: Graphic Press.

Alexander, J. F., Barton, C., Schiavo, R. S., & Parsons, B. V. (1976). Behavior interventions with families of delinquents: Therapist characteristics and outcome. *Journal of Consulting and Clinical Psychology, 44,* 656–664.

Alexander, J. F., & Parsons, B. V. (1973). Short term behavioral intervention with delinquent families: Impact on family process and recidivism. *Journal of Abnormal Psychology, 81*(3), 219–225.

Alexander, J. F., & Parsons, B. V. (1982). *Functional family therapy.* Pacific Grove, CA: Brooks/Cole.

American Association for Marriage and Family Therapy. (1991). *AAMFT Code of Ethics.* Washington, DC: Author.

American Association for Marriage and Family Therapy. (2001). *AAMFT Code of Ethics.* Washington, DC: AAMFT.

American Association for Marriage and Family Therapy. (2002). *AAMFT membership categories.* Retrieved August 2002 from www.aamft.org

Anderson, W. J. (1989). Client/person-centered approaches to couple and family therapy: Expanding theory and practice. *Person-Centered Review, 4,* 245–247.

Anonymous. (1972). On the differentiation of self. In J. Framo (Ed.), *Family interaction: A dialogue between family researchers and family therapists.* New York: Springer.

Aponte, H. J., & Van Deusen, J. M. (1981). Structural family therapy. In A. S. Gurman & D. P. Kniskern (Eds.), *Handbook of family therapy.* New York: Brunner/Mazel.

Babcock, D., & Keepers, T. (1976). *Raising kids ok.* New York: Grove Press.

Bader, E., Pearson, P. T., & Schwartz, J. D. (2000). *Tell me no lies.* New York: St. Martin's Press.

Bandura, A. (1969). *Principles of behavior modification.* New York: Holt, Rinehart, & Winston.

Bandura, A. (1977). *Social learning theory.* Englewood Cliffs, NJ: Prentice Hall.

Barker, P. (1992). *Basic family therapy.* New York: Oxford University Press.

Barton, C., & Alexander, J. F. (1977). Treatment of families with a delinquent member. In G. Harris (Ed.), *The group treatment of family problems: A source learning approach.* New York: Grune & Stratton.

Barton, C., & Alexander, J. F. (1981). Functional family therapy. In A. S. Gurman & D. P. Kniskern (Eds.), *Handbook of family therapy.* New York: Brunner/Mazel.

Bateson, G., Jackson, D. D., Haley, J., & Weakland, J. (1956). Towards a theory of schizophrenia. *Behavioral Sciences, 1,* 251–264.

Bateson, G., Jackson, D., Haley, J., & Weakland, J. (1971). Toward a theory of schizophrenia. In G. Bateson, *Steps to an ecology of the mind.* New York: Ballentine.

Baucom, D. H., & Epstein, N. (1990). *Cognitive-behavioral marital therapy.* New York: Brunner/Mazel.

Bauer, R. (1979). Gestalt approaches to family therapy. *American Journal of Family Therapy, 7*(3), 41–45.

Beck, A. (1976). *Cognitive therapy and the emotional disorders.* New York: International University Press.

Beck, A. (1991). Cognitive therapy: A 30 year retrospective. *American Psychologist, 46,* 368–375.

Beck, A., Rush, A., Shaw, B., & Emery, G. (1979). *Cognitive therapy of depression.* New York: Guilford *Press.*

Bell, J. E. (1961). *Family group therapy.* Public Health Monograph 64. Washington, DC: U.S. Government Printing Office.

Benedek, E. P. (1982). Conjoint marital therapy and spouse abuse. In A. S. Gurman (Ed.), *Questions and answers in family therapy* (vol. 2). New York: Brunner/Mazel.

Berg, I. K. (1991). Letter to the editor. *Journal of Marital and Family Therapy, 17,* 311–312.

Berger, M. (1982). Predictable tasks in therapy with families of handicapped persons. In A. S. Gurman (Ed.), *Questions and answers in family therapy* (vol. 2). New York: Brunner/Mazel.

Berger, P. L., & Kellner, H. (1977). Marriage and the construction of reality. In P. L. Berger (Ed.), *Facing up to modernity: Excursion in society, politics and religion.* New York: Basic Books.

Bergin, A. (1967). Some implications of psychotherapy research for therapeutic practice. *International Journal of Psychiatry, 3,* 136–150.

Bergin, A. (1971). The evaluation of therapeutic outcomes. In A. Bergin & S. Garfield (Eds.), *Handbook of psychotherapy and behavior change.* New York: Wiley.

Bergin, A., & Lambert, M. (1978). The evaluation of therapeutic outcomes. In A. Bergin & S. Lambert (Eds.), *Handbook of psychotherapy and behavior change: An empirical analysis* (2nd ed.). New York: Wiley.

Berne, E. (1961). *Transactional analysis in psychotherapy.* New York: Grove Press.

Berne, E. (1972). *What do you say after you say hello?* New York: Grove Press.

Black, L., & Piercy, F. P. (1991). A feminist family therapy scale. *Journal of Marital and Family Therapy, 17,* 111–120.

Bodin, A. M. (1981). The interactional view: Family therapy approaches of the Mental Research Institute. In A. S. Gurman & D. P. Kniskern (Eds.), *Handbook of family therapy.* New York: Brunner/Mazel.

Bowen, M. (1960). A family concept of schizophrenia. In D. Jackson (Ed.), *The etiology of schizophrenia.* New York: Basic Books.

Bowen, M. (1961). Family psychotherapy. *American Journal of Orthopsychiatry, 31,* 40–60.

Bowen, M. (1971). Family therapy and family group therapy. In H. Kaplan & B. Sadock (Eds.), *Comprehensive group psychotherapy.* Baltimore: Williams & Wilkins.

Bowen, M. (1976). Theory in the practice of psychotherapy. In P. J. Guerrin, Jr. (Ed.), *Family therapy: Theory and practice.* New York: Gardner Press.

Bowen, M. (1978). *Family therapy in clinical practice.* New York: Jason Aronson.

Bray, J. H., & Jouriles, E. N. (1995). Treatment of marital conflict and prevention of divorce. *Journal of Marital and Family Therapy, 21*(4), 461–474.

Broderick, C. B., & Schraeder, S. S. (1991). The history of professional marriage and family therapy. In A. S. Gurman & D. P. Kniskern (Eds.), *Handbook of family therapy* (Vol. 2). New York: Brunner/ Mazel.

Buckley, W. (1967). *Sociology and modern systems theory.* Englewood Cliffs, NJ: Prentice Hall.

CACREP Connection. (2001, Summer). Directory of accredited programs.

Campbell, T. L., & Patterson, J. M. (1995). The effectiveness of family interventions in the treatment of physical illness. *Journal of Marital and Family Therapy, 21*(4), 545–584.

Canfield, B. S., Hovestadt, A. J., & Fenell, D. L. (1992). Family-of-origin influences upon perceptions of current family functioning. *Family Therapy, 19,* 55–60.

Carkhuff, R. (1969a). *Helping and human relations. Vol. 1: Selection and training.* New York: Holt, Rinehart, & Winston.

Carkhuff, R. (1969b). *Helping and human relations. Vol. 11: Practice and research.* New York: Holt, Rinehart, & Winston.

Carter, E. A., & McGoldrick, M., (Eds.) (1980). *The family life cycle: A framework for family therapy.* New York: Gardner Press.

Chamberlain, D. (1996). Past and future birth. *APPPAH Newsletter,* Summer, 1–2.

Chamberlain, P., & Rosicky, J. G. (1995). The effectiveness of family therapy in the treatment of adolescents with conduct disorders and delinquency. *Journal of Marital and Family Therapy, 21*(4), 441–460.

Clarke, J. (1978). *Self-esteem: A family affair.* Minneapolis: Winston Press.

Clarke, J., & Dawson, C. (1989). *Growing up again: Parenting ourselves, parenting our children.* Minneapolis: Hazelden.

Colapinto, J. (1991). Structural family therapy. In A. S. Gurman & D. P. Kniskern (Eds.) *Handbook of family therapy.* (vol. 2). New York: Brunner/Mazel.

Conye, J. (1987). Depression, biology, marriage and marital therapy. *Journal of Marriage and Family Therapy, 13*(4), 393–407.

Coombs, R. H. (1991). Marital status and personal well-being: A literature review. *Family Relations, 40,* 97–102.

Corey, G. (1991). *Theory and practice of counseling and psychotherapy* (4th ed.). Pacific Grove, CA: Brooks/Cole.

Corey, G. (1996). *Theory and practice of counseling and psychotherapy* (5th ed.). Pacific Grove, CA: Brooks/Cole.

Corey, G. (2000). *Theory and practice of group counseling* (5th ed.). Belmont, CA: Brooks/Cole.

Corey, G. (2001). *Theory and practice of counseling and psychotherapy* (6th ed.). Belmont, CA: Brooks/Cole.

Corey, G., Corey, M., & Callahan, P. (1993). *Issues and ethics in the helping professions* (4th ed.). Pacific Grove, CA: Brooks/Cole.

Davidson, T. (1978). *Conjugal crime.* New York: Hawthorne.

Davis, R. F., & Borns, R. F. (1999). *Solo dad survival guide: Raising your kids on your own.* New York: NTC Contemporary.

deMause, L. (1982). *Foundations of psychohistory.* New York: Creative Roots.

Denton, W. (2002). Relational diagnosis and the DSM. *Family Therapy Magazine, 1*(3), 18–19.

DeWitt, K. (1978). The effectiveness of family therapy: A review of the outcome research. *Archives of General Psychiatry, 35,* 549–561.

Dilts, R., & Green, J. D. (1982). Neuro-linguistic programming in family therapy. In A. M. Horne & M. M. Ohlsen (Eds.), *Family counseling and therapy.* Itasca, IL: Peacock.

Doherty, W. J. (1991). Beyond reactivity and the deficit model of manhood: A comment on articles by Napier, Pittman, and Gottman. *Journal of Marital and Family Therapy, 17,* 29–32.

Duhl, F. J., Kantor, D., & Duhl, B. S. (1973). Learning, space and action in family therapy: A primer of sculpture. In D. Bloch (Ed.), *Techniques of family psychotherapy*. New York: Grune & Stratton.

Edwards, M. E., & Steinglass, P. (1995). Family therapy treatment outcomes for alcoholism. *Journal of Marital and Family Therapy, 4,* 475–509.

Ellis, A. (1962). *Reason and emotion in psychotherapy*. Secaucus, NJ: Citadel Press.

Ellis, A. (1974). *Techniques of disrupting irrational beliefs*. New York: Institute for Rational Living.

Ellis, A. (1977). *Self-help report form*. New York: Institute for Rational Living.

Ellis, A. (1991). Rational-emotive family therapy. In A. Horne & A. Passmore (Eds.), *Family counseling and therapy* (2nd ed.). Itasca, IL: Peacock.

Ellis, A. (1992). First order and second order change in rational-emotive therapy: A reply to Lyddon. *Journal of Counseling and Development, 70,* 449–461.

Ellis, A. (1993). The rational-emotive therapy approach to marriage and family therapy. *The Family Journal, 1,* 292–307.

Ellis, A. (1995). Rational emotive behavior therapy. In R. J. Corsini & D. Wedding (Eds.), *Current psychotherapies* (5th ed.). Itasca, IL: Peacock.

Epston, D. (1994). Extending the conversation. *The Family Therapy Networker, 18*(6), 30–37.

Erikson, E. H. (1946). *The psychoanalytic study of the child*. New York: International Universities Press.

Erikson, E. H. (1950). *Childhood and society*. New York: Norton.

Erikson, E. H. (1959). *Psychological issues*. New York: International Universities Press.

Estrada, A. U., & Pinsof, W. M. (1995). The effectiveness of family therapies for selected behavioral disorders of childhood. *Journal of Marital and Family Therapy, 21*(4), 403–440.

Everett, C., & Volgy, S. (1991). Treating divorce in family therapy practice. In A. Gurman & D. Kniskern (Eds.), *Handbook of family therapy* (vol. 2). New York: Brunner/Mazel.

Eysenck, H. (1952). The effects of psychotherapy: An evaluation. *Journal of Consulting Psychology, 16,* 319–324.

Fairbairn, W. (1954). *Object-relations theory of the personality*. New York: Basic Books.

Falloon, I. (1991). Behavioral marital therapy. In A. S. Gurman & D. P. Kniskern (Eds.), *Handbook of family therapy* (vol. 2). New York: Brunner/Mazel.

Fenell, D. L. (1982). Counseling dual career couples. *Arizona Personnel and Guidance Journal, 7,* 8–10.

Fenell, D. L. (1990, March). Unpublished paper presented at University of Colorado, Colorado Springs.

Fenell, D. L. (1991). Critical issues in long-term marriages. *International Association for Marriage and Family Counseling Newsletter,* spring, 1–2.

Fenell, D. L. (1993a). Characteristics of long-term first marriages. *Journal of Mental Health Counseling, 15,* 446–460.

Fenell, D. L. (1993b). Using Bowen's differentiation of self scale to help couples understand and resolve marital conflict. In T. S. Nelson & T. S. Trepper (Eds.), *101 interventions in family therapy*. New York: Haworth Press.

Fenell, D. L., & Hovestadt, A. J. (1986). Family therapy as a profession or professional specialty: Implications for training. *Journal of Psychotherapy and the Family, 1*(4), 25–40.

Fenell, D. L., Hovestadt, A. H., & Cochran, S. (1985). Characteristics of effective administrators of rural mental health centers. *Journal of Rural Community Psychology, 8*(1), 23–35.

Fenell, D. L., Hovestadt, A. J., & Harvey, S. J. (1986). A comparison of delayed feedback and live supervision models of marriage and family therapy. *Journal of Marital and Family Therapy, 12*(2), 181–186.

Fenell, D. L., Martin. J., & Mithaug, D. E. (1986). The mentally retarded child. In L. B. Golden & D. Capuzzi (Eds.), *Helping families help children: Family interventions with school-related problems*. Springfield, IL: Charles C. Thomas.

Fenell, D. L., Nelson, R. C., & Shertzer, B. (1981). The effects of a marriage enrichment program on marital satisfaction and self-concept. *The Journal for Specialists in Group Work, 6*(2), 83–89.

Fenell, D. L., & Wallace, C. (1985). Remarriage: The triumph of hope over experience: A challenge for counseling professionals. *Arizona Counseling Journal, 10*, 12–18.

Fields, N. S. (1983). Satisfaction in long-term marriages. *Social Work, 28*, 37–41.

Fisch, R., Weakland, J. H., & Segal, L. (1982). *The tactics of change: Doing therapy briefly.* San Francisco: Jossey-Bass.

Fish, V. (1993). Poststructuralism in family therapy: Interrogating the narrative/conversational mode. *Journal of Marital and Family Therapy, 19*, 221–232.

Flowers, B. J. (2000). *Beyond the myth of marital happiness.* San Francisco: Jossey-Bass.

Flugel, J. D. (1921). *The psychoanalytic study of the family.* London: Hogarth Press.

Foley, V. D. (1974). *An introduction to family therapy.* New York: Grune & Stratton.

Framo, J. L. (1981). The integration of marital therapy with family of origin sessions. In A. S. Gurman & D. P. Kniskern (Eds.), *Handbook of family therapy.* New York: Brunner/Mazel.

Framo, J. L. (1982). *Explorations in marital and family therapy.* New York: Springer.

Freud, S. (1909). Analysis of a phobia in a five-year-old boy. *Standard Edition, 10*, 3–152. (original work published 1909)

Freud, S. (1949). *An outline of psychoanalysis.* New York: Norton.

Freud, S. (1963). *Collected papers* (vol. 4). New York: Collier Books.

Fried, S., & Fried, P. (1996). *Bullies & victims: Helping your child survive the schoolyard battlefield.* New York: M. Evans and Company.

Friedman, E. H. (1991). Bowen theory and therapy. In A. S. Gurman & D. P. Kniskern (Eds.), *Handbook of family therapy* (vol. 2). New York: Brunner/Mazel.

Fromm, E. (1941). *Escape from freedom.* New York: Holt, Rinehart, & Winston.

Fromm, E. (1947). *Man for himself.* New York: Holt, Rinehart, & Winston.

Gaylin, N. L. (1989). The necessary and sufficient conditions for change: Individual versus family therapy. *Person-Centered Review, 4*, 263–279.

George, R. L. (1990). Counseling the chemically dependent: Role and function. Englewood Cliffs, NJ: Prentice Hall.

Gill, S. J. (1982). Professional disclosure and consumer protection in counseling. *Personnel and Guidance Journal, 60*, 443–446.

Gladding, S. T. (2002). *Family therapy: History, theory, and practice* (3d ed.). Columbus, OH: Merrill.

Gladding, S. T., Burggraf, M. Z., & Fenell, D. L. (1987). A survey of marriage and family therapy training within departments of counselor education. *Journal of Counseling and Development, 66*(2), (p. 90–92).

Glang, C., & Betis, A. (1993). Helping children through the divorce process. *PsychSpeak, 13* (4), 1–2.

Glenn, N. D. (1990). Quantitative research on marital quality in the 1980s: A critical review. *Journal of Marriage and the Family, 52*, 818–831.

Glick, P. (1989). Remarried families, stepfamilies and stepchildren: A brief demographic analysis. *Family Relations, 38*, 24–27.

Goldenberg, I., & Goldenberg, H. (2000). *Family therapy: An overview* (5th ed.). Belmont, CA: Brooks/Cole.

Goldstein, M. J., & Miklowitz, D. J. (1995). The effectiveness of psychoeducational family therapy in the treatment of schizophrenic disorders. *Journal of Marital and Family Therapy, 21*(4), 361–376.

Goodrich, T. J., Rampage, C., & Ellman, B. (1989). The single mother. *The Family Therapy Networker,* Sept.–Oct., 52–56.

Goodrich, T. J., Rampage, C., Ellman, B., & Halstead, K. (1988). *Feminist family therapy: A casebook.* New York: Norton.

Gottman, J. M. (1991). Predicting the longitudinal course of marriages. *Journal of Marriage and Family Therapy, 17*, 3–7.

Gottman, J. M. (1993). *Why marriages succeed or fail.* New York: Simon & Schuster.

Gottman, J. M. (1999). *The marriage clinic: A scientifically based marital therapy.* New York: W.W. Norton.

Gottman, J., Notarius, C., Markman, H., Bank, S., Yoppi, B., & Rubin, M. (1976). Behavior exchange theory and marital decision making. *Journal of Personality and Social Psychology, 34,* 14–23.

Goulding, M., & Goulding, R. (1978). *The power is in the patient: A Gestalt approach to psychotherapy.* San Francisco: TA Press.

Goulding, M., & Goulding, R. (1979). *Changing lives through redecision therapy.* New York: Brunner/Mazel.

Greenburg, L. S., & Johnson, S. M. (1988). *Emotionally focused therapy for couples.* New York: Guilford Press.

Grof, S. (1985). *Beyond the brain.* New York: SUNY Press.

Gumper, L. L., & Sprenkle, D. H. (1981). Privileged communication therapy: Special problems for the family and couples therapist. *Family Process, 20,* 11–23.

Gurman, A. S., & Kniskern, D. P. (1978a). Deterioration in marriage and family therapy: Empirical, clinical and conceptual issues. *Family Process, 17,* 3–20.

Gurman, A. S., & Kniskern, D. P. (1978b). Research on marital and family therapy: Progress, perspective and prospect. In S. L. Garfield & A. E. Lambert (Eds.), *Handbook of psychotherapy and behavior change: An empirical analysis* (2nd ed.). New York: Wiley.

Gurman, A. S., & Kniskern, D. P. (1981a). Family therapy outcome research: Knowns and unknowns. In A. S. Gurman & D. P. Kniskern (Eds.), *Handbook of family therapy.* New York: Brunner/Mazel.

Gurman, A. S., & Kniskern, D. P. (Eds.) (1981b). *Handbook of family therapy.* New York: Brunner/Mazel.

Gurman, A. S., & Kniskern, D. P. (Eds.) (1991). *Handbook of family therapy* (vol. 2). New York: Brunner/Mazel.

Haley, J. (1963). *Strategies of psychotherapy.* New York: Grune & Stratton.

Haley, J. (1971). Family therapy: A radical change. In J. Haley (Ed.), *Changing families: A family therapy reader.* New York: Grune & Stratton.

Haley, J. (1983). *Problem solving therapy.* San Francisco: Jossey-Bass.

Hamberger, L. K., & Hastings, J. E. (1993). Court mandated treatment of men who batter their partners: Issues, controversies and outcomes. In Z. Hilton (Ed.), *Legal responses to wife assault.* Newbury Park, CA: Sage.

Hansen, J., & Schuldt, J. (1984). Marital self-disclosure and marital satisfaction. *Journal of Marriage and the Family, 46,* 923–936.

Harris, T. (1967). *I'm o.k., you're o.k.* New York: Harper & Row.

Hatcher, C. (1978). Intrapersonal and interpersonal models: Blending Gestalt and family therapies. *Journal of Marriage and Family Counseling, 4*(1), 63–68.

Hatcher, C. (1981). Managing the violent family. In A. S. Gurman (Ed.), *Questions and answers in family therapy.* New York: Brunner/Mazel.

Havighurst, R. (1972). *Developmental tasks and education.* New York: David McKay.

Hendrick, S. (1981). Self-disclosure and marital satisfaction. *Journal of Personality and Social Psychology, 40,* 1150–1159.

Herrington, B. S. (1979). Privilege denied in joint therapy. *Psychiatric News, 14,* 1.

Horne, A., & Ohlsen, M. (Eds.) (1982). *Family counseling and therapy.* Itasca, IL: Peacock.

Hovestadt, A. H., Fenell, D. L., & Canfield, B. S. (2002). Characteristics of effective providers of marital and family therapy in rural mental health centers. *Journal of Marital and Family Therapy, 28*(2), 225–231.

Hovestadt, A. J., Fenell, D. L., & Piercy, F. P. (1983). Integrating marriage and family therapy within counselor education: A three-level model. In B. F. Okun & S. T. Gladding (Eds.), *Issues in training marriage and family therapists.* Ann Arbor, MI: ERIC/CAPS.

Huber, C. H. (1994). *Ethical, legal and professional issues in the practice of marriage and family therapy* (2nd ed.). New York: Merrill.

International Association of Marriage and Family Counselors. (1993). *Ethical Code for IAMFC*. Denver: Author.

International Association of Marriage and Family Counselors. (2001). *Ethical Code for IAMFT*. Denver: Author.

Jackson, D. (1965). Family rules: The marital quid pro quo. *Archives of General Psychiatry, 12*, 589–594.

Jacobsen, N. (1978). Stimulus control model for change in behavioral marital therapy: Implications for contingency contracting. *Journal of Marriage and Family Counseling, 4,* 29–35.

Jacobson, N. (1989). The maintenance of treatment gains following social learning based marital therapy. *Behavior Therapy, 20,* 325–336.

James, M., & Jongeward, D. (1971). *Born to win.* Reading, MA: Addison-Wesley.

Johnson, H. C. (1987). Biologically based deficit in the identified patient: Indications for psychoeducational strategies. *Journal of Marital and Family Therapy, 13,* 337–348.

Johnson, J., & Odent, M. (1995). *We are all water babies.* Berkeley, CA: Celestial Arts.

Jones, C. (1995). *Childbirth choices today.* New York: Citadel Press.

Jurich, A. P. (2001). Suicidal ideation and behavior. *AAMFT Clinical Update, 3*(6), 1–8.

Kaplan, L. (1978). *Oneness and separateness: From infant to individual.* New York: Simon & Schuster.

Kaplan, M., & Kaplan, N. (1978). Individual and family growth: A Gestalt approach. *Family Process, 17,* 195–206.

Kaufman, E., & Kaufman, P. (1979). *The family therapy of alcohol and drug abusers.* New York: Gardner Press.

Kempler, W. (1965). Experiential family therapy. *The International Journal of Group Psychotherapy, 15,* 57–71.

Kempler, W. (1968). Experiential therapy with families. *Family Process, 7*(1), 88–99.

Kempler, W. (1981). *Experiential therapy with families.* New York: Brunner/Mazel.

Kempler, W. (1991). Gestalt family therapy. In A. Horne & J. L. Passmore (Eds.), *Family counseling and therapy* (2nd ed.). Itasca, IL: Peacock.

Kerr, M. E. (1981). Family systems theory and therapy. In A. S. Gurman & D. P. Kniskern (Eds.), *Handbook of family therapy.* New York: Brunner/Mazel.

Kerr, M., & Bowen, M. (1988). *Family evaluation.* New York: Norton.

Kitson, G., & Morgan, L. (1990). Multiple consequences of divorce: A decade review. *Journal of Marriage and the Family, 52,* 913–924.

Klaus, M., Kennell, J., & Klaus, P. (1993). *Mothering the mother: How a doula can help.* Reading, MA: Addison-Wesley.

Klaus, M., Kennell, J., & Klaus, P. (1995). *Bonding.* Reading, MA: Addison-Wesley.

Klein, N. C., Alexander, J. F., & Parsons, B. V. (1977). Impact of family systems interventions on recidivism and sibling delinquency: A model for primary prevention and program development. *Journal of Consulting and Clinical Psychology, 45,* 469–474.

Knapp, M. L., & Vangelisti, A. L. (1991). *Interpersonal communication and human relationships* (2d ed.). Boston: Allyn & Bacon.

Kniskern, D. P., & Gurman, A. S. (1979). Research in training marriage and family therapists: Status, issues, and directions. *Journal of Marital and Family Therapy, 5,* 83–96.

Krumboltz, J., & Thoresen, C. (1969). *Behavioral counseling: Cases and techniques.* New York: Holt, Rinehart, & Winston.

Krumboltz, J., & Thoresen, C. (Eds.) (1976). *Counseling methods.* New York: Holt, Rinehart, & Winston.

Lambert, M. J., Bergin, A. E., & Collins, J. L. (1977). Therapist induced deterioration in psychotherapy. In A. S. Gurman & A. M. Razin (Eds.), *Effective psychotherapy: A handbook of research.* New York: Pergamon Press.

Lambie, R., & Daniels-Mohring, D. (1993). *Family systems within educational contexts: Understanding students with special needs.* Denver, CO: Love.

Lauer, J. C., & Lauer, R. H. (1986). *'Til death do us part: A study and guide to long-term marriages.* New York: Harrington Park.

Lazarus, A. (1971). *Behavior therapy and beyond.* New York: McGraw-Hill.

Lazarus, A. (1981). *The practice of multimodal therapy.* New York: McGraw-Hill.

Leboyer, F. (1975). *Birth without violence.* New York: Knopf.

Levant, R. (1978). Family therapy: A client-centered perspective. *Journal of Marriage and Family Counseling, 4*(2), 35–42.

Levant, R. (1984). *Family therapy: A comprehensive overview.* Englewood Cliffs, NJ: Prentice Hall.

Levin, P. (1988a). *Becoming the way we are.* Deerfield Beach, FL: Health Communications.

Levin, P. (1988b). *Cycles of power.* Deerfield Beach, FL: Health Communications.

Lewis, R., & Spanier, G. (1979). Theorizing about the quality and stability of marriage. In W. Burr, R. Hill, F. I. Nye, & I. Reiss (Eds.), *Contemporary theories about the family (Vol. 2).* New York: Free Press.

Liberman, R. P. (1970). Behavioral approaches to couple and family therapy. *American Journal of Orthopsychiatry, 40,* 106–118.

Liddle, H. A. (1991). Training and supervision in family therapy: A comprehensive and critical analysis. In A. S. Gurman & D. P. Kniskern (Eds.), *Handbook of family therapy* (vol. 2). New York: Brunner/Mazel.

Liddle, H. A., & Dakof, G. A. (1995). Efficacy of family therapy for drug abuse: Promising but not definitive. *Journal of Marital and Family Therapy, 21*(4), 511–544.

Liddle, H., Davidson, G., & Barrett, M. (1988). Pragmatic implications of live supervision: Outcome research. In H. A. Liddle, D. C. Breunlin, & R. C. Schwartz, (Eds.), *Handbook of family therapy training and supervision.* New York: Guilford Press.

Liddle, H., & Halpin, R. (1978). Family therapy training and supervision: A comparative review. *Journal of Marriage and Family Counseling, 4,* 77–98.

Lowe, R. N. (1982). Adlerian/Dreikursian family counseling. In A. M. Horne & M. M. Ohlsen (Eds.), *Family counseling and therapy.* Itasca, IL: Peacock.

Luborsky, L., Singer, B., & Luborsky, L. (1973). Comparative studies of psychotherapies. *Archives of General Psychiatry, 29,* 719–729.

Lyddon, W. J. (1990). First and second order change: Implications for rationalist and constructivist cognitive therapies. *Journal of Counseling and Development, 69,* 122–127.

Lyddon, W. J. (1992). A rejoinder to Ellis: What is and is not RET? *Journal of Counseling and Development, 70,* 452–454.

Mackey, R. A., & O'Brien, B. A. (1995). *Lasting marriages: Men and women growing together.* Westport, CT: Praeger.

Magid, K., & McKelvey, C. (1987). *High risk: Children without a conscience.* New York: Bantam Books.

Mahler, M. (1968). *On human symbiosis and the vicissitudes of individuation, Vol. 1, Infantile psychosis.* New York: International Universities Press.

Mahler, M. S., Pine, F., & Bergman, A. (1975). *The psychological birth of the human infant.* New York: Basic Books.

Margolin, G. (1982). Ethical and legal considerations in family therapy. *American Psychologist, 7,* 788–801.

Margolin, G. (1987). The multiple forms of aggressiveness between marital partners: How do we identify them? *Journal of Marital and Family Therapy, 13*(1), 77–85.

Maslow, A. (1968). *Toward a psychology of being* (2nd ed.). New York: Van Nostrand Reinhold.

Maslow, A. (1971). *The farther reaches of human nature.* New York: Viking Press.

McClendon, R. (1977). My mother drives a pick-up truck. In G. Barnes (Ed.), *Transactional analysis after Eric Berne.* New York: Harper & Row.

McFarlane, W. R. (1991). Family psychoeducational treatment. In A. S. Gurman & D. H. Kniskern (Eds.), *Handbook of* family therapy (vol. 2). New York: Brunner/Mazel.

McGoldrick, M., & Gerson, R. (1985). *Genograms in family assessment.* New York: Norton.

McGoldrick, M., Pearce, J. K., & Giordano, J. (1982). *Ethnicity and family therapy.* New York: Guilford Press.

McGoldrick, M., Preto, N. G., Hines, P. M., & Lee, E. (1991). Ethnicity and family therapy. In A. S. Gurman & D. P. Kniskern (Eds.). *Handbook of family therapy* (Vol. 2). New York: Brunner/Mazel.

McGoldrick, M., & Rohrbaugh, M. (1987). Researching ethnic family stereotypes. *Family Process, 1,* 89–100.

Meichenbaum, D. (1977). *Cognitive behavior modification.* New York: Plenum.

Miller, A. (1981). *The drama of the gifted child.* New York: Basic Books.

Miller, A. (1983). *For your own good.* New York: Farrar, Straus, Giroux.

Miller, A. (1986). *Thou shalt not be aware.* New York: New American Library.

Miller, A. (1988). *Banished knowledge.* New York: Doubleday.

Miller, A. (1991). *Breaking down the wall of silence.* New York: Dutton.

Mindell, A. (1983). *Dreambody.* Santa Monica. CA: SIGO Press.

Mindell, A. (1985a). *River's way.* Boston: Routledge, Kegan, Paul.

Mindell, A. (1985b). *Working with the dreaming body.* Boston: Routledge, Kegan, Paul.

Mindell, A. (1987). *The dreambody in relationship processes.* Boston: Routledge, Kegan, Paul.

Minuchin, S. (1974). *Families and family therapy.* Cambridge, MA: Harvard University Press.

Minuchin, S., & Fishman, C. (1981). *Family therapy techniques.* Cambridge, MA: Harvard University Press.

Minuchin, S., Montalvo, B., Guerney, B. G., Jr., Rosman, B. L., & Schumer, F. (1967). *Families of the slums: An exploration of their structure and treatment.* New York: Basic Books.

Minuchin, S., Rosman, B., & Baker, L. (1978). *Psychosomatic families: Anorexia nervosa in context.*

Cambridge, MA: Harvard University Press.

Mitchell, K. M., Bozarth, J. D., & Kraft, C. C. (1977). A reappraisal of the therapeutic effectiveness of accurate empathy, nonpossessive warmth, and genuineness. In A. S. Gurman & A. M. Razin (Eds.), *Effective psychotherapy: A handbook of research.* New York: Pergamon Press.

Montalvo, B., & Thompson, R. F. (1988). Conflicts in the caregiving family. *The Family Therapy Networker,* July-Aug., 30–35.

Moreno, J. L. (1951). *Sociometry, experimental method and the science of society.* Boston: Beacon.

Moreno, J. L. (1983). Psychodrama. In H. Kaplan & B. Sadock (Eds.), *Comprehensive group* (2nd ed.). Baltimore: Williams & Wilkins.

Morgan, L. A. (1990). The multiple consequences of divorce: A decade review. *Journal of Marriage and the Family, 52,* 911–924.

Murphy, J. P. (1984). Substance abuse and the family. *Journal for Specialists in Group Work, 9,* 106–112.

Murstein, B. I. (1976). *Who will marry whom?* New York: Springer.

Murstein, B. I. (1987). A clarification of the SVR theory of dyadic pairing. *Journal of Marriage and the Family, 49,* 929–933.

Napier, A. Y., & Whitaker, C. A. (1978). *The family crucible.* New York: Harper & Row.

Nichols, M. P., & Schwartz, R. C. (2001). *Family therapy: Concepts and methods* (5th ed.). Boston: Allyn & Bacon.

Noler, P., & Fitzpatrick, M. A. (1990). Marital communication in the eighties. *Journal of Marriage and the Family, 52,* 832–843.

Norton, A. J., & Mooreman, J. E. (1987). Current trends in marriage and divorce among American women. *Journal of Marriage and the Family, 49,* 3–14.

Nylund, D., & Thomas, J. (1994). The economics of narrative. *The Family Therapy Networker, 18*(6), 38–39.

O'Hanlon, B. (1994). The third wave. *The Family Therapy Networker, 18*(6), 18–29.

O'Leary, C. J. (1989). The person-centered approach to family therapy: A dialogue between two traditions. *Person-Centered Review, 4,* 308–323.

Olin, G. V., & Fenell, D. L. (1989). The relationship between depression and marital adjustment in a general population. *Family Therapy, XVI,* 11–20.

Olson, D. H., Russell, C., & Sprenkle, D. H. (1980). Marriage and family therapy: A decade review. *Journal of Marriage and the Family, 42,* 973–993.

Olson, D. H., & Sprenkle, D. H. (1983). Circumplex model of marital and family systems VI: Theoretical update. *Family Process, 22,* 69–83.

Olson, D. H., Sprenkle, D. H., & Russell, C. (1983). Circumplex model of marital and family systems IV: Theoretical update. *Family Process, 22*(1), 69–83.

Orr, L., & Ray, S. (1977). *Rebirthing in the new age.* Millbrae, CA: Celestial Arts.

Pais, S., Piercy, F., & Miller, J. (1988). Factors related to family therapists' breaking confidence when clients disclose high-risks-to-HIV/AIDS sexual behaviors. *Journal of Marital and Family Therapy, 24,* 457–472.

Paolino, T. J., Jr., & McCrady, B. S. (Eds.) (1978). *Marriage and marital therapy: Psychoanalytic, behavioral and systems theory perspectives.* New York: Brunner/Mazel.

Papp, P. (1980). The Greek chorus and other techniques of paradoxical therapy. *Family Process, 19,* 45–57.

Parry, A. (1991). A universe of stories. *Family Process, 30,* 37–54.

Parsons, B. V., & Alexander, J. F. (1973). Short-term family intervention: A therapy outcome study. *Journal of Consulting and Clinical Psychology, 41,* 195–201.

Patterson, G. (1971). *Families: Application of social learning in family life.* Champaign, IL: Research Press.

Patterson, G. (1976). *Families: Application of social learning in family life.* Champaign, IL: Research Press.

Patterson, G., Reid, J., Jones, R., & Conger, R. (1975). *A social learning approach to family intervention: Families with aggressive children.* Eugene, OR: Castalia Publishing.

Pattison, E. M. (1982). Family dynamics and interventions in alcoholism. In A. S. Gurman (Ed.), *Questions and answers in the practice of family therapy* (vol. 2). New York: Brunner/Mazel.

Paul, G. L. (1967). Strategy of outcome research in psychotherapy. *Journal of Consulting Psychology, 31,* 109–118.

Perls, F. (1969). *Gestalt therapy verbatim.* Moab, UT: Real People Press.

Piaget, J. (1951). *The child's conception of the world.* New York: Humanities Press.

Pinsof, W. M., & Wynne, L. C. (1995a). The effectiveness and efficacy of marital and family therapy: Introduction to the special issue. *Journal of Marital & Family Therapy, 21*(4), 341–343.

Pinsof, W. M., & Wynne, L. C. (1995b). The efficacy of marital and family therapy: An empirical overview, conclusions, and recommendations. *Journal of Marital & Family Therapy, 21*(4), 585–613.

Prince, S. E., & Jacobson, N. S. (1995). A review and evaluation of marital and family therapies for affective disorders. *Journal of Marital and Family Therapy, 21*(4), 377–402.

Rabin, M. (1980). *The field of family therapy: A paradigmatic classification and presentation of the major approaches.* Paper presented at the annual meeting of the American Personnel and Guidance Association, Atlanta, GA.

Raskin, N., & Van der Veen, F. (1970). Client-centered therapy: Some clinical and research perspectives. In J. Hart & T. Tomlinson (Eds.), *New directions in client-centered therapy.* Boston: Houghton Mifflin.

Reid, J., & Patterson, G. (1976). The modification of aggressive behavior in boys in the home setting. In A. Bandura & E. Ribes (Eds.), *Behavior modification: Experimental analysis of aggression and delinquency.* Hillsdale, NJ: Erlbaum.

Roberto, L. G. (1991). Symbolic-experiential family therapy. In A. S. Gurman & D. P. Kniskern (Eds.), *Handbook of family therapy* (vol. 2). New York: Brunner/Mazel.

Robinson, L. C., & Blanton, P. W. (1993). Marital strengths in enduring marriages. *Family Relations, 42,* 38–45.

Rogers, C. R. (1957). The necessary and sufficient conditions of therapeutic personality change. *Journal of Consulting Psychology, 21*, 95–103.

Rogers, C. R. (1961). *On becoming a person: A therapist's view of psychotherapy.* Boston: Houghton Mifflin.

Rogers, C. R. (1980). *A way of being.* Boston: Houghton Mifflin.

Rowe, G. P., & Meridith, W. H. (1982). Quality in marital relationships after twenty-five years. *Family Perspective, 16*(4), 149–155.

Rudestam, K. E. (1982). *Experiential groups in theory and practice.* Pacific Grove, CA: Brooks/Cole.

Russell, P. (1979). *The brain book.* New York: Hawthorne Books.

Sager, C. J., et al. (1971). The marriage contract. *Family Process, 10*, 311–326.

Satir, V. (1983). *Conjoint family therapy* (3rd ed.). Palo Alto, CA: Science and Behavior Books.

Satir, V. (1988). *The new peoplemaking.* Palo Alto, CA: Science and Behavior Books.

Schiff, J. (1970). *All my children.* New York: Pyramid Books.

Schiff, J. (1976) *The cathexis reader.* New York: Harper & Row.

Schumm, W. R. (1985). Beyond relationship characteristics of strong families: Contrasting a model of family strengths. *Family Perspective, 19*(1), 1–9.

Schwartz, R. C. (1995). *Internal family systems therapy.* New York: Guilford Press.

Segal, L. (1991). Brief therapy: The MRI approach. In A. S. Gurman & D. P. Kniskern (Eds.), *Handbook of family therapy* (vol. 2). New York: Brunner/Mazel.

Serovich, J. M., & Mosack, K. E. (2000). Training issues for supervisors of marriage and family therapists working with persons living with HIV. *Journal of Marital and Family Therapy, 26*, 103–111.

Shadish, W. R., Ragsdale, K., Glaser, R. R., Montgomery, L. M. (1995). The efficacy and effectiveness of marital and family therapy: A perspective from meta-analysis. *Journal of Marital & Family Therapy, 21*(4), 345–360.

Shapiro, A. F., Gottman, J. M., & Carrere, S. (2000). The baby and the marriage: Identifying factors that buffer against decline in marital satisfaction after the first baby arrives. *Journal of Family Psychology, 14*, 59–70.

Shea, M. T., Elkin, I., Imber, S. D., Sotsky, S. M., Watkins, J. T., Collins, J. F., Pilkonis, P. A., Beckham, E., Glass, D. R., Dolan, R. T., & Parloff, M. B. (1992). Course of depressive symptoms over follow-up: Findings from the National Institute of Mental Health Treatment of Depression Collaborative Research Program. *Archives of General Psychiatry, 49*, 782–787.

Shields, C. G. (2002). Interview with Lyman Wynn: The role of diagnosis in family therapy. *Family Therapy Magazine, 1*(3), 20 –25.

Smith, M. L., & Glass, G. V. (1977). Meta-analysis of psychotherapy outcome studies. *American Psychologist, 32*, 752–760.

Spanier, G. (1976). Measuring dyadic adjustment: New scales for assessing the quality of marriages and similar dyads. *Journal of Marriage and the Family, 38*, 15–28.

Sperry, L., & Carlson, J. (1991). *Marital therapy: Integrating theory and technique.* Denver, CO: Love.

Spitz, R. (1965). *The first year of life.* New York: International Universities Press.

Sporakowski, M., & Hughston, G. A. (1978). Prescriptions for happy marriage: Adjustments and satisfactions of couples married 50 years or more. *Family Coordinator, 27*, 321–327.

Sprenkle, D. H. (1990). Continuity and change. *Journal of Marital and Family Therapy, 16*, 337–340.

Stanton, M. D. (1978). Some outcome results and aspects of structural family therapy with drug addicts. In D. Smith, S. Anderson, M. Buxton, T. Chung, N. Gotlieb, & W. Harvey (Eds.), *A multicultural view of drug abuse.* Cambridge, MA: Schenkman.

Stanton, M. D., & Todd, T. (1979). Structural family therapy with drug addicts. In E. Kaufman & P. Kaufman (Eds.), *The family therapy of drug and alcohol abuse.* New York: Gardner Press.

Stanton, M. D., & Todd, T. (1981). Family treatment approaches to drug abuse problems. *Family Process, 18*, 251–280.

Stevens, P., & Smith, R. L. (2001). *Substance abuse counseling: Theory and practice* (2d ed.). Upper Saddle River, NJ: Prentice Hall.

Stinett, N., & Sauer, K. H. (1977). Relationship characteristics of strong families. *Family Perspective, 11*(4), 3–11.

Storm, C. L. (1991). Placing gender at the heart of MFT masters programs: Teaching a gender sensitive systemic view. *Journal of Marital and Family Therapy, 17,* 45–52.

Strupp, H. H., & Hadley, S. W. (1979). Specific vs. nonspecific factors in psychotherapy: A controlled study of outcome. *Archives of General Psychiatry, 36,* 1125–1136.

Stuart, R. (1980). *Helping couples change: A social learning approach to marital therapy.* New York: Guilford Press.

Sullivan, H. S. (1947). *Conceptions of modern psychiatry.* Washington, DC: William Alanson White Psychiatric Foundation.

Sullivan, H. S. (1953). *The interpersonal theory of psychiatry.* New York: Norton.

Sullivan, H. S. (1954). *The psychiatric interview.* New York: Norton.

Swensen, C. H., Eskew, R. W., & Kohlhepp, K. A. (1984). Five factors in long-term marriages. *Lifestyle: A Journal of Changing Patterns, 7,* 94–106.

Taub-Bynum, E. (1984). *The family unconscious.* Wheaton, IL: Theosophical.

Thayer, L. (1991). Toward a person-centered approach to family therapy. In A. M. Horne & J. L. Passmore (Eds.). *Family Counseling and Therapy* (2nd ed.). Itasca, IL: Peacock.

Thomas, D., & Rogharr, H. B. (1990). Postpositivist theorizing: The case of religion and the family. In J. Sprey (Ed.), *Fashioning family theory: New approaches.* Newberry Park, CA: Sage.

Toman, W. (1961). *Family constellation.* New York: Springer.

Training of clinical psychologists. (1981). *Psychology Today, 16*(2), 85.

Truax, C. B., & Carkhuff, R. R. (1967). *Toward effective counseling and psychotherapy: Training and practice.* Chicago: Aldine.

Truax, C. B., & Mitchell, K. M. (1971). Research on certain therapist interpersonal skills in relation to process and outcome. In A. E. Bergin & S. L. Garfield (Eds.), *Handbook on psychotherapy and behavior change: An empirical analysis.* New York: Wiley.

US Army Secondary Education Transition Study. (2001). *Parent guidebook.* Military Child Education Coalition.

Usher, M. L., & Steinglass, P. J. (1981). Responding to presenting complaints in an alcoholic family. In A. S. Gurman (Ed.), *Questions and answers in the practice of family therapy.* New York: Brunner/Mazel.

Van der Veen, F. (1977). Three client-centered alternatives: A therapy collective, therapeutic community and skills training for relationships. Paper presented at annual meeting of the American Psychological Association.

Verny, T. (1981). *The secret life of the unborn child.* New York: Dell.

Visher, E. B., & Visher, J. S. (1979). *Stepfamilies: A guide to working with stepparents and stepchildren.* New York: Brunner/Mazel.

von Bertalanffy, L. (1968). *General systems theory: Foundation, development, applications.* New York: Brazillier.

Wachtel, E. F. (1999). *We love each other, but....* New York: Golden Books.

Waite, L. J., & Gallagher, M. (2000). *The case for marriage.* New York: Doubleday.

Wallerstein, J. S. (1992). Children after divorce. In O. Pocs (Ed.), *Marriage and Family.* Guilford, CT: Dushkin.

Wallerstein, J. S., & Blakeslee, S. (1995). *The good marriage: How and why love lasts.* Boston: Houghton Mifflin.

Wallerstein, J. S., Lewis, J. M., & Blakeslee, S. (2000). *The unexpected legacy of divorce: A twenty-five year landmark study.* New York: Hyperion.

Walsh, R., & Vaughan, B. (Eds.) (1980). *Beyond ego: Transpersonal dimensions in psychology.* Los Angeles: J. P. Tarcher.

Watson, R. (1977). An introduction to humanistic psychotherapy. In S. Moore & R. Watson (Eds.), *Psychotherapies: A comparative casebook.* New York: Holt, Rinehart, & Winston.

Watzlawick, P. (Ed.) (1984). *The invented reality.* New York: Norton.

Watzlawick, P., Weakland, J. H., & Fisch, R. (1974). *Change: Principles of problem formation and problem resolution.* New York: Norton.

Weiner, N. (1954). *Cybernetics, or control and communication in the animal and the machine* (2nd ed.). Cambridge, MA: MIT Press. (original work published 1948)

Weiner-Davis, M. (1992). *Divorce busting.* New York: Summit Books.

Weinhold, B. K. (1982). *A transpersonal approach to counselor education.* Colorado Springs: Author.

Weinhold, B. K. (1991). *Breaking free of addictive family relationships.* Walpole, NH: Stillpoint Publishers.

Weinhold, B. K. (Ed.). (2001). *Spreading kindness: A program guide for reducing youth and peer violence in the schools.* Colorado Springs, CO: CICRCL Press.

Weinhold, B. K., & Hendricks, G. (1993). *Counseling and psychotherapy: A transpersonal approach.* Denver: Love.

Weinhold, B. K., & Weinhold, J. B. (1989). *Breaking free of the co-dependency trap.* Walpole, NH: Stillpoint Publishers.

Weinhold, B. K., & Weinhold, J. B. (1994). *Soul evolution: The spiritual uses of conflict in relationships.* Walpole, NH: Stillpoint Publishers.

Weinhold, J. B., & Weinhold, B. K. (1992). *Counter-dependency: The flight from intimacy.* Colorado Springs, CO: CICRCL Press.

Weinhold, B. K., & Weinhold, J. B. (1993). Building partnership families: A psychosocial approach. *Family Counseling and Therapy, 1,* 1–20.

Weinhold, B. K., & Weinhold, J. B. (2000). *Conflict resolution: The partnership way.* Denver, CO: Love Publishing.

Weishaus, L., & Field, D. (1988). A half century of marriage: Continuity or change. *Journal of Marriage and the Family, 50,* 763–774.

Weiss, L., & Weiss, J. (1989). *Recovery from co-dependency.* Deerfield Beach, FL: Health Communications.

Wells, R. A., & Dezen, A. E. (1978). The results of family therapy revisited: The non-behavioral methods. *Family Process, 17,* 251–274.

Whitaker, C. A. (1976). The hindrance of theory in clinical work. In P. J. Guerrin, Jr. (Ed.), *Family therapy: Theory and practice.* New York: Gardner Press.

Whitaker, C. A., & Keith, D. V. (1981). Symbolic-experiential family therapy. In A. S. Gurman & D. P. Kniskern (Eds.), *Handbook of family therapy.* New York: Brunner/Mazel.

White, M. (1986). Negative explanation, restraint, and double description: A template for family therapy. *Family Process, 25,* 169–184.

White, M., & Epston, D. (1990). *Narrative means to therapeutic ends.* New York: Norton.

Wilber, K. (1980). *The Atman project: A transpersonal view of human development.* Wheaton, IL: Quest Books.

Wilcoxon, S. A., & Fenell, D. L. (1983). Engaging the nonattending spouse in marital therapy through the use of a therapist-initiated written communication. *Journal of Marital and Family Therapy, 9,* 199–203.

Wilcoxon, S. A., & Fenell, D. L. (1986). Linear and paradoxical letters to the nonattending spouse: A comparison of engagement rates. *Journal of Marital and Family Therapy, 12*(2), 191–193.

Winch, R. (1958). *Mate selection: A study of complimentary needs.* New York: Harper & Row.

Wolpe, J. (1958). *Psychotherapy by reciprocal inhibition.* Stanford, CA: Stanford University Press.

Wolpe, J. (1969). *The practice of behavior therapy.* New York: Pergamon Press.

Working with military children. (2001). Military Child Education Coalition.

Wynne, L. C., (Ed.) (1988). *The state of the art in family therapy research: Controversies and recommendations.* New York: Family Prouss Press.

Wynne, L. C., McDaniel, S. H., & Weber, T. T. (1987). Professional politics and the concepts of family therapy, family consultation and systems consultation. *Family Process, 26,* 153–166.

Wynne, L. C., Ryckoff, I. M., Day, J., & Hirsch, S. I. (1958). Pseudomutuality in the family relationships of schizophrenics. *Psychiatry, 21,* 205–220.

Name Index

A

Abbot, D. A., 351, 355
Ackerman, N., 27
Adler, A., 24, 93–94
Alexander, J. F., 39, 161, 177, 178, 179, 181, 183
Anderson, W. J., 201
Aponte, H. J., 168, 169, 170, 177

B

Babcock, D., 282
Bader, E., 351
Baker, L., 162, 344
Bandura, A., 152
Barker, P., 12
Barrett, M., 389
Barton, C., 161, 177, 181
Bateson, G., 25, 26, 38, 43, 184, 284, 345
Baucom, D. H., 139
Bauer, R., 207, 213
Beck, A., 139, 143
Bell, J., 27
Benedek, E. P., 326
Berg, I. K., 322
Berger, M., 318
Berger, P. L., 352–353, 360
Bergin, A., 341, 342
Bergman, A., 89
Berne, E., 98, 99, 100, 281
Berry, M., 351, 355
Bertalanffy, L. von, 32
Betis, A., 333
Black, L., 322
Blakeslee, S., 349, 353
Blanton., P. W., 351, 353, 355, 360
Bodin, A. M., 26
Borns, R. F., 8

Subject Index

theoretical constructs of, 202–203
therapeutic interventions for, 203–206
Personality formation, 24
Phenomenological orientation
explanation of, 94
in person-centered family therapy, 201–202
Philadelphia Child Guidance Clinic, 162, 175
Placaters, 239
Post-traumatic stress disorder (PTSD), 299
Postmodernists, 28
Premarital counseling, 314
Prenatal psychology, 275
Presentation of other, 219
Privilege, 380
Problem definition, 53–54
Problem solving, 54–55
Professional journals, 362
Professional organizations, 367–372
Projection
explanation of, 212
marriages based on, 125
onto children, 112
Pseudomutuality, 27
Pseudoself, 109
Psychoanalytic approaches
of corrective parenting, 282
explanation of, 85
historical background of, 24, 25, 88–89
philosophical tenets of, 89
theoretical constructs of, 89–90, 92–93
Psychodrama-oriented family therapy
case example of, 217
historical background of, 214–215
limitations of, 220
philosophical tenets of, 215
theoretical constructs of, 215–216, 218–219
therapeutic interventions of, 219–220
Psychodynamic approaches
advantages and disadvantages of, 87–88
case example of, 91
explanation of, 85
goals of, 85–86
process of, 86–87
transactional analysis as, 98–103
Psychodynamic systems theories
family-of-origin theory, 118–129
family systems theory, 107–118
internal family systems theory, 129–135
The Psychodynamics of Family Life (Ackerman), 27
Psychological birth, 89
Psychosexual stages, 88
Psychosis, 92
Psychotherapists, 18–19. *See also* Family therapists
Psychotherapy
historical background of, 24
research on, 341–343
theories of, 23

Q

Questions, information gathering by asking, 63

R

Raising Kids OK (Babcock & Keepers), 282
Rapport building
in cognitive/behavioral approaches, 141–142
in group counseling, 61–62
in individual counseling, 61
joining with each family member and, 62
joining with family, 62–63
in marriage and family counseling, 62
Rational emotive behavior therapy (RET)
case example of, 148–149
explanation of, 143–145
goals of, 150
limitations of, 150
philosophical tenets of, 145
theoretical constructs of, 145–147
therapeutic interventions for, 147–149
Reauthored narrative, 256–257
Recovery from Co-dependence (Weiss & Weiss), 282
Redefining the problem, 76
Reflecting content, 67–68, 204
Reflecting feelings
explanation of, 68–69, 205
feeling cross technique for, 70–71
importance of, 69–70
Reframing
in brief therapy, 190, 191
explanation of, 76
relationship conflicts, 291–292
Regression-progression
breaking free from, 301–302
explanation of, 299, 300
problems related to, 300–301
Reinforcement, 140, 153
Relationships
developmental stages of, 289–291
dominator, 295–297
double-bind, 26
partnership, 293–297
reframing, 291–292
stages in family, 297–298
Religion, 355
Remarriage, 332–333
Research
early, 341–343
major reviews of, 343–344
summary of, 361–363
Respect, need to show, 206
Restraining change, 191
Restructuring, 169–170
Retroflection, 212
Reverse psychology, 28
Right to refuse treatment, 380–381

Rigid families, 37
Role playing, 219
Rules, subsystem, 163
Rural families
    explanation of, 336–337
    family therapy for, 15–16

S

Schizophrenia
    family communication and, 25–27, 38
    family therapy for, 107–108, 345
    treatment of, 88
School phobia, 10–11
School-related problems, 10–12
Scientific realism, 89
Self-acceptance, 147
Self-actualization, 198, 220
Self-awareness, Gestalt approach and, 207,
    208
Self-concept
    in person-centered family therapy, 201
    value of strong, 234, 235
Self-disclosure
    explanation of, 205
    function of, 72–73
Self-esteem
    development of, 238–239
    violent individuals and, 326
Self-presentation, 219
Self-transcendence, 228–229
Self-worth, 237, 241
Separated families, 37
September 11 terrorist attacks, 334
Sex roles, 382–383
Sibling subsystems, 165–166
Signals, amplification of, 262–264
Single-parent families, 8
Social constructivist approaches, 28
Social learning theory, 151
Solid self, 109
Spiritual bypass, 227
Spiritual dimension
    in marriage, 351
    in relationships, 295
    transpersonal theory and, 222, 224
Spousal subsystems, 164–165
Spouses. *See also* Families
    individual treatment for, 7
    of substance-abusing individuals, 9–10
Story telling, 62
Strategic family therapy, 27
Stress management, 143
Strokes, 99
Structural family therapy. *See also* Brief
        therapy; Functional family therapy
    activating family transaction patterns and
        structural assessment in, 169
    case example of, 175
    effectiveness of, 344
    explanation of, 27, 161

historical background of, 161–162
homeostasis and disequilibrium and, 163
joining and, 167–169
philosophical tenets of, 162
reasons for seeking, 166–167
restructuring family transaction patterns
    in, 169–176
strengths and limitations of, 177
subsystems and, 163–166
Structural modification, 174–176
Structured families, 37
Structuring
    function of, 64–65
    in marriage and family therapy, 65–66
Subjective experience, 202
Substance abuse, 8–10, 319–321, 347
Subsystems. *See also* Family systems
    boundaries in, 35
    explanation of, 163
    individual, 163–164
    joining with family, 62, 63
    as living system, 29–31
    parental, 165
    sibling, 165–166
    spousal, 164–165
    types of, 33
Suicide
    adolescent, 12, 13
    families and, 328–330
Summarization, 72, 78
Surface process, 261, 264
Symbolic-experiential family therapy
    battle for structure and initiative in, 246
    case example of, 251
    co-therapy and, 247–249
    historical background of, 243–244
    limitations of, 250
    philosophical tenets and theoretical
        constructs of, 244–245
    strengths of, 250
    therapeutic interventions for, 245–246
    three-generation approach in, 250
Symptom prescription, 191
Symptoms
    altering effect of, 172
    deemphasizing, 173
    exaggerating, 172–173
    expanding, 172
    focusing on new, 173–174
    relabeling, 171–172
System recomposition, 170
Systems consultants, 27
Systems theories
    individual vs., 45, 47–51
    rural families and, 337
Systems therapists
    as experts, 52–54
    function of, 30, 49
Systems therapy
    evaluating effectiveness of, 77
    locus of pathology and, 49